Ethics and
Governance

Ethics and Governance

Business as Mediating Institution

TIMOTHY L. FORT

OXFORD
UNIVERSITY PRESS

2001

OXFORD
UNIVERSITY PRESS

Oxford   New York
Athens   Auckland   Bangkok   Bogotá   Buenos Aires   Cape Town
Chennai   Dar es Salaam   Delhi   Florence   Hong Kong   Istanbul   Karachi
Kolkata   Kuala Lumpur   Madrid   Melbourne   Mexico City   Mumbai   Nairobi
Paris   São Paulo   Shanghai   Singapore   Taipei   Tokyo   Toronto   Warsaw

and associated companies in
Berlin   Ibadan

Published by Oxford University Press, Inc.
198 Madison Avenue, New York, New York 10016

Oxford is a registered trademark of Oxford University Press.

Library of Congress Cataloging-in-Publication Data
Fort, Timothy L., 1958–
Ethics and governance : business as mediating institution / by Timothy L. Fort.
    p.   cm.   (The Ruffin series in business ethics)
Includes bibliographical references and index.
ISBN 0-19-513760-4
1. Business ethics.   2. Business ethics—Philosophy.   3. Business—Religious
aspects—Christianity.   4. Social contract.   I. Title.
HF5387 .F677   2001
174′.4—dc21   00-055800

9 8 7 6 5 4 3 2 1

Printed in the United States of America
on acid-free paper

To Nancy

Acknowledgments

This book, in one form or another, has been part of my life for so long, I scarcely know where to begin in acknowledging all those who have helped me think it through. To start, I would like to thank Bob Solomon and Bill Frederick, who recommended that I write it and helped me convince the editors at Oxford to publish it.

There were also several folks who spent a tremendous amount of time reading through the manuscript and making very helpful comments. They include Jeff Nesteruk, Robbin Derry, Mike Naughton, Tom Dunfee, Bill Frederick, Steve Salbu, Joshua Margolis, Bob Kennedy, Dana Muir, and Tom Shaffer. In addition, no significant work leaves my hands unless my wife, Nancy Nerad, has had a chance to look at it. Her editorial help makes my thoughts sound better than they really are.

I would also like to thank the University of Michigan Business School, which provides a marvelous place for scholarly development. Dean Joe White has provided wonderful leadership as have my departmental mentors and friends Cindy Schipani and George Siedel. I have also been fortunate that several ethics scholars have visited Michigan over the past six years. Tom Dunfee, Steve Salbu, Jeff Nesteruk, Caryn Beck-Dudley, and Fran Zollers have helped me considerably. Two other, longer-term collaborations with LaRue Tone Hosmer and Joshua Margolis made life considerably more fun at Michigan and my ethics work more productive. My thanks to them.

Because portions of nearly every chapter have appeared in some form in a journal, there are probably a couple dozen reviewers whose comments assisted in the development of the ideas. I may have grumbled about the comments when I first read them, but they proved helpful.

Two scholars with whom I collaborated on published articles have graciously allowed me to use substantial portions of our work in this book. Cindy Schipani and I previously published most of what is chapter 5. I split the article I wrote with Jim Noone so that major parts of it comprise chapters 4 and 7. Versions of previously published material have also been adapted into chapters, and at the end of this section I formally recognize these journals and publishers for allowing me to use this material. My thanks also to Cheryl Strickland, Becky Sad, and Tassie Zahner-Palylca for helping me put the manuscript together.

There may be some truth to the thought that this book is simply an intellectualization of my experiences growing up in a rural community. Mediating institutions, real ones, abound in such places. I thank the folks and family in Stronghurst and Henderson County, Illinois, for teaching me lessons about ethics. I think they have something to tell the world, too.

Finally, I want to note the members of my house. Nancy's support in all things has been a blessing beyond measure. And last but not least, Scooby the sheepdog and Rose the basset hound helped by curling up at my feet while I typed away on the computer. I am tempted to connect the errors in this book to those times when they broke my concentration by wanting me to get up and play ball with them, but alas, the errors in the book are wholly my own.

A portion of chapter 2 was originally published in volume 6 of *Business Ethics Quarterly*, copyright 1996, and is reprinted with permission. All rights reserved. Another portion of chapter 2 was originally published in volume 14 of *Business & Professional Ethics Journal*, copyright 1995, and is reprinted with permission. All rights reserved. Another portion was originally published in a chapter entitled "The Nature of Business as a Mediating Institution," from *Rethinking the Purpose of Business*, University of Notre Dame Press, copyright 2001. Permission granted by Michael Naughton, editor.

A portion of chapter 3 was originally published in volume 62 of *Law and Contemporary Problems*, copyright 1999, and is reprinted with permission. All rights reserved. Another portion of this chapter was originally published in volume 38 of the *American Business Law Journal*, copyright 2001, and is reprinted with permission. All rights reserved. Another portion of this chapter was originally published in volume 33 of the *Cornell Journal of International Law*, copyright 2000, and is reprinted with permission. All rights reserved.

A portion of chapter 4 was originally published in volume 62 of *Law and Contemporary Problems*, copyright 1999, and is reprinted with permission. All rights reserved.

A portion of chapter 5 was originally published in volume 33 of the *Vanderbilt Journal of Transnational Law*, copyright 2000, and is reprinted with permission. All rights reserved.

A portion of chapter 6 was originally published in volume 73 of the *Notre Dame Law Review*, copyright 1997, and is reprinted with permission. (The publisher bears responsibility for errors that occurred in reproduction and editing.) All rights reserved. Another portion of this chapter was originally published in volume 15 of the *Journal of Law and Commerce*, copyright 1995, and is reprinted with permission. All rights reserved.

A portion of chapter 7 was originally published in volume 62 of *Law and Contemporary Problems*, copyright 1999, and is reprinted with permission. All rights reserved.

A portion of chapter 8 was originally published in volume 23 of the *Journal of Corporation Law*, copyright 1998, and is reprinted with permission. All rights reserved. Another portion of this chapter was originally published in volume 8 of *Business Ethics Quarterly*, copyright 1998, and is published with permission. All rights reserved. Another portion of chapter 8 was originally published in volume 36 of the *American Business Law Journal*, copyright 1999, and is reprinted with permission. All rights reserved.

A portion of chapter 10 was previously published in volume 12 of the *Notre Dame Journal of Law, Ethics, & Public Policy*, copyright 1998, Thomas J. White Center on Law & Government. Further reproduction is strictly prohibited.

Oxford University Press granted permission for certain quotations from *Natural Law Theory: Contemporary Essays*, edited by Robert P. George (1992).

Seton Hall University Law School granted permission for quotations by Terry Morehead Dworkin and Ellen R. Pierce, copyright 1997.

University of California–Davis Law Review granted permission for quotations taken from Michael J. Perry, "Religion in Politics," originally published in volume 29, copyright 1996, by the Regents of the University of California. All rights reserved.

Terry Morehead Dworkin, William C. Frederick, LaRue Tone Hosmer, Robert G. Kennedy, Jeffery Nesteruk, James J. Noone, Donald A. Mayer, Michael J. Perry, Ellen R. Pierce, Steven R. Salbu, and Cindy A. Schipani all granted permission for extensive quotation of their work.

Contents

1. Touchstones 3

PART I: BUSINESS AS MEDIATING INSTITUTION

2. Some Catholic Notions 21

3. Natural Law and Laws of Nature 39

4. Nature and Self-Interest 62

5. The Velvet Corporation 87

PART II: BUSINESS AS MEDIATING INSTITUTION AND OTHER
LEADING BUSINESS ETHICS FRAMEWORKS

6. Stakeholder Theory 119

7. Social Contracting 136

8. Business as Community 155

PART III: THEOLOGY AND BUSINESS

9. Theological Naturalism 181

10. The Dark Side of Religion in the Workplace and
Some Suggestions for Brightening It 199

11. Bright Dots, Dot Coms, and Camelot? 222

Notes 231

Bibliography 279

Index 297

Ethics and
Governance

1

Touchstones

During the mid-1980s, I primarily practiced business and tax law. One exploding area was employee benefits law. Pension plans, of course, had been around for some time, but many companies found that there were more efficient and inexpensive ways for a corporation to provide retirement benefits than through traditional defined-benefit plans. A proper execution of the termination of a defined-benefit plan, which had been the mainstay of corporate retirement programs, could result in substantial excess cash that a company could convert for other corporate purposes.

In the rural area where I practiced, few companies had adopted pension plans. Most of the companies in the area were small, with a total payroll of fewer than ten. There were, however, a few somewhat larger companies, which had defined benefit plans. Some had been informed by the trustee of the plan that there were several ways to sponsor a plan in addition to the company's traditional plan. This led to a local company wanting to terminate its defined-benefit plan and replace it with a defined-contribution plan. The local company needed legal counsel to execute the termination and set up a new plan, so it hired my firm, which handled its other legal work.[1]

Although the field of employee benefits was mostly new to my firm, my youth and inexperience prompted me to have the illusion I could do the job. One of the initial steps in the process, however, revealed exactly why this termination and replacement maneuver was so economically beneficial. It raised significant problems not only for me but for my client as well.

3

The basis of a defined-benefit plan is that a company guarantees that an employee will receive a targeted amount at retirement. Thus, employees have assurances of what they can expect and plan their retirement accordingly. The amount is based on a formula, which can vary from company to company. A typical target would be an amount equal to one-half of the employee's average income during her five highest years of compensation, a time frame generally measured during the ten years prior to retirement. Often, the company would not pay a full 50 percent of the highest five years' income, but reduce that 50 percent figure by the employee's estimated social security income, a variation known as an offset plan. Having calculated the 50 percent amount and reduced it by the expected social security benefits, the company would estimate the amount currently required to contribute to an employee's account. Given the compounding of interest expectations and the number of years until the employee reaches retirement age, this would often be a relatively small portion of the final amount to be distributed.

From this brief description, one can see that extensive actuarial calculations are required to make each of these estimates. An actuary would need to calculate the 50 percent figure, the estimated social security benefits, and the amount required currently to fund a retirement benefit that would not begin to be distributed until the employee reached retirement age five, twenty, or forty years later. These calculations would need to be made for each and every employee, provided that he or she had been employed long enough to qualify for coverage.

For relatively small companies, these annual actuarial expenses could be nearly as large as the contribution made for the employees. In part by avoiding these expenses, savings could be realized through a defined-contribution plan. This was the thinking of my client. It wanted its contributions to fund retirement benefits rather than actuarial costs. To do this, the old plan would have to be terminated and the employees guaranteed the funds that had already been contributed on their behalf.

At the termination of the plan, employees of my client would receive a lump sum equal to what would be necessary to purchase an insurance annuity, which would equal the targeted benefit. Essentially, the insurance company would be paid to guarantee the original benefit promised by my client. The employees could choose to keep the money (subject to tax consequences), purchase the annuity, or roll over their lump sum into the new defined-contribution plan.

In a defined-contribution plan, the company simply designates a particular amount to be contributed to each employee's retirement plan account annually. This annual contribution could be, for instance, 2 percent of an employee's salary or 2 percent of corporate profits divided by the number of eligible employees. The board of directors could also reserve the right to refuse to fund an annual contribution. In a defined-contribution plan, the employer does not guarantee a final retirement benefit. The risk shifts from the employer to the employee, who keeps track of what is in the account and how that amount compares to what she will need at retirement.

Not only does this defined-contribution alternative increase risk for the employee, but the process of terminating a defined-benefit plan also produces surprises. Because of the many actuarial variables, an employee in her upper fifties, who had worked at a company for six years, could have a higher lump sum distribution than a person in his thirties who worked at a higher salary for fifteen years.

For my client, this anamoly became apparent quickly. Since it was a small company, the various final amounts for each employee became known throughout the company, and the disparities raised many questions among the employees about the fairness of the process. By law, my client had to provide informational hearings to explain the process. In addition, it provided an unlimited amount of my time to meet individually with any employee who had a question. Company executives also offered their own time to meet with employees to explain what was happening.

Moreover, the executives of the company were themselves surprised at some of the variations in benefits and were quite concerned that the process was unfair. In particular, because the company had traditionally been very careful to fully fund and even overfund its annual obligations, there was an excess beyond what was necessary to fund employees' lump sum benefits resulting from the plan termination. The company could use this excess for any purpose.

My client decided to return this overfunding back to the employees, a move that was wholeheartedly endorsed by shareholders of the company who, being from a small community, were family and friends of the employees as well as investors. They did so by plowing the excess back into the new plan (which commenced shortly before the end of the calendar year), followed by a second contribution immediately after the new year began a few weeks later. The amounts contributed exceeded what the company expected to contribute annually, but it made these larger contributions anyway because, quite simply, the board felt that it should.

Thus, although my client could have utilized the overfunding for more luxurious offices, increased executive salaries (increased attorney fees), or increased shareholder dividends, the board felt that it was important that the employees felt they were treated fairly. Legally and even economically, the prescribed method of termination did treat the employees fairly. Employees would not receive less than what they were initially promised had my client kept the excess. But the executives of my client knew that there were other criteria than legal and economic fairness at stake.

Why did my client take these steps? One could apply any number of influential business ethics frameworks to describe and justify my client's actions. Certainly, my client practiced a form of stakeholder management. It was concerned with its shareholders, but saw a clear link between shareholders and employees. That link took the form of nearly all of the shareholders and employees being members of the same rural community who obtained an instrumental benefit of having happy employees. My client was not particularly concerned with other stakeholders, except to the extent that those stakeholders were legally empowered to approve my client's action. Thus, stakeholders such as the Pension Benefit Guarantee Corporation, the Internal Revenue Service, and the U.S. Department of Labor were important, but suppliers, competitors, and even customers were only marginally considered. The company, however, did view employees as stakeholders whose moral sentiments and economic productivity were essential elements of the business.

A communitarian analysis could also describe my client's action. Not only were employees (including managers) and shareholders part of the same geographic community, they were also part of a community as a business. The business was a place in which there was a strong sense of identity, where individuals often worked for forty years, and where particular virtues were critically important. Frequently, the employees or their families were stockholders. The annual meeting was, and remains, an anticipated community festival. It simply was inconceivable for anyone in the business to envision an approach other than one that was completely transparent. Dishonesty could never have been remotely efficacious. Similarly, notions of loyalty and solidarity inspired my client to do more than what was legally required in directing the overfunding to the employees.

This kind of community formed, disciplined, and nourished the virtues necessary for this or any other admirable business. Practicing integrity virtues, such as truth telling and promise keeping, made sense because there was an immediate feedback mechanism. Community solidarity led to loyalty and friendship. In short, it is exactly this kind of community where virtue theory makes the most sense. Although tangential, another example may help to illustrate this relationship between virtue and a small community.

On many occasions I have asked students or corporate audiences how forthcoming they would be in trading in an old car to a car dealer. Almost always, people indicate that they would disclose a clear problem and would not mislead the dealer, but basically they feel that it is up to the dealer to check out the car to determine the extent of any defects. On the other hand, the same audiences also agree with me fully that when I sold my used car to my nephew-in-law, it was quite a good idea that I had the car completely checked out by my own mechanics in order to head off any potential problems. They also agree that it was wise of me to pay for any repairs to fix any things that might be potentially worrisome.

The search for truth in this second scenario was much more necessary because I happen to enjoy pleasant Thanksgiving dinners with my in-laws. The gravy on my potatoes might have settled a bit heavily if folks felt that I had taken advantage of my wife's nephew. Occasionally, the audiences with whom I share this story think that the professional status of the car dealer makes an important difference. Yet, when I then change the story to one situated in the same rural community as my pension client and propose to deal with a very professional car dealer whom I had to see (and immensely liked) every day, they agree that what is most important is not the professional expertise of the dealer, but the relational connection. Indeed, to the extent the expertise of the dealer would make a difference, it would have been to heighten the need for honesty; my friend/car dealer would know that I had tried an underhanded maneuver. Thus, the same audiences also think the increased importance of truthfulness would be necessary in the kind of rural community in which I practiced law because the car dealer was a friend.

In the case of the small-town car dealer and my nephew-in-law, the feedback mechanisms provided by the small community made dishonesty nothing less than stupid. Of course, truth telling would still be a virtue in dealing with the large-city car dealer, but the point is that small communities—mediating institutions—are the most effective cohort for integrity virtues. This was certainly true of the actions of my pension client. A communitarian analysis would virtually mandate my client's course of conduct.

A contract analysis would also shed light on my client's action. My client's executives felt that not only was there a legal contract between the business and the employees to provide a specific retirement benefit, but there was also a psychological contract that required respect. That psychological contract necessitated the extensive time and expense of counseling employees and explaining the process to them as well as directing funds to them. This psychological contract was further reinforced by a social contract of fairness. I clearly remember one of the executives commenting to me that "if I were one of the employees, I would wonder about the fairness of this."

I use this example not only because I personally find it an inspiring action, but also because it demonstrates that differing ethical frameworks may provide similar solutions. Indeed, a central thrust of this book is that one might be able to articulate a notion of business ethics that integrates various influential theories into a central governance approach. By doing so, we may be able to articulate a unifying metaphor for much of business ethics.

Of course, one must not simply conflate ethical approaches that have incommensurable methodological assumptions. Nevertheless, I believe that a business as mediating institution approach (BMI) can combine particular features of the major business ethics approaches in a useful way. This is beneficial because business ethics needs a metaphor that stands in constructive opposition to a nexus-of-contracts view of the firm that emphasizes profit maximization. To date, stakeholder theory has largely supplied this metaphor, although social contract and virtue theories also offer alternative conceptions. As part II argues, BMI draws upon each of these approaches, and by minimizing the weaknesses of each of them, BMI can become this needed metaphor for business ethics.

Before engaging in this academic proposal, however, I would like to finish the story about my client. My client was a mediating institution. It was a relatively small institution, where individuals within the organization were confronted with the consequences of their actions. Families, neighborhoods, religious institutions, and voluntary associations are the most commonly known mediating institutions.[2] They provide face-to-face interaction where specific virtues are nourished in microcommunities. But my client, as a business, was also a mediating institution. Executives could no more avoid the consequences of their pension decisions than they could avoid the consequences of telling their children that they were breaking their promise to pay for college. The leaders of my client could not make decisions apart from this realization.

Moreover, the consequences had impact because those affected by the action, the employees and shareholders, had implicit mechanisms for counteracting the power held by executives of the corporation. Those mechanisms included being members of the same church, the same families (in some cases), and the same village council. In a sense, the employees were not only members of a business community, but they were also citizens of that community because executives could not ignore their voices. As citizens, they were enfranchised participants in their work life.

This status as citizen was of a more complex nature than what is often thought of as worker empowerment. I do not wish to diminish notions of empowerment, but the heart of the relationship between my client and its employees was a concrete moral realization that the employees were human beings whose interests, feelings, and identities were important and were also powerful. They were powerful because executives, shareholders, and employees lived in a community in which moral treatment was an acknowledged criterion of value.

The creation of such small business communities can be part of a similar system of checks and balances in large multinational corporations with a payroll many hundreds of times larger than that of my client's. Such a system requires a legal architecture: a legal regime that allows and even requires the creation of mediating institutions within large corporate megastructures. These mediating institutions are necessary to foster ethical business behavior.

As a lawyer and theologian, I am primarily interested in proposing a legal architecture, which has space for the inspirational aspirations of those whose lives are extensively intertwined with a business. I wish to articulate this notion of BMI from what can be called "natural law theory in light of the laws of nature." That is, I will rely on certain natural law concepts that are supported by anthropological and biological findings. This combination suggests that there are limitations to the number of relationships individuals can process. If ethics is concerned with the rules that sustain and govern relationships, such limitations are important. Thus, findings from biological anthropology will be used to ground a natural law approach. Just as natural law has often been used by lawyers and theologians, law and religion have central roles in BMI.

To be sure, law and theology will have major philosophical components. This is true of BMI because I borrow from leading business ethics frameworks—stakeholder, social contract, and virtue—which are driven by philosophy. For purposes of grounding my argument, however, I am interested in working out of a different, albeit complementary, set of methodological frameworks.

Indeed, providing an integration of business ethics frameworks is one of the three goals of the book. I hope to persuade the reader that BMI provides a framework in which the most persuasive aspects of stakeholder, social contract, and virtue theory are implemented while minimizing their drawbacks and also not conflating them. Second, beyond integration, I want to propose this mediating institution model as an independent corporate governance alternative for enhancing ethical business behavior.

Third, in doing these two things, I hope to initiate a dialogue concerning the legal modifications to corporate governance laws necessary to foster ethical business behavior. Much like a lawyer arguing a case, I will present evidence—in this case often from anthropology—about human nature that must be taken into account in constructing business organizations that foster ethical business behavior.

As optimistic as I am that BMI can initiate a dialogue around what legislative action can take place, my argument is limited to the corporate governance structures that foster ethical business behavior. I am interested, for purposes of BMI, in issues of ethical business behavior more than in corporate social responsibility. In other words, for purposes of this particular book, I am not so interested in the role corporations might play in helping the environment or the poor as I am in formulating a way for ethical conduct within the organization to be enhanced. I believe BMI provides a construct in which ethical concerns can be more regularly and efficaciously considered and virtuous behaviors inculcated than in other theories of the firm.

ON RULES AND FAMILIES

One might think that a lawyer would propose strict rules in order to construct these kinds of organizations. While I will argue for the importance of legal architecture and modifications of current law, the emphasis on rules is problematic. Oliver Wendell Holmes argued that the law tends to move toward external standards of conformity and away from moral standards such as guilt, malice, or conscience.[3] Similarly, legal intervention in business affairs often takes the form of specific legislation requiring specific behavior. This can range from harassment laws to minimum wage laws. Sometimes these are necessary, but the kind of legal modifications I am interested in are different. They entail the creation of a structure in which there is openness for moral intentions rather than a Holmesian external mandate of required action.

Corporate governance needs an architecture providing a general framework in which there is room for flexibility and even inspiration from within the business community. To see the difference between a law mandating specific behavior and one that provides a forum within which more complex relationships take place, take the notion of contracts.

Legal scholars group contracts into various categories. Doctrinally, the common categories are express contracts, implied contracts, and quasi contracts.[4] Such doctrinal categories assist judges and attorneys in interpreting agreements in accordance with relevant statutory and judicial authority. These are not, however, the only categories. Intellectually, scholars have also differentiated between transactional and relational contracts. One of the most articulate champions of this differentiation is Ian MacNeil.[5] MacNeil describes transactional contracts as being of "short duration, limited personal interaction, precise measure of money and goods subject to the exchange, a minimum of future cooperation, no expectation of altruism and no entangling strings of friendship within the deal," which he contrasts with a relational contract that works over long periods of time with expectations of friendship, cooperation, virtues, and solidarity.[6]

Steven Salbu writes that neoclassical contracts, of which relational contracts are an important part, "have more ethical content than legalistic classical contracts."[7] This is because relational contracts are more "flexible" and entail a much larger degree of freedom than do classical contracts that are based on rigorous rules of order.[8] Precise articulation of rules and principles often help, but do not necessarily encourage moral development. Indeed, precise rules and principles can foster legalistic casuistry that makes rules and principles into games of manipulation by lawyers.[9] In short, transactional contracts depend on specific external constraints for enforcement. Relational contracts provide a structure within which parties work on their cooperative goals. Transactional contracts depend on Holmesian external standards and are akin to building a house. Relational contracts are frameworks within which human beings cooperate and are akin to homes.

Salbu's position is not one of hypothetical thought experiments, but a view of law as standing within the particular context in which it is developed. It is a view of law that sees human interaction as something more than rule-based. When abstract principles are anachronistically applied, one loses the sense of participation in the law's meaning, purpose, and content.[10] Indeed, when anachronistic legalisms are applied, the law ceases to be a constitutive part of the lived life of members of a community, and instead becomes an object.[11] Because it is then an object, it becomes easier to manipulate, and popular confidence in it then decreases.[12]

Salbu applies the notion of relational contracts beyond its legal context to the field of corporate strategy. By doing so, he borrows the law's wisdom without its anachronisms. He writes that the classical model of contracts arose in a relatively stable time of the Middle Ages when unchanging conditions make it relatively easy to predict foreseeable contractual problems.[13] In this kind of environment, contract language simply adds more stability to predictable events.[14] In a dynamic global environment, however, one cannot predict potential consequences because business conditions change so rapidly.[15]

Salbu argues that in rapidly changing, unpredictable conditions, the use of traditional contracts becomes "dysfunctional."[16] Moreover, because Anglo-American contract law has traditionally been framed in adversarial, transactional terms, the goal of contracts became control.[17] Rather than focusing on control, however, contemporary business transactions focus on cooperation.[18] This strategy looks at the opportunities provided by the market and attempts to place relationships with others in terms of "win-win" (i.e., cooperative) contexts rather than in competitive, adversarial forms.[19] Legal contracts for contemporary, dynamic, global business then require a relational form in which cooperation becomes central. To create an analogy for this relationship, Salbu argues that

[t]he functional family provides a useful analogy here. Like the family members who genuinely wish one another success, transactional allies will naturally constrain self-interest through concessions made for the ultimate good of others and of the alliance. Those who interact functionally and familially have little use for formalization of obligation, and indeed such formalization would be wasteful and ineffective. Like the organically moderated relationships that comprise the cohesive family, close business network allies have a reduced need for compulsory rules and obligations, both the establishment and the implementation of which are costly and superfluous in function. Innovations in relationship management forms may better serve emerging, nonadversarial forms of cooperative linkages.[20]

The picture Salbu paints is that of a need for legal doctrine to develop notions of contracts that take into account the ethical, relational commitment to a common good in a particular historical context. Rather than adversarial attempts to control and predict the elaboration of a transactional exchange, there is instead a need to provide models that accord with the realities of global business practices.

I want to build on Salbu's notion of the efficacy of the functional family as a model for mediating institutions. The family, after all, is a mediating institution. What is important is not that the business becomes a substitute for a family, but that the processes that make a family function are replicated in business so that it becomes a mediating institution. In a popular vein, Tom's of Maine CEO Tom Chappell describes this extension to corporate life when he compares the corporation to a family:

In the family we learn love, patience, respect, nurturing, affirmation, and health. The family also teaches us about competition, domination, selfishness and deceit. The family is thus a relatively efficient learning system for the development of mind, spirit, and body. It involves the whole self. Certainly it has its own hierarchy and power centers, but it also can be egalitarian. Members of a happy, thriving family will do anything for each other; they devote themselves to maintaining that happiness and increasing it. Substitute the word company for family . . . and you get an idea of what I envision a company community to include. In my experience, employees will run through walls for a company that understands them, gives them some freedom, encourages their creativity, appreciates their work, and rewards it fairly. Treat an employee like a cog in a machine, and you'll get a cog's work. Treat that same person as a member of your family, and you'll get loyalty.[21]

Going further, Chappell argues that business ethics do not come from business school courses, but from bonds developed in family, church, schools, neighborhoods, and self-help groups; in other words, from mediating institutions.

In a scholarly vein, Robbin Derry uses a similar model when she applies Virginia Held's "mother-child" paradigm to business ethics.[22] Derry's argument has two central points. First, it is a mistake to compartmentalize personal and professional life; the experiences of the one pour over into the experiences of the other.[23] She argues that personal experiences and models of parenting relationships may have something important to say about how to blend economizing and ecologizing values in business.[24] Second, she notes that rather than individuals' finding themselves in the position of autonomous and/or rational actors, parents find themselves in an obligatory bond of responsibility, a characteristic of enmeshment that is rarely acknowledged in business,[25] but is ever present in a mediating institution.

Moral development in such families is best effectuated through authoritative (neither authoritarian nor permissive) parents who remain open to questioning and explanation.[26] In a vein similar to Chappell, influential family therapists Salvador Minuchin and H. Charles Fishman provide a Western view of a family structure, one that supports "individuation while providing a sense of belonging."[27] This requires differentiation of roles that will change as the family changes over time and place, boundaries that both must be set and will be challenged, creation of subgroups (such as sibling or spousal relationships), and a relationship to a larger culture that inevitably influences the family itself.[28]

Obviously much more can be said about families beyond these scant paragraphs. Moreover, there are many kinds of families in many different cultures. There are, however, several important reasons why the articulated notion of functional family is helpful for corporate purposes. First, if one assumes some form of liberal, economic structure, such as capitalism, then these descriptions of functional family dynamics are particularly relevant in describing the balancing between individual autonomy and communal belonging. While one may be hesitant to argue that Western ideas of the family should be universal (a position I do not take), one can look at these functional notions as guides to this balancing.

This leads to the second point. In functional families there is a relationship between the well-being of the family unit (the common good) and the individuals within it. The bonds within this unit are more complex than economic sustenance. They also entail moral, emotional, and spiritual values. Similarly, even if businesses are designed to focus on economic efficiency, the relationships within the firm are human ones and the bonds that sustain these relationships will also entail moral, emotional, and spiritual values. Such values may be encouraged by a particular kind of structure, but they cannot be reduced to philosophical principle or legal rule.

Here it may be helpful to briefly note an argument made by legal scholar–business ethicist Jeffrey Nesteruk. For Nesteruk, business ethics suffers because it has an impoverished view of the law as a set of rules, obligations, or constraints.[29] Beyond specific rules, Nesteruk emphasizes the rhetorical power of the images created by the law.[30] Beyond rules and even institutions, law acts as a script in which the use of law as a language provides us a mechanism to constitute and develop character, culture, and community.[31] In other words, language such as "fiduciary duty" or even economic efficiency becomes not a rule to be followed, but that which, in turn, forms our lives and communities.

There is a tension in Nesteruk's view of law as a device creating constitutive identity and that of the earlier reference to Holmes for whom law moves standards toward external criteria. My task in elaborating BMI is along the lines of balancing these two views, both of which state important truths. I am interested in sketching a regime of corporate governance laws (a Holmesian external standard) that also provides a rhetoric for understanding the life of those in a business organization (a Nesterukian constitutive identity). The proposed governance structures establish a level playing field of corporate mediating institutions in which meaning is found in respectful working relationships.

Third, the family structure must remain open to the outside world to some degree. The functional family does not quarantine its members, or separate them from society. It *mediates* between individuals and society. Any grouping that fosters identity, such as an inner-city gang or a rural militia, could be described as a mediating institution. In this book, I want to distinguish between a descriptive and normative mediating institution. A mediating institution integrates an individual's good into the common good of others and their associations. It neither quarantines its members nor does it organize itself on the basis of alienation, fear, or superiority. It socializes its members to see the connection between individual self-interest and the good of others through the means of ethical behavior.

In a business corporation, the influence of the outside world is ever present because of the need to respond to demands of the market. What might be of more concern in structuring a business so that it works like a family is perhaps not the need to be open to the outside world as much as it is to develop the bonds mentioned in this opening chapter. Having said this, however, openness to the outside world, as I shall argue more thoroughly later in the book, is an adaptive survival trait.

What Salbu and the others provide is a concrete metaphor for a forum in which healthy interaction occurs. This metaphor is an architectural form describing the contours of the "organization." But the architecture has space for many kinds of rooms, furniture, and décor. In this book, I would like to extend this architecture to a broadly based notion of mediating institution. Legal supports are necessary for this kind

of structure. Ultimately, however, it is not the structure but the participants living in the house who create a home.

BACK TO BUSINESS

These images explain the actions of my pension client. Certainly, employment within the company provided income, and work for the company provided profits. In addition to the economic relationship, there
was a distinct sense of moral, emotional, and spiritual well-being in the
corporate community. Individuals not only believed that they benefited
from being affiliated with the company, but they also questioned, as
enfranchised members of the corporation, the decisions made by corporate executives. Openness to question does not require workplace
democracy. The willingness of an authoritative, centralized decision-
making unit (the CEO and/or the board of directors) to be open to
questioning is something more akin to a constitutional republic.

It is useful to ask if this model is something appropriate only to family
businesses. In some ways, the answer is yes, but families and family businesses offer lessons for multinational corporations. To draw upon another example, I was once hired by a family business that was a leader in
its market.[32] The shareholders of the business were third- and fourth-
generation owners. What was once a tightly knit family—everyone lived
in the same town and had similar values—was now a very diverse group
from all over the country with a full range of religious views, all devoutly
practiced. Although the business was a model of how businesses could
ethically treat employees and contribute to the welfare of the community, the shareholders, frankly, did not get along with one another. They
were distant, separated, and (to a large degree) alienated from one another. Seeing their problem as one of a difference in values and concerned that ultimately the frictions produced by value conflict would
tear the company apart, I was hired, in part as a theologian, to articulate
a normative direction to their company.

Rather than listing the relevant values and virtues they might adopt, I
and a colleague instead listened to the concerns of all of the shareholders and then asked them to write a story about something they thought
represented their values. The stories were photocopied, bound, and distributed to all the members of the family. At a shareholder/family meeting, some of them took turns reading their stories and talking about
them. What we quickly discovered was that the willingness to share stories and to communicate and listen enhanced empathy and respect
among them. Even those who disagreed quite strenuously with a particular viewpoint discovered a human being behind that viewpoint.
Without the opportunity to express what was important, the atmosphere

of caring for one another had been absent. Now, seven years later, the family has difficulty recalling why they ever needed a consultant: didn't they always get along with each other?

The difference between what existed prior to this exercise and what existed afterward was the difference between a collection of individuals who shared an abstract relationship to something called "family" and an actual mediating institution. This "family" had interacted on the basis of superficial constructs rather than real, lived lives. After the meeting, the family returned over time to what it had been originally—a mediating institution—where there was a sense of empathy and compassion for one another that made them want to treat each other well. The very nature of their diverse backgrounds required them to be attentive to the outside world, but they also found reasons to have a heightened sense of the need for treating others fairly within their mediating institution because they were fully confronted with the personal lives of others in their family.

Because BMI is about mediating institutions and not only about families, however, it is also much broader than family business. There are other kinds of mediating institutions. Religious institutions, voluntary associations (such as a softball team, a chamber singer ensemble, a PTA, or a self-help group), and neighborhoods are all mediating institutions. Thus, while the "family" probably provides the most direct experiential connection to mediating institutions, it is not an exclusive model. As a result of this, and because I hope to demonstrate that there is an innate human need for mediating institutions if, in fact, moral behavior is to be inculcated, a more expansive notion of mediating institutions is offered and is applicable to a wide array of business organizations, including public, multinational corporations.

My pension client was a mediating institution, nurturing trust, honesty, solidarity, loyalty, transparency, accountability, and commitment to a common good. The way it did so was by an almost instinctive integration of the wisdom of stakeholder, virtue, and contract theories. The family business with which I worked returned to being a mediating institution. What each mediating institution did was to provide a relatively small context in which members of the organization learned that other human beings were directly impacted by their actions, human beings whose well-being was concretely tied to their own. As I will argue in the next two chapters, there are limits to the number of individuals that can be in such communities in order to provide this kind of experience. Because anthropological evidence suggests this limitation and because corporations today can be huge organizations, there is a need for a legal architecture that allows members of corporate communities to have these empathic experiences. Moreover, to preserve the *normative* character of BMI as opposed to it being simply a *descriptive* term, it will be important to distinguish further between a normative (mediating) institution and what I will term a quarantining (descriptive and even problematic) institution. Chapters 4 and 5 will examine further notions of checks and balances necessary to construct this kind of a firm in comparison to international examples of corporate governance. Thus, part I's task is to elaborate the normative basis of BMI and to sketch the legal requirements necessary to create these kinds of firms.

I

Business as Mediating Institution

2

Some Catholic Notions

In Richard Attenborough's film *Gandhi,* the title character is on his way
to negotiate with Muslim leaders in conjunction with India's freedom
from Great Britain. That freedom lifted the lid off the simmering ha-
treds between Muslims and Hindus. Gandhi was preparing to negotiate
a power-sharing arrangement to prevent Muslim secession (which eventually became Pakistan). As Gandhi began to drive past Hindus protest-
ing these negotiations, he scolded the protesters claiming that he
(Gandhi) was a Muslim and a Christian and a Jew: all this from a devout
Hindu. His example is a model for a commitment to a particular identity and simultaneously profound openness to others. His commitment
is not simply one of tolerance but of integration and openness. This is
the orientation produced by a normative mediating institution.

Perhaps the best word to characterize Gandhi's spirituality is a profound sense of solidarity. Indeed, at the heart of his ethic of nonvio-
lence was a profound commitment of not only respect, for but also empathy with his enemies. Even in the midst of his battles with Great
Britain to gain Indian independence, he refused to characterize the
British as enemies, but considered them to be friends. In his ashram, he
brought together diverse individuals to live together in a community
that transcended ethnic and religious identity. Interestingly enough, the
population of Gandhi's ashram hovered around 130, a number that will
be important later in the book.[1] Bonding with this close association of
diverse individuals in the ashram also reinforced Gandhi's embrace of
all India as his family.[2] Compare then, Gandhi's spirituality with Pope
John Paul's description of solidarity.

21

This then is not a feeling of vague compassion or shallow distress at the misfortune of so many people, both near and far. On the contrary, it is a firm and persevering determination to commit oneself to the common good; that is to say to the good of all and of each individual, because we are all really responsible for all. This determination is based on the solid conviction that what is hindering full development is that desire for profit and that thirst for power already mentioned. These attitudes and "structures of sin" are only conquered—presupposing the help of divine grace—by a diametrically opposed attitude: a commitment to the good of one's neighbor with the readiness, in the Gospel sense, to "lose oneself," for the sake of the other, instead of exploiting him, and to "serve him" instead of oppressing him for one's own advantage.[3]

One hesitates to think how "at home" Gandhi would be in a multinational corporation. Still, there is a sense in which it is exactly his attitude that would be at the heart of an effective business ethic and which practices the solidarity the pope advocates. In this chapter, I would like to elaborate two notions: solidarity and mediating institutions. To do so, I will rely upon what might be called catholic social thinking. It is *catholic* rather than *Catholic* because I want to emphasize a universality of these ideas. Nevertheless, it is very dependent upon Catholic social thought. To do this, I want to first extend the argument that compassion and empathy are catholic principles. Second, I want to show how Catholic social thought has emphasized the importance of mediating institutions to develop the responsible exercise of these principles, primarily vis-à-vis governmental structures. Third, I want to apply these thoughts to corporate life.

NURTURING EMPATHY, SOLIDARITY, AND COMPASSION

As an example of the catholicity of solidarity, empathy, and compassion, I extend the twin examples of the Hindu Gandhi's essential practice of solidarity and John Paul's articulation of this practice to LaRue Tone Hosmer's summary of world religions. In analyzing world religions, Hosmer offers these summaries from the religions themselves:

Buddhism . . . "Harm not others with that which pains yourself."
Christianity . . . "All things whatsoever you would that others should do unto you, do ye even so unto them, for this is the law and the prophets."
Confucianism . . . "Loving kindness is the one maxim Which ought to be acted upon throughout one's life."Hinduism . . . "This is the sum of duty; do naught to others which if done to thee would cause thee pain."Islam . . . "No one of you is a believer until you wish for everyone what you love for yourself."
Jainism . . . "In happiness and suffering, in joy and grief, we should regard all creatures as we regard our own self."

Judaism . . . "What is hurtful to yourself, do not do to others. That is the whole of the Torah, and the remainder is but commentary. Go and learn it."

Sikhism . . . "[A]s thou deemest thyself, so deem others. Then shalt thou become a partner in heaven."Taoism . . . "Regard your neighbor's gain as your gain, and regard your neighbor's loss as your loss."[4]

One could think of these religious injunctions as variations of the Golden Rule (or the Golden Rule itself) and, of course, one sentence will rarely summarize the richness of any religion. Nevertheless, Hosmer states a fundamental religious perspective, and he notes two interesting aspects of the injunctions. First, they are aimed at creating a sense of community.[5] The second aspect is that although religious beliefs are tied to more specific injunctions for a particular community, at the heart of them is the compassion necessary to form a community. In fact, Hosmer entitles the chart above the quoted summaries "Examples of Compassion in the World's Religions."[6]

There is abundant evidence in human history that religions can be part of an "us versus them" attitude. The religions of Gandhi's own India are proof of this. Yet, the spirituality of Gandhi and John Paul is precisely to foster the compassion that can also be extended to a wider community. One's mediating institution, in this context, becomes the incubator for the compassion, solidarity, and empathy that extends to those outside of one's "in-group." Mediating institutions, in contrast to quarantining institutions, do this.

The contemporary rebirth of mediating institutions as a social means of analysis can be traced in large part to the work of Peter Berger and Richard John Neuhaus, who defined them as "those institutions standing between the individual in his private life and the large institutions of public life."[7] Berger and Neuhaus clearly identified the state as the key "large institution" that could be alienating, but they left open the possibility that other large structures such as multinational corporations and labor unions could also be alienating megastructures.

The important point is that it is within these mediating institutions that solidarity, empathy, and compassion (I do not think it is overly beneficial to separately define each of these terms) are cultivated. At one level, this produces significant problems. One can view militias or gangs as small groups that foster in-group solidarity on the basis of alienation from the rest of the world. These are quarantining institutions, which do not possess the normative *mediating, connective* character of the metaphor I am advocating. The examples of the last chapter provide examples of more ideal mediating institutions. My pension client, for instance, was a mediating institution that fostered solidarity among its various internal constituents, which led to the practicing of positive virtues such as loyalty, truth telling, promise keeping. My consulting client became an institution whose members grew in empathy as they (re)discovered the complexities and humanness of others in the family.

Viewed in this light, what is *catholic* is the importance of nurturing this spirituality of solidarity or, if one prefers, empathy or compassion. Although these notions are not identical, they share a sense of finding one's self interest in the well-being of others. The way this attitude or spirituality is nurtured is through an identification of oneself with others, which might be most deeply understood in the context of relatively small communities. In such communities, one can experience solidarity through a shared commitment to a common good or a common need.

What small communities do that larger stuctures do not are (1) to provide a more immediate feedback mechanism for how actions affect others; (2) to enhance the relative power of individuals vis-à-vis their community (a) by inculcating a sense of moral identity (which rules out certain choices as unacceptable) and (b) by leaving communal decisions more amenable to individual actions (because the number of individuals are relatively few); and (3) to reinforce a disposition about why treating others well is important and desirable.

Perhaps more important, small groups provide a greater likelihood of human beings interacting with other multifaceted, complex human beings. Think of the examples from the previous chapter. The family business changed when members saw others as complex persons rather than as unidimensional opponents. It was when they heard the stories important to others that they found the other person was more than a projected Other. Similarly, my pension client was concerned about the fairness of the switch to the new plan because employees were not labor inputs but friends.

To switch to a larger setting, Charles Hampden-Turner found that when Annheuser-Busch made its culture more "high context" (meaning that feelings, beliefs, and ideas of members were woven into the fabric of the corporate culture), its productivity, product quality, and plant safety all improved, resulting in decreases in absenteeism and grievances.[8] From this, it is at least plausible to suggest that solidarity, empathy, and compassion may be heightened when fuller selves are engaged at work. And in small institutions, the chance for seeing fuller selves may be increased. With that engagement comes the possibility of treating others as human beings whose interests transcend economic efficiency.

This emphasis on small institutions relates, but is not identical to another Catholic notion called subsidiarity, which has to do with the specification of authority. Indeed, one of the tasks of chapters 4 and 5 is to apply subsidiarity to corporations (as opposed to governments) and to suggest that corporations ought to rely upon subsidiary. That is, it should devolve some kinds of decisions to smaller groups within the corporation in order to nurture the compassion that would encourage a person to want to treat others in an ethical manner.

As is clear from the terminology I am using, this chapter will draw heavily upon Catholic social thought, primarily because that tradition has done excellent work in developing the concepts. Moreover, the Catholic tradition's reliance on natural law, a methodology I will draw upon in the following chapter, contemplates the possibility of all human beings acquiring moral knowledge. It then is inherently catholic, as is reinforced by the opening paragraph, which focused on a Hindu. Hosmer's survey of world religions suggests that concepts such as compassion, empathy, and solidarity have a universality to them. Thus, while giving full credit to Catholic social thought for developing the categories I use in this book, and in particularly in this chapter, I, as a non-Catholic, want also to emphasize their *catholic* potential.

In this chapter, then, I want to begin to connect solidarity and mediating institutions in an effort to show why business organizations should be constructed as mediating institutions and not just collections of individuals contracting in a self-interested way. These concepts are cornerstones upon which one can build a new model of corporate governance.

CORE PRINCIPLES OF CATHOLIC SOCIAL THOUGHT

William Byron, a Jesuit priest and former president of Catholic University, recently distilled from various Roman Catholic ecclesial documents, ten core principles of Catholic social thought. They are human dignity, respect for human life, right of association, participation, preferential option for the poor and vulnerable, solidarity, stewardship, subsidiarity, human equality, and the common good.[9] I do not wish to argue against these principles. In looking at them, however, it would seem that one could group seven of these principles (human dignity, respect for human life, association, participation, preferential option for the poor and vulnerable, stewardship, and human equality) as practical principles and practices that lead to the creation of a common good.

Moreover, they relate to not just any common good, but to a particular kind of common good. That is, the principles Byron articulates relate to a common good of caring for others. I emphasize this because the attitude or spirituality of solidarity can be linked to a common good in relation to a quest for an important objective, such as a World Series crown, an election to the Senate, or a 30 percent return on equity. In such quests, people can *minimize* their complex selves in order to reach the particular goal. While at certain times and places these kinds of quests can be good, the common good of which Byron writes and about which I write, is a common good of mutual respect of the dignity of all people. The principles I have noted in Byron's list are those that lead to this kind of common good. Byron's other two principles, solidarity and subsidiarity, seem to have, or at least may have, a different orientation.

Solidarity conveys an attitude or spiritual orientation. A person practicing "a firm and persevering determination to commit oneself to the common good; that is, to the good of all and of each individual"[10] would likely be a person who also respects human dignity, the right to associate, and the other principles summarized by Byron. Thus, in addition and perhaps prior to the implementation of these principles is this attitude or spirituality of solidarity we have already seen. To put it another way, these other principles are actualized by individuals with an orientation manifesting solidarity.

The question is how one cultivates such an orientation. In chapters 3 and 4, I will present evidence from anthropology and biology that suggest cognitive, neural reasons for why such groups are the place where empathy develops. Before getting to these sources, one can look to more traditional ways in which one cultivates solidarity. Acceptance of a religious faith calling for compassion may be one valid way of doing this. The principle of subsidiarity also suggests a particular structure that also cultivates such an orientation via the government. Subsidiarity, as Byron describes it, relates to the proper role of government. More specifically, it states that "no higher level of organization should perform any function that can be handled efficiently and effectively at a lower level of organization by human persons who, individually or in groups, are closer to the problem and closer to the ground."[11] In such instances, those closer to the ground are more likely to *care* about resolving the problem.

This notion of subsidiarity is also a Jeffersonian notion and one often neglected in critiques of government. Governmental bodies are not monolithic, but themselves must be broken down in smaller segments in order to effectively respond to needs.[12] The Postal Service comes to mind. Although a massive bureaucracy, it must also have a local office. The primary question for chapter 5 is how a large corporate bureaucracy, like the U.S. Postal Service, integrates *meaningful* suboffices (mediating institutions) that reduce the alienation that large bureaucracies (like the Postal Service and also like a multinational corporation) can produce of those working for them. The simple point, to be more fully developed, is that the principle of subsidiarity may describe a moral preference for noncentralized decision making that may be applicable to corporate life as well as governmental.

Preliminarily, how might Catholic social thought be applied to business? Robert Kennedy provides the acronym PARTNERS:

Participation (of all employees);

Access (to work for as many people as possible);

Respect (of the dignity of the worker in taking into account the gifts and vocations of individuals);

Trust (as a duty to be developed by making employment stable and permanent as possible and not to view employees as variable expenses);

Needs (in matching work to the human need for meaningful work);

Expression (of employees to express their freedom through work and to make it part of their identities);

Rewards (of a wage for a decent life and that rewards individuals for the contributions they make to the organization); and

Success (in terms of a duty, within moral bounds, towards efficiency and productivity and by eliminating laziness and waste).[13]

It seems again that at the heart of Kennedy's directives is a spirituality of solidarity as applied to work. The identification of one's self-interest with another's well-being would be an experience that would also lead a person to implement PARTNERS. It is exactly when corporate life is linked to a meaningful, spiritual commitment to the dignity of those with whom one works that Kennedy is at his most persuasive, as he writes:

> Most authors tend to agree that the overriding purpose of business is to create a profit and that, at the end of the day, this is the unavoidable measure of business success. The result, of course, is to turn things upside down. Instead of subordinating business activities to genuine human goods (as an Aristotle or Aquinas might say), we instrumentalize ethics (the study of genuine human goods) and make it serve as a tool for the acquisition of money, the instrumental good *par excellence*. This is rather like saying that the ultimate purpose of building a house is to give the carpenter practice in using his hammer.[14]

Of course, such hammering in terms of providing meaningful work for the carpenter is important. Kennedy's point, however, is that the criterion for measuring moral worth is human goods, not simply facilitated choices for later decisions. Instead, the purpose of building a house is not even the completion of the structure, but the creation of a structure that can become a home. Within the context of this book, the idea is to propose a legal architecture in which residents are more likely to develop the bonds and affections that inspire them to practice principles such as those Byron and Kennedy champion and as exemplified by the stories of chapter 1. That corporate structure is one of creating workplace mediating institutions in which individuals bond and connect with one another so as to inspire an attitude of solidarity. In short, among the applicable principles of Catholic social thought are the importance of nurturing empathy (or solidarity) in the workplace. In order to cultivate this attitude, mediating institutions become a practical embodiment of subsidiarity that provides a structure to nourish all the principles of Catholic social thought.

THE IMPORTANCE OF MEDIATING INSTITUTIONS

American culture has long been noted for the degree to which individuals voluntarily form associations in order to solve social problems. Alexis de Tocqueville noted this habit and credited it (along with religion) for preventing the individualism inevitable in a nonaristocratic culture from becoming excessively self-centered. The dependence upon others to achieve one's own goals resulted in what Tocqueville described as "self-interest rightly understood," a concept of virtue Tocqueville saw not as noble, but as a trait that on the whole raised the morality of all.[15]

Generally speaking, mediating institutions (leaving aside business communities for now) provide a socialization process whereby identity is developed. Years ago, sociologist Robert Nisbet argued that human beings have a set of very fundamental social needs, usually met by family, local community, and church. These institutions engender notions of affection, friendship, prestige, and recognition and have also engendered or intensified notions of work, love, prayer, and devotion to freedom and order.[16] Mediating institutions, of course, do not meet these needs, but they provide a context in which one deals with other human beings in a way that socializes all the participants. In such contexts, one learns interdependence. Mediating institutions break down an individual's interaction with the rest of the world into more manageable personal interactions with other human beings.

One aspect of this social importance lies in the continuing activation of individual moral concern and contribution to solving social problems. For instance, John Haughey has written that the spiritual weakness of Solomonic Israel occurred with the establishment of the monarchy. Rather than each person being responsible for the welfare of others, such responsibility was transferred to the king and his bureaucracy.[17] Similarly, James Burtchaell writes:

> Somehow we have managed to shift all responsibility for need beyond our immediate reach to officials and organizations. And thus we are morally dwarfed. It is surely ironic that in the very age when citizens have insisted that their governments be more active in socially constructed activity, individuals have been encouraged to transfer any long-distance moral responsibility to appropriate agencies, and to turn into their social torpor, caring not for those who never come into personal touch with them.[18]

Unless one is able to see tangible results of one's efforts (something that is difficult on the level of national politics or in the large global corporation), the incentive to sustain social responsibility can be diminished. Nisbet warns that the most powerful resources of democracy lie not in state protections, but

> in the cultural allegiances of citizens, and that these allegiances of citizens are nourished psychologically in the small, internal areas of family, local community, and association . . . [I]t is the liberal concentration of interest upon the individual, rather than upon the associations in which the individual exists, that serves, paradoxical as it may seem, to intensify the processes that lead straight to increased governmental power.[19]

Here again, it is important to at least raise the question of the extent to which this is a peculiarly American phenomenon. In fact, the experience of learning empathic responsibilities to others is broader. For instance, in writing about Japanese ethics, Iwao Taka has written about the notion of concentric circles. In this understanding, one has the most intense responsibilities to those with whom one is close, such as family, with decreasing responsibilities as one extends further out into the world.[20] Certainly there is a danger in this creation of an "us versus them" attitude. An emphasis on the importance of "us" can threaten to dehumanize a "them." At the same time, at what point will persons learn that people are affected by their actions and take those consequences into account in places other than small groups? The danger is not that these affections are fostered in the small group, which they practically will have to be, but in whether one also learns a way to further extend them toward others as well. As a corollary, however, if one does not participate in a structure where normative lessons are learned in small groups but are emphasized vis-à-vis a large megastructure (governmental or corporate), then a person may see no reason to think that her vote, her embezzlement, or her voice makes a difference. If this is true, how does one go about proposing a structure for a multinational corporation to attend to the importance of these small groups while maintaining the efficiencies of the large megastructure (which, for better or worse, is probably with us to stay)?

One response is to follow a structure similar to the constitutional system of checks and balances as well as federalism, diffusion of power among groups, which also fosters a social defense against the acquisition of power by any narrow person or faction. This reason not only acts as a rationale against state power, but as normative constraint within the corporation, because it too can be organized with a centralization of power that prevents the meeting of individual social needs.

In addition to these character-forming aspects, corporations, in fact, are dependent upon mediating institutions in important ways. For instance, economic benefits flow to a society in which mediating structures flourish. Economic freedom relies upon institutions that temper self-interest. Robert Bellah and his co-authors write that Adam Smith situated his free market only within the context of a larger public sphere with a "myriad of voluntary associations."[21] Patricia Werhane has made a similar analysis of Smith and free market capitalism, noting that "Smith presupposes a foundation of government, law, and social and religious institutions in which he locates his political economy. Smith does not imagine that a political economy could function without such support, and this crucial point is often neglected by commentators on the Wealth of Nations."[22]

Even free market proponent F. A. Hayek has argued that family and religious institutions efficiently inculcate the morality needed by capitalism.[23] Of course, it is one thing to say that capitalism flourishes in a society populated by mediating institutions. It is another thing to suggest that businesses ought to be mediating institutions. Such institutions may be necessary for capitalism to flourish, but should businesses be places where moral values are inculcated?

BUSINESS AS MEDIATING INSTITUTION

Much of a person's conscious life will be involved with work, in addition to traditional forms of mediating institutions. Because so much time is spent working, perhaps more so than has been spent in previous eras of human history, there is also a need to consider the extent to which businesses should also be mediating institutions.

Harvard economist Juliet Schor has argued that prior to capitalism, people did not work long hours and they enjoyed significant leisure time. She calculates that an adult male peasant living in England in 1200 A.D. worked 1,620 hours annually. By the year 1840, the average U.K. laborer worked 3,688 hours, a figure similar to her 3,650-hour estimate for Americans working in the year 1850. While those numbers had declined to 1,949 hours in the United States and 1,856 hours in the United Kingdom by the late 1980s, she argues that work itself was a far more casual affair in the early part of the millennium than that of the industrialized capitalist countries today.[24]

The time available for family, guilds, and associations may be simply less than it once was. Of course, one can argue about the extent to which Schor has fully captured all the work that may have been engaged in throughout history. Nevertheless, if mediating institutions are important, formative moral institutions, it may be better to create more time for traditional mediating institutions rather than to argue that businesses should become mediating institutions regardless of the precise arithmetic. There is little reason, however, to believe that businesses' influence will lessen in the near future. The question then becomes whether businesses can be made into organizations in which, like traditional mediating institutions, each participant gains some of the moral knowledge typically provided by family, church, or voluntary organizations.

Neoconservatives' Classical Understanding of the Corporation

Berger and Neuhaus propose their notion of mediating structures in order to address a "double crisis" in meaning. That is, they see that "megastructures" of society are alienating in that they do not provide "meaning and identity for individual existence."[25] Those individuals who handle this crisis of meaning, they argue, have access to institutions that mediate between individual private life and public life in megastructures.[26] Mediating structures such as neighborhood, family, church, and voluntary associations have a private face in which individuals obtain identity, and a public face where the megastructures gain their meaning and value. The central theme of such structures, according to Berger and Neuhaus, is the empowerment of individuals to have an impact on the actions that affect them. Such empowerment entails responsibility as well as individuals directly witnessing the consequences of their actions on others.

Are business corporations already mediating institutions? Except in family businesses, corporations are not family. They typically are neither neighborhoods nor religious institutions. They might be voluntary associations, but Berger and Neuhaus write: "For our present purposes, a voluntary association is a body of people who have voluntarily organized themselves in pursuit of particular goals. (Following common usage, we exclude business corporations and other primarily economic associations.)"[27]

At least two others, however, extend the notion of mediating institutions to corporations. The difficulty is that in doing so, the normative content of mediating institutions is emptied. Richard Madden provides a classic description of corporation and weds that description to the mediating analogy when he writes that a large corporation diminishes risks for individuals and allows opportunities for "group insurance, pensions, credit unions, and even more unusual benefits—day nurseries, for example. In addition, the corporation provides alternatives for suppliers, customers, and investors in the communities in which it operates. Finally, the resources of a corporation can be used to support other mediating structures that improve the social climate."[28]

In this notion, what the corporation mediates is the relationship between the individual and an amorphous ambiguity of life by providing the monetary return so that individuals can have financial security, so owners can realize profit, and so charities can be funded. Virtually noth-

ing is said about obtaining identity except as that identity is characterized by the ability of the individual to choose what he or she can do with
this monetary return.

There is nothing necessarily objectionable when the corporation creates wealth for its constituents, but it does stretch the notion of mediating institution beyond any recognizable form. Like Michael Novak, who
also calls the corporation a mediating institution, Madden is clear that
ethical virtues are necessary for the proper functioning of business, but
he also argues that size "has relatively little to do with whether or not an
organization can serve as a mediating structure."[29] If, however, Berger
and Neuhaus are correct in describing these structures as "the face-to-
face institutions, the people-sized institutions, the mediating institutions
where people act as neighbors,"[30] then the large corporation is not necessarily, if it can be at all called, a mediating institution. A small business, like those of my two clients in chapter 1, may more easily fit Berger
and Neuhaus's description of a mediating institution, but a large multinational corporation, if not carefully structured, can be an alienating
megastructure. The reason size has everything to do with the analysis is
that the large bureaucratic corporation hides the consequences of individual action, so that a person acts without knowledge or concern of
how actions affect others.

What is missing from the classical description of the corporation
(which is the description offered by Madden) is the communal element
necessary to provide meaning and identity. Of course, the corporation,
even as a megastructure, can very well foster the common good by satisfying customers, making a return for investors, creating new wealth and
jobs, generating upward mobility, promoting invention and ingenuity,
promoting progress in arts and sciences, and diversifying the interests of
the republic.[31] But such goods are not goods of creating meaning and
identity. Nor are such institutions necessarily communities that foster
virtue and solidarity. Thus, although there is a sense in which some may
wish to characterize businesses as mediating institutions, they do not
necessarily nourish solidarity, compassion, empathy, and respect for others. Saying that they are not necessarily mediating institutions does not
mean, however, that they cannot become so.

Business as Community and Business Virtues

The compelling critique of the capitalist corporation comes from the
(religious) neoconservatives' guide: Pope John Paul II. In his 1991 encyclical, *Centesimus Annus,* John Paul dwelled on the importance of work
to human identity. Like the notion of mediating structures, John Paul
noted the personal dimension of meaning and the connection of that
dimension to the common good in another encyclical: "Work thus be-

longs to the vocation of every person; indeed, man expresses and fulfills himself by working. At the same time work has a 'social' dimension through its intimate relationship not only to the family, but also to the common good."[32]

Of course, human beings work for their own material needs too, but in doing so they are involved in a "progressively expanding chain of solidarity."[33] Novak, however, had previously warned that solidarity was a "more proper term for the hive, the herd, or for the flock, than for the democratic community," concepts that were more Marxian than American.[34] Nevertheless, the pope had also endorsed a "market economy" that did embrace solidarity with the poor and within the workplace, and each required a wider conception of business than the classical notion.

The difference between these two capitalisms—and they are both versions of the free market—is that the classical version views identity as that which takes place separately from the material production of goods, whereas the spiritual alternative recognizes the doing of work as inherently moral, educational, and social. It is the worker's identification with the product of her work and with those with whom she has collaborated in producing something that teaches her responsibilities to those around her. I will elaborate upon this version at length in chapters 3 and 4. The spiritual version recognizes our "self" in others, so that moral obligations are not "choices" but our interconnected nature.

Novak addresses the moral, social dimension in part by concentrating on the notion of business as a vocation. But he also rightly understood that to be a vocation in which an individual practiced certain virtues required business to also be a community. For Novak, businesspeople are always building community, because business success depends upon high levels of creativity, teamwork, and morale. Apart from ethical requirements imposed on business from those outside the corporation, business requires internal moral integrity. An important element of community is a relative closeness of managers to the actions of employees. Without that, quality controls can suffer.[35]

Business can be the kind of community Novak describes. It can be an organization in which cooperation, trust, honesty, and commitment flourish. It can also be the kind of place in which bureaucracy overwhelms individual identity and responsibility, just as it can when the bureaucracy is political. In his arresting book, *Moral Mazes*, Robert Jackall describes interviews he conducted with managers in which success was determined by luck, fealty to "the king," milking a division and leaving before long-term realities caught up, and such factors as appearance, self-control, perception as a team player, style, and patron power.[36] Very important to success, he found, was adeptness at inconsistency. Thus, "what matters in the bureaucratic world is not what a person is but how closely his many personae mesh the organizational ideal; not his willingness to stand by his actions but his agility in avoid-ing blame."[37]

This is not to say that all people in an organization behave this way or even that those who do behave this way do so at all times. It would be difficult for an organization to survive if everyone always acted in this fashion. Nevertheless, the large bureaucratic organization does provide the opportunity to act in this manner before consequences catch up. A simple, quasi-business example may help to demonstrate this point. If a college football coach violates National Collegiate Athletic Association (NCAA) regulations by improperly recruiting star athletes, the coach and the athletes could easily be starring in the National Football League before the NCAA can discover and punish the transgression. The coaches and players of the university who do pay the price in the form of probation and lost scholarships quite likely have had nothing to do with the transgressions. Such events do not happen in all places at all times, and even those coaches who do violate NCAA rules do not do so all the time. But the repetition of such incidents indicates the failure of bureaucratic rules to be able to adequately govern moral behavior. (It also demonstrates how subgroups—here a college—also cannot rely on overarching laws, but must preemptively inculcate moral behavior even if they are simply to stay out of trouble.)

Decentralization is thus necessary so that decisions are made as close to the problem as possible. In theological terms, this is known as the principle of subsidiarity, which neoconservatives have used to critique the federal government. In business terms, Novak correctly writes that "[a] successful corporation is frequently based on the principle of sub-sidiarity. According to this principle, concrete decisions must be made on the level closest to the concrete reality. Managers and workers need to trust the skills of their colleagues. A corporate strategy which over-looks this principle—and many do—falls prey to all the vices of a com-mand economy, in which all orders come from above.[38]

It is important to note, as Berger and Neuhaus have, that "the man-agement mindset of the megastructure—whether of the U.S. Depart-ment of Health, Education, and Welfare, Sears Roebuck, or the AFL-CIO—is biased toward the unitary solution."[39] In political terms, the danger of this absence of mediation is that "the political order becomes detached from the values and realities of individual life. Deprived of its moral foundation, the political order is 'delegitimated.' When that hap-pens, the political order must be secured by coercion rather than by consent. And when that happens, democracy disappears."[40]

This is not to argue that corporations ought to become economic democracies, but, as Neuhaus argues, it is "to make democratic capital-ism more genuinely democratic . . . A person deprived of freedom cannot do work that is truly his, nor can he enjoy the benefits of that work."[41] Just as political megastructures undermine meaning, identity, and responsibility, so can economic ones. If we learn at work that our self-interest is best enhanced by intrigue, deception, and more self-interest, rather than by virtues of cooperation, honesty, and solidarity, then we have created a bigger hurdle, one that prevents individuals from being citizens interested in republican well-being in any public setting. Using these ideas, one can summarize six reasons why businesses should be mediating institutions.

First, meeting human needs is a good thing for individuals and society. As a good, meeting these needs should be done, whether profitable or not. Robert Greenleaf aptly describes the priority of the motivations for pursuing such a good:

> When George Fox gave the seventeenth-century English Quaker business-men a new business ethic (truthfulness, dependability, fixed prices—no haggling) he did it because his view of right conduct demanded it, not because it would be more profitable. It did, in fact, become more profitable because those early Quaker businessmen quickly emerged out of the seamy morass of that day as people who could be trusted. But the new ethic was a radical demand on those people and they must have had apprehensions about it when it was urged upon them.[42]

Second, since business is the place where people spend a great deal of their waking hours, there is the opportunity to satisfy human needs and socialize workers and managers in interpersonal responsibility. A great deal of learning (of some kind) will inevitably occur on the job. If the lessons of the workplace are different from lessons of solidarity, responsibility, and fairness, workers and managers will rarely see practiced the idea that self-interest is nourished in terms of fulfilling the needs of others in any public economic or even political context.

The third reason is that business has annexed the time previously utilized for meeting associational needs. Just as an acquiring company is liable for the obligations of an acquired company, business should be liable for the needs met in previously nonbusiness time.

Fourth, if one assumes that the legal system will (rightly) insist upon nondiscrimination in the workplace, businesses have the unique opportunity (and concomitant responsibility) to develop a language of common good within the context of multiculturalism. In his book *A Different Mirror*, Ronald Takaki writes that "on their voyage through history, Americans have found themselves bound to each other as workers."[43] It is by our labor that we come to our identity and to understand others who may not be like us. Businesses can be public grounds where people of different faiths, nationalities, races, and genders can work out commonality among diversity. Nondiscriminatory businesses provide a public forum for diversity. This kind of dialogue is likely to produce social models and languages for multiculturalism on a larger political context.

A fifth reason is that the mediating institution concept is particularly well suited for the limitation of business responsibility. The business as mediating institution view is a limited view of corporate action, because a traditional mediating institution such as family, church, or voluntary organization has primary loyalty to its own members. Those members are quite often devoted to a particular external cause, but the organization exists by virtue of a commitment to one another that may lead to addressing that external cause. Similarly, people work in businesses to achieve many external goals other than profitability, satisfying a customer, or feeding one's family. But, in order for them to do so, the organization must have community of people working together.

A chief duty of an organization then is to its members. In a corporation, that would include shareholders and managers, as has often been noted. Without arguing whether a corporation may have duties to the community at large and that meeting those duties may have positive economic consequences in the form of goodwill and reputation, a corporation first has a duty to its other internal members: its employees. In fact, as I will argue in this book, a mediating institutions approach primarily demands heightened duties to all internal members, while duties to external constituents ought to take the form of corporate obedience to legal and economically sustainable concerns.

Sixth, there are contemporary management strategies that argue that profitability can be maintained or increased if business does attempt to meet the moral needs of its members. If business does have a duty of wealth creation, then it is morally compelled to create profitable organizational structures. Thus, business does have a moral duty to reinvent itself along the lines of a mediating structure because it has the (perhaps only broad-based) opportunity to address a significant number of people in a way that provides meaning to them while confronting the critical social issues of our days with tools that can make businesses themselves more profitable.

RED AND YELLOW LIGHTS

As I indicated earlier in this chapter, I do not want to be Polyannaish about mediating institutions. They carry with them dangers as well. For instance, does the fact that a gang in an inner city provides identity to its members mean that its actions of drug dealing and murdering are ethical? Does the fact that militias form in small rural areas in reaction to the federal government mean that we should champion the Michigan Militia? The answer is too obvious to require an answer. Yet there is a dangerous potential for clannishness in my proposal that flashes a red light. Berger and Neuhaus, in fact, recognize that "[o]f course, some critics will decry our proposal as 'balkanization,' 'retribalizaton,' 'parochialization,' and such."[44] Still, there are times when clannishness is more problematic than at other times. In Madisonian terms, the multiplicity of organizations itself can be a corrective for those who would otherwise be trapped in organizations from which there is not escape. Berger and Neuhaus again write: "The relevance of the Balkan areas aside, we want frankly to assert that tribe and parochial are not terms of derision. . . . *Liberation is not escape from particularity but discovery of the particularity that fits.*"[45] In other words, the diversity of business mediating institutions enhances the individual's ability to find the community in which she is most at home.

Moreover, our shrinking world intrudes on the kinds of borders that oppressive institutions erect to maintain their evil. With cameras, televisions, fax machines, telephones, and the Internet lurking around every corner, exposure of wrongdoing is not too difficult. Thus, the possibility of oppressive communities is not as significant as it might have been in an earlier time. Nevertheless, minimizing the problems that mediating institutions may possess is something I will expand upon in subsequent chapters.

One can distinguish between different kinds of groups. To avoid the trap of an ambiguous metaphor and my normative mediating institutions model, I would like to elaborate on an earlier differentiation I made between a quarantining institution and a mediating institution, with some help from another business ethicist who draws upon naturalist categories.

In an extraordinarily challenging integration of complexity theory and morality, Bill Frederick argues that a corporation, like any other living organism, from plant life to the nation-state, is a "complex adaptive system."[46] That is, a corporation is an organization of separate parts that mutually support one another within the context of their life as an organization.[47] Putting to the side a remarkable array of other terms, Frederick poses the question of how to relate the corporation to the community at large. He responds that *"[a] community is an ecological system—an ecosystem—consisting of interlinked organisms living within an abiotic (non-living) setting. "*[48] But such a community is open also because no community can escape basic natural processes whether those be thermodynamics or El Niño.[49] The corporation, he concludes, is itself a community, but it is a community that has no choice but to be open to the realities of natural forces.[50] One could say, although Frederick himself does not, that a community that attempts to insulate itself acts contrary to nature.

Thus, business organizations are communities, but they cannot avoid interacting with the outside world. Communities require attention to the lives of individual members that comprise it in order to provide individuals with the context for meaning-making. Communities must also, however, "flirt" with the outside world lest they become anachronistic. If they do not flirt, their inevitable interaction with the outside world could become oppressive or violent or at the very least, create insularity. While such insularity may work within the context of a particular community, such as the Amish, it is not likely to have much utility in a global business environment.

To the extent a community focuses on itself only and does not remain open to the larger community, it acts as a quarantining institution. In a quarantine, the outside world is closed off (or more accurately, the local world is prevented from going out). Regardless of who is supposed to be going in and out, the important point is that there is a separation of the local community and the outside world. Interactions between the two are dangerous and should be avoided. When there is interaction, it could result in violence.

This is an imperfect, but helpful way to look at the difference between a mediating institution and a quarantining institution. A quarantining institution is closed off. Groups may close themselves off for a variety of reasons, including being alienated from a society in which they have no meaningful ability to participate. While the participation that could occur within the institution may be admirable and while the solidarity and loyalty within the organizational structure may be profound, it is insufficient. Instead, a mediating institution both promotes internal goods such as participation, solidarity, and loyalty while also "mediating"; that is, interacting (not quarantining) with the outside world. As such, a mediating institution is an adaptive mechanism for living in the world at large, not a survival mechanism in which the world at large is an enemy.

There is also a yellow light. This chapter is obviously assuming that religious belief is admissable to corporate life. This is an assumption many will not be willing to accept. As Neuhaus writes, however, "It is spiritually eviscerating that what millions of men and women do fifty or seventy hours of most every week is bracketed off from their understanding of their faith."[51] In part III of this book, I will address the question of the reasonableness of allowing such spiritual language to intrude into the workplace (and will not surprisingly conclude that I think this is a good thing). For now, however, I simply want to turn on the warning light myself to the concern that the resolution of the appropriateness of this spiritual sense raises significant, secular workplace issues to which I will attend.

In the meantime, having presented notions of solidarity and subsidiarity and their relationship to business ethics, I want to go further down this path to sketch a natural law view of corporate life that extends these thoughts and that also provides a platform from which one can develop a legal architecture to institutionally take advantage of the strengths of this approach.

3

Natural Law and
Laws of Nature

My instinct is to entitle this chapter "Natural Law (Sort Of)." This is because what I present in this chapter is a limited version of natural law. It certainly does not pretend to be a full rendering of the natural law tradition. The spokesperson on whose work I mostly rely, legal scholar John Finnis, is not often applied to corporate theory. Moreover, in addition to this selective use of normative natural law categories, I plan to begin to introduce some notions from biology and anthropology. Natural law is no stranger for such integration with science: Aristotle was, after all, also a biologist. But it seems that normative versions of natural law are often less reliant on such sciences, with some important exceptions that will be noted. Thus, this chapter will be a version of natural law a bit different from what a philosopher, theologian, or academic lawyer might typically expect when seeing the term.

This chapter seeks to build on the notion of mediating institutions, a construct arising out of the notions of subsidiarity and solidarity, from the standpoint of the philosophical version of natural law offered by Finnis, as further modified by contemporary science. (The scientific element will be further detailed in the following chapter.) The result is natural law, sort of, at least as is commonly presented.

The claim I wish to make in this chapter is simple. Natural law helps us to define certain structures that should be present in corporations. As in the analogy to relational contracts in chapter 1, my emphasis is on structures rather than on specific virtues. For instance, rather than attempting to discern what the Golden Rule has to say about a particular dilemma (say, about affirmative action), I am interested in what organizational characteristics foster the development of individuals who wish to take the Golden Rule seriously. My hope is that in making this move, I will be able to avoid some historical difficulties that have plagued natural law and to do so in a way that simultaneously provides some degree of universality and openness to diversity.

As a start, however, it is worth noting an odd feature of this entire argument. Nearly every week, the media reports another colossal merger creating a yet bigger corporation. In such an era, doesn't my emphasis on small organizations seem, at best, quaint? To show that it is not simply quaint, I would like to briefly consider a moral premise underlying this phenomenon of colossal size and relate it to why an Aristotelian notion of the corporation makes sense. To do this, I would like to look at mergers and acquisitions and then use the insights regarding the need for a commitment to tradition to proceed to the natural law description of the corporation.

In mergers and acquisitions, one can certainly find economic rationales for and against takeovers. Other concerns revolve around the strategic and ambitious goals of the participants in merger and acquisition activity. Lawyer–deal maker Bruce Wasserstein argues that, while economic determinism may make it likely that mergers will occur, there is also a distinctly human element provided by the ingenuity, stubbornness, ruthlessness, and charm of the executives in charge.[1] Robert Jackall, in his study of multinational corporations has compared chief executive officers to kings in a feudal society.[2] He is not alone in his characterization.[3] Take, for instance, this description of the kingdom of RJR Nabisco and F. Ross Johnson by LaRue Tone Hosmer:

> Executives were very well paid. Mr. F. Ross Johnson, the chairman and chief executive officer, received $3,500,000 in 1988. The next 31 persons (whose salaries were published in total, not individually, in the 10K annual report for that year) received an average of $458,000 each.
>
> Executives also received numerous "perks." All of the senior managers at corporate headquarters, and many of the functional and technical people at the divisional offices, were given an allowance of $10,000 a year for estate planning, tax assistance, and investment counseling. Everyone at the managerial rank received at least one country club membership and was given at least one company car. Executives could select their own country club and their own car model. Some managers received multiple club memberships; Mr. Johnson held the record with over 24 club memberships spread across the country. Some managers selected very luxurious cars; the record here was a special Mercedes Benz said to have cost over $200,000.
>
> Office decorations at the corporate headquarters matched the managerial salaries, perks, and cars. The *Wall Street Journal* reported that Mr. Johnson's office included a $51,000 vase, a $36,000 table, and a $100,000 rug. Expensive furnishings even extended to the corporate jet hangar at the Atlanta airport.

The RJR Nabisco jet hangar was not a sheet metal building of the type that is commonly seen at airports. Instead, it was a three-story building of tinted glass, surrounded by $250,000 in landscaping. A visitor entered through a tall open "atrium," with a roof made of glass marble, floors laid in Italian marble, and walls panelled with Dominican mahogany. $600,000 in furniture was spread through the pilots' lounge and control room, which were also decorated with $100,000 in paintings and statuary.

RJR Nabisco employed 36 pilots and co-pilots and maintained 10 corporate jets in a fleet commonly known as either the RJR Air Force or Air Johnson. The pilots and planes were used to carry managers to workday meetings and inspection tours, of course, but they were also used to bring sports figures, entertainment stars, and elected officials to Atlanta for weekend outings. The sports figures and entertainment stars were paid to be representatives for the company but spent much of their time playing golf and socializing with senior executives. . . .

It was said that many of the representatives for RJR Nabisco did very little "representing." Jack Nicklaus [paid $1 million a year] for example, refused to make more than six appearances a year, and he didn't like to play golf with RJR Nabisco's largest customers or meet with them at the evening cocktail parties and dinners.[4]

In response to these extravagancies and six-figure payments for no-shows such as O. J. Simpson, F. Ross Johnson said, "A few million dollars . . . are lost in the sands of time."[5]

Beyond these "kings," a takeover specialist must have a certain degree of single-mindedness in order to discipline the resources to engage in a successful acquisition. Thus, the successful deal maker is someone who can take advantage of regulatory and environmental changes and does so to impose a new order of economic reality within a given industry or company (as in the aftermath of Johnson's rule of RJR when it was taken over). It is the shrewd, tough, strong-willed deal maker—whom one ethicist has called Masters of the Universe[6]—who takes advantage of opportunities and efficiencies with minimal regard for other constituencies—sometimes not even of shareholders. Although the actions of such a king sometimes offend moral sensibilities, they are also justified as evolutionarily advantageous and are glorified. These CEOs are comparable to Nietzsche's Zarathustra.[7]

NIETZSCHE'S DELIGHT

If this claim seems far-fetched, consider some of Zarathustra's challenges to traditional moral views and compare them to those of the titans of mergers and acquisitions. Zarathustra argues that the good and the just, as well as believers of all faiths, hate and despise the lawbreaker; yet the lawbreaker is the creator of new values.[8] While CEOs do not necessarily break legal rules—instead, they take advantage of regulatory change—they often break rules of employment expectations, community commitment, and risk shifting. In doing so, they break old moral customs in favor of new contracts, and thereby create and ratify notions such as corporations being a "nexus of contracts"[9] rather than corporate citizens engaged in a communal endeavor.[10]

The leader who can create such value is a person of iron will. Zarathustra would find this totally appropriate, as he says: "Indeed, in me there is something invulnerable and unburiable, something that explodes rock: that is *my will*."[11] This iron will is central to economic developments, even if it is destructive. If the efficiencies it creates also maximize opportunities for stakeholders, they would hardly be expected to be considered by the overman. Instead, the appeal to self-interest is paramount and transforms selfish vice to virtue. A commitment to equality, such as limiting excessive CEO compensation, would therefore be ridiculed by Zarathustra: "I do not wish to be mixed up and confused with these preachers of equality. For, to *me* justice speaks thus: 'men are not equal.' Nor shall they become equal! What would my love of the overman be if I spoke otherwise?"[12]

To be sure, this comparison is a caricature of business leadership. Yet it also describes a logical conclusion of the forces driving mergers and acquisitions and hardly seems incompatible with the likes of an F. Ross Johnson, not to mention a Donald Trump. Some executives will not be modern-day Zarathustras. That they are not, however, is a testament to their character, because the logic of capitalism leads to exactly the ruthlessness described, at least insofar as mergers and acquisitions are concerned. One could hardly expect a rosy view of an impediment like the corporate constituency statutes, and neither would Zarathustra who says, "*Do not spare your neighbor!*"[13]

The Nietzschean dimension is important for several reasons. First, I am not the first to note this dimension, although it may not have been "Zarathustraized" before. Bringing in this dimension in terms of mergers and acquisitions, however, helps to see what is at stake. Second, the Nietzschean justification of such a quest for power also helps to explain why autonomy-based ethics struggle to respond to a hard individual will lusting for power. One could, as many have, critique mergers and acquisitions on the basis of liberal notions of autonomy and dignity. The impact mergers have on workers and communities, because of plant closings for instance, is amenable to critiques concerning the importance of treating these constituents as ends rather than as simply means to an end (of wealth maximization).

While I would like to embrace versions of stakeholder theory and contract theory in critiquing mergers and acquisitions, a central difficulty with both is that an autonomous creator of universal principles, or a consent giver, can also "choose" to do evil. Without a set of goods to which one aspires and which is fostered by a community, standard liberal theory—for all its valuable insights into protections of rights and dignity—has no real answer for Zarathustra's choice to lust for power and to spare no neighbor. This is exactly Alasdair MacIntyre's critique of liberal morality through the lens of Aristotle.

AN ARISTOTELIAN VIEW

The central difficulty with the Nietzschean justification for the lust for power and selfishness is not what it illuminates but what it obscures. Certainly, one can make a series of sophisticated assessments regarding the costs and benefits of merger and acquisition activity. The difficulty, however, is that hidden within this assessment are many other dimensions of human life that are not so easily monetized and which if monetized grossly distort the value itself.

In recent years, Alasdair MacIntyre has provided the most telling critique of its kind with this argument. For MacIntyre, the contemporary world is Weberian; that is, a decision made by, say, corporate managers, "disguises and conceals and it depends for its power on its success at disguise and concealment."[14] What does it conceal? In a bureaucratic system, one assumes that one cannot ultimately adjudicate among various moral traditions, so one does not ask ultimate questions. One brackets them off, and instead relies upon a process that will generate choices so individuals can determine autonomously what particular thing maximizes individual self-interest. Free market economics is based on precisely this. It is based not on determining the "good" of a product, but on how to efficiently produce a product that meets market demand.

Consumer choice, legal regulation, and competition then make assessments of what products are acceptable. The manager does not ask ultimate questions; asking them is simply not his job as an agent. The argument is that the model depends upon its power (of managerial efficiency) on the ability to conceal the fact that deep values are at stake in corporate affairs.

Indeed, this project of concealment, in MacIntyre's terms, hides the fact that the moral arguments available to us are fragments of earlier traditions.[15] Arguments about morality are notoriously indeterminate, because they are concealed rather than argued; they are shorn from historical traditions that allow such rationales to be intelligible.[16] As an example of this, MacIntyre, in two separate books, draws upon Hawaiian history to demonstrate his point.

A Trip to Hawaii

MacIntyre reports that when Captain James Cook made his third voyage to the Polynesian islands in 1778, his crew was surprised that while sexual mores there were very lax, there were strict prohibitions on women eating with men.[17] When asked why, the sailors were simply told that the practice was *taboo*.[18] No one, though, could really understand what "taboo" meant. In fact, anthropologists concluded that a few decades later, the natives themselves did not really understand what "taboo" meant.[19] According to MacIntyre, this is why Kamehameha II, whom MacIntyre compares to a Nietzschean overman and whose father "merged" the Hawaiian islands for the first time,[20] had an easy time overthrowing the taboo system in 1819.[21] While I think that MacIntyre's assessment of Kamehameha II is overdrawn, he is correct that if a cultural rule of behavior is predicated simply on a prohibition without any other understanding of its rationale, then it is hardly persuasive.[22]

In actuality, the notion of a taboo prohibiting women and men from eating together was based on the creation myth of Hawaiians called the Kumulipo, a myth taken with great seriousness in pre-Western Hawaii.[23] So too, for that matter, was a freewheeling attitude toward sex with multiple partners and spouses throughout life a logical participation in the highly sexually charged creation myth of Kumulipo.[24] Without this creation myth, its religious system collapsed, and so did the taboos. Abstracted from that myth, witnessed by the lack of harsh consequences that did not follow the breaking of taboo in conjunction with Cook's arrival, applied in a way that systematically (and by definition) "discriminated" against commoners, and further undermined when the ruling class—the *ali'i nui* (essentially, the nobles) and the *mo'i* (king)—used taboo for commercial profitability with the West, the practice of taboo became an ineffective moral fragment that was only barely understood by the native Hawaiians themselves.[25] What was once a behavioral system connecting individuals with cosmic identity was undermined, so that the rules of behavior no longer made any sense to those governed by them.

MacIntyre argues that we are in the same moral position today that the Hawaiians were in then. In fact, he argues that the Enlightenment project—perhaps best exemplified in Kantian universal duty and in utilitarianism—would be seen as degenerative in the pre-Cook Hawaiian mind because of how the "detachment of European moral rules from their place within an overall theological moral scheme, embodying and representing a highly specific conception of human nature, corresponds to the similar detachment of taboo rules."[26] With moral rules serving as abstract principles derived from an earlier history that we no longer know, moral rules and duties are disembodied fragments with no real authority except that which can be willed by a powerful person and imposed on others.[27] Such an authority, of course, is filled by a positivist view of law and the powerful authority is filled precisely by Nietzsche's overman.

MacIntyre's argument against Nietzsche is not that Nietzsche was able to defeat an Aristotelian view of moral behavior. Instead, it is that the Enlightenment made a drastic mistake in reacting against the Aristotelian tradition and that Nietzsche brilliantly prevailed against the Enlightenment thinkers.[28] A positivist application of utilitarian calculations that tally up what satisfies the most utiles for the most people can be every bit as rational and logical as any Kantian view of universalizing logic. Moreover, no utilitarian, Kantian, nor contractarian position can identify goods more valuable than others for an individual to prefer. In short, if one contents oneself with an economic assessment—which in our day will be utilitarian in some fashion—of the pros and cons of an activity, there are few alternatives that can combat this liberal notion of maximizing self-interest. Thus, Nietzsche's epigrammatic battle cry: "The greatest evil is necessary for the overman's best,"[29] is, according to MacIntyre, perfectly logical and essentially the end result of Kantian autonomy.

MacIntyre invites a consideration of some kind of Aristotelian/ Thomistic engagement with the modern world. Admittedly, this is an enormous project. Moreover, I am not at ease with the entirety of MacIntyre's approach, for reasons that will become apparent. I do, however, want to view corporations through another set of Aristotelian lenses, provided by legal philosopher John Finnis.

A Natural Law View

Integrating natural law with corporate life faces several significant hurdles. Epistemologically, it is open to question whether human beings can actually know what the natural law is, even if one assumes that there is such a thing.[30] Moreover, natural law can tend to lend itself to coercive punishments of those who deviate from what has been articulated as the natural law.[31]

Epistemological Problems of Natural Law

Even if there is something like natural law that is a set of universal principles, Steve Salbu is right to argue that the "inability of natural law theories to convince either that there is one truth or that we can know that truth is, respectively, its ontological and its epistemological failure."[32] This is a good argument. To counter it, natural law theorists must carefully consider three elements that must be present in natural law itself.

First, any attempt to make natural law into a specific set of fine-grained analytical principles will be problematic. This, of course, is true of nearly any global moral theory. Philosophical business ethicists routinely fall into this dilemma when they claim that their raison d'être is fine-grained analysis.[33] Natural law theories that attempt casuistry will always tend toward legalisms and maddening exceptions to situational complexity. This problem does not mean, however, that broad themes are not useful. Natural law may be able to provide broad themes that circumvent the problems of casuistry.

A second response is that there will always be opposition to moral theory. Even if one can develop a natural law theory that fully recognizes cultural diversity, some may have reasons to not care if they are moral, some may rationalize why their actions are an appropriate departure from natural law, or some may simply be bad people.[34] This response, however, does not effectively challenge Salbu's critique. Salbu is not concerned with the fact that certain people may find ways to weasel out of a moral principle, but whether people sincerely seeking to find moral principles can come to the same conclusions. This again raises the question of the level of generality of the natural law principles.

A third response to the question of whether we can know universal principles then, is whether there is a level of generality where natural law is self-evident. Natural law theorists have traditionally relied upon rationality as a language through which one understands principles and articulates them. Finnis goes so far as to fully equate moral and rational thought when he writes "moral thought is simply rational thought at full stretch, integrating emotions and feelings, but *undeflected* by them.[35] Because of this, he rejects the notion that "self-evident principles" are the result of feelings or certitude.[36] Rather, principles are the criteria to evaluate feelings, no matter how intense, irrational, unwarranted, or delusive they may be.[37]

Rather than relying upon notions of self-evidence of rational thought, one can instead consider anthropological evidence of what goods and what rules seem to be natural to human sociability. Two examples illustrate this. First, one can study religious belief, not for doctrinal pronouncements of what one must do, but as evidence of cross-cultural moral norms. When one does this, one finds that a notion of "Golden Rule reciprocity" grounds nearly all ethical systems, as we saw in chapter 2[38]: Confucius is reported to have said that at the core of his entire ethical system is the principle of reciprocity, Maimondes makes a similar summary of Jewish law, and Jesus exposes the commandments to love God with all one's heart and one's neighbor as oneself as a core ethic of his ministry. The Golden Rule and reciprocity undergird Kant's categorical imperative, according to which actions can be morally evaluated.[39] The generality of this ethical principle, of course, does not provide specific resolution of a given complex moral issue. But it is again worth cautioning that there is a trade-off between the level of fine-grained ethical analysis that can be performed and its cross-cultural efficacy.

For instance, a Hawaiian *ali'i nui'i* would have to practice reciprocity very rigorously to maintain his social position. Strict demands would be made, for instance, regarding gift giving. But the *ali'i nui'i* would have little obligation to a *maika'aina*, who could be killed if the shadow of the *ali'i nui'i* fell upon the unfortunate commoner. The social categories of Hawaiian society would therefore provide a very different idea of who should be treated in a reciprocal manner and who should not. I have no hesitance in using contemporary Western notions arguing that a system in which commoners could be killed based on their physical proximity to a noble should be changed. Prior to trying to make such an argument, however, one needs to situate oneself in the cultural realities of the time and place in order to propose any kind of remedy that might be sensible. My argument is that, prior to attempting to make definitive judgments about specific cases, one might attempt to bring some sense to basic structures first before making fine-grained analysis.

A second example of the universality of certain rules and structures is that current anthropological data indicate that cross-cultural norms may be more expansive than generalized notions of the Golden Rule. Finnis characterizes the current evidence in the following extended way:

> These surveys [of philosophers studying anthropological literature] entitle us, indeed, to make some rather confident assertions. All human societies show a concern for the value of human life; in all, self-preservation is generally accepted as a proper motive for action, and in none is the killing of other human beings permitted without some fairly definite justification. All human societies regard the procreation of a new human life as in itself a good thing unless there are special circumstances. No human society fails to restrict sexual activity; in all societies there is some prohibition of incest, some opposition to boundless promiscuity and to rape, some favour for stability and permanence in sexual relations. All human societies display a concern for truth, through education of the youth in matters not only practical (e.g. avoidance of dangers) but also speculative or theoretical (e.g. religion). Human beings, who can survive infancy only by nurture, live in or on the margins of some society which invariably extends beyond the nuclear family, and all societies display a favour for the values of co-operation, of common over individual good, of obligation between individuals, and of justice within groups. All know friendship. All have some conception of *meum* and *tuum* title or property, and of reciprocity. All value play, serious and formalized, or relaxed and recreational. All treat the bodies of dead members of the group in some traditional and ritual fashion different from their procedures for rubbish disposal. All display a concern for powers or principles which are to be respected as superhuman; in one form or another, religion is universal.[40]

In short, while it may be dangerous to articulate a specific set of natural law principles that govern particular situations, one may be able to appeal to our human nature, discovered by anthropology, to find some basic universal capacities and interests.

Limiting Coercion

If the caution to avoid casuistry is not followed, then any moral theory attempting cross-cultural analysis is vulnerable to the second problem that natural law has experienced. That is, when a given group has convinced itself that it "knows" what the natural law is, then those who deviate from it may be justifiably punished. Here again, Salbu summarizes the situation aptly: "The ostensibly universal character of superior choices under natural law provides the justification for those contending to understand its valuation priorities to try to impose those priorities universally. Ethical systems based on natural law tend in this way to become coercive, and the belief that morality is absolute renders a legalistic form of moral reasoning."[41]

The appropriate response to Salbu's legitimate charge is that a natural law theory that is not open to either individual judgment or adaptive change violates the laws of nature and should therefore be rejected. MacIntyre may be right (I believe he is) that moral beliefs are essentially community property,[42] but naturalism does not require forfeiture of personal judgment. Further, any attempt to claim universal rules ought to also be humble enough to be open to changes in any particular formulation of governing rules. Just as a family must be open to the larger culture in which it is situated, so must any community guard against quarantining itself in the development of its moral knowledge.

Contemporary science holds an analogy, and perhaps a structure, for understanding a dialectic among universal goods, adaptive openness, and individual freedom. Contemporary science argues that there is both chaos and simplicity in the physical world.[43] Chaos, unfortunately, is typically used to note that nothing is sure.[44] In fact, it refers to the unpredictability of specific times and events. Chaos is also "complex." That is, there is order within the chaos. While individual events, like cultures, may be strongly differentiated, certain patterns, like the perception of natural law, emerge over time. For instance, in the early "discoveries" of chaos, both variability and patterns were immediately apparent.[45] Thus, "[n]ature forms patterns. Some are orderly in space but disorderly in time, others orderly in time but disorderly in space. Some patterns are fractal, exhibiting structures self-similar in scale. Others give rise to steady states or oscillating ones."[46] Complexity theory demonstrates these recurring patterns and laws that govern human life.[47] Within that order, however, individual events are chaotic; they are unpredictable.

They are both subject to individual influences and part of recurring patterns.

With this in mind, one can view natural law as describing the large-scale patterns of human history in which moral principles of goodwill and reciprocity mandate a method of discourse in which the community's pursuit of its common good is preeminent, but must also protect individuals and their judgments and preserve their ability to adapt.

One example of an ordered capacity is the size of the groups that human beings can live in. Wasserstein noted that while there were evident deterministic drives toward largeness in corporations, there was also evidence of a strong attempt to reduce size.[48] Both natural law and laws of nature suggest that human beings may be most "at home" in small groups. Normatively, this could suggest a ratification of subsidiarity. This principle leads significant autonomy and responsibility in the hands of particular communities. Its corollary, however, is that it requires a level of participation by individuals within the community. Thus, it is both ordered and open.

Finnis describes the importance of the individual within the context of a community and its common good in much the same way as did Tom Chappell, quoted in chapter 1: "one who is never more than a cog in big wheels turned by others is denied participation in one important aspect of human well-being."[49] Rather than being opposed to individuality, a natural law approach emphasizes that decisions should be made in the closest proximity to individual control. Natural law does insist upon a normative principle of supporting the common good, but it does so in a way that balances good with the development of individual responsibility and creativity. Biological anthropology confirms this emphasis I have been giving to small groups.

Laws of Nature

The point to be made is that human beings, while having a good deal of plasticity in the development of their culture, do not have infinite flexibility. Much as we would like, we cannot make our arms into wings so that we can fly. We must build things like airplanes, which take into account our inability to fly by our own physical means. Similarly, while we may want to think that we have a Lockean plasticity in the development of our moral sentiments and our rational achievements, biology suggests that there are limitations. Those limitations impact how we relate to other individuals. If ethics is about how we relate to other individuals, these biological limitations make a significant difference as to how we go about proposing ethics in corporate life or anywhere else.

First, anthropologists have found consistent group sizes among aboriginal populations. These tend to cluster between twenty-five and thirty-five (the band) and four hundred to six hundred (the macro-band), which is the largest community that interacts regularly.[50] One of the difficulties in larger groupings is that scalar stress—increasing numbers of disputes within the group—increases exponentially rather than arithmetically when membership in the group exceeds these "magic numbers."[51] All of these relatively small numbers suggest a simple numerical empowerment of individuals. In such groups, morality may be communal, but the individual's influence on her relevant community is arithmetically more powerful. The relationship between the empowering efficacy of these small groups and the large megastructures, such as the multinational corporation, will be explored more fully throughout this book. For present purposes, it is sufficient to see that studies of human behavior indicate ways to blend individual power and communal good.

In his study on the development of human language, psychologist Robin Dunbar reported accounts for the genesis of its development. He noted that a typical explanation for the difference between humans and other animals is the large size of the human brain.[52] But whales and elephants have larger brains than humans, so he instead examined the ratio of the neocortex—that part of the brain responsible for cognition as opposed to the controller of bodily functions and movement—to body mass.[53] In doing this, he found general groupings of neocortex ratios; that is, reptiles were in a certain range, fish in another, primates in another, with human brains having, by far, the highest ratio.[54]

Dunbar also noticed that primates tend to limit the size of their group. Above a certain number, the group fissions.[55] He then plotted a graph with coordinates of primate neocortex ratios and group size.[56] Extending the results, he predicted the maximum size of a human group to be 150.[57] This is in the range of the hunter-gatherer numbers we just saw, but does it have any contemporary ratification? In fact, in looking at other studies Dunbar noted that religious groups, such as the Hutterites, have pursued their life in communal farms for nearly four centuries in Europe and in North America. According to Dunbar the mean size of their communities is 100 and the communities split if they reach a size of 150. Above this number, the Hutterites believe that it is hard to control membership by peer pressure alone.[58] Why is this? Dunbar writes:

> Indeed, there is a well-established principle in sociology suggesting that social groupings larger than 150–200 become increasingly hierarchical in structure. Small social groups tend to lack structure of any kind, relying instead on personal contacts to oil the wheels of social intercourse. But with more people to coordinate, hierarchical structures are required. There must be chiefs to direct, and a police force to ensure that social rules are adhered to. And this turns out to be an unwritten rule in modern business organizations too. Businesses with fewer than 150–200 people can be organized on entirely informal lines, relying on personal con-

tacts between employees to ensure the proper exchange of information. But larger businesses require formal management structure to channel contacts and ensure that each employee knows what he or she is responsible for and whom they should report to.[59]

Dunbar has other examples as well. He goes on to note that the Mormons followed a pattern similar to the Hutterites. He writes that when Brigham Young led the Mormons to Utah, he divided his flock of 5,000 into groups of 150.[60] Dunbar also reports that a study conducted by the Church of England found that the ideal congregation size is less than 200, and he also found that over the past one hundred years, the military company unit has ranged from 130 (the number in Gandhi's ashram) to 170.[61] These anthropological realities suggest that certain capacities are universal among human beings. The findings themselves do not suggest universal norms, but do indicate basic human capacities that may have an impact on how human beings relate to each other.

Such small institutions, of course, are in a sense "mediating institutions." They stand between the individual and society.[62] They socialize and empower the individual and thereby, ideally, make such individuals into citizens who enter society with the tools to negotiate, knowing that they are social creatures depending upon a community.[63] That is the rosy view. The thorn is that these groups can be insular, violent, and reclusive.[64] The difference between the petals and the thorns is the distinction, made in chapter 2, between a mediating institution and a quarantining institution. A mediating institution provides a community for its members, but it does mediate, so that it is open to the outside world. It therefore is always negotiating and adapting. While a mediating institution must also have a unique identity, it also contains feedback mechanisms—its cybernetics[65]—open to environmental changes.

The point is that biological anthropology (laws of nature) confirms the natural law (as articulated by Catholic social thought) emphasis on the desirability (and necessity) of small groups. Human beings relate to one another in small groups, where they have feedback mechanisms for the consequences of their actions. If ethics has to do with how we treat others, then this cognitive limitation makes a difference to doing ethics well. Put individuals in large groups, and one loses the sense of community that nurtures ethical behavior. Who will really notice if I embezzle a bit of money from this huge employer? At the same time, an attempt to quarantine a company may lead the company to the continued manufacture of buggy whips in an age of automobiles.

The natural law position, if it does not attempt too much specificity, can helpfully account for this order and change. The order includes cognitive limitations, which suggest a structure necessary for notions such as empathy, solidarity, and compassion with the correlative virtues, such as truth telling and promise keeping, that arise from these dispositions. The ordered structure, however, is also open for cultural diversity and for historical development in which one can converse about the superiority of some moral systems and virtues over others. In this sense, natural law provides an awareness of structure, but it remains open to Kantian or other philosophical assessment of particular moral conduct.

Thus, natural law is a repository of a global ethic, not only in contemporary society but throughout other lives and cultures on this planet. As Joseph Boyle puts it, "The tradition of natural law stretches over more than five hundred years and has been carried out by people in very different cultural circumstances within communities which certainly seem distinct."[66] If there is a unity of thought concerning what universal principles might be, then natural law's historical perspective may be a rich source of information, but it also must be attentive to the reality of the laws of nature. The proposal I am making is only a small step in recognizing that by studying human activities and primate activities as well, we may be in a position to determine some universal structures and if we maintain a commitment to a level of generality, rather than overemphasizing the attempt to derive specific judgments in specific cases, we may be in a position to actually provide more assistance to business practitioners on how to organize their institutions to enhance ethical business behavior.

A TRADITIONAL NATURAL LAW APPROACH

Reflecting the importance of generality, there is no "one" natural law position. Instead, there appropriately is diversity, as general patterns are applied to specific historical conditions. One article recently distinguished among four natural law traditions, just within the United States.[67] This includes a traditionalist approach, which contends for specific goods and virtues that differ, to some extent, from those proposed by Aquinas.[68] Actions are wrong if they destroy other goods, even in pursuit of a basic good itself.[69] John Finnis is an influential spokesperson for this approach, and the seven goods he identifies are life, knowledge, play/work, aesthetic experience, sociability, practical reasonableness, and religion.[70] An example of the application of this approach would be a condemnation of the tobacco industry. Regardless of the goods promoting by a legal business—in terms of profit and work for instance—there is a violation of a basic good of life (through undermining human health).[71]

To abbreviate a great deal, a second approach is that of proportion, with its distinguishing moral calculus, called the principle of double effect.[72] In particular, an assessment about the proportion of the good and evil involved in the action gives rise to the "proportionist" label this tradition carries.[73] An example of this approach would be affirmative action, where providing a job to a minority applicant is not evil, but it does have a bad effect of "reverse discrimination."[74] One can then argue about the proportionate good of bringing about a more just society, outweighing the current evil effect.[75]

A third natural law approach is that of "right reason."[76] This approach places heavy emphasis upon human ability to determine the foundations of natural law with or without theology.[77] Business ethicists who follow this approach have linked natural law to contemporary philosophical categories of utility, rights, and justice.[78]

Finally, the historicist approach to natural law emphasizes the adaptability of natural law; that is, that the Church changed its views, through natural law categories, on issues such as usury, divorce, slavery, abortion, and religious toleration.[79] An example of this would be bribery, which may not be absolutely immoral, depending upon the conditions of the time and culture in which it takes place.[80] One can also justifiably view the founding of the United States and the creation of the Constitution as a part of a long tradition of natural law dialogue, so that American notions of government structure and legal principles are rooted in natural law.[81] For purposes of this chapter, I will use Finnis, MacIntyre, and the American legal order as baselines for analysis, because I view them as reasonably comprehensive articulations of natural law positions and because the other approaches are implicitly and explicitly a part of the argument.

Finnis's Natural Law

As just mentioned, Finnis identifies seven basic human goods: life, knowledge, play/work, aesthetic experience, sociability, practical reasonableness, and religion. I would like to focus on two of them: sociability and practical reasonableness.

Sociability and a Human Social Nature

Aristotle bases his philosophy on the claim that human beings are inherently social. While Finnis's notion of sociability is not explicitly based on this fundamental claim, Aristotle's insight can be demonstrated empirically. Central to this argument is rooting human nature in nature itself, because, unlike Hobbes's theories, Aristotle's theories of social behavior are essentially biological and thus compatible with Darwin.[82] Inherent in Aristotle's political thought was a biological understanding of human nature with "an ambivalent combination of individualistic competition and social cooperation, and the view that the full development of human moral and political capacities requires a complex interaction of nature and nurture."[83] If human social behavior rests upon a biological nature, then one can compare basic human and nonhuman goods. In doing exactly this, Larry Arnhart lists twenty natural desires present in all human societies throughout history: "a complete life, parental care, sexual identity, sexual mating, familial bonding, friendship, social ranking, justice as reciprocity, political rule, war, health, beauty, wealth, speech, practical habituation, practical reasoning, practical arts, aesthetic pleasure, religious understanding, and intellectual understanding."[84] MacIntyre himself now looks to biology to, at least in part, provide some kind of telos for his philosophy.[85]

Anthropologists Carol and Melvin Ember, says Arnhart, confirm this listing.[86] It may be too strong to argue that human beings have a moral sense, as Hume and recently James Q. Wilson argued.[87] It is not too risky, however, to argue that human beings are by nature social and that survival, while being social, requires working out principles of social life. This is an important point and one that can both reinforce normative reflection on ethics and avoid the trap of naturalistic determinism.

In a recent book, Alasdair MacIntyre added biology to his virtue-based approach. His argument, which I believe strikes the right balance between nature and philosophy, has four critical elements. The first is that human beings are not only social, but vulnerable and dependent creatures.[88] The second is that because we are vulnerable and dependent, our survival and flourishing depend on virtues that teach us to care for others.[89] The third element is that the mark of a good community and a good person is when individuals choose to exercise their judgments in a way so as to value those who, like them, share some disability.[90] Fourth, only certain kinds of communities, which for MacIntyre do not include the nation-state and the modern family, can meet the standard of teaching individuals these lessons.[91]

While there may be many interesting philosophical implications to MacIntyre's argument, I would like to emphasize four of my own corporate extensions of this argument. First, the emphasis on human vulnerability is potentially contradictory to notions that human beings act in a rationally self-interested way, as economists often like to assume. Rational self-interest, at least insofar as it includes the notion that one does not have to take into account various externalities because others can take care of themselves, does not take into account the particular vulnerabilities and disabilities with which a person makes a decision. Second, experiencing empathy with the vulnerable is exactly what transformed my family-business client, described in chapter 1, into a mediating institution: it was the vulnerability they felt in sharing one another's stories that opened the eyes of each of them to the humanness of the others in the family.

Third, this emphasis seems correct. Let me provide a classroom example. Over the past twelve years, I have nearly always begun my ethics course with an exercise in which students must tell me a story about an action they personally witnessed in business that they thought was ethical and to tell me why they thought it was ethical. At least 70 percent write a story about how someone in a firm made an exception to the rules for an employee who was having some sort of personal (physical, emotional, or otherwise) difficulty. No doubt my assessment would fail standards of empirical analysis, but 70 percent of more than two thousand stories does suggest a moral disposition at work. What seems to be at work is a general notion that moral behavior has something to do with the recognition that human beings are not always capable of taking care of their own self-interest. To survive and flourish, they rely not only on others, but on others who, even in business life, have learned to see their responsibility to the vulnerable.

This then leads to the fourth and final point: how do we link our social, vulnerable, dependent nature to the practices and virtues that take these natural characteristics into account? It is exactly in institutions small enough to recognize vulnerability and disability that virtues supporting individual and communal flourishing are reinforced: when businesses are mediating institutions.

Practical Reasonableness:
An Architecture of Legal Reasoning

For Finnis, there are the following requirements of practical reasonableness: a coherent plan of life, no arbitrary preferences among values or persons, detachment and commitment, limited value of efficiency, respect for every basic value, following one's conscience, and attention to the needs of the common good. The sum of all of this is morality. In natural law thinking one hopes to have a community governed by natural law principles in which individuals will flourish. Thus, "[i]t asserts that there are principles of sound social architecture, objectively given, and that these principles, like those of physical architecture, do not change with every shift in the details of the design toward which they are directed."[92]

To create an architectural design of reason requires the existence of a coherent plan. But how does one claim such a telos for human nature when an Enlightenment reason for rejecting Aristotle was that science largely decimated the telos accepted by Aristotle, not to mention Aquinas?[93] In revitalizing Aristotle's relationship to biology and ethics, Masters argued that "Aristotle's teleological conception of nature was based primarily on his biology rather than his physics."[94] Biologically, one may be able to find an organism's telos. To "pursue these goods in the right order, to the right degree, at the right time to avoid contradiction

requires good habits of choice—the moral and intellectual virtues that
Aristotle examines in the *Ethics*."[95] Thus, if human beings are social,
there may be ways in which living together is a telos. A natural law approach is one that would take into account the variety of goods that
human beings, in corporations or elsewhere, view as important.

Central to this legal architecture is to recognize that efficiency is a
necessary but not sufficient criterion for moral corporate life. Efficiency
is itself a value necessary to sustain corporate life.[96] It is a standard creed
of contemporary corporate governance, as the following two chapters
will emphasize, that efficiency is itself sort of a telos. Yet we have already
seen Robert Kennedy, in chapter 2, as well as the members of the two
clients I described in chapter 1, emphasize that efficiency is only part of
the story of any human community. In short, economic efficiency is not
the whole story of life, corporate or otherwise. And because goods are
not necessarily commensurable, it is a mistake to attempt to describe
any human good as amenable to economic analysis. Anthropologist Roy
Rappaport writes:

> Money degrades meaning, but not only meaning. Living systems require
> a great variety of distinct and incommensurable substances to remain
> viable. Monetization, however, forces the great range of things and pro-
> cesses to which it is applied into a specious commensurability. . . . Deci-
> sions made in terms of simple-minded monetary considerations, freed
> from the surveillance of higher-order meanings, are in their very nature
> unmindful of the uniqueness and incommensurability of elements in the
> objective world upon which life depends, and the deployment of large
> amounts of mindless energy under the guidance of money is almost
> bound to be brutal and destructive.[97]

These notions underscore a crucial natural law point: that in any decision one must respect *all* the values, not just one. Indeed, such respect is
at the heart of business ethics and is applicable in particular to mergers
and acquisitions. While a takeover may be economically efficient and
may maximize wealth, at least among deal makers and perhaps among
shareholders, there are other goods involved in the corporate community that make a difference. Stakeholder and contract theory are exactly
right to emphasize these other interests that constituents may have in
the corporate organization. Does natural law have resources for addressing these concerns? Finnis would respond that it does through legal
reasoning.

Why is this process of legal reasoning important? Finnis answers that
its importance lies in the fact that law provides heuristic devices necessary for individual and community flourishing so that affairs will be predictable and power not become arbitrary.[98] In tapping such wisdom,
one must consult the dead. That is precisely what natural law does. It
consults the dead to understand what kinds of rules are appropriate for

a lifetime. That is why Michael Perry says that "when consulting a rule we consult with the dead and by so doing we enrich the quality of the conversation."[99] Or as Chesterton put it: "Tradition means giving votes to the most obscure of all classes, our ancestors. It is the democracy of the dead. Tradition refuses to submit to the small and arrogant oligarchy of those who merely happen to be walking about. All democrats object to men being disqualified by accident of birth; tradition objects to their being disqualified by the accident of death."[100] The question thus becomes, what specific structures does tradition, a resource significant to natural law, teach to help us live together—and to do so in order to create order that is also open to change and to multiple goods within the corporate community? Using Finnis, I will elaborate two aspects: checks and balances and then five specific pillars that can be a corporate legal architecture to build such checks.

Checks and Balances. While the American system of separation of powers, federalism, and checks and balances immediately springs to mind when thinking about this matter, there are other options. Within American history itself, the first state constitution (Connecticut's Fundamental Orders of 1639) was based on a tripartite separation of powers, but a separation very different from our contemporary political structure.

The Reverend Thomas Hooker specified the Fundamental Orders' moral contours.[101] His 1636 sermon to the General Court relied upon the notion of an interventionist God active in community life. Within that "check," citizens were to choose their ruling magistrates according to what they believed to be the will of God and were then to restrain the power of the elected magistrates.[102] Hooker believed that people would be more likely to love their rulers if allowed to elect them.[103] In this system, all judicial, legislative, and executive power was vested in the General Court,[104] but the outside checks of the laws themselves (produced from a historical consultation with the dead) and the people (acting in order to enforce the will of God) restrained the power of elected officials.[105] This system of checks and balances obviously differs from our contemporary context, but it demonstrates that a system of natural law checks and balances need not simply replicate that of constitutional democracy. This insight has two direct implications.

First, it will have implications for corporations themselves. There are no requirements, even in contemporary corporate constituency statutes, that corporations be operated in a democratic fashion. Nevertheless, a requirement that they be operated within a system of checks and balances is a necessary principle of justice. In the sense that they do operate within a legal and economic system, of course, executives do not have unfettered discretion. But, as we shall see, there are more demands placed upon corporations in a natural law theory: demands related to the moral responsibilities corporations have toward members of their organizations.

Second, global businesses offer other models of reaching a system of checks and balances without a democratization of the community. For instance, in the strongly hierarchical patterns of Confucian thought, obedience to those in power (whether rulers or fathers or others in the morality of Confucianism) is surrender not to despotic discretion but to a discretion strongly bounded by moral principles.[106] While democratization can accomplish great goods, these other models cannot be dismissed.

Content of the Law. What then are the relevant elements of a theory of natural law? I would like to identify five central, appropriately general yet substantive elements, each of which is, in essence, a normative principle manifesting a system of checks and balances.

The first element is impartiality. We have already seen that reciprocity, described in terms of the Golden Rule, is the central principle of natural law theory. Much of the legal system of the United States is, in fact, an attempt to build in principles of impartiality with respect to due process and of holding all persons responsible under the same law. This is not to argue that United States law does it perfectly, but it is to provide an example of the extant application of the principle itself.

The second element is the criterion of the common good. Aquinas argues that "nothing stands firm with regard to the practical reason, unless it be directed to the last end which is the common good; and whatever stands to reason in this sense, has the nature of a law."[107] No system of laws is just unless it promotes the common good of the community. Those who have power direct the danger toward which this is the criterion of justice. It points the person with authority to the restraints on his or her exercise of power. In fact, Finnis takes this point to the extent that he denies any reason for a person to obey authority unless that authority is, in fact, exercised for the common good (an action that all too often can mean the good of the rulers, but which should mean the good of all).[108]

A third principle is that of communication. In an important sense, communication is simply a practical safeguard to ensure that rulers are acting for the common good and to provide a method of articulating why a person is acting in an impartial manner. Yet its self-standing importance has been made preeminent by Lon Fuller, who states that the central natural law injunction is "Open up, maintain, and preserve the integrity of the channels of communication by which men convey to one another what they perceive, feel, and desire."[109]

These three principles reinforce the general notion of subsidiarity described previously. Participating in the decisions and activities affecting them and locating problems on the level appropriate for their resolution develops the moral character of individuals, so that they may live a flourishing life. It is the dialectical interaction of order and freedom, through which one learns the lessons appropriate for one's life while preserving a freedom to be creative.

Subsidiarity also acts as its own (fourth) check against abusive power in the form of mediating institutions. If individuals have their own decision-making authority, then leaders are less likely to abuse power, because they have other power with which they must contend. Subsidiarity also promotes communication, so that those with power (through subsidiarity) understand the reasons provided for the exercise of power over them. That process guarantees the impartiality of the norms that are being implemented. Moreover, in an age where individuals may be members of multiple communities, subsidiarity provides a meaningful way for individuals with exposure to other mediating institutions to build in an internal adaptability to the outside world.

The fifth principle is the establishment of property rights. Historian Richard Pipes has recently argued that property rights are natural institutions.[110] Whether found in animals, children, hunter-gatherers, or urbanites, animal life entails property ownership.[111] Rejecting a romantic notion of noble savages practicing socialism, Pipes points out that collective land systems among "primitive" peoples were nearly always family ownership systems.[112] Moreover, individuals claimed private ownership to incorporeal rights to songs, legends, designs, and magic incantations, which were fiercely defended.[113] Similarly, anthropologists have found that hunter-gatherer bands sometimes stake out land territories,[114] and more often to particular objects such as trees.[115] When agriculture and, later, industrial economics appeared, the importance of land ownership became critical.[116] The philosophical notion of the value of owning private property, according to Pipes, traces to Aristotle, who in opposition to Plato argued that property is an attribute of a household not of the state.[117] Moreover, Aristotle argued that property was better cared for in the hands of private owners.[118] This notion was built upon by Aquinas and even more enthusiastically by the Protestant reformers,[119] and philosophically by Locke.[120] A central attribute of private property ownership undermines feudal ownership of wealth, where land always reverts to the lord and is only derivatively held by vassals.[121] This counterweight to centralized power, according to Pipes, also gave rise to democratic politics in England and the securing of basic human rights and freedoms.[122]

Thus, one can conclude that one of the most effective checks on royal power has always been property rights. This is corroborated by biologist Matt Ridley, who argues that the most effective protection of a commons is not socialized ownership, but private property.[123] Moreover, legal historian Stephen Presser contends that the "theory was that ownership of property conferred a stake in the community, and led one better to act in the interests of all."[124]

The result of the implementation of the substantive content of the law must be tested against the moral principles themselves. Reciprocity is an element that is readily seen; all the substantive principles described are implementations of reciprocity. But does their implementation lead to a flourishing life? Finnis responds:

> This sense of "(basic) reason for action" holds for all the other basic human goods: *knowledge* of reality (including aesthetic appreciation of it); *excellence in work and play* whereby one transforms natural realities to express meanings and serve purposes; *harmony between individuals and groups* of persons (peace, neighbourliness, and friendship); *harmony between one's feelings and one's judgements and choices* (inner peace); *harmony between one's choices and judgements and one's behaviour* (peace of conscience and authenticity in the sense of consistency between one's self and its expression); and *harmony between oneself and the wider reaches of reality* including the reality constituted by the world's dependence on *a more-than-human source of meaning and value.*[125]

We can therefore say that natural law emphasizes the importance of checks and balances and that five pillars—commitments to impartiality and the common good of all, communication through the institution, vibrant mediating institutions, and invigorated property rights of those who are members of the institution—can support the creation of a corporation that is open to a variety of human goods and that creates order while remaining open to change. There may be a simpler way to organize these pillars by turning again to the laws of nature.

William Frederick, who is the pioneer of using laws of nature to reconsider business ethics, provides a framework for making sense of these competing "values." Indeed, one of the checks against natural law's proclivity toward projecting parochial visions of the good coercively onto others is to require natural law to be open to the critique of the laws of nature. Frederick, for instance, notes that there are three value clusters that are in tension in all of nature.[126] Economizing values are those drives for the efficient utilization of resources for survival.[127] Power-aggrandizing values "work toward the acquisition, accumulation, and retention of coercive power by and for those who hold commanding positions within organizations."[128] Ecologizing values "interweave the life activities of groups in ways conducive to the perpetuation of an entire community."[129] These three clusters pervade all of nature—from plants to humans, but in addition, humans have a fourth value set: technologizing (or technosymbolic) values.[130]

Related to this division of natural forces is a description of contemporary political economy in our natural law framework. Michael Novak divides society into three forces: economic, political, and cultural/

moral.[131] The obvious connections are that these basic forces pervade human as well as other forms of natural life. While business may be more prone to economizing values because its social function is to convert (i.e., to metabolize) resources into useable goods and services, all three of these forces can be expected to "extrude" into all life, including corporate life.[132] This might not be happily accomplished. Frederick notes, for instance, that these forces are incompatible in business and hopes at best for a blending of ecologizing and economizing values while seeing little hope for constructive engagement with power-aggrandizing forces.[133] Novak is more optimistic about integrating these forces in an interdependent way.[134]

Essentially, these characterizations represent "natural" systems of checks and balances. Dominance of any one may throw a system out of balance. Moreover, if a shift occurs rapidly in the relationship among these forces, one might expect revolutionary changes in social make-up. Biologist Lyall Watson notes a number of coincidences, whose existence result in a world that is "finely wrought and delicately balanced."[135] Its fine-tuning creates conditions "just right" for life: the "Goldilocks Effect."[136] Nature is always in flux; the ideal of a perfect balance is illusory,[137] but Watson may have a point when he notes that humans become most warlike when populations become too big to be personable or too small to be secure.[138]

Moreover, this tripartite dialectic may provide an organizational scheme for the pillars. Chapter 5 will elaborate on the notion that one can group property rights with economizing values, power aggrandizement with notions of subsidiarity and mediating institutions, and communication with ecologizing values. In each grouping, the natural law precept acts either as a check (on unfettered economizing or aggrandizing) or as a method to facilitate ecologizing. The commitment to impartiality and the common good, along with the emphasis on checks and balances itself, will become results of these pillars once implemented.

Thus, a natural law theory of corporations is one in which corporations will be mediating institutions in order to foster individuals' goods as those goods are defined in a social sense. In addition, a series of other checks and balances are necessary in order to restrain the kind of arbitrary, centralized power that threatens mediating institutions and individuals in them. Natural law emphasizes the importance of checks and balances and that five pillars—commitments to impartiality and the common good of all, communication through the institution, vibrant mediating institutions, and invigorated property rights of those who are members of the institution—can support the creation of a corporation that is open to a variety of human goods and which creates order while remaining open to change. The next chapter extends the legal principles that may accomplish this task.

4

Nature and Self-Interest

There are a spate of books . . . that suggest that business is a "mystical experience [or] a "religious happening." And their mantra is lifted directly from the lips of Yoda—"experience the force." No matter how sincere and well intentioned some of these texts are—enough already, please![1]

Size matters not. Look at me. Judge me by my size, do you? Hm? Mmmm. And well you should not. For my ally is the Force. And a powerful ally it is. Life creates it, makes it grow. Its energy surrounds us and binds us. Luminous beings are we . . . not this crude matter. You must feel the Force around you. Here, hidden between you . . . me . . . the tree . . . the rock . . . everywhere! Yes, even between this land and that ship.[2]

Basing a theory of moral business on a celluloid science fiction creation may not foster its intellectual stature. But one could substitute quotes similar to Yoda's from Buddhism,[3] Hinduism,[4] many yogis,[5] many "native" religions,[6] and the Christian tradition,[7] to name just a few religious sources.[8] Indeed the connectedness of reality has philosophical support from Spinoza[9] to Whitehead,[10] as well as in the writings of many feminists[11] and philosophers of science.[12] The engagement with a connected, transcendent reality in these theologies and philosophies is

62

often a starting point for formulating ethical duties. With such a pedigree, "experience the force" deserves neither ridicule nor neglect. Yet the metaphor "force" can easily be used in ways that provide little enlightenment and, as *Star Wars* itself elaborates, can have both "good" and "dark" sides.

In the previous two chapters, I began the development of a natural law model of corporate life with occasional reference to how these principles are substantiated by certain anthropological data. In this chapter, I want to reverse the emphasis. Here I want to develop some models from nature and relate them to natural law. This chapter does not seek to formulate a theory of "business ethics according to Yoda." It does, however, relate business ethics to notions of transcendence found in nature and anthropology.[13] Like Yoda's "force," nature (human and nonhuman) has a "good" and a "dark" side: it is ambiguous and it emphasizes small sizes.

Of course, the issues at stake in formulating a corporate governance framework are a good deal more serious than a science fiction character. Nevertheless, the insight into ambiguity is important. In particular, therefore, this chapter addresses the notion of "contracts" within corporate legal theory because "contracts" are used as a model both by those who advocate minimalist, agency business duties and by others who propound a broad business ethic. The agency use of the term by theorists such as Frank Easterbrook and Daniel Fischel,[14] F. A. Hayek,[15] and Oliver Williamson[16] is quite different from social contract business use by ethicists such as Steven Salbu,[17] Michael Keeley,[18] and especially Tom Donaldson and Tom Dunfee.[19]

The agency theory of contracting is ultimately unpersuasive because it fails to take into account adequately the cultural embeddedness of rationality and choice. Agency contractarians concentrate on a one-sided, dark notion of human nature, and do not account adequately for the coercion necessary to sustain the "choice" that supposedly validates their approach.

To make this argument, the chapter first poses a question about the use of metaphor in business ethics. This question is important for two reasons. First, ethical constructs are essentially arguments of metaphors.[20] Whether one follows "stakeholder,"[21] "virtue ethics,"[22] "rights,"[23] "contracts,"[24] "naturalism,"[25] or another theory, one is selecting a metaphor to describe a model for the way business ought to be conducted.

Second, it is precisely the question of metaphor that becomes problematic for a contractual approach to the corporation. In particular, nature and evolution have been used narrowly as justifications for agency contractarianism. A basic problem arises when corporate governance trades upon a notion of methodological individualism that is at the heart of a nexus-of-contracts approach to corporate governance. The chapter concludes with an elaboration of the difficulties of this nexus-of-contracts approach when contemporary anthropological assessments of human nature are applied.

A dialectical epistemology that follows the work of philosopher Errol Harris underpins my view of nature.[26] By this, I mean three things. First, any description of reality must take into account the relationship of the parts and the whole of the given organization.[27] Any part of an entity, whether a biological body or an organizational structure, is always defined in relation to its whole, and conversely, any whole is always defined in relation to its parts.[28] A description that "brackets off" or compartmentalizes phenomena does violence to the reality of the entity itself.[29] Unfortunately, according to Harris, positivism in the form of mathematics and most economics describes reality in compartmentalized, unrelated units. In particular, what is bracketed off are the metaphysical assumptions that provide meaning for the interaction of components of those units.[30]

Take, for instance, the simple theorem, *If P, then Q.* P and Q do not exist independently of a context of historical connectedness. The very P that leads to Q is comprised of internal relations that make P itself comprehensible. In a context of pure logic, the very identity of P and Q, as well as the relationship of P to Q, may bracket off the outside world sufficiently and remain a complete analysis of a given situation. If P is a market sample, however, conducted by a corporation which leads to Q, which is a marketing strategy that takes advantage of the existence of P, the theorem is not complete. P may lead to Q, but what does P mean? What if P is a set of empirical data indicating a strong demand for child pornography? That may lead to Q (providing such material); but, when stripped of what P means (done by bracketing off moral analysis of the connection of P to the reaction people have to P), neither P nor Q alone fully explains whether P leads to Q. Not only is the normative question of whether we should allow child pornography to be sold left out, but there is insufficient description of reality itself. Business persons, including business students, make this mistake in advocating transactions that they assume to have no relevant data other than quantifiable cost-benefit analysis. The very P that leads to Q, however, is comprised of internal relationships that make P itself comprehensible.[31]

Similarly, Kantian analysis also fails to describe any given whole, not because it brackets off normative considerations, but because it assumes that an autonomous, subjective ego is able to undertake universalizing conceptions of ethical rule-making.[32] It mistakenly assumes that such an ego is able to describe any given whole. Metaphor, on the other hand, is powerful because of the range of meaning that can be encompassed in its usage. Appropriately proposed, a metaphor can be inclusive rather than exclusive, and can provide an immediate orientation as to what a proper action might look like.

Second, a dialectical description is inherently relational. Since relationships are never fixed, a dialectical theory will emphasize context more than self-interest and duties. An emphasis on relationships and context, however, exposes a vacuum of uncertainty that humans generally want to fill. Thus, the history of dialectical thought is frequently linked to strong accompanying teleological constructs. This is true of Hegel's notion of the *Geist* of human history, and the communist dialectics of Marx and Mao.

Given my favorable view of Catholic social thought, I am not opposed to notions of an ultimate telos working itself to some kind of eschatological fullness in human history. (I also am open to some of the "religious happenings" Al Gini seems to discount in the opening epigraph.) I doubt that humans are able to describe religious finality sufficiently to develop specific universal criteria for determining moral action. I do believe, however, that nature provides sufficient evidence of human nature to allow and even to require normative inclusions of natural phenomena, albeit in existential terms, and does so by recognizing characteristics of human nature that constrain the choices we can realistically make.

In particular, what human beings need in order to make business behavior more ethical is a more significant experience of moral empathy. That empathy is rooted in relational experience, where individuals observe the consequences of their actions. They most markedly have such experiences in small mediating institutions. In contrast, contractual accounts tend to emphasize arm's-length transactions inhibiting the development of moral empathy, particularly in large organizations where bureaucracy separates consequences from actions.

EVOLUTION, NATURE, AND ECONOMICS IN BUSINESS

One difficulty with using the notion of "contracts" as an organizing corporate metaphor is that it can mean so many different things. By itself, this may not be a problem because that openness also can be inclusive. However, agency contractarianism does not follow this inclusive path. As a result, it has to rely upon greater elements of coercion and hierarchy to maintain its argument concerning the firm being a nexus-of-contracts and to suppress our innate social instincts which encourage empathy.

A simple contract is essentially an agreeement between autonomous strangers.[33] A relational contract is an agreement among members of a community.[34] A social contract is a commitment to an ideal.[35] One's view of human nature makes a difference in how one characterizes the contracts negotiated by individuals, even when the agreement is a social contract. American legal history provides an example of this anthropological assessment.

A social contract based upon the premise that human beings are self-interested, deceptive, opportunistic strangers[36] will produce a different ideal social contract than one founded upon a view of individuals as altruistic, noble, and committed to the common good. Some legal historians have argued that the U.S. Constitution's system of checks and balances was the result of the realization that Americans as a group had the former characteristics rather than the latter, an inference based on the profiteering that occurred during the Revolutionary War.[37] A rosy view of human nature hardly requires countervailing balances. But an opportunistic human nature requires a social contract governed, if not by a strong Hobbesian sovereign, at least by a system that limits "evil" persons and groups from acquiring the power to abuse individual rights.

Not only does human nature affect the construction of a social contract, but the establishment of a social contract also gives rise to rules of ethical behavior that help to shape the moral character of the individuals subject to it.[38] For instance, a social contract ideal that corporations should provide lifelong employment to workers would have an impact on the nature of specific employment agreements. It may well foster virtues such as loyalty and trust among those working for the corporation.

I begin by arguing that free market theory, as exemplified by one of its most sophisticated spokespersons, F. A. Hayek, misleadingly uses evolutionary theory to justify the superiority of the free market over collectivist structures. I then describe how methodological individualism in particular misuses evolution and point out that individualism's focus on individual life, like dialectical theory, provides a vacuum of purposelessness. Hayek fills this vacuum with a teleology of the market itself, an approach that is not necessarily inappropriate in moral terms, but which is not mandated by evolution, as Hayek seems to think. I go on to summarize this misuse of evolution in relation to a more accurate way of using evolutionary metaphors and discuss the constructive model that describes multi-level selection theory. I then apply this understanding of evolution to the nexus-of-contracts theory of the firm.

Evolution and Economics

F. A. Hayek often used evolutionary justifications in his free market theory. Hayek believes that the free market offers an advance over collectivist social structures, simply because it allows humanity to survive.[39] Hayek, however, does not ignore the importance of moral and legal structures in the free market. He proposes a view of morality as a kind of cultural evolution that allows individuals to transform a collectivist sense of self-interest.

Disagreeing with Hobbes, Hayek argues that there was never a set of solitary individuals who engaged in a war of all against all.[40] Instead, human beings existed in small bands of hunters and gatherers whose instincts were collectivist and whose survival depended heavily upon basic instincts of solidarity and altruism toward members of a group.[41] We have not shed these instincts, and such instincts lead to a collectivist longing for economic solidarity,[42] as manifested in the theory of socialism.[43] Thus, Hayek's free market morality, which places limitations on these instincts for solidarity and altruism, is always hated. Any human community depends upon cultural constructs; there is no magic differentiation in Hayek's dichotomy of "natural" versus civilized.

Contemporary global business clearly does not replicate small bands. Indeed, Hayek observes that we live and work in an environment in which we serve people we do not know and obey rules we have never played a part in making. In fact, we rarely understand our relationship to others regarding what we manufacture.[44] In such a system, he argues, notions of cooperation and solidarity are anachronistic, and such sentiments press against contemporary civilization.[45]

The "value" of this "fact," according to Hayek, is that this "adaptation" to living in large groups allows for an "extended order" (for example, a civilization) to develop, and that development allows us to survive without the protection of small groups.[46] The extended order promotes self-interest better than individual experiences and understandings. "Innate morality," based on solidarity, altruism, and group decisions, makes sense in small groups with similar habits and knowledge facing known problems, but it does not make sense when attempting to "adapt" to unknown circumstances in an extended order.[47] In civilization, the important virtues form an "evolved morality," consisting of values such as savings, contract protection, and honesty, that allow the group to discover more material resources and to obtain and preserve more from those resources.[48] The logic of Hayek's market morality emphasizes virtues largely abstracted from those of a community in which individuals witness the consequences of their actions.

How do we go about juggling these two moralities? Hayek argues that the idea that human beings can consciously structure a fair society to juggle them is a "fatal conceit."[49] Instead of reason, Hayek relies on the cultural adaptations of moral behavior found in custom and tradition: "Just as instinct is older than custom and tradition, so then are the latter older than reason: Custom and tradition stand between instinct and reason—logically, psychologically, temporally."[50]

Hayek's position raises two concerns. First, his argument implies a critique of more than socialism, it also ctitiques any liberal social contractarian position favoring distributive justice.[51] Thus, his approach seems intractably opposed to many, if not all social contractarian notions of business ethics.

Second, and more fundamentally, Hayek's view is on shaky anthropological ground. His statement that "custom and tradition stand between instinct and reason" is contrary to standard anthropological understandings of human beings. Custom and tradition always have significant amounts of reason as well. The evolution of human cultural behavior, as informed by the studies of modern and past cultures and of our primate cousins, indicates that cultural behavior and the ability to think abstractly evolved mutually and gradually. Without the ability to construct or conceive of abstract notions such as "uncle," as opposed to "this man, the brother of my mother," most mechanisms that keep groups of persons together in band-sized groups could not work. In short, one cannot make the clean differentiations within human societies that Hayek attempted; any culture requires consciously constructed social norms that trade on custom, instinct, *and* reason.

Third, how does one go about learning virtues such as honesty, truth telling, and promise keeping? As I have already argued, the best places for the development of such virtues are in the small groups Hayek finds antithetical to large-scale adaptation. But if large-scale enterprise does not have room for small groups, its very stability may be weakened.

Evolution, Economics, and Methodological Individualism

In his deconstruction of the attempt to link evolution and economics, Geoffrey Hodgson bluntly states that Hayek "does not seem to realize that [economists'] work is not equivalent to Darwinian evolution or natural selection in a fully specified sense."[52] There are several reasons this is true. One reason is simply that social evolution is of a different character from biological evolution; analogies between the two are fraught with danger.

Hodgson points out another reason, noting that Hayek "slurs over the fact that the typical story of the emergence of 'spontaneous orders,' as found in the works of the Scottish School, is ontogenetic in character. Thus, it is not strictly analogous either to a Darwinian process of natural selection or even to evolution of a Lamarckian kind."[53] If Hayek's notion of evolution and natural selection were Darwinian, it would be phylogenetic in character, meaning a description of the "the complete and ongoing evolution of a population, including changes in its composition and gene pool."[54] Rather than the entire population, the carrier of Hayek's evolution is the individual as economic being. Jon Elster describes this methodological individualism as "the doctrine that all social phenomena (their structure and their change) are in principle explicable only in terms of individuals. . . . The individual, along with his or her assumed behavioral characteristics, is taken as the elemental building block in the theory of the social or economic system.[55]

Methodological individualism, at least insofar as it is limited to a narrow, economic view of human nature, is very much contrary to the anthropological assessment of the character of individual actions. It is a long-standing tenet of anthropology that culture is an emergent property.[56] That is, culture is greater than the sum of its parts. Anthropologists who were working on the problem of "culture" in the early days of the discipline—indeed, who were instrumental in the construction of the anthropological concept of "culture"—were very concerned with the role of the individual within groups, the primacy of the individual, and the explanatory power of a focus on the individual.

Perhaps best known is Emile Durkheim, whose concept of culture is usually translated from French to mean "collective mind" or "collective conscience."[57] His basic point, which remains powerful, is that a culture is an emergent property of a group of individuals. It is not reducible to the individual, but is defined by the sum total of all of the perspectives, feelings, and behaviors of those who participate in it: "The determining cause of a social fact should be sought among the social facts preceding it and not among the states of the individual consciousness."[58]

The work of Durkheim is complemented by the work of another well-known anthropologist, Bronislaw Malinowski.[59] Malinowski makes an equally strong case for the error in attempting to explain cultural or group behavior solely by examining individuals. Malinowski focused on the concept of "institutions" in society. Malinowski defined an institution as "definite groups of men united by a charter, following rules of conduct, operating together a shaped portion of the environment, and working for the satisfaction of definite needs."[60] This definition, and Malinowski's approach to the individual and culture, places institutions squarely between individuals and their needs, and between the greater society and its needs—in short, as mediators.

Despite being contrary to anthropological analyses of human society, methodological individualism has had an enormous impact on economic thought, and on corporate governance, in which individual choice is preeminent.[61] Allegedly first named by Joseph Schumpeter,[62] methodological individualism focuses on the individual as the relevant datum of economic analysis. Thus, individuals and the "contracts" they make for their own self-interest are the governing economic exchange. Collections of individuals, such as the corporation, are a nexus of methodologically individualistic contracts. Hodgson argues, however, that methodological individualists have provided no reason why social phenomena are individual rather than social. "It is simply arbitrary to stop at one particular stage in the explanation and say 'it is all reducible to individuals' just as much as to say it is 'all social and institutional.'"[63] Instead, it is important to account for both social and individual dimensions. Hayek's evolutionary descriptions of the market selectively employ a metaphor in which adaptation takes place on an individual level. But this ontogenetic approach is neither consistent with the Darwinian theory on the legitimacy of which Hayek trades, nor is it consistent with the "spontaneous orders" championed by Scottish philosophers upon whom he relies for the transference of naturalist theory to free market economics, unless one adopts a deterministic biological naturalism predicated on selfish genes.

Teleology and the Free Market

While some theologians and other supporters of the anthropic principle[64] wed a teleology to evolutionary processes, that typically is not the way in which evolutionary accounts proceed. Hayek, however, argued that the suppression of human nature's instincts is a necessary action for the rise of civilization.[65] But, as Hodgson argues, "Surely instincts of self-interest, competition, rivalry and even aggression are part of our biological inheritance, along with other dispositions towards caring and cooperation. Hayek dogmatically assumes that we inherit one type of instinct but not the other."[66] This dogmatism is based on an ideology that evaluates political and social institutions in terms of those which maximize individual liberty within a minimalist government.[67]

The flaws in the kind of classic liberal utopia proposed by Hayek and Spencer are both to conceive of a perfectible type of system based on a ubiquitous kind of economic arrangement and to limit the indigenous diversity to that of agency rather than structure. Rather than a faith in evolution toward perfection, Hayek believes that socioeconomic intervention must be pushed down a particular track precisely by the creation of institutions and "general rules" that are necessary for the formation and sustenance of the liberal utopia.[68]

Hodgson argues that the emphasis on nonintervention and the goodness of free markets is obscured because free markets are the dominant norm in today's economy.[69] But in developing economies in the former communist block, the twin impulses of competition and cooperation run headlong into each other.[70] Free market theorists favor a particular kind of government conducive to a particular free market economy. Thus, use of the metaphor "evolution" and implicitly grounding the authority of the free market in natural processes demonstrates commitment to a teleological belief that free markets produce a desired state of affairs. But does nature inevitably lead to markets in which individuals freely trade and evolve? Under Hayek's own theory, they do not; individual instincts must be suppressed first. What is apparent in Hayek's notions of nature and evolution is the selective, idealized aspects of nature, and the use of the rhetoric of evolutionary and natural descriptions of the world to justify free markets. Yet nature and evolution are more complex than Hayek conceded, and that complexity has implications for the kinds of contracts individuals and groups make.

Metaphors of Evolution

Terms such as "evolution" have an aura of authority to them. Yet, when described incompletely, they carry that authority illegitimately. This is precisely what happens when theorists describe economic and business competition as "self-interest" and "survival of the fittest." In fact, although a part of common knowledge, the very term "survival of the fittest" is a misnomer that incorrectly summarizes a basic concept of Darwinian evolution. More accurately, natural selection acts to prevent the survival of the unfit, and, by so doing, fosters the survival of the fit. The danger of using a term like "survival of the fittest" is that one single thing can be thought to encompass what it means in order to be fittest and so, for instance, wealth maximization becomes the proof of adaptive fitness, and self-interest (characterized in economic terms) becomes a tool to predict how that wealth maximization will and should take place. If evolution is more complex than one single thing, however, then the effort to specify the single one thing to enhance fitness can be seen as an overwhelming task for limited human brain power. The notion of "survival of the fit" can provide more criteria to determine fitness than "survival of the fittest" because it does not designate any one proof or any one element of the self that is to be maximized.

Anthropologist Kent Flannery argues that the uniqueness of humanity is that it has undergone "two fundamentally different types of evolution."[71] Biological evolution proceeds from an adaptation from a previous phylogeny. Thus, "[m]ammals arose from reptiles, which arose from amphibians, which arose from bony fishes."[72] Social evolution, conversely, generates human societies in multiple ways. In Egypt and Mexico, "rank" societies evolved from autonomous villages, but in different ways and for different reasons.[73] When a change to a more complex state of social organization—for example, bands to chiefdoms—fails, humans may return to the more basic band. When such a failure confronts a mammal, however, the mammal does not return to being a reptile but becomes extinct or adapts to give rise to a new species suitable to the altered environment.[74] The more basic band is not a default social institution requiring no social maintenance. Human beings can adapt to living in the prior form of society when a more recent social structure fails.

Flannery argues that societies are more akin to organs. Eyes, for instance, have evolved independently in various kinds of animals.[75] Different species' eyes did not all evolve from a common ancestor's eyes; instead, each species' eyes evolved independently from various seeing mechanisms to survive and adapt.[76] This means that notions of evolution are useful, but the analogies must be to comparable structures. In particular, a view of economics and corporate governance that assumes methodological individualism does not account for the communal values and character of human nature. Thus, the difficulty one finds in Hayek's analysis is that he uses a powerful rhetoric of evolution to justify a socioeconomic system by selectively focusing on certain aspects of nature. While I agree that nature and natural processes can be used in the formulation of socioeconomic considerations, they should be used with more attention to their complexity.

Multilevel Selection Theory

To make the evolutionary metaphor work, I would suggest that it be employed through multilevel selection theory. For purposes of this chapter, I want to make a narrow but important methodological point in concluding an argument for the use of nature for business. Evolutionary adaptation and natural selection take place on multiple levels. That is, adaptive selection may occur in different ways on differing levels. The notion is that selection operates on individual species or perhaps broader levels.[77] One cannot apply the evolutionary adaptations of earthworms to that of human economic systems operating on a kind of Darwinism. Instead, one needs to carefully consider what analogies are suitable and what are not.

The acceptance of multiple levels of evolution cuts to the heart of contemporary analyses of business ethics. To analyze business behavior in terms of Darwinian competitive markets introduces a teleology that depends on a moral justification based upon an appeal to nature that simply is inaccurate. A multilevel selection process, however, incorporates the complexity in nature, and acknowledges that human nature depends upon solidarity, cooperation, and altruism as much as it does on cunning, competitiveness, and struggle.

Multilevel selection theory is not new: Darwin himself recognized it.[78] One can study the adaptive behavior of groups as one does individuals, but this does not mean that groups and individuals are the same things. The important task is to learn from comparisons without conflating their separate aspects. For example, individuals who practice altruism toward everyone are relatively less fit than others in the group.[79] But subgroups of altruists are more fit than subgroups of nonaltruists.[80] The fitness of the whole group is enhanced by repressing the nonaltruistic behavior of individuals within the group.[81] Interestingly enough, the terms biologists use in the suppression of individual genes, which may have genetic adaptive advantages for the individual but which produce relatively less fit social organisms in the aggregate, are "outlaws," "sheriffs," "police," "parliaments," and "rules of fairness."[82]

Thus, within any particular group, individuals are prevented from undertaking selfish behavior because it is in the self-interest of the individual to behave altruistically. Groups thus perform a "socializing" function on individuals, for the benefit of both the group and the individual. For instance, the individual human body exercises social control over individual genes. But social control is at least partially necessary for both individual and group survival.[83]

The application of multilevel section theory seems to be at the heart of Alasdair MacIntyre's integration of biology and the virtues introduced in the previous chapter. In critiquing Heidegger's grouping of humans on the one hand and all nonhuman animals on the other, MacIntyre argues that such an approach fails to distinguish the crucial differences among various kinds of animals.[84] Earthworms and crabs, on the one hand, and dolphins, apes, and dogs (on the other) do not differ insignificantly.[85] Dolphins, apes, and dogs differ from other animals and are more similar to human beings because, as MacIntyre argues, they have greater neocortex development in terms of the ratio of body mass to size,[86] a position quite compatible with that of Robin Dunbar, as we saw in the previous chapter. As a result, these animals have at least prelinguistic reasoning capacities.[87]

MacIntyre grasps the critical point that it is important to seek meaningful comparisons. Compatible with my argument in chapter 3, he also engages in a level of comparison that emphasizes the socialness of humanity as being hardwired without falling prey to notions that other characteristics are malleable according to the community in which one learns, or fails to learn, virtues. These kinds of multilevel distinctions prevent an uncritical acceptance of hardwired behavior.

Human socialization is not simply biology, but culture as well.[88] Culture shapes individual fitness as well as the group's collective fitness. Culture is also the product, in significant part, of individual choices. Thus, it is a mistake to think that human societies, whether clans, nation-states, or corporations, operate according to deterministic, naturalistic, evolutionary processes identical to that of cells and genes. But the importance of a group's fitness to an individual's own fitness is apparent in both cases. Individual relationships with the community can be identified, but their particular manifestations differ at differing levels of adaptation.

At the same time, the community, however, may require significant sacrifice from its individual members. This demand that an individual sacrifices does not mean that the sacrifice need be particularly costly. Wilson argues that "[v]irtually all individual-level adaptations evolve in the form of genes that benefit the collective at little or no cost to themselves. Yet, when individuals benefit their groups at little or no cost to themselves, their traits are not classified as group-level adaptations."[89] Why don't we see this? Because it demonstrates a social nature of self-interest not readily accommodated by economic (or liberal) notions. The social nature of self-interest suggests that actions benefiting a community are not necessarily sacrifices of (autonomous) self-interest, but that self-interest is a result of a communal human nature. In a liberal age, it is sometimes hard to conceive of this social self-interest.

Moreover, this social self is much more complex than kinship affinity, found even in nonhumans. For instance, one study shows that buffalo herds engage in a form of communal decision making similar to that of honeybees even though, unlike honeybees, buffalo do not share nearly as tightly related a kinship breeding.[90] Once in the "same boat," however, individuals are benefited by acting in the interest of everyone in the "boat."[91] There are times when group altruism is not smart— for example, when the group surrenders itself voluntarily to a pack of wolves. But generally, what benefits the individual benefits the community and vice versa. In short, the analysis cannot be reduced to that of either the group or the individual. A more complex dialectic is at work: individual welfare and individual identity are tied to a social nature that expresses itself not in a predetermined formula but in a pattern of concrete, historical (and necessarily social) relationships.

In terms of business, then, rejecting Hayek's misuse of the market as the natural individual construct eliminates the ideology coercively requiring a nexus-of-contracts view of the corporation. Economic affairs depend upon the organization of people. Organizing them depends upon attributes they possess as human beings, attributes that are not simply characterized as the result of an arm's-length contract, but that also depend upon solidarity, empathy, and compassion. The corporation is more complex than the description given by methodological individualism and the nexus-of-contracts theory; the corporation is also comprised of social beings who value many things besides the bottom line, but who are also not automotons at the mercy of groupthink.

For example, the members of my pension client's corporation (from chapter 1) were neither robots slavishly following a social script nor honeybees nor strangers evaluating the wisdom of the decision to terminate the pension plan and recreate a new one. They were people who cared about one another—some more and some less—but who were benefited by each other individually and collectively in economic and in noneconomic ways. Their actions were simply not tractable to economic analysis alone in the sense of whether the excess of plan assets was to be directed to the new plan. No one would have been economically hurt had the company kept the excess. One could place a dollar figure on the psychological "cost" of keeping the money, but that would be a strange calculation for the participants. The executives rechanneled the money into the new plan because it was what people who care about their mediating institution do.

This analysis leads to two important preliminary conclusions. First, behavior that benefits an individual is often related to that which benefits the group, and behavior that benefits the group often benefits the individual. In fact, an individual always exists within some greater group context, a culture or the environment generally. To have a more accurate notion of the self, one must relate the individual to her community and, dialectically, the community to the individual.

Second, norms of behavior will have a different content depending upon the nature of the "same boat" in which individuals find themselves. The same rules of behavior do not apply to individuals who live within the same group and those who live among different groups. Rules of behavior well suited to one level are not necessarily suitable to another. For instance, a rule may require that an individual tell the truth to others. Within the context of a tightly knit group, this may well be an efficient, adaptive behavior. Selling a used car to one's nephew requires honesty; otherwise, the community (family) will punish the dishonest uncle. But to require the same uncle to be equally honest to a carjacker, or even to a car dealer, applies the rule of honesty in a context in which its meaning, as well as its adaptive benefits, are quite different.[92]

With this as background, we can now see how agency contract notions of the firm are dangerous. Basically, they are troubling because they do not fully account for the social nature of human beings. Thus, the notion that autonomous individuals negotiate a real or hypothetical contract immediately trades on an assessment of human nature that can be strongly challenged.

THE CORPORATION AS A NEXUS OF CONTRACTS

In this section, I make two main arguments. I begin by describing the nexus-of-contracts theory of the firm, relate it to the assumptions Hayek uses concerning the free market, note the narrow sense of responsibility suggested by this approach, and assess the ways in which exemplars of this approach utilize aspects of human nature. I then discuss three flaws in agency contractarianism: a lack of attention to social embeddedness, an incomplete view of human nature, and the attention directed at the level of coercion necessary to sustain the freedom of the market. I conclude by summarizing the assessment of agency contractarianism.

Microcontracts on the Corporate Level

The nexus-of-contracts theory is the predominant theory that accounts for today's modern corporation. Simplifying a great deal of legal history, the theory states that "[e]verything to do with the relation between firm and the suppliers of labor (employees), goods and services (suppliers and contractors) is contractual."[93] In step with free market economic theory, autonomous individuals are freely able to choose whether to form a company, to be an employee, investor, or other constituent, and to accept the responsibilities accompanying such roles.[94] Indeed, the freedom of individuals to choose is one of the justifications typically offered for the moral legitimacy of a contractual approach. In addition to the moral justifications, however, there are other important questions to consider: with whom do people contract, what responsibilities do corporations then bear, and when, if ever, does contract not work?

Justification of Contracts

The ability of those associated with the corporation to choose freely is a central justification for traditional contract theory. For instance, in perhaps the leading contemporary articulation of the theory, Easterbrook and Fischel argue that this freedom includes the power to put things other than profits first:

> If the *New York Times* is formed to publish a newspaper first and make a profit second, no one should be allowed to object. Those who came in at the beginning consented, and those who came later bought stock the price of which reflected the corporation's tempered commitment to a profit objective. . . .
>
> . . . If [another] firm suddenly acquired a newspaper and declares that it is no longer interested in profit, the equity investors have a legitimate complaint. It is a complaint for breach of contract, not for derogation from some ideal of corporate governance.[95]

Business ethics scholar John Boatright turns the common presumption that corporations should maximize shareholder value on its head when he argues that, because the theory itself is indifferent to financial structures, the theory is also then open to having corporate managers consider and protect other constituents.[96] This is exactly what happens, he argues, in employee and customer-owned firms.[97] At the bottom of each of these conceptions is the notion of choice.[98]

Beyond this notion of choice is a related justification for the nexus-of-contracts theory. Agency contractarianism is more efficient and produces more material goods and services. This is a commonplace notion verified by nearly any examination of market activities. Consistent with Hayek's free market capitalism, efficient companies tend to be profitable. Boatright acknowledges this when he writes, "Although many structures are possible, some are more efficient than others, and over time more efficient structures tend to predominate through a Darwinian struggle for survival."[99] Because corporations are good at producing more material goods and services, however, Easterbrook and Fischel argue that shareholder profitability is also good for stakeholders other than the shareholders because "each party to a transaction is better off. A successful firm provides jobs for workers and goods and services for consumers."[100] This is true, they argue, even in situations involving plant closings, because the benefits to "workers and communities in the new locale . . . must be greater, or there would be no profit in the move."[101] Their view, of course, assumes that the only reason a company would in fact relocate is for economic reasons, and treats particular constituents as having interests in the corporation that are freely exchangeable.

Limited Responsibility of the Corporation: Two Masters or Too Many Masters

Easterbrook and Fischel assert that the normal model of corporate responsibility in agency contractarianism is maximizing shareholder welfare. To do anything else, such as to consider the impact on nonshareholder constituents, would be to serve too many masters: "A manager told to serve two masters (a little for equity holders, a little for the community) has been freed of both and is answerable to neither."[102] This argument is erroneous. Corporate executives do serve multiple masters, including shareholders, creditors, and a variety of political officials.[103] Serving more than one master is part of the job. There may be a point, however, at which too many masters results either in gridlock, or in the enhancement of managerial power by an executive shrewd enough to play various constituencies against one another.[104] On the other hand, it is dangerous to undermine a successful institutional organization by "do-gooding" treatment of other constituencies.[105] I will dwell at some length on these issue of stakeholder theory in chapter 6, but it is important for now to see that Easterbrook and Fischel cannot prove their case for agency contractarianism by the too-many-masters argument.

Against what potential dangers must a contract theory protect? For Easterbrook and Fischel, the key problem is the possibility that managers can take advantage of investors.[106] Investors hold firm-specific assets in the corporation in the form of shares of stock. Nevertheless, Boatright notes that other constituents also have firm-specific assets. If the total rents or quasi-rents fail to cover the promised wages or leave too little for shareholders, then the investment might be considered a failure by the shareholders—even if the firm is highly profitable as measured by the rents and quasi rents generated by the firm. In such a situation, the shareholders might prefer to liquidate the firm rather than deliver on the promises of higher wages, and the shareholders could not be held to these promises because of their limited liability. In short, shareholders can close down an otherwise profitable firm that generates great wealth for its employees and society at large merely because the profits are flowing to these other groups instead of the shareholders themselves.[107]

Thus Boatright argues that employees, like shareholders, are residual claimants.[108] What these two positions demonstrate, at least in part, is what Eric Orts calls "shirking" and "sharking."[109] "Shirking" refers to the fears that employees will not fulfill their obligations to those who employ them.[110] "Sharking" refers to the abuse of power by those who control the organization when they take actions that benefit some individuals rather than the entire firm.[111] Both Easterbrook and Fischel's position and the Boatright position are concerned that some members of the firm will take benefits from or abuse the rights of a group of stakeholders who ought to be protected. The only question is who ought to be protected: shareholders or other constituencies. Beyond this common concern, albeit on behalf of different interests, is another commonality: both assume the primacy of autonomous choice. Even Boatright's more broadly concerned model seems to include a rationally self-interested person who cannot rely on the goodness of others. But are human beings really that selfish? The autonomous individual required by the market must repress the very instincts of altruism and solidarity that could counteract shirking and sharking.

To Contract or Not to Contract

Some agency contractarians are willing to consider human nature in their normative theory. Oliver Williamson, for example, discusses two fundamental aspects of human nature that accompany the traditional view that human beings act in self-interested ways. First, Willliamson follows Herbert Simon's seminal insight that human beings have "bounded rationality."[112] This includes both computational limits and limits in the ability to communicate through language.[113] Second, he recognizes that opportunistic human beings exhibit a "lack of candor or honesty in transactions, to include self-interest seeking with guile."[114] Joined with these traits are the additional problems of uncertainty and populations of small numbers (which prevent a market check on the actions of any self-interested individual).

From his analysis, Williamson concludes that firms are better constructed as hierarchical organizations than as market transactions. The firm becomes a sole source supplier to itself for those transactions that are shifted out of the market and into the firm; relevant prices are known or, in any event, bids are presumably solicited less frequently as a result. The firm substitutes a single incomplete contract (an employment agreement) for many complete ones. Such incomplete contracts purportedly economize on the cost of negotiating and concluding separate contracts.[115]

Williamson's theory is complex, but it is logically coherent, given presumptions of methodological individualism and a fairly limited description of human nature. He considers how to place individuals into a context in which they are the most efficient producers for an organization. That context does not mean consensus decision making, nor does it depend upon notions of altruism, solidarity, or the other instincts Hayek views as inappropriate in the free market.

Williamson, however, does provide, implicitly or otherwise, a view of multilevel selection. That is, Willliamson understands that some organizing principles may be better than others, depending on the level of analysis. Among firms, or individuals acting as consumers, price generally serves as the organizing principle for decision making. The same is not true within the firm.

While the price system has advantages where remote parties to a transaction are not apprised or do not need to be apprised of details of transactions, internal organization allows parties to deal with uncertainties in part because "efficient codes are more apt to evolve and be employed with confidence by the parties. Such coding also economizes on bounded rationality."[116]

For Williamson, transactional contracts serve individuals best, because they encourage opportunistic representations and haggling, but a corporate system is better served without such transaction costs.[117] The three advantages of internal, hierarchical organizations are that individuals "are less able to appropriate subgroup gains" as a result of opportunism, such organizations can be more effectively audited, and an organization can more effectively resolve disputes.[118] These rationales are hardly the stuff of ethical inspiration, but they demonstrate Williamson's understanding of the human need for cooperation and satisfactory work environments.

Williamson argues that "atmosphere" makes a difference in a transaction.[119] As Kenneth Arrow writes, "People just do not maximize on a selfish basis every minute. In fact, the system would not work if they did. A consequence of that hypothesis would be the end of organized society as we know it."[120] Arguing explicitly against the "standard economic model," Williamson notes that transactions are often not neutral and instrumental; individuals require a satisfying exchange relation, so "quasi-moral" considerations are relevant.[121] While there are quasi-moral "associational benefits," increased profitability also requires checks on shirkers.[122] The importance of constructing a community, however, does not by itself legitimate a consensus form of decision making. A peer group making decisions based on information flowing to all members, in a sort of modern band fashion, would simply overload communications and would preempt valuable time individuals could use for other purposes.[123] Instead, Williamson argues, a simple hierarchy can provide, as well as a peer group, the sense of community that individuals need, along with the sense of cooperation necessary for a satisfying exchange experience.[124] Moreover, a hierarchy can do so much more efficiently.[125] Thus:

> An authoritative order is usually a more efficient way to settle minor conflicts (for instance, differences of interpretation) than is haggling or litigation. . . . In addition, outside arbitration, as compared with inside conflict resolution, has a less easy (more costly) access to the facts and tends to (1) employ restrictive rules of evidence, (2) consider the issues narrowly, from the point of view of what is actionable rather than in terms of what really is at stake, (3) cast the problem in the context of legal precedent for the class of cases to which it is related rather than in firm-specific terms, and (4) favor equity in relation to efficiency considerations where these goals are in conflict.[126]

Thus, Williamson relies upon a conception of human nature that is apparently one-sidedly dark and extended to develop a corporate governance system based on acquiescence to authority. I shall point out the weaknesses of this approach, but Williamson does offer a hierarchical construct that at least pays close attention to the dynamics of human nature.

Three Critiques of Agency Contractarianism

If the nexus-of-contracts theory of the firm relies upon justifications of free choice and human agency as normative rationales for the firm's legitimacy, then an understanding of such choice and agency is necessary. In seeing such understanding, however, one again runs into the difficulty of relying upon individual choice for socioeconomic systems. I do endorse, of course, the goodness of free choice, but the reality of evolution is that explaining organizational development requires more than methodological individualism. If a model of methodological individualism is applied on a phylogenetic rather than an ontogenetic level,[127] what it means to freely consent to an action can be distorted, particularly if the model uses only a partial view of human nature. The coercive nature of the system itself may be obscured.

Social Embeddedness

Mark Granovetter argues that both the model of atomized individual-ism, resulting from the social contract theories of Rawls and Hobbes, and the "embedded" model traced to tribal societies in which economic action is the determined result of social kinship patterns, are problem-atic.[128] The embedded model provides an oversocialized view of human nature, while the atomized view provides an undersocialized view.[129]

Persons have a dual nature: we are constrained and informed by our communitarian norms, and we retain an ability to transcend that com-munity. Granovetter uses this dual nature to reach a new insight: in both over- and undersocialized views of human nature, an atomized actor de-cides and carries out economic action.[130] In Hobbes's theory, for in-stance, the wholly atomized residents in the state of nature surrender their rights to an authoritarian power and willingly obey an oversocial-ized state.[131] In the oversocialized condition, social influence is an ex-ternal force that is internalized by the individual.[132] Ongoing social re-lations existing outside of the mind of oversocialized persons cease to be a factor in understanding what the individual will do.[133] But, in reality, human beings act neither as atoms outside of a social context nor as au-tomatons slavishly following a script written for them by their commu-nity's institutions.[134]

Granovetter's analysis raises an important point for business ethics. "Individuals" are not autonomous decision makers, nor are they simply the product of their community. More factors than authoritative institu-tions and autonomous choices affect economic behavior. Between an oversocialized and undersocialized account of human action are con-crete patterns of social relations. These are patterns of relationships often outside of any formal norm or rule and, while concrete, can be very difficult to define. For example, the trust developed between a sup-plier and purchaser may lead to firm loyalty, and the parties may bend the formal rules to accomplish their mutual objectives. Such concrete-ness is a very real relationship of significant importance within a rela-tionship and within communities. They are too specific and concrete, and too important to the participants, to be evaluated simply in terms of generalized norms. Thus, Granovetter does not and cannot make "sweeping (and thus unlikely) predictions of universal order or disorder but rather assumes that the details of social structure will determine which is found."[135] That is, the variety and complexity of the internal contracts are too varied and diverse to apply anything but the most basic universal rules. Similarly, Steven Salbu argues that international joint ventures have difficulties, because "[c]ontractual terms have no ab-solute meaning independent of the context in which they are created;

and socio-linguistic differences between contracting parties create breeding grounds for contextual ambiguities."[136]

Extant social contracts thus cannot be only formal institutional rules, nor can ethics be left to autonomous decision makers. Instead, moral reflection is a mediating process within communities. Rogene Buchholz and Sandra Rosenthal aptly describe the dialectic of community life in which the individual and the common perspective becomes worked out through a negotiated, mediated process and whereby the community constitutes itself though "the ongoing communicative adjustment between the activity constitutive of the novel individual perspective and the common or group perspective, and each of these two interacting poles constitutive of community gains its meaning, significance, and enrichment through this process of participatory accommodation or adjustment."[137]

The difficulty with agency contractarianism is that it assumes an individual capable of free consent without attempting to demonstrate that such free consent in fact exists. From a sociological perspective, human beings develop categories of thought, choice, and meaning within a social, not autonomous, context.

An Incomplete View of Human Nature

Contemporary findings concerning the natural moral dispositions of primates, and studies of psychological development, prompt sociobiologists such as Frans de Waal to optimistically conclude that science is beginning to "wrest morality from the hands of philosophers."[138] Citing the work of Richard Alexander, Robert Frank, James Q. Wilson, and Robert Wright, de Waal embraces a naturalist, evolutionary account of morality. Such a focus on nature is compelling insofar as it helps to ground normative theory, but the work of sociobiology is dangerous if it precludes philosophical or theological reflection, analysis, and prioritization of natural dispositions. If sociobiologists are correct that human beings develop their "moral sense" through small communities, however, can such an approach be reconciled with the powerful analytical tools of social contract theory?

Using these ideas requires great care. The difficulty with sociobiology, as perhaps with evolutionary psychology, arises when it is used with excessive confidence in its explanatory power and comprehensiveness. Sociobiology, like methodological individualism, is too single-mindedly confident in its ability to explain life. Though antipodal to methodological individualism, sociobiology lurches to determinism with similar confidence. While making use of biological facts in my critique, I want to describe both the benefits and the difficulties of a human nature most at home in small groups. Because I view human cognitive abilities as evolutionary adaptive advantages, I believe that one can incorporate human nature's preference for small groups into a broader cultural construction that emphasizes its positive features rather than its negative ones. I want to offer anthropological assessments in a provocative rather than a definitive form.

In his controversial book *The Moral Animal*, Robert Wright argues that human beings are adapted—at this stage of our evolutionary development—not to live in our contemporary, urban and suburban environment, but in a band organization.[139] The disjunction between this evolution and our current lives, he argues, results in a good deal of our contemporary psychopathology.[140]

Wright is not alone in noting this need for small communities. In espousing sociobiology, James Q. Wilson argues that, while Darwinian evolutionary theory suggests that altruism is an adaptive mechanism for survival,[141] the nurturing characteristics of human beings result from the development of our moral sense within small communities.[142] Wilson provides several examples from experimental psychology and anthropology. He concludes that children in rural, economically simple communities with strong kinship ties are more willing to help and comfort others not only within their own group, but outside of the group as well.[143] The study of these same children and the history of tribal warfare, however, indicate that such small groups have little conception of universal rights and duties and have less intense commitments to those who are unlike them.[144] Nevertheless, Wilson argues that to a stranger in need of help, residents of "small towns are in fact and not just in legend more helpful than those [living] in big cities."[145] If small groups encourage nurturing, then fostering that role while reining in their destructive aspects is an admirable goal.

Many years ago, Jacob Bronowski noted that the communication skills of our hunter-gatherer ancestors were almost entirely internal.[146] Colin Turnbull suggests that hunting societies are typically larger than one or two families but remain small,[147] and Julian Jaynes, drawing on archeological evidence from Glynn Issac,[148] estimates that the optimal number for such groups is approximately thirty.[149] Peace and good relations are more important in these groups than adjudicating rights and duties,[150] and responsibility is more communal than personal.[151] Norms become so embedded in the lives of individuals that the norms become constitutive of what it means to be a member of that group. The socially derived identity was by its very nature dependent on society. In premodern times, that identity was based on accepted social categories, but today identity, according to Charles Taylor, is gained through exchange, a process that can fail.[152]

Thus, in addition to a sociological component of human nature, there is a biological component as well. Human beings are a communal species and, to the extent that organizational structure forces them into large bureaucratic groups and then justifies such systems according to an insufficient account of autonomous identity, modern society literally forces us to live in a way where we are distanced from our empathic nature.

The Coercion Necessary for Freedom

It is a standard rule of contracts that agreements are not enforceable if coerced, or uninformed, or if any of the parties lack the requisite capacity to enter into the contract.[153] All three of these are at risk in contemporary capitalism if the theory of methodological individualism is at the heart of the system's justification. Individuals do not have a full, free choice, and coercion is necessary to sustain a social order promoting the free market. As William Frederick has noted, power aggrandizing is a naturally occurring value cluster in plant, animal, and human life.[154] One need not even accept the conclusions of critical legal studies to acknowledge that a legal structure is about the coercive enforcement of values. The important point is to avoid a Hayekian confusion between what is natural and what is ideologically preferred.

The bone of contention is not whether freedom and consent are good or bad values. Generally speaking, they are very good values. The question, rather, is whether freedom and consent mean anything outside an account of a culture and nature. If they do not, using them as if they do strains the metaphor of nature to contract to the point where the metaphor can be sustained only through coercion.

Individuals often are also uninformed about the decisions they make. This is, in part, an aspect of Williamson's uncertainty principle. In fact, individuals account for their lack of information, lessening the risks associated with uncertainty, but not removing uncertainty. Structures exist in the market to assist individuals to become informed and to participate in the market with limited information.

Participation in corporations is uniquely amenable to contracting because even the ignorant have an army of helpers. The stock market is one automatic helper. Employees work on terms negotiated by unions (and nonunion employees can observe the terms offered at other firms, which supply much information).[155] As with freedom and consent, recognizing the degree of information available is necessary for deciding when to bind individuals to promises.

Finally, there is the issue of capacity to make binding decisions. Bounded rationality suggests that there are limits to capacity. Most individuals who contract, however, do have the requisite ability to understand the terms of the transaction proposed to them. Here again, anthropology may help.

Clearly, human beings live in small groups and in large groups. The difficulty is that in living in large groups, increasing coercion is necessary to keep these societies together. Peter Richerson and Robert Boyd argue that while command-and-control institutions lead to more productive economies, more internal security, and better resistance to external aggression, they also lead to a social stratification benefiting those in high positions, a problem because there "is every evidence . . . that humans' Pleistocene evolutionary experience did not prepare us to tolerate more than the most minimal command and control institutions. Nor were we prepared to tolerate much inequality."[156]

Because we are not biologically prepared to live in such large societies, Richerson and Boyd argue that human beings have developed several "work-around" mechanisms. These include (1) "coercive dominance" backed up by force, which subjugates members of an organization; (2) "segmented hierarchies," which can be brutally exploitative and also represented, insofar as membership in hierarchies can be, by using mixtures of achievement and ascription; (3) "exploitation of symbolic systems," which attempts to connect individuals as part of a large in-group through identification with cultural symbols; and (4) "legitimate institutions," which are rational, with lively markets, protected property rights, widespread participation in public affairs, efficient distribution of public and private goods, and a measure of protection of individual liberties.[157]

These techniques provide some optimism that fair megastructures might be constructed, but they also suggest that doing so will be much more complex a task than agency contractarianism suggests. In a fashion similar to the natural law and Catholic social thought, concepts described in chapters 2 and 3, these anthropological notions suggest that the construction of "legitimate institutions" depends upon practices and values such as property, participation, impartiality, and individual dignity. Without such structuring, the mechanisms to build large social structures such as the multinational corporation are more prone to rely only ideology and hierarchy, coercively reinforced.

Moreover, Richerson and Boyd note that to enhance solidarity, small groups are necessary. For examples, they turn to modern military organizations, which are obviously massive bureaucratic structures. They find that those militaries, that pay close attention to the bonding of fighting units, such as those of Israel and (ironically) World War II Germany, have more effective and foster greater solidarity than militaries such as the Anglo-American ones, which rely on more classical managerial techniques.[158] Thus, the small sizes that foster empathy, compassion, and solidarity are important to those people who belong to them.

The point is twofold. First, with increased size often comes increased coercion and ideology in order to hold the system together. There is also a threat to solidarity and the empathy that makes people interested in ethical behavior. Second, there are mechanisms that may allow us to utilize the larger megastructures, and they will entail notions such as small groups, open participation in organizational affairs, and property protection that agency contractarianism does not call for. Agency contractarianism does not call for such protection because its appropriation of evolutionary theory is focused on methodological individualism to the exclusion of the social nature of the human self. Without that conception of human nature, a conception linked to the embedded nature of the self, the risk for coercion and the disconnect of empathy increases.

Summary of Agency Contractarianism

These critiques of the free market do not suggest that capitalism is an ill-conceived system. Instead, my point is that free market theorists have borrowed the authority of nature to justify a particular kind of capitalism, a borrowing that is not merited by a fuller understanding of nature itself. Agency contractarianism lacks a sufficiently developed normative model of the relationships between the corporation and its stakeholders. It also lacks a sense of the "rules of the game." In other words, agency contractarianism lacks a sense of social contractarianism. A statement by Easterbrook and Fischel demonstrates both the need to appeal and the reluctance against appealing to such broader notions of norms:

> The normative thesis of the book is that corporate law should contain the terms people would have negotiated, were the costs of negotiating at arm's length for every contingency sufficiently low . . . [A]rguments about social contracts are problematic. They are constructs rather than real contracts . . . Perhaps the corporate contract, like the social contract, is no more than a rhetorical device. After all, investors do not sit down and haggle among themselves about the terms. Investors buy stock in the market and may know little more than its price. The terms were established by entrepreneurs, investment bankers, and managers. Changes in the rules are accomplished by voting rather than unanimous consent. So why not view the corporation as a republican government rather than a set of contracts?[159]

Indeed, why not apply models of republican governments to a theory of corporate governance? It is in that spirit that I turn to chapter 5.

5

The Velvet Corporation

The point is that capitalism, albeit on another level and not in such trivial forms, is struggling with the same problems [as communism]. . . . [I]t is well-known, for instance, that enormous private multinational corporations are curiously like socialist states; with industrialization, centralization, specialization, monopolization, and finally with automation and computerization, the elements of depersonalization and the loss of meaning in work become more and more profound everywhere. . . . IBM certainly works better than the Skoda plant, but that doesn't alter the fact that both companies have long since lost their human dimension and have turned man into a little cog in their machinery, utterly separated from what, and for whom, that machinery is working, and what the impact of its product is on the world.[1]

At the conclusion of the last chapter, I intimated that Easterbrook and Fischel's sardonic suggestion that we style corporations after republican governments was not such a bad idea. Presumably, the republican government they have in mind is one based on treating stakeholders as citizens who can vote and protect their rights rather than as agents whose actions can be coordinated efficiently.

Most likely, styling corporate governance according to republican ideals would reduce efficiencies, but it would also require those associated with any given corporation to consider a broader sense of goods than profitability. In this chapter, I would like to suggest that it is an alternative worth considering. Chapter 8 will extend the particular comparisons of republicanism and corporate communitarianism. In this chapter, I would like to delve into legal history and legal doctrine to fashion this governance model. With regard to legal history, there is no better starting point than U.S. legal history, where the country's framers debated issues similar to the ones I have been considering. They do so through a mixture of natural law and liberal theory. Given the debates in business ethics and corporate governance concerning liberal and Aristotelian approaches, reconsidering some constitutional framing issues will be, I believe, beneficial. I then want to consider the corporate governance structures of three countries: the United States, Germany, and Japan. The combination of these three subjects leads to a notion of partnership, which is a republican model for corporate governance that also becomes the legal manifestation of BMI.

The structure necessary to teach this kind of balanced, collective effort cannot be based on some of the "workaround structures" Boyd and Richerson have explained if one is to also respect notions of individual rights, dignity, and empowerment. Specifically, because reliance on coercion and ideology will inevitably require excessive sacrifice of the individual for the common good, one needs to rely on what Richerson and Boyd call "legitimate institutions," which balance the importance of individual human beings with communal goods.[2] Those institutions take into account the importance of small groups combined with property protection and individual rights.[3] Anthropologist Roy Rappaport calls this kind of institution a "cybernetic form." This denotes "a *structure* or *form* of a particular sort, that of the closed causal loop. *Intrinsic to*, or *entailed by*, the operation of a *simple* cybernetic structure is 'negative feedback,' such that deviations of the states of components of the loop from reference values initiate processes tending to return those states to their reference values.[4]

In short, a balanced corporation would be one where participants within the organization have the requisite voice and power to have economic and noneconomic concerns expressed and integrated into their business communities. Put another way, in such structures, there is a sense of partnership among the participants because of a rich feedback loop. It is this notion of partnership that I want to elaborate in the chapter, a concept that I want to derive from comparative corporate governance laws in the United States, Germany, and Japan, and through the natural law approach I have already elaborated.

In chapter 3, I set out a notion of natural law whereby a legal architecture would assemble a system of checks and balances through the following five pillars: (Golden Rule) impartiality, the common good, communication, subsidiarity, and property. Generally speaking, a commitment to the common good of a corporate community that produces impartial treatment of its (at least) internal constituents will require a system of checks and balances. Thus, practicing impartiality and being commited to the common good are the marks by which a good corporation can be known and will be known only if everyone in a corporation, including leadership, is accountable.

The remaining pillars—communication, subsidiarity, and property—can be welded together by the human technosymbolic capacity to recombine these three elements into a cybernetic corporate community. Thus, we can match the natural law principle with a law of nature to create a corporate model. Because these clusters interact, neat divisions of them is impossible, but one can usefully fit them into this structure to fashion a system of corporate checks and balances.

FEDERALISTS, SIZE, AND VIRTUE

The traditional story of American constitutional law is that the Federalists won and the Anti-Federalists lost. The Federalists wanted a strong federal government to avoid the weaknesses of the Articles of Confederation. The debates about the Constitution revolved around several issues, key among them being the need for a bill of rights and, more fundamentally, whether a republic could even exist in a large form. The Anti-Federalists, following Montesquieu, are reported to believe that a republic had to be small in order to govern a homogeneous society, which would produce virtuous citizens. I say "reported to believe" because conventional wisdom has been seriously challenged by legal historian Larry Kramer.[5]

Kramer notes that in *The Federalist* No. 10, James Madison argued that a large republic could better handle the factions that would inevitably arise by having these factions compete with each other.[6] Because of the success of the United States, Madison and his Federalist friends have been hagiographically lauded ever since.[7] One problem, according to Kramer, is that Madison's argument about the superiority of an extended republic was ignored by friends and foes alike.[8] Why would it be ignored? Kramer argues that the real debate, and one that has been overlooked ever since, is the Anti-Federalist concern about the *size* of a large republic for reasons *other* than homogeneity. More specifically, the Anti-Federalists were concerned whether a large republic would be able to able to obtain and maintain the "confidence of the people."[9] This is a concept distinct from homogeneity. It is a concept dealing with why individuals would trust their leaders when they could never know their leaders in a large republic. Indeed, although Kramer does not make this argument, contemporary politics manifests this natural human desire to connect personally with the powerful. The false intimacy fostered by political campaigns reflects this, so that, for instance, candidates for the presidency are willing to answer questions on whether they wear boxer shorts or briefs.

Like the Federalists, the Anti-Federalists were concerned about the distinctiveness of factions, but the Anti-Federalists intuitively knew that for the people to have confidence in their leaders, they needed to have some personal attachment and trust in them. This view is "a critique that goes to the very heart of republican government—a critique that the Federalists failed to address and that we have ignored altogether."[10]

How does one gain the confidence of the people? To Madison, it would be won by the creation of wise laws and better administration, something more likely to be accomplished through the "breathing room" representatives would achieve by being distanced from their constituents.[11] This distancing, of course, resulted from the size of the republic, which would separate representative from citizen. Thus, both the Federalists and the Anti-Federalists agreed that in a democracy, obtaining and maintaining the confidence of the people was critical. They could agree that unless government obtained and maintained the confidence of the people, it would have to resort to "force and the coercion of the sword."[12] Winning this confidence depended on " people believing that government is, in a word, theirs."[13]

Obtaining this confidence, according to the Anti-Federalists, was dependent upon personal interaction between representative and citizen.[14] The Anti-Federalists believed in a relationship between governed and governor that was fairly rich. It was not based on a particular interest, but on the character of a more complex relationship of people within their community. The Anti-Federalists were more like my pension client, described in chapter 1, where relationships between "line workers" and executives was significantly enriched (and complicated) by the fact that everyone was also neighbor and friend. Unlike George Washington, who, like Madison, believed that representatives would have sufficient "wisdom" and "virtue" to perform well and through such wise performance of the function of governing would secure that confidence,[15] the Anti-Federalists believed that public confidence would be gained when individuals had "personal knowledge" of their leaders' characters, a knowledge gained by intermingling with those leaders.[16]

In actuality, the Anti-Federalists correctly predicted the tensions that have resulted from the Constitution. During the 1790s, the republic was in trouble, with threats of civil war in the air; the commander of the U.S. army considered invading Virginia, and several governors organized militias in preparation for a possible civil war.[17] Even Thomas Jefferson and John Adams later agreed that "terror" and "terrorism" "were apt descriptions of what had transpired."[18] It was probably George Washington's own virtue and the nation's trust in him that kept the country from unraveling.[19] I would agree that if a leader can be as universally respected and singularly impressive as George Washington, many checks and balances safeguards could be done away with. Nevertheless, why was the confidence of the people unsecured so that they engaged in "terror" and "terrorism"? The Anti-Federalist writer Brutus, invoking analogies to agency law, explained that without intermingling and closeness, "a perpetual jealousy will exist in the minds of people against" the leaders.[20]

In small electoral units, leaders had to mix with and even prostrate themselves before votes.[21] As wild as some of these campaigns may have been, the leaders got to know voters and visa versa. This style of politics, however, was seen as doomed by the constitutional opponents, who foresaw "that representatives who were not known personally and could not mix with voters would lose the confidence of the people. Distancing politicians from politics, they understood, would come with a cost."[22]

Eventually, according to Kramer, it was Madison and Jefferson who formed the first political party as a response to this problem.[23] This reliance on parties, which are sometimes classified as a kind of mediating institution,[24] is one also noted by organizational theorist–business ethicist Michael Keeley.[25] Keeley rightly notes that the founders' solution for avoiding the religious and other warfare of the centuries leading to the American Revolution was to place governance in the hands of the people.[26] While Keeley does not address the size argument raised by Kramer, he does rightly note that this constitutional history (for Keeley, primarily with respect to the importance of popular governance) has important lessons for business ethics.[27]

Keeley notes that Aristotelian views of ethics, such as those expressed by Anti-Federalists and contemporary business ethicists relying on virtue, are not bad, but may not be enough to prevent "abuses of power by bosses or cynical reactions by workers."[28] What more is needed, according to Keeley, and I agree, is an emphasis on governance structures.[29]

Keeley goes on to review the stakeholder-stockholder debates that have dominated the field of business ethics to argue for a special status for employee stakeholders.[30] Liberals also seek common goods, Keeley argues, but they may disagree on which goods are common.[31] "These commitments can be personally motivated. But they are not always selfish—for individuals are willing to sacrifice personal interests for the good of the organization, as they see it."[32] And there is no reason to believe that powerholders will be impartial or ethical unless they are held accountable to do so.[33]

This view of a liberal "common good" fits into Kramer's description of the real Anti-Federalist argument and my position on BMI. It is in small groups that members of those organizations obtain confidence in the leadership, precisely because the attachments between governor and governed are thicker than mere interests, gender, race, or any other one thing. Absent a heroic Washington, whose reincarnation one cannot depend upon, the safeguard for persons is a republic in which individuals form real common goods among themselves. Yet, if large organizations are inevitable—a fair assumption, I think—then one must find ways to preserve this confidence. Thus, if the Anti-Federalists described by Kramer were right, as I think they were, one has to find a way to secure the confidence of those associated with the organization and in the organization's leaders. In particular, employees are those to whom special status should be given above all other constituents. Why? Keeley responds that managers don't expect customers, temps, or investors "to put the good of the organization above their own interests. . . . Generally, it's only expected of full-time employees. It seems reasonable for employees, in return, to expect some say in the larger good they are supposed to place before their own."[34]

Beyond this, the cognitive abilities of individuals to process relationships makes it more likely that the community with which they can identify at work will be one of work. It will be in these contexts of regular, repeated, frequent, face-to-face interactions that virtue (of some sort) will be formed. As Madison and the Anti-Federalists saw, the development of such small groups or factions is inevitable. It is inevitable because of the laws of nature I have elaborated through this book. Thus, an important question is whether such factions are to organize themselves in alienation from larger social organizations—the corporation or nation-state—or whether these large groups attempt to respond to this natural need with a structure that obtains and maintains the confidence of those most directly involved in corporate life: the employees and shareholders.

Employees, like shareholders, are thus a special case of stakeholders. Keeley concludes his view of the issues for twenty-first-century business in saying that the challenge is "to devise more popular theories of the corporation, to close the gap between governing fiction and reality in the workplace."[35] It is this kind of model, with special attention to participatory form of governance, to which I wish to turn.

COMPARATIVE NOTES AND EXTANT
LEGAL DOCTRINE

Capitalism has an enviable record of creating wealth, opportunity, and technological advances. No other economic system in human history has produced an equivalent standard of living. Yet apart from the important issues raised by environmentalists and abstracted from the passion of protests in Seattle[36] and Davos,[37] there is an unease associated with capitalism, an unease captured by Václev Havel, the president of the Czech Republic, in the opening quote. On the one hand, it is absurd to compare the dreariness of an Eastern European plant with the clean efficiency of a U.S. technology firm, even one as large as IBM. On the other hand, the unease that Havel expresses is one in which human beings lose a sense of their personhood in the midst of a centralized, controlling, corporate megastructure. Although people in free market capitalism undoubtedly have vastly superior freedom to choose what companies they work for, the logic of efficiency and bureaucracy requires them to adopt roles that can change persons into cogs.

This problem has not gone unnoticed. Indeed, it is a central concern of what can be called communitarianism. Communitarians worry that human beings lose a sense of their social identity in free market economics, a free market dominated by a contractarian approach to business relationships.[38] As a result, a substantial portion of the twentieth century featured debates among American corporate theorists as to whether corporations should be considered a natural entity with responsibilities for its stakeholders, or instead a web produced by a nexus of contracts among individuals who are self-interested and who measure the success of the firm through profitability.[39] This question of the meaning of the purpose of the firm is one raised in comparative literature, where Japan and Germany are seen as emblematic of countries with communitarian corporate governance structures, in contrast to the United States and United Kingdom, which feature contractarian models.[40]

Overview of Comparative Governance Structures

What differentiates the governance structures of the United States, Japan, and Germany are the roles the various stakeholders play in monitoring and controlling the firm. For example, in the United States, the primary stakeholder has been the shareholder, whereas in Japan and Germany, labor historically has also had a relatively strong voice. However, none of these countries takes an all-or-nothing approach. Rather, it appears that some of the more communitarian features of Japan and Germany are finding their way into U.S. governance practices,[41] as the more contractarian features of the United States are gradually being incorporated into Japanese and German practices.[42]

The structure that typifies U.S. capitalism traditionally has been differentiated from both Japan and Germany in the way it configures the factors that create accountabilities. In focusing on the well-being of the shareholder, the U.S. governance system has emphasized efficiency, with impressive results. A market designed to transparently provide information to a wide range of investors has been able to generate effective discipline for managers to run efficient operations.

The contractarian governance model prevalent in the United States may in large part be the result of the greater reliance placed by U.S. corporations on external capital markets to provide corporate funding. Investors in such markets are concerned with returns on their investments and thus demand efficiently run businesses. This has resulted in a much larger equity market with relatively liquid funds. There are more than 9,000 firms listed in the three major stock exchanges in the United States, the New York Stock Exchange, the American Stock Exchange, and NASDAQ.[43] In contrast, Japan lists only 1,800 firms,[44] while in Germany fewer than 700 firms are listed in the equity markets, although there are nearly a half million German corporations.[45] Listed firms account for only about 20 percent of the corporate revenue in Germany,[46] and stock market capitalization as a percentage of GDP is less than 40 percent, compared to 57 percent in Japan and 136 percent in the United States.[47]

The liquidity provided by American markets also makes possible contested ownership of corporations themselves. In recent years, the United States has accounted for more than half of all merger and acquisition activity worldwide.[48] The combination of liquidity and potential competition provides further incentive to executives to manage their businesses efficiently, lest they lose control.

In contrast, the market for corporate control is relatively inactive in Japan. Between 1985 and 1989, mergers and acquisitions accounted for just over 3 percent of the total market capitalization, and all were friendly transactions.[49] The words used to describe takeovers in Japan include *miurisura* (to sell one's body), *baishu* (bribery), and *notorri* (hijack), suggesting a cultural aversion to takeovers.[50] Antitakeover defenses such as poison pills and golden parachutes are rarely found in corporate charters or by-laws. Cross-shareholding is used as an antitakeover device, although it is limited by Japanese law. Cross-shareholdings by subsidiaries in their parents is prohibited, and voting by companies with large cross-shareholdings is restricted under the Japanese Commercial Code.[51]

The market for corporate control is also poorly developed in Germany. Between 1985 and 1989, only 2.3 percent of the market value of listed stocks were involved in mergers and acquisitions, compared with more than 40 percent in the United States.[52] Corporate combinations tend to be friendly, arranged deals, rather than hostile takeovers and leveraged buyouts.[53] While there are informal guidelines, there is no commonly accepted formal German takeover law, and antitakeover provisions, poison pills, and golden parachutes have not been introduced.[54]

Disclosure rules also distinguish the United States from Germany and

Japan, in part due to the dependency of U.S. corporations on the stock market for external financing. For example, the Organization for Economic Cooperation and Development (OECD) has collected survey data to rate corporations on their disclosure based on three standards: "full disclosure," partial disclosure," or "not implemented." Two-thirds of U.S. firms surveyed met the full disclosure standard, with the remaining one-third meeting the partial disclosure standard.[55] In contrast, in Japan, only 1 percent of the firms met the standard of full disclosure, while in Germany, no firms met the full disclosure standard.[56] The high level of disclosure in the United States is likely due in large part to the Securities and Exchange Act of 1934, which mandates disclosure of corporate activity and delegates power to regulate proxy communications to the Securities and Exchange Commission (SEC).[57]

Rather than focus on the protection of creditors, employees, or other stakeholders, U.S. accounting rules emphasize the provision of accurate economic information to potential investors and shareholders.[58] Thus, for example, U.S. securities are evaluated at market price rather than historical cost.[59] In Germany, marketable securities are carried at historical cost, and tangible fixed assets are carried at cost, less depreciation, resulting in an understatement of true asset values.[60] Despite the emphasis on shareholder wealth, few people see the current U.S. style of corporate governance as blindly profit-oriented at the expense of the community. While employees suffered greatly at the hands of corporate downsizing in the 1980s, such pain generally was not associated with the takeovers of the 1990s. Further, employees can use stock ownership to protect themselves and force management to consider their interests as part of the fiduciary duty to shareholders. According to a recent study by the National Center for Employee Ownership, employees now control more than 8 percent of total corporate equity in the United States,[61] compared with 1–2 percent ten years ago.[62] NCEO estimated that as of August 1997, employees owned $663 billion of the estimated $8 trillion in corporate equity, $213 billion through employee stock ownership plans, $250 billion through 401(k) and profit-sharing plans and $200 billion through broadly granted stock options and other broad ownership plans.[63] The growth and impact of employee ownership is illustrated by the July 1994 acquisition of 55 percent of United Airlines by the pilots and machinists unions in exchange for $4.9 billion worth of salary and other concessions.[64] Five years later, the company was operating profitably, and the unions had realized a profit of several billion dollars.[65] It is therefore no coincidence that the attitude of labor toward management also has become less confrontational. Despite some high-profile strikes such as the United Parcel Service strike in August 1997[66] and the General Motors strike in June 1998,[67] the number of major strikes in the United States reached a record low of seventeen in 1999, idling a total of 73,000 workers for an average of sixteen days per strike.[68]

Recent events suggest that the traditional distinctions between the U.S., Japanese and German systems may be changing. The Tokyo Stock Exchange recently has ruled that in filing their results, all listed companies must disclose their efforts to improve corporate governance.[69] Increasing pressure for transparency and corporate accountability has led to the implementation of significant accounting reforms over the past year.[70] In Germany, landmark legislation was passed last spring to authorize share option schemes and share buybacks, curb voting restrictions, and allow companies to use more liberal, non-German accounting standards.[71] New financial disclosure rules also have been suggested,[72] and insider trading laws have been introduced.[73]

With the apparent convergence toward a more open, transparent, and liquid external market, it is worth comparing the corporate governance features of the United States, Japan, and Germany in an attempt to pull from each approach the best practices that might be included in a blended model. The next part thus compares the corporate governance features of the United States, Japan, and Germany along the following lines: (1) goals of the corporation; (2) ownership structure; (3) board composition; (4) managerial labor markets; and (5) executive compensation.

Features of Corporate Governance

Goals of the Corporation. In the United States, federal law has not been involved in the internal workings of the corporation and has not weighed in with a corporate purpose. Instead corporate law has primarily been the province of the states. Historically, legislatures only granted corporate status to organizations that would benefit the public generally, such as municipalities and public utilities.[74] Through the dynamics of nineteenth-century industrialization, the rise of the influence of Adam Smith's "invisible hand" theory of social benefits from self-interested economic acts, and the populist reforms that swept the nations after the presidential election of Andrew Jackson, the granting of corporate charters became ministerial rather than a legislative act.[75] This move undermined the cronyism that accompanied legislative grants of corporate charters, but it also minimized the public purposes for which a corporation had to be accountable.[76] Thus, historically, even in the United States, there was a tension between public and private accountabilities of the corporation, a tension that has raised its head throughout American corporate legal history.[77]

Nevertheless, for the past one hundred years or so, it has been possible to form a corporation for no more specific purpose than to "engage in any lawful act or activity for which corporations may be organized."[78] In 1919, the Michigan Supreme Court made it clear that "[a] business corporation is organized and carried on primarily for the profit of the stockholders."[79] The American Law Institute also asserts that a corporation's primary objective should be "corporate profit and shareholder gain."[80] However, the adoption of other constituency statutes by most states has changed long-standing conceptions of corporate purpose. Previously, shareholder primacy was based upon, and ensured by, the director's exclusive duty to shareholders. Other constituency statutes alter the nature of a director's fiduciary duty by allowing, and in some circumstances requiring, consideration of noncapital stakeholders.[81] This change is not as fundamental as it may appear, however, because Delaware, the place of incorporation for more than 300,000 American corporations,[82] has not adopted legislation allowing or mandating directors to consider the interests of nonshareholder constituencies. In addition, although there have not yet been efforts to repeal the statutes, they have been heavily critiqued as nothing more than a shield used to expand the discretion given to directors, making the board less accountable to all stakeholders.[83] Another school of thought argues that constituency statutes "simply ratify preexisting corporate law" and therefore will not produce social change.[84]

Traditionally, Japanese corporations have operated to benefit a small group of owners, rather than to maximize shareholder value.[85] The corporate governance system emphasizes the protection of employee and creditor interests as much or more than shareholder interests.[86] Management has had few direct incentives to enhance shareholder value.[87]

German law clearly defines the goals of German corporations.[88] In 1937, the German government adopted a new business corporations statute, consolidating nearly fifty years of corporate laws and amendments. The law reads: "The managing board is, on its own responsibility, to manage the corporation for the good of the enterprise and its employees, the common weal of the Volk [citizens] and the Reich [state]."[89] The law also provides that if a company endangers public welfare and does not take corrective action, it can be dissolved by an act of state.[90] Although this statute thus contains the first nonshareholder constituency clause, it is equally noteworthy for its omission of shareholders from the constituencies to be considered in management decisions. Shareholders were not specifically mentioned until the statute was revised in 1965.[91] Still, German corporate law clearly shows that mangers must operate the firm for the benefit of multiple stakeholders, not just shareholders.[92] The propagandist language used throughout the 1937 act was common to Nazi propaganda of the interwar period urging Germans to sacrifice personal interests in the name of the Reich.

However, modern Germany clearly demonstrates that this scheme of corporate governance does not inevitably lead down the road to statism, collectivism, and the destruction of individual entrepreneurialism. This history of the German statute allows me to anticipate a central claim of this chapter, to be developed in chapter 8. To the extent that the German structure is an example of a communitarian regime that attempts to link an individual to a megastructure, it can pose serious risks of coercion and excessive sacrifice of individual needs to those of the community. Human beings authentically develop the sentiments communitarianism champions—for example, empathy, solidarity, and commitment to the common good[93]—in much smaller "mediating institutions," not in large communities where such sentiments often are rhetorical fig leaves covering coercive leadership.

Ownership Structure. In the last twenty years, the role of the institutional investor in U.S. corporations has grown dramatically. In 1997, public mutual funds and other similar investments accounted for almost 50 percent of all equity in U.S. corporations.[94] Pension funds hold close to 25 percent of U.S. shares.[95] U.S. households own slightly more than 50 percent of all outstanding domestic shares, representing more than double the percentage owned by German or Japanese households.[96] Ownership by banks and other U.S. corporations is small relative to other developed nations.[97]

Traditionally Japan's industrial organization system has been defined by the *keiretsu*, groups of networked firms with stable, reciprocal, minority interests in each other.[98] Typically the firms in a *keiretsu* are separate, independent, joint-stock companies that have implicit and relational contracts with each other on such matters as ownership, governance, and commercial contacts. A *keiretsu* can be either vertical or horizontal. A vertical *keiretsus* is a network consisting of a loose collection of firms from the supplier to the distributor chain. A horizontal *keiretsus* is a network consisting of a loose collection of businesses in similar product markets. A large main bank that conducts business with all of the member firms and holds minority equity positions in each of the firms usually will be a member of a horizontal *keiretsu*.[99] Relative to the total number of joint-stock companies, the number of *keiretsu* in Japan is small. However, collectively, *keiretsu* firms represent approximately 25 percent of the total sales in the Japanese corporate sector and close to 50 percent of the value of all listed stock in Japan.[100]

History provides a good illustration of how a *keiretsu* operates. In 1974 Mazda Motors faced bankruptcy when sales of its rotary-engineered cars plummeted as a result of the oil crisis.[101] Mazda was a member of the Sumitomo *keiretsu*, and the group's chief bank, Sumitomo Trust, was a major lender and shareholder in the car company. Sumitomo Trust took the lead in reorganizing Mazda, dispatching seven directors and forcing it to adopt new production techniques. The other members of the *keiretsu* switched their automobile purchases to Mazda, the parts suppliers reduced prices, and lenders provided the necessary credit. As a result, Mazda survived without requiring any layoffs, although management and workers received smaller bonuses.[102] Taken alone, none of the decisions to save Mazda by the members of the Sumitomo *keiretsu* made economic sense. Whether the decisions taken together made economic sense remains a much-debated question.[103] The example, however, serves to illustrate the degree of sacrifice members of a *keiretsu* are willing to undertake to prevent one of its members and that member's stakeholders from experiencing the pains of market change, pains that American management would argue ensures efficiency. Many people contend that the painful downsizing of U.S. corporations in the 1980s is at least in part responsible for the U.S.'s current economic boom and, similarly, that Japan's refusal to accept such pain has created its current economic crisis.[104]

Evidence suggests that many of the *keiretsu* bonds are now beginning to soften or break. For example, parts procurement in the auto industry has long been viewed as a model of Japanese vertical keiretsu, but Japanese automakers purchased $15.5 billion of U.S.-made parts in 1993, a sixfold jump since 1986.[105] In 1994, Japanese car companies did business with 1,245 U.S. companies, compared with only 298 in 1987.[106] Purchasing companies, pressured by global competition, have sought lower-cost suppliers outside of their *keiretsu* networks.[107] The merger of the Industrial Bank of Japan (IBJ), Fuji Bank, and Dai-Ichi Kangyo Bank (DKB) announced in the fall of 1999, and any further banking consolidation, will undoubtedly have a significant impact on the *keiretsu* system.[108] The most likely effect will be the dilution of the major keiretsu groups' power and influence. In addition, banks involved in the mergers may have to divest at least part of their stakes in related industrial companies in order to comply with Japanese law.[109]

Frequently, in Japan, a small group of four or five banks will control between 20 and 25 percent of the stock.[110] Thus, despite a prohibition on Japanese banks' holding more that 5 percent of a single firm's stock, banks may be the only shareholders who can easily influence a firm's management.[111] In practice, however, bank shareholders often will not intervene in firm management unless the firm performs poorly.[112] The largest bank shareholder is also usually the largest debtholder.[113]

The role of banks in financing has been decreasing in the past decade. Historically Japan's legal and regulatory regime was heavily biased against nonbank forms of finance; however, since the mid-1980s, these restrictions gradually have been relaxed.[114] Cross-shareholding is declining, as companies recognize that they may no longer have practical value and in fact may even create obligations that are not good for business in the long term.[115] Between 1992 and 1998, company cross-shareholding decreased from a high of 52 percent to 45 percent.[116]

The ownership structure of equity in Germany also differs substantially from that in the United States. Ownership in Germany is concentrated and controlled in large part by banks. Banks own approximately 14 percent of shares of German corporations, while roughly 40 percent are owned by other German corporations.[117] Bank ownership is high in Germany, in part because a substantial portion of equity in Germany is in the form of bearer stock and left on deposit with banks.[118] Banks are permitted to vote the shares on deposit by proxy unless the depositors explicitly instruct the bank not to do so.[119] However, here, too, there are signs of change. For example, banks are being encouraged to divest their corporate shareholdings and to reduce their lending exposures to individual companies.[120] In addition, new laws require German investors to disclose the details of share ownership of greater than 5 percent in a company,[121] and foreign ownership in Germany corporations has increased as a result of relaxed foreign share ownership rules.[122]

Board Composition. In the United States, shareholders typically elect directors at annual shareholders meetings. Similarly, shareholders have the power to remove directors either with or without cause, unless the articles of incorporation or by-laws limit this power to removal for cause only.[123] Labor is rarely involved in the corporate governance system. In the majority of U.S. corporations, several directors will be named from outside of the company.[124] The role of the board of directors is to monitor a management team that it hires to carry out the day-to-day operations of the company.

Japan, like the United States, uses a single-tier board structure.[125] Traditionally, Japanese boards have been large, increasing with the size of the firm.[126] One of the primary reasons for the large board size is that directorships were given to company managers as rewards for loyalty and long service.[127] Some of the largest Japanese firms have had more than fifty directors.[128] Another traditional characteristic of Japanese boards has been a domination by older men, nearly all of whom are insiders of the company.[129] Most typically, board members will be current or former senior and middle management.[130]

There are, however, signs of sweeping change within the Japanese boardroom. For example, in April 1999, Nissan announced a reduction in its board size from thirty-seven to ten, with a younger average age and three new directors from Renault, the French car maker that purchased a 36.8 percent stake in the company.[131] Sony was one of the first Japanese companies to reform its board, reducing the size from forty to ten in 1997 and including three independent, nonexecutive directors.[132]

Following the changes commenced by Sony and Nissan, nearly two hundred other companies, including trading houses, leasing companies, insurers, and supermarket chains, have announced plans to shrink their boards.[133] Reasons for the reductions range from simple cost cutting to, in Sony's case, a deliberate effort to remove day-to-day managers and enable the board to focus on hard strategic decisions.[134]

Some Japanese firms have retained large boards but shifted management decisions to other forums. For example, Matsushita is now run by a group management committee that meets weekly and consists of four board members, who bring in other managers as needed.[135] This enables the company to make much faster decisions than the traditional approval method.[136] Other companies similarly have shifted away from consensus decision making to a more top-down management system. Mitsubishi now has a single management committee, composed of the heads of its previous multiple committees system.[137] In addition to shrinking their boards, Japanese companies have discussed importing outsiders to their decidedly inward-looking boards. The Keizai Doyukai, an association of corporate executives, has recommended that at least 10 percent of board directors come from outside the company.[138]

The system used in Germany is significantly different from those in either the United States or Japan. In large German firms, employees select half the board of directors.[139] It is speculated that this practice—known as codetermination—traditionally influenced firm management and stockholders to limit the flow of information to the board and otherwise minimize its functions.[140] Modern German companies manifest the codetermination philosophy through a two-tier board structure. Large firms with more than five hindred employees are required to have this structure, which divides the oversight role into two functions. A supervisory board performs the strategic oversight role, while a management board performs the operational and day-to-day management oversight role.[141] There can be no membership overlaps between the two boards; membership overlaps between boards of different corporations are restricted and rare.[142] In firms with more than two thousand employees, employees of the firm must comprise half of the supervisory board; shareholder representatives make up the other half.[143] Typically, the supervisory board chairperson is a shareholder and has the tie-breaking vote.[144] Supervisory boards also may include representatives of firms with whom the corporation has vertical relationships, such as suppliers and customers.[145] The supervisory board appoints and oversees the management board. The management board is comprised largely of the firm's senior management.[146] Consequently board members tend to possess technical skills related to the firm's product(s), as well as substantial firm- and industry-specific knowledge. The German board structure thus functions to explicitly represent the interests of nonshareholder constituents and ensures that major strategic decisions cannot be made without the consent of employees and their representatives.[147]

Managerial Labor Markets. While the United States has an active market for managerial labor, intercorporate mobility is limited in Japan and Germany. Historically, employees in these countries have tended to stay with one company for most of their careers. In Japan this has been due primarily to the practice of "lifetime" employment, which causes closure of the external labor market.[148] Employees have been encouraged to remain at firms, which traditionally have provided much greater levels of responsibility, discretion, benefits, and guarantees to their employees than comparable U.S. corporations.[149] An early retirement age of fifty-five years also has contributed to the limited managerial labor market.[150] In Germany limited intercorporate movement may be due to extensive apprenticeships and training, which build firm-specific human capital.[151]

Executive Compensation. In the past few years, U.S. newspapers and magazines have headlined rising U.S. executive compensation levels. Last year, the average U.S. chief executive officer's total pay was 442 percent higher than in 1990.[152] The pay increases largely have been due to the growing use of stock options, a measure initially introduced to better align executive and shareholder interests by rewarding CEOs for driving up stock prices. A bull market has made stock options especially lucrative. As a result, in 1998 the average total pay for a U.S. CEO was 419 times greater than the average pay of a blue-collar worker.[153] This compares with a multiple of 15–20 in Japan and Germany.[154]

Stock options were behind the huge differential between the compensation levels of the heads of Chrysler and Daimler-Benz at the time of the 1998 merger of the U.S. and German companies. While Bob Eaton and Jurgen Schrempp had similar salaries, in the $1–2 million range, Eaton's total pay was seven times that of his counterpart, largely because he received a $1.2 million performance-share payment and $10 million in options.[155] In 1988, the average CEO who was a member of the Financial Executive Institute received four times his or her base salary in stock options.[156]

Outside of the United States, stock options are infrequently used as compensation, and when they are, it is to a much lesser degree.[157] This may in part be due to complicated laws and cultural conditions. Stock options were illegal in Japan until 1997.[158] Now, in order for a U.S. multinational with more than fifty employees to issue stock options, it must go through a cumbersome annual notification process with the Ministry of Finance.[159]

The Japanese culture traditionally has supported an egalitarian pay structure. Directors' pay has been low and fixed.[160] Although change to pay arrangements has been slow, recently some large companies have announced plans to give more weight to individual performance rather than length of service.[161] This shift is likely to be buttressed by government-initiated reform. For example, the Japanese government recently has announced plans to further deregulate the banking, securities, foreign exchange, and insurance sectors by 2001.[162] In Germany, stock options became legal in 1998.[163] However, the response of German Daimler-Chrysler shareholders to the compensation discrepancy between Eaton and Schrempp suggest significant cultural resistance to stock-option programs. Few major Germany companies have introduced stock option schemes.[164] Instead, management compensation is usually in the form of fixed salaries and bonuses.

Benefits and Shortcomings of the Various Approaches

Shareholder primacy, though slightly amended, is still the rule in the United States, but with a greater swath of the population owning shares and the unsurprising fact that bad community relations hurt profits, the adoption of communitarian values in this still very contractarian regime is understandable. If it is true that a contractarian regime produces more wealth, it is also true that a community of shareholders can reinvest that wealth as they see fit—a very American twist on the centralized control of corporate social conscience as exercised by Germany and Japan.

The benefits of free markets, transparency, and efficiency provide opportunities for large organizations that can take advantage of efficiencies of scale in intraorganizational synergies and in increasing market share. This risks, however, simultaneously turning the human beings who work in large corporations into mere labor inputs. To use Havel's term, it makes them "cogs." Two conditions particularly affect this kind of alienation. One is the extent to which workers, whether managers or line-workers, have a sense of ownership of their jobs and, with such ownership, a right as citizens of the corporation to participate in the governance of the institution.[165] The second is the extent to which the corporation acts as a social construct where important relationships are formed among those who work there.

The heart of the problem is that the anonymity of markets and the anonymity of large corporate bureaucracies tend to overwhelm the individuals working in them.[166] Contemporary governance structures tend to make individuals into what Havel feared: cogs. While efficiency is a good value, it must be balanced with work that is valued by the worker. Ironically, although purporting to provide a social connection to work, communitarian regimes have similar problems of alienation when they attempt to provide "community" in megastructures.

The German system, for instance, is not immune to its own creation of elites in opposition to a full-fledged participatory notion of corporate governance.[167] To be sure, employees do have a greater potential role in shaping German corporate behavior. To the extent such a voice can be raised, the German system has a mechanism to broaden corporate concern beyond that of monetary goals. Yet an insular group of creditors and investors could be even more dangerous to social concerns. One reason this could be true is the lack of accountability. Centralized control of information and a lack of American-style sensitivity to pluralistic concerns could make a board less concerned with a broad range of stakeholder issues. To the extent the U.S. system requires significantly enhanced disclosure to the public and investors, it counteracts the sort of elitism found in the German model. Thus, a model like the German model, that allows key stakeholders such as employees to have a vote may be an improvement for the protection of their stakeholder interests, but to avoid a new set of cronyism, governance decisions should also be transparent, as U.S. governance requires.

Two important lessons can be gleaned from the German situation. First, a mechanism for enhancing stakeholder concerns can be designed in the form of oversight boards. Second, in doing so, it is important to not simply create another "in-group" that can dominate corporate policy. If an oversight board is to be designed, it must be small enough to be practical, yet diverse enough to function as a proxy for pluralistic interests. Joined with the transparency of an American system, such a board would have the benefits of a protected group of stakeholders—the employees—subject to the review of other stakeholders.

Many of the benefits and shortcomings of the German model also apply to Japan. What is highlighted in the Japanese model is the view of corporate life as a social one. Perhaps more accurately, the Japanese model is more a family model. It is not surprising then that the Japanese corporation is described as being seen by employees as a social entity as well as an economic one.[168] The reasoning connects with a normative framework in Japan that is more relational than what we might expect to acknowledge in the United States.[169] In Japanese thinking, "a person becomes a full person only through a social network, and an independent person without a social network is, even if it is possible, a deviation or negation of its original form."[170] This social network is part of a person's life, but the relationships also continue after death.[171]

In this relational context, it has been argued that the task of ethics "is to define the structure and the mechanism of this relationship that already exist in our social life through customs and mores."[172] Rather than beginning with a Western notion of self-consciousness of one's autonomy, this structure "starts with the two-person community, the smallest unit of human relationships."[173] This two-person community may be that of husband and wife or parent and child, but can also be a relationship between friends.[174] The kinds of trust involved in these relationships differ according to the relationship itself. Thus, there are three kinds of relationships.

In the first context, there is a close-knit relationship such as family and intimate friends, where the presumption of mutual basic trust is beyond reasonable doubt. In the second context, one has a relationship akin to neighbors and casual acquaintances, where mutual trust is reasonable. In the third context, there are no reasonable presumptions of trust: people are strangers.[175] This stage is akin to what the law considers to be arm's-length transactions. For the Japanese philosopher Umezu, the kinds of relationship we have and the rules associated with those relationships differ. He is critical of the Western approach of analyzing business relationships in an arm's-length way. This may be a helpful model for negotiating with strangers, but it the nature of the relationship and the moral principles governing that relationship are very different in the community where one works. In that community, one at least has the opportunity for bonding in the form of casual acquaintance and neighbor and possibly even more intimately as close friends and colleagues. Umezu's approach suggests that between the notion of individualism and communitarianism associated with megastructures—Germany or IBM—there may be models where communitarian sentiments can flourish in a contractarian global setting.

A BLENDED MODEL: BUSINESS AS A MEDIATING INSTITUTION

The U.S. governance model offers advantages of freedom and transparency, the German governance model provides notions of citizenship and participation, and the Japanese model offers a sense of communal identity. Each offers advantages, but each also threatens to overwhelm the human beings working in a megastructure. The business as a mediating institution approach (BMI) may provide a framework for blending these three factors.

Because reliance on coercion and ideology will inevitably require excessive sacrifice of the individual for the common good, it is necessary to rely on "legitimate institutions" that balance the importance of individual human beings with communal goods.[176] Those institutions take into account the importance of small groups combined with property protection and individual rights.[177] In short, a balanced corporation would be one where participants within the organization have the requisite voice and power to have economic and noneconomic concerns expressed and integrated into their business communities. Put another way, in such structures there is a sense of partnership among the participants because of a rich feedback loop.

As already noted in chapter 1, the most tangible mediating institution is a family, which is the most basic community. Yet "[f]amily members do not ordinarily experience themselves as part of this family structure. Every human being see herself as a unit, a whole, interacting with other units."[178] In order to preserve the reality of autonomy with the reality of one's networked identity, family therapist Salvador Minuchin has created the term "holon" to describe the idea of *holos* (whole) and the suffix "on" suggesting a particle or part, as in a proton or neutron.[179] Holons belong to the whole of the family, but are also part of other wholes as well.[180] Thus, families are examples of systems thinking in which one looks at a world in which "objects are interrelated with one another."[181] In such systems, a feedback loop is necessary in order to grow and maintain a state of dynamic equilibrium.[182] By analogy, the basis of a corporation acting as a mediating institution is one that provides a way for individuals to act within the mediating unit while being linked to other systems. What fosters interaction and empathy is the enhanced opportunity to actually communicate with others in a "human-sized" setting. It is this interactive engagement that develops communitarian sentiments of affection and empathy. In family businesses—unique combinations of two kinds of mediating institutions—an important way to develop a notion of community spirit is the unsurprising, and often unpracticed, solution of "listen, establish two-way performance evaluations, encourage open communication in the family."[183] In short, one central way of creating a system which functions in a state of balance is to engage the most relevant stakeholders in the system unit. And, in fact, a leading proposal for a self-enforcing model of corporate law suggests a "direct participation of shareholders, directors, and managers rather than judges regulators, legal and accounting professionals as well as the financial press."[184] Yet, shareholders are not enough. Employees are also a special case of stakeholders, and, as two scholars of corporate culture note, "[l]ike family, villages, schools, and clubs, businesses rest on patterns of social interaction that sustain them over time or are their undoing. They are built on shared interests and mutual obligations and thrive on cooperation and friendships."[185] Corporations are the loci for a good deal of other social interaction which, in fact, is directly related to the financial success of the corporation itself. To be a self-enforcing model attuned to the realities of the workplace, corporate governance should be configured to foster an active engagement of shareholders and employees. It may be true that involving all stakeholders in corporate governance creates "too many masters, reinforces managerial authority, and risks gridlock."[186] A

limited set of stakeholders—shareholders and employees—would significantly diversify the voices heard in corporate governance. These parties
could act as proxies for the concerns of other stakeholders, since employees are also members of the community at large. Thus, by adding employees to the corporate governance structure, both empathy and efficiency are given voice.

Three Governance Prongs

Economizing and Property

As I have already argued, economizing is a priority of any corporation.
As Frederick describes it, economizing acts as a culture's metabolism,
converting raw materials into useful products and services.[187] To do so
in an adaptive way places a priority on efficiency. To the extent corporations can maximize the value they produce in relation to the cost in-
curred by their effort, they are rewarded with profit and a higher market
valuation.[188] The optimal goal of this process of efficiency is survival
and growth of the organization. As a result, efficiency and the transparency that makes corporations efficient (through vibrant and liquid
capital markets) promote an adaptability to be valued.

One key governance step, then, is to encourage the open markets
that the United States is known for. This is already occurring in other
countries. They see the efficiency and competitiveness that an open,
transparent system provides and the obvious economic rewards associated with it. Strong disclosure laws, accounting principles that value assets according to their market value, liquidity of markets, and free trans-
ferability of shares all promote this kind of corporate efficiency. In
short, corporations ought to be accountable for their economic performance, and these legal regimes foster that accountability.

In addition to this kind of efficiency, there is the dimension of how
each significant stakeholder can maximize her economic utiles. The
open market mechanism described in the previous paragraphs go a
long way to achieve this for shareholders. We have already argued that
employees are a special group of shareholders. One traditional way of
ensuring that individuals have the ability to control their own work is to
emphasize the property interest they have in their work.

Anthropologists and historians have noted cultures' recognizing
property rights in songs and rituals,[189] and today, of course, we recognize property rights in patents and copyrights.[190] Similarly, following
John Locke's logic linking an individual's work to a property interest in
his work,[191] and Abraham Lincoln's emphasis on the priority of labor
over capital,[192] the notion of property rights could be enhanced in an
individual's work. Property rights enable individuals to feel more like

they have an ability to influence the factors that affect their lives. Mediating institutions have this kind of influence; the individual is not simply at the mercy of an amorphous "society," but instead is a constitutive part of that community with an influence on it. In particular, by strengthening the right of employees to vote in their corporate community, they become citizens of their corporate community. This could be done in the following ways (ways that are meant to be suggestive rather than exhaustive).

One way would be for employees within various divisions or teams to state what their norms are and should be. Without that, the members of the organization do not relate to one another as human beings, but as interests, stereotypes, and ciphers. By engaging in the development of aims or norms, or by simply telling stories, the individual presents a richer revelation of his person. In addition to the norms required by laws such as the Federal Sentencing Guidelines, the members of these smaller communities-within-a-corporation at least should have the ability to vote for the norms that govern the behavior within their group and to put it in writing. For instance, subgroups can meet to determine what values they believe their subgroup should respect. Evidence suggests that the list of values may not be as diverse as one might think.[193] But there is a psychological difference created by contributing to the norms by which one is governed rather than by being told those norms.[194] The ownership one then has in those rules acts as a ratification of the rules themselves. Because small groups can also lurch toward tribalism, writing the rules down further acts as a transparent protection against the kind of oppression a small group can perpetrate.[195]

This kind of ownership over one's direct work experience is akin to models of workplace engagement advocated by quality theorists.[196] The heart of their argument is twofold: first, that refined statistical measures are necessary in order to properly understand whether a product or service is being produced in a high-quality way; and second, that to make things in a high-quality way; one must directly engage the person working on the product to contribute his ideas of how the product can be improved.[197]

Another way to provide this kind of citizenship voting, matched with property, is to expand the use of employee stock ownership plans (ESOPs). ESOPs link efficient work with a direct property right. With the traditional property interest—in this case, a share of stock—comes a right to vote for items such as the corporate board of directors, provided that the employee does not simply transfer the right to vote to someone else. Indeed, a significant portion of this first pillar's objectives could be accomplished by a greater set of incentives for the utilization of ESOPs.

Power Aggrandizement and Subsidiarity

As the framers of the Constitution knew, owning property itself provided an important check against unbridled executive power. They knew this because of evidence that individual property rights neutralized royal power in England.[198] The foregoing proposal relative to property rights thus has implications for checks against executive power as well. Beyond this, however, the notion of subsidiarity checks excessive centralized power. Sociologist Robert Nisbet argues that centralized government's chief opponents are mediating institutions.[199] These institutions—families, guilds, churches, and voluntary associations—command allegiance from members at the expense of loyalty to megastructures.[200] Rather than allowing such groups to form on the rallying point of alienation, it would seem more constructive to nourish them within a context of corporate and global good.

In corporate terms, some significant degree of autonomy should be given to subunits within the corporation. The "team" concept of contemporary management does this, although turnover makes equating "team" and "community" dangerous.[201] J. Irwin Miller, longtime CEO of Cummins Engines, required that no plant have more than five thousand workers.[202] Beyond this number, he thought, one could not generate a unifying culture. Thus, a second check designed to create a system in which corporate governance fosters impartial treatment of its members and inspires its members to community to a common good is that of creating mediating institutions within the corporate structure.

First, as already suggested, the mediating institutions within the corporation can establish their "aims." It is important to establish clear aims in order to force psychological attention to the multiplicity of goods that human beings in fact do possess and value.[203] Without concrete expression of those goals, it is difficult for any organization to attend to the multiplicity of values that its members may bring to the workplace. Instead, a default to efficiency and only efficiency may replace it. As has already been noted, however, this emphasis on efficiency may not fully account for all interpersonal dynamics within the firm.

Thus, a mediating institution either could ask its members to nominate, discuss, and vote on what values it holds important or it could tell stories about what is meaningful to individual members of the group. These techniques elicit the moral goods of the constituents, which can become aims to which members aspire and hold each other accountable in addition to (not instead of) the traditional corporate aim of profitability. It is theoretically possible that these aims could be destructive. A group could aim, for instance, to abuse minorities. My proposal, however, is made with the expectation of a regulatory environment in which there will be limits on such activity and with transparency of those aims so that groups are accountable for their actions.

In between communal moral aims and the capacity (through property rights and voting) to influence corporate policy lie the various layers of corporate bureaucracy. It is important then to link the notions described herein so such bureaucracy does not eliminate them. Institutional economists argue that consensus decision making is inefficient.[204] Instead, they argue for hierarchies, so that there are clear lines of power and authority.[205] These are similar to what anthropologists call simultaneous hierarchies.[206] In legal terms, this economic argument for hierarchical control of corporate decisions makes the master-servant aspect of agency law one that characterizes employer-employee relationships.[207]

Another model is that of sequential hierarchies. In these structures, small (mediating) groups elect a representative to articulate the group's consensual decisions with other small groups "up the ladder."[208] This process continues so that any decision is made within a small group where there is face-to-face interaction. Often, the representative of the initial group changes according to the issue, so a group has multiple leaders reinforcing that consensus.[209] These varying representatives are known as "sodalities," and they serve to keep each separate mediating institution open to the views of others. Having such a process helps to preserve the adaptability of the mediating institution. These structures require the face-to-face interaction necessary for the development of moral empathy and to provide a structure to make clear the moral aims that exist within the corporation in addition to its economic aims.

In short, the creation of vibrant subgroups creates communities where empathy, commitment to the common good, and concern for the welfare of a variety of stakeholders take place. These kinds of subgroups can be integrated within the corporation itself. The authority of these groups does not necessitate capitulation of strategic thinking to full-fledged workplace democracy. It does provide an opportunity for individuals to maximize their influence on those things that matter directly to the workers.

Ecologizing Values—Communication

So what do these mediating institutions equipped with a kind of property right within corporations do? They link personal moral identity with corporate policy and bring to corporate discussions the variety of human goods and experience that exist within any organization. It has been argued that communication serves as the central natural law principle.[210] Similarly, this construct is a mechanism for configuring institutions so that communication can be more fully developed. While I do not wish to suggest that all intractable moral disputes are simply a matter of needing a good chat, open communication is a powerful tool. Not only can it reveal inconsistencies and commonalties, allowing people to find ways to work together, the very commitment to communicate is a validation of human respect and dignity. Indeed, in the 1980s revival of civic republicanism, the commitment to dialogue was a central tool to transform self-interested individuals into citizens concerned with the common good.[211]

In corporate terms, the importance of open communication among constituents can be demonstrated by a recent study that suggests ways to handle downsizing. For instance, to mitigate the "downside" of downsizing, a four-step process is often recommended.[212] The process is one that can beconsidered a way to enhance a sense of partnership, even in situations where one is being removed from the partnership.

In step 1, the decision to downsize is made only as a last resort, where it is necessary as part of a long-term vision for the company.[213] In step 2, actually planning the decision, a cross-functional team that has insights into constituent needs and can speak on behalf of stakeholders should be formed.[214] This team should identify all the affected constituents, use experts (such as outplacement companies or government training programs) to assist downsized workers, train managers how to communicate the decision, and supply information to employees about the realities of the business.[215] In step 3, announcing the decision, the company should explain the business rationale for the decision, have senior managers announce it, notify employees in advance of the effective date, beat the media to the announcement, and offer employees the day off.[216] Finally, in implementing the decision, the company should tell the truth and "overcommunicate."[217] It should also involve employees in downsizing decisions, exercise fairness (in terms of some kind of objective criteria) as to separation, keep its promises with respect to its timetable, help department employees find other jobs, allow for voluntary separations, provide generous benefits and career counseling, and train survivors.[218] Through this process, the corporation will maintain trust and minimize productivity losses.[219]

Impact on Comparative Criteria

The tripartite model thus emphasizes the importance of property rights with citizenship participation. This is both an American and a German strategy. It is American to the extent that it relies upon transparent disclosure of each subgroup, and it is German to the extent that it features employee participation in the governance process. The model also emphasizes the importance of mediating institutions, or subgroups, within the organization in order to balance power. This is both an American and a Japanese strategy. It is American to the extent that mediating institutions have historically been an integral component of civil society[220] and in its concern for creating checks to accumulation of power. It is Japanese in that it relies upon subgroups within the organization to be akin to families or, in even more Japanese terms, to be like quality circles.[221] In such small groups, work is social as well as productive. In fact, the two often go together. Finally, the model also emphasizes communication. This is an aspect of all three structures, although the members of the governance structure among whom communication takes place differ. In BMI, it takes place not simply among creditors, nor officers, nor capital markets, but among those who finance and operate, truly operate, the business.

Goals of the Corporation

As I have indicated, the goals of U.S., German, and Japanese governance structures differ. Corporations must compete in global markets and doing so has advantages of efficiency as measured by profitability. Corporations, as collective entities, should operate according to contractarian models in this competitive environment. In BMI, these institutions do compete with each other and their activities will be disciplined by external capital markets. Yet, in addition to the goal of shareholder protection, there is also a goal that those who work for the organization are allowed to be involved in work that enables them to flourish as human beings. BMI thus stands as a possible regime that allows individuals to voice their concerns in a small, familial setting while being open to competitive market moves. The remaining comparative factors are ways that this is accomplished.

Ownership Structure and Composition of
Board of Directors

Rather than an ownership structure focused only on shareholders or on a small clique of creditors, BMI blends shareholder and employee ownership. The ownership structure has three components. One component is in ownership of shares of the company. As I have argued, a transparent model, as followed by the United States, provides protection to shareholders by emphasizing full disclosure and liquid markets. These act as disciplinary mechanisms against managerial misfeasance and provide a a model superior to the secretive workings of German and Japanese systems. ESOPs then enhance the ownership interests of employees.

The second component of ownership is that employees have a sense of ownership over their environment and the work they do. This ability to have control brings a communitarian dimension to work in a forum small enough to truly be a community. Recognizing this dimension of "ownership" is an important supplement to financial notions of ownership. By recognizing it, a communitarian sentiment of living in a workplace community can be combined with contractarian competitiveness in the marketplace through the collective action of the corporation as a whole.

Finally, there is ownership in a system of checks and balances that represents to the board the variety of values, both economic and noneconomic, that members of the corporate community bring with them to work. As the research from Hampden-Turner on Anheuser-Busch suggests, making the workplace ownership broad-based may in fact not be inimical to productivity; a high-context environment may actually make the workplace more productive.[222]

Thus, "ownership" has several nuances to it. Each of these nuances can be captured by BMI, and, in doing so, BMI can provide a blended model.

Managerial Labor Markets and Executive Compensation

The U.S. model also provides significant opportunities for managers to migrate to other firms and to do so with significant compensation. As a result, there is competition for talented managers and a system leading to a higher differential between highest and lowest paid workers in the corporation. Undoubtedly, complex business organizations need talented individuals, and there may be a correlation between that talent and concrete returns on investment. Nevertheless, there is a danger in the differentiation between highest and lowest paid. Anthropologists advise that there "is every evidence . . . that humans' Pleistocene evolutionary experience did not prepare us to tolerate more than the most minimal command and control institutions. Nor were we prepared to tolerate much inequality."[223] The German and Japanese models create less differentiation in compensation.

One way to mitigate the kind of resentment that could occur with high differentiation, assuming that such a differentiation is needed to be competitive and attract desired managers, is to have all of those in the organization have a voice in corporate decisions. This would occur in a republican, representative model rather than a democratic model of corporate governance. Nevertheless, it seems likely that significant differentiation would be more tolerable if it has wide-based support within the organization.

At the same time, of course, it is possible that such a scheme would prevent such differentiation. Although this could cause a competitive disadvantage, there may be countervailing factors to limit this danger. First, with information about competitive markets, employee engagement may not be so parochial as not to realize the necessity of paying top talent well. Second, if the more broad-based governance structure brought with it concerns and values to make the corporation a satisfying place to work, more than money may be available to attract top talent. In short, a broad-based model, the BMI model I propose, has the potential not so much to reduce competition for top talent as to make the allocation of resources for such talent more acceptable and to create nonmonetary benefits for talented executives.

Two Legal Notes

The proposed partnership structure is one that integrates the five pillars of natural law elaborated in chapter 3, with an emphasis on economizing, ecologizing, and power aggrandizing. It corresponds to an evolved notion of property rights, for efficiency for everyone in the organization, and power equilibrium, for development of the sizes of groups where individuals' social nature is nourished; it also requires transparent communication. This is a model that may or may not develop on its own. More likely, it will require legislation to change current corporate governance structure. Yet corporate governance structures have changed historically and can change, and should change, again.

In proposing such legislative change, I must note, however, two things. First, Rappaport warns that "the lawful and the meaningful are *never* coextensive, and they are differently known. . . . As law cannot do the work of meaning neither can meaning do the work of law."[224] While one can create an architecture that allows life to flourish, an architect, in the last analysis, can only build a house not a home. The laws necessary to implement this proposal *will not* magically make individuals in corporations ethical. It will support the sentiments that make it more likely for people to care about being ethical.

Second, should these structures be mandatory? In other words, should all corporations be required to adopt these governance structures? I don't think so. One can legally support a scheme of doing things without requiring an individual or corporation to follow them. The tax code is the primary example of this. One can offer incentives for charitable contributions, but it is up to the individual or corporation to determine whether or not the charitable deduction is utilized. Moreover, a federal tax incentive scheme makes corporation law, itself a state law, less complicated than overturning the laws of fifty states. Rather than federalizing corporate law, I instead simply propose that legislation be drafted to provide tax incentives for companies adopting these kinds of programs. Thereafter, states can determine whether to authorize these kinds of governance structures. In this way, I would rely upon the interest of the political community to force enactment of alternative mechanisms of corporate governance and rely on business persons to determine whether this model is attractive.

CONCLUSION

Corporations, after all, are not communities without a human element. Corporations are institutions comprised of human beings, and the issues that arise with any kind of human community also arise in corporate life. The social existence of corporations, however, depends upon their successfully taking on the responsibility of being economically efficient producers of goods and services and the organized practitioners of economizing values that battle entropic disintegration.[225] They are not only that. They remain human institutions, but one must take into account the special role that wealth production and property values have in corporate responsibility.

Those institutions should provide a system of checks and balances producing impartial treatment of (at least) internal constituents, a commitment to the common good, and adaptive openness to the outside community.[226] Doing this requires a balancing of economizing, power aggrandizing, and ecologizing values. These values can be manifested through increasing recognition of property and voting rights, fostering the creation of mediating subunits within the corporation, and by having those mediating institutions regularly identify and discuss the moral norms of its members. These steps would allow for the efficiency of markets to discipline corporations while preserving the moral goods of human lives lived in such corporations.

Providing this corporate governance structure would establish room for mediating institutions to be developed within the corporation. If these communities can be developed, their sizes predict that one will have a greater reason to be ethical, because one will develop moral empathy. The elements of that structure are:

1. Maintenance of open, transparent markets
2. Heightened emphasis on internal (employee) control of the organization through
   a. creation of citizen-like property rights for employees in the organization
   b. development of subcommunities within the corporation, which state the aims of its group
   c. empowerment over control of one's work product as a central aspect of one's property rights, and/or
   d. expansion of ESOP-like rights

3. Establishment of authentic mediating institutions within the corporation, where individuals witness consequences of their actions and where lessons of vulnerability and disability are recognized and virtues taught through
   a. establishment of sequential hierarchies and sodalities
   b. telling of stories such as those told by my family business client, where vulnerabilities are expressed and discussion about values engaged
   c. mandating of employee representation on various levels of corporate enterprise, including the board of directors
4. Creation of enhanced lines of communication in the organization by linking these mediating institutions through processes such as sequential hierarchies, storytelling, and empowered rights
5. Implementation of this model through tax incentives

II

Business as Mediating Institution and Other Leading Business Ethics Frameworks

Part I elaborated the business as mediating institution (BMI) framework as a normative model for business ethics. It is based on the theory that human beings develop their moral orientation in relatively small groups. This is confirmed by the laws of nature and natural law. Natural law also suggests that notions of impartiality, a commitment to the common good, subsidiarity, participation, and communication are necessary to construct a balanced company that allows for ethical business behavior. Using the structural model of German corporate governance law and social aspect of Japanese employment, I proposed a legal structure that would follow the American model, but with a greater social function for employees of the corporation, with their participation reinforced by governance presence within the organization itself, reaching up to representation on an oversight board. The approach, therefore, is primarily concerned with a richer understanding of the internal dynamics of the corporation as opposed to focusing on the social responsibilities of the corporation to external stakeholders.

Part II compares this approach to that of three leading business ethics frameworks: stakeholder, social contract, and virtue theories. In doing so, I will argue that the business as mediating institution approach is consistent with some of the best aspects of each of these theories and welds them into a model that is practical for corporations. Although there are important philosophical differences in the approaches, I hope to show that the approaches can still be integrated.

6

Stakeholder Theory

No approach has been more prominent in contemporary business ethics than stakeholder theory. Led by the work of Ed Freeman, the theory has successfully played off the typical focus on corporate duties to "shareholders" to identify duties toward employees, suppliers, community, and perhaps many others besides.[1] More than half the states have enacted statutory forms of stakeholder theory known as "corporate constituency statutes."[2] These statutes, like stakeholder theory itself, are open-ended in two ways. First, they generally allow, but do not require, managers to take into account nonshareholder constituents in making corporate decisions. Second, it is unclear exactly what weight managers ought to give to the various nonshareholders in the corporation.[3] In addition to these philosophical ambiguities, the debate surrounding "corporate constituency statutes" has shed more heat than light on who is entitled to what.[4]

In this chapter, I wish to suggest that criticisms of stakeholder theory do not fatally wound it when the corporation is viewed as a mediating institution.[5] In a mediating institution, duties primarily flow to the internal members of the corporation. When corporate responsibilities are arranged so there is a mandatory requirement for management to be accountable to internal members of shareholders and employees—but not legally accountable to external members such as suppliers, the environment, and the host community—the corporation can do what it does best. Primarily, corporations should owe duties to internal constituents. Duties to external constituents are important, and specific legislation will be necessary to prevent corporate abuse of, for instance, the

119

environment. Management may also find that "good business" dictates "good ethics" in how customers, suppliers, and host communities are treated. But as a matter of corporate governance, businesses ought to be mediating institutions.

As we have already seen, mediating institutions are communities that socialize their members. "Mediating" between the individual and society as a whole, they provide a community. They require individuals to grasp their responsibilities to others, at least within their group, so that a person's very identity is developed.[6] Mediating institutions teach individuals that they are not autonomous beings accountable only to their own wants and desires. Instead, a series of relationships comprise personhood, and human beings obtain their identity by becoming accountable for the relationships.[7] In short, mediating institutions teach us that we are relational not autonomous beings. Because we are relational beings, our very "self" is dependent upon ethical responsibilities.[8] In mediating institutions, we develop bonds of affection that motivate individuals to treat others well. A manager who "sees" that her person is affected by just relations with employees learns to inculcate responsibility, just as a parent's identity is developed by being responsible for a child who has (at least sometimes) less power. Managers learn that their "selves" are tied up with those who are lower on the corporate hierarchy. In a dialectical sense, employees who have more power may also be more likely to sympathize with the needs of managers.

In making this argument, my argument is consciously normative. Thomas Donaldson and Lee Preston have criticized the stakeholder approach as confusing descriptive, instrumental, and normative dimensions. The approach is descriptive insofar as it attempts to characterize what a corporation actually is; it is instrumental when arguing that attention to stakeholders may be efficient and effective; it is normative when it claims that stakeholders are entitled to certain considerations.[9] To the extent that I argue that contemporary managerial practices demonstrate that a mediating institutions approach is a practical method of organizing affairs, I also take an instrumental and, to a lesser extent, descriptive assessment of a limited form of stakeholder theory. That is, it is limited to the extent that a certain group of stakeholders— internal constituents such as shareholders and employees—are integrated more fully into a decision-making process. Yet the rationale for getting to this stage is normative: internal stakeholders are entitled to more consideration than other stakeholders. Thus, while BMI has all three aspects implicit within it, it is primarily normative.

Moreover, the argument in this chapter is not interpretative. Rather than delineating the differences among the various state constituency statutes, or detailing the differences among the variations of stakeholder theory (except in brief), or analyzing the ways courts have interpreted the statutes, I argue that corporations ought to be operated for the primary benefit of all internal constituents; the approach is therefore normative. Other duties may be derivative of those mandatory duties or may be expressed in other specific legislation.

To make this argument, I begin by briefly describing corporate constituency statutes and the debate concerning them. The debate can be enriched by understanding the normative positions taken in the debate concerning stakeholder theory; that is the second part. Next I integrate the concept of business as mediating institution (or the mediating institutions approach) that provides a limited model of stakeholder management, one grounded in prudential and normative rationales so as to make stakeholder theory a workable model for business ethics and corporate governance.

CORPORATE CONSTITUENCY STATUTES

What They Are and Why They Were Enacted

Corporate constituency statutes have been enacted in over half the states[10] and have generated significant academic commentary.[11] They are, however, only the latest in a very old debate. While tracing its origin to the charter amendments of the 1970s[12] and to the opposition of the corporate takeovers of the 1980s,[13] the debate is probably best known from the Berle-Dodd exchanges of the 1930s.[14] In fact, the notion of what the corporation is has changed throughout American history.[15]

The judicial source for this malleability is Chief Justice John Marshall's *Dartmouth College* opinion in which he ruled that a corporation is an artificial creation of the state and thus subject to whatever duties the state imposes upon it.[16] This reason, along with other more philosophical rationales, prompts business ethicist John Boatright to declare that "except for the useful role they play in corporate governance, there is nothing special about shareholders."[17] We, or at least a legislature, can alter corporate duties; they are not immutable laws of nature.[18]

When the duties of corporations are viewed in the light of a public policy struggle,[19] the stage is set for the fierce polemic of politics, a fact that explains Eric Orts's conclusion that commentators have tended toward extremism.[20] I do not wish to join that battle, but suggest that there is a moderate (mediating) position that has prudential and moral advantages.

The rationale for the statutes is simply that corporate actions affect and have always affected (often significantly) nonshareholders.

Whether the corporate decision is "downsizing" or discharging toxic waste, nonshareholders feel the impacts of this artificial creation of the state. In the wake of the takeovers of the past decades, those nonshareholder constituents have sought protection from their legislatures.[21] Given the pain corporate decisions can cause in human lives and in communities, and given the legal precedent for the malleability of corporate duties, what could be wrong with requiring corporations to take into account the impact of their actions on nonshareholder constituents? One can summarize four key areas of difficulty.

Four Problems with the Statutes

Too Many Masters

First, when one requires a corporation to take into account all the stakeholders affected by an action, one creates "too many masters" for management.[22] That is, having many bosses makes it difficult for management to effectively manage the firm. This could happen in two ways.

One way is that the statutes will allow managers to play off constituencies against one another, thereby enhancing managerial power.[23] The second way is that multiple constituents, if actually powerful, could create corporate gridlock, allowing nothing to get done.[24] Either result does little to protect those that the statutes are presumably designed to protect. If either result is true, the statutes could even make things worse.

Is this criticism valid? Jonathan Macey argues that it is overstated.[25] Macey argues that managers typically have to deal with many conflicting goals and masters.[26] Balancing multiple forces, such as shareholders, bondholders, and other creditors, does not necessarily overburden management.

While this may be true, any organization's ability to respond to multiple demands is finite. Corporations may be able to process demands of some additional constituents, such as employees, but can they process the demands of community organizations, suppliers, customers, governments, and (in the case of environmental matters) constituents who may not be born for years to come?

While I am open to models that can make such a complex integration, it may well be true that if we wish corporations to be productive organizations, there may be limits to the number of constituents they can serve. One reason for a mediating model is that it limits the number of constituents to whom management is accountable; that limitation, however, may be sufficient for management to fulfill such responsibilities.

Slippery Slope to Socialism?

If a model can integrate these various constituencies contemplated by the states, is it still a corporation? This leads to the second problem for constituency statutes and the further development for the notion of a mediating notion of stakeholder theory. A corporation that fully engages all its affected constituents requires business to be an "unelected governmental entity."[27] As F. A. Hayek has argued:

> So long as the management has the one overriding duty of administering the resources under its control as trustees for the shareholders and for their benefit, its hands are largely tied; and it will have no arbitrary power to benefit this or that particular interest. But once the management of a big enterprise is regarded as not only entitled but even obliged to consider in its decisions whatever is regarded as the public or social interest, or to support good causes and generally to act for the public benefit, it gains indeed an uncontrollable power—a power which could not long be left in the hands of private managers but would inevitably be made the subject of increasing public control.[28]

Implicit in this criticism is the fear of socialism. If private property of shareholders must be used for purposes other than what they desire, then their money has been, in some sense, confiscated.[29] Moreover, if corporations do become redistributive vehicles, society is not likely to allow such distribution to take place without giving those constituents a voice. Hayek's "slippery slope" argument is that the public is not likely to entrust corporate executives with such power. The logical next step, then, is public control of corporations.

As the statutes are currently written, these concerns seem overdrawn. Most statutes simply permit, but do not mandate, the consideration of nonshareholders. Even if such duties were mandated in part, such as through employee representation on the board of directors, one could argue that the corporation, like a state, becomes more autonomous, not less. That is, there may be less reason for the state to micromanage corporate affairs if the corporation itself is a more just organizational structure. The danger of socialist collectivism is not in making individuals accountable for their actions, but in undermining accountability itself. It may well be true that "too many masters" undermine accountability. But making management accountable to employees can make the corporation more independent from state control.

In limiting attention to employees, external stakeholders remain represented by forces that can have an impact on the corporation.[30] The environment can be protected through a variety of legal mechanisms. Special protection of employees does not eliminate the fact that legal or economic incentives (economic in the sense that there can be good business reasons for being ethical in terms of goodwill and reputation)[31] may foster corporate responsibility. Moreover, if employees have a say in corporate decision making, then they are likely to consider concerns such as community welfare important for corporate action. Indirectly, they also represent the community of which they are a part. The effect on external constituents may not be as great as one might fear. The mediating approach allows for social accountability without socialism.

Adjudicatory versus Utilitarian Rationality

A third criticism of the statutes concerns the way in which corporations operate. Joseph Biancalana argues that corporations operate according to a "utilitarian rationality," maximizing preferences as opposed to "adjudicatory rationality," which depends on normative reasoning.[32] Simply put, corporations are not designed to determine justice or fairness. They maximize preferences within the context of normative rules established by others. Because preferences are so fluid, a utilitarian rationality is not able to make normative judgments unless those judgments are imposed, such as in the traditional legal doctrine of *ultra vires* actions.[33] Without such specificity, vague notions of "fairness" supply no criteria for regulating corporate actions, and actually undermine notions of fiduciary duty.[34]

This criticism, of course, begs the question of how corporations actually do operate. Are they economic preference maximizers or something else? For purposes of this argument, let us assume that they are preference maximizers. While Biancalana identifies one way to set limits to this utilitarianism—through specific legal constraints—the other way is to broaden the preferences that are maximized. This is exactly what stakeholder theory does. It expands relevant preferences. The problem of utilitarianism is the problem of determining whose preferences are, in fact, being maximized and at whose expense. For what "number" is a "greatest good" being sought? The answer provided by the corporate constituency statutes is that one must ask nonshareholders this question.

It is, however, practically impossible to ask all of one's suppliers or representatives of future generations (regarding environmental issues). But it is not so difficult to consult internal members of the organization. A mediating approach broadens the concern of a preference-maximizing entity without making stakeholder theory impractical.

Do the Statutes Make a Difference?

William Carney has argued that corporate constituency statutes will not make a difference in a corporation's decisions because an "enlightened board" will have already factored in the best interests of all parties.[35] This may well be true, but it begs the question of whether a board is enlightened. The fact that many boards are not enlightened suggests that they need a framework that requires them to become enlightened. In interpreting Illinois's corporate constituency statutes, for instance, Thomas Bamonte writes that the legislature was not convinced that boards were already enlightened. Thus, directors needed direction toward the correct scope of their duties, since "if all section 8.85 did was to codify the existing common law rules, it was hardly necessary. . . . Section 8.85 does, in fact, do more. [It] establishes that the director's primary fiduciary duty is to the corporate entity."[36]

If a board is already "enlightened," then the statutes should pose no particular burden on it. Such boards will continue to operate as they always have. If such boards are not "enlightened," then the statutes require them to become enlightened.

Corporate Constituency Statutes: A Summary

There are important truths to these criticisms of the statutes. The statutes may create too many masters. Corporations may become unelected and unaccountable public bodies. The statutes may confuse the very ways in which corporations work. But a limited notion that requires managers to take into account internal constituents—shareholders and employees—dramatically simplifies these concerns. BMI, which looks primarily to internal constituents, may allow corporate constituency statutes to avoid these criticisms while significantly expanding the responsibilities of management.

In addition to the benefits of avoiding these criticisms, there are positive, normative reasons for the mediating institution approach. These can be better addressed within the context of the business ethics debate regarding stakeholder theory.

STAKEHOLDER THEORY

The Theory and Its Development

As with the statutes, stakeholder theory argues that the corporation ought to be managed for the benefit of all affected by corporate actions, not simply the shareholders. A central rationale for the theory lay in a Kantian principle that all human beings should be treated as ends, not as means to ends.[37] This was extended to what is known as the stakeholder theory of the firm, in which managers owe fiduciary duties to stakeholders as well as shareholders.[38]

Evan and Freeman summarize their theory first in terms of the "Principle of Corporate Legitimacy," in which the corporation should be managed for the benefit of all its stakeholders and that those stakeholders (customers, suppliers, owners, employees and local communities) ought to participate in the decisions that substantially affect them.[39] Second, the "Stakeholder Fiduciary Principle" places a fiduciary duty on management toward the stakeholders of the corporation as an entity in safeguarding the long-term stakes of each group.[40]

Who comprises the stakeholder group? Drawing on the Berle-Dodd debate (and demonstrating the linkage between corporate constituency statutes and stakeholder theory), Boatright says that: "Dodd's position . . . is that the fiduciary duties of management should be extended now to include all other constituents."[41]

Stakeholder theory has been amended in various ways by those who would retain fiduciary duties toward shareholders and extend important, but nonfiduciary, duties to other stakeholders.[42] Others, as we have seen, argue that there is nothing morally special about shareholders; our imposition of fiduciary duties is a choice of public policy that could just as easily be extended to various other stakeholders.[43] Recent stakeholder theory has gone beyond the Kantian commitment to persons to embrace a feminist theory of the firm. In this theory, our very "self" is understood as being relationally interconnected with others: "The stakeholder concept, understood in feminist terms, makes explicit how the boundaries of the self extend into areas far beyond what we can easily recognize and into areas clearly 'outside' the corporation."[44]

According to this approach, the corporation should incorporate a variety of internal and stakeholder concerns. Thus, in responding to the question of what managers should do, Wicks, Freeman, and Gilbert urge "managers [to] drop the quest for objectivity and embrace the quest for solidarity and communicatively shared understandings."[45]

This feminist reinterpretation is subject to the same difficulties that give rise to the "too many masters" criticism and the other criticisms in the previous section. But it makes a significant advance in understanding the communal notion of the self. Human selfhood is not simply autonomous, if it is at all, but is stitched together through interaction with others in a community.[46]

In addition to the feminist critique, Donaldson and Preston offer a normative justification for stakeholder theory in terms of property rights. According Donaldson and Preston, the notion of property rights is based on a deeper understanding of rights as mediating (my term) affairs among individuals. Thus, to offer an ironic twist to one of the greatest champions of "nexus of contracts," Donaldson and Preston quote Coase as noting the limitations of property rights. According to Coase, they argue, property rights are not unlimited; if rights were unlimited, we would live in a system in which there were no rights to acquire.[47] Instead, property rights are part of a greater system of rights in which there are limitations on any particular right. Property rights are thus associated with and circumscribed by other kinds of human rights as well. If so, then the use of a property right to harm the right of another person is a situation that suggests modification of the extent of the harmful use.[48] As Donaldson and Preston indicate, this does not go so far as to indicate what kind of property use ought to be restricted and which stakeholders ought to count more than others.

In attempting to answer the question of who may count the most, Donaldson and Preston avoid taking a position as to whether utilitarianism, libertarianism, or social contract theory best describes the principles of distributive justice they believe form the cornerstone of justifying the allocation of property rights among stakeholders.[49] They use this pluralistic problem, however, to their advantage. They argue that because various stakeholders would have their various needs justified by any of these approaches, this overlap is sufficient to demonstrate that concern for such stakeholders is real.[50]

Thus, one might justify stakeholder theory by traditional Kantian principles, by principles of distributive justice, by feminist thinking, and by property theory. Regardless of which of these normative justifications one uses, however, it appears that each of them would lead one to endorse one of the more precise specifications of stakeholder obligations known as "the Clarkson Principles":

Principle 1: Managers should acknowledge and actively monitor the concerns of all legitimate stakeholders and take their interests appropriately into account in decision-making and operations.

Principle 2: Managers should listen to and openly communicate with stakeholders about their respective concerns and contributions, and about the risks they assume because of their involvement with the corporation.

Principle 3: Managers should adopt processes and modes of behavior that are sensitive to the concerns and the capabilities of each stakeholder constituency.

Principle 4: Managers should recognize the interdependence of efforts and rewards among stakeholders, and should attempt to achieve a fair distribution of the benefits and burdens of corporate activity among them, taking into account their respective risks and vulnerabilities.

Principle 5: Managers should work cooperatively with other entities, both public and private, to insure that risks and harms arising from corporate activities are minimized and, where they cannot be avoided, appropriately compensated.

Principle 6: Managers should avoid altogether activities that might jeopardize inalienable human rights (e.g., the right to life) or give rise to risks which, if clearly understood, would be patently unacceptable to relevant stakeholders.

Principle 7: Managers should acknowledge the potential conflicts between (a) their own role as corporate stakeholders, and (b) their legal and moral responsibilities for the interests of stakeholders, and should address such conflicts through open communication, appropriate reporting and incentive systems, and, where necessary, third party review.[51]

This kind of widely focused approach is found in many statements of corporate responsibility, such as the Caux Roundtable and the Interfaith Center on Corporate Responsibility. Each contains important and helpful directives of the kinds of concerns corporations ought to internalize. Yet the question remains: why do nonshareholder constituents have a claim to a greater role in corporate governance? That question can be answered in a more systematic critique of stakeholder theory.

Four Critiques of Stakeholder Theory

The Agency Critique

The most direct critique of stakeholder theory comes from agency theory and is utilized in defense of a free market approach that directs fiduciary duties only toward shareholders. According to this theory, agents have moral duties to carry out the instructions of their principals. Anyone is free to establish a corporation, and those who decide to take such a risk (shareholders) ought to have their instructions carried out by agents who have decided not to take the risk of investing in a business. Thus, according to Ian Maitland, corporations do not violate stakeholders' rights to self-determination, but are the result of stakeholders who choose to form or invest in a corporation rather than choosing to do something else.[52] If nonshareholders want to become shareholders, they can do so. If they do not, then they can choose to carry out the duties of those who have become shareholders.

Rejecting the stakeholder position that current corporate structure defeats individual stakeholders' rights to self-determination, Maitland argues, "Both sides endorse the principle of self-determination—but they disagree about whether the corporation respects that principle."[53] Thus, one argument against stakeholder theory is that it ignores the free choices that were made to establish corporations. Moreover, an agency approach does not harm self-determination according to Maitland, but, as an empirical matter, better protects it.

As an empirical matter, Maitland offers evidence that employee-run firms and cooperatives do not seem to possess competitive advantages when, if it is true that participatory management is a preferable way of organizing corporations, it should: "despite their supposed attractiveness to employees, such firms have repeatedly failed."[54]

There are two difficulties with this argument. First, although Maitland also acknowledges that employees may be willing to sacrifice efficiency in a trade-off to obtain governance input,[55] he leaves out the criteria for determining how well employee-run companies protect rights to self-determination in terms of economic, competitive advantages. Of course, there is a truth to this position: without competitive advantages, there may not be a business organization in which anyone will have rights to self-determination. But to more accurately determine if such structures do better protect self-determination, one would need to evaluate other criteria supplied by those who work for the firm. Employees, for instance, may not make competitive advantages a high priority. This prioritization may make them less profitable, but better places to work.

The important point is that the determination to become an investor does not prescribe the totality of duties that result from such a decision. Deciding to become an investor is an important decision, the risk of which ought to be compensated (for instance in the form of capital growth). But a person may not have capital to invest and thus may not be able to choose. Even if an individual has made such a choice, the principal-agency relationship remains a relationship. As a relationship, one must at least hear the concerns of the other party in the relationship. Neither a principal alone nor a law can hear. Thus, Cohen is right to argue that "[t]he process of making a decision about what is to the advantage of a group or what advances *that group's* welfare should often (usually) involve considering *that group's* opinion."[56]

An example of the complexity of stakeholder voice and self-determination can be seen in another institution that can be a mediating organization: the military. When a soldier joins the military, there are clear rules he or she must follow. Even if one has been conscripted (as opposed to having voluntarily joined), there are very specific roles soldiers must carry out. As such, their position is very much like an agent-employee who has decided to join a corporation rather than set up her own company.

Being in such an organization, however, neither allows the agent-soldier to comply exclusively with the orders of superiors nor does it allow superiors to ignore the welfare of the soldiers. The Nuremberg Trials demonstrated the fact that soldiers have duties to question some orders of their superiors. The ancient Chinese general Sun-Tzu argued that a primary responsibility of a general is to treat soldiers with warmth and beneficence.[57] If an organization as hierarchical as the military requires "stakeholder" input, responsibility, and concern, then corporations might consider at least allowing employees to have a voice in corporate governance.

There is no doubt that competition and contracting can protect many nonshareholder interests as agency theory would suggest. But with less than 20 percent of the American workforce unionized,[58] this strength of contract may not be what it once was. In retirement years, for instance, employees are particularly vulnerable.[59] Traditional contracting and competition mechanisms may not be sufficient to give employees the voice that accurately reflects their "stake" in the organization.

Moreover, it is hard to think some downsizing activities would not have evolved into a different form had employees had a greater voice. This is not to argue that workers cannot be fired, but it is to argue that employee participation is necessary for proper protection of today's economy.

In short, while Maitland may have a point that agency theory protects the right to self-determination, it only does so incompletely. Evidence shows that there may be economic advantages to including more employee control of the firm.[60]

The Social Contract Critique

For Thomas Donaldson and Thomas Dunfee, stakeholder theory suffers from two problems. First, it does not consider the community standards in describing an account of business ethics, and second, it does not have any normative foundation to determine who counts as stakeholders and what weight ought to be given to particular stakeholders.[61] At least in part because of these weaknesses, Donaldson and Dunfee offer their integrative social contracts theory (ISCT) which attempts to specify weights and duties according to extant social contracts constrained by universal hypernorms.[62]

Where do contracting relations take place? All over, of course, but in particular, the specification of rights and duties occurs within a community. In mediating institutions such as families, churches, and voluntary organizations, individuals learn the impact of their actions, and learn to internalize their responsibilities.[63] Through community interaction, one learns to contract with others.

For instance, a person who wants to volunteer for her church's soup kitchen does not thereby become a minister in charge of the entire church. Instead, she learns the duties of a role specified through ongoing contracts between the church and the leaders of the soup kitchen, between the leaders of the kitchen and the volunteers, between volunteers and the recipients of the food, and a myriad of other agreements. Those contracts develop the character of the participants. Even more important, however, they also develop the bonds of affection and the moral vision of the participants. The participants contract to join an organization, but thereafter the community itself becomes a participant in the life of the volunteer. After being in the organization, the volunteer no longer sees the soup kitchen, the guests served in the soup kitchen, and the church in the same way.

In short, community life requires ongoing contracts between the various stakeholders of the institution. Mediating institutions require social contracting, but that kind of contracting develops a different character (a relational contract) and different characters (persons), whose moral vision grows with the engagement with a mediating institution.

Ultimately, in fact, one learns to contract with oneself while internalizing the responsibilities one has to other members of the community. In negotiating what activities are acceptable and unacceptable, an individual gradually, although not inevitably, develops a character that internally regulates one's behavior. That is, one develops a conscience.[64] Put another way, one is formed in virtues that make responding to others possible.

ISCT, which is the subject of the following chapter, attempts to provide a specificity in terms of what duties ought to have more weight. In a mediating institutions framework, one's community—including a corporation—takes priority. Whatever the relationship may be among various external stakeholders, the internal stakeholders are a community.[65] The place where one is most likely to learn ethical duties toward others is, first, in one's community. The place where business is likely to develop ethical behavior is also internal.

A common way of describing this today is as "corporate culture."[66] A company's culture can hold it together in the midst of turmoils such as decentralization, delayering, and downsizing.[67] To be sure, individual companies have much different cultures; they are not identical.[68] Different as they may be, however, a corporate culture is important to the individuals who comprise them, because a sense of community matters to people.[69] At the heart of Donaldson and Dunfee's respect for community is an understanding of human nature that becomes particularly potent in an emerging naturalist approach to business ethics.

Naturalist Critique

In his book *Values, Nature and Culture in the American Corporation*, William Frederick somewhat whimsically summarizes contemporary business ethics in the formula EBB= $f(R_k+J_r+U)$, where EBB stands for ethical business behavior.[70] In this "Philosophers' Formula," ethical business is a function of Kantian rights (R_k), Rawlsian justice (J_r), and utilitarianism (U).[71] While the characterization has limits, it does roughly characterize the field. Most business ethics theories do not simply address one of these elements, but emphasize certain elements within the formula.

Frederick notes that his endorsement of the value of utility is the area of biggest disagreement between himself and other ethicists.[72] With economizing values central to survival in a naturalist theory, the utility of corporate actions is not only something to put up with, but the very justification for business. Without it, there would be no reason for us to have business. They provide "the vital link between business economizing and technologizing and the humanly vital needs and satisfactions by the members of the society."[73] By endorsing utility and expanding it to include all persons by virtue of its "naturalness," Frederick expands the preferences that a corporation must maximize.

As we have already seen, one can take Frederick's naturalist framework even further by considering the limited group size in which individuals can understand the consequences of their actions. Robin Dunbar's work and the work of anthropologists in the last century—who found that hunter-gatherer societies did not simply live in small groups but that their groups were related to larger social organizations—relate to this idea, as demonstrated in part 1. Thus, "overnight camps" of thirty to thirty-five people (comprising five or six families) collaborate with other such groups for hunting and foraging and ultimate belong to tribes of 1,500 to 2,000 people.[74] This matrix ties together the already noted findings of Jaynes and Turnbull to suggest that individuals find their identity best in small organizations, which can be linked to larger units.

Is this development of moral identity in small organiaztions, however, a good idea? Anthropologist Lawrence Keeley has studied the degree of violence in these small, hunter-gatherer communities and has found the rate of deaths in warfare to be twenty times higher than they are in what we call a bloody twentieth century.[75] Clearly, the fostering of small groups in order to obtain a sense of moral identity has to be circumscribed, or else one's moral identity can be gained through unacceptable behavior. Nevertheless, when James Wilson finds that children in rural, economically simple communities with strong kinship ties are more willing to help and comfort others, not only within their group, but outside the group as well,[76] one can see that finding a place for a natural need for small communities in order to encourage moral development is not a bad idea either.

Speaking in the business context, perhaps we best learn our moral responsibilities in small, mediating institutions in which there are face-to-face consequences of our actions rather than in large, abstract structures bound by rules that may seem to have little to do with the everyday life of the individual person affected by them.[77] Of course, one cannot simply turn back the clock so as to put human beings into small tribes roaming the countryside, but the point is that within our large nation-states and corporations, we need to foster the communities, the mediating institutions, in which individuals have some significant control over the rules of their community and learn to internalize moral responsibilities.

While evolutionary psychology is geared toward explaining reproduction,[78] our genetic similarity with our ancestors suggests that we do need small groups to form our identity and to learn our moral responsibilities. Evidence suggesting that the communication skills of such small groups are almost entirely internal to one's community[79] supports the notion that we may be similarly disposed. In short, we may not be wired to have a moral sense. But we are wired to have a social sense, and that social sense is most acute in small organizations, where we have face-to-face interaction and communication with others.

Rather than attempting to grasp our responsibilities to far-flung stakeholder groups, perhaps our corporate responsibilities ought to focus on those things which we are best able to do: develop corporate communities with duties flowing primarily to internal members. This is exactly the position of the business as mediating institution approach, as I have already described.

The Mediating Critique

Stakeholder theory incorporates a good deal of the Philosophers' Formula. It attempts to protect Kantian commitments to the individual. It also incorporates utilitarianism. Evan and Freeman broaden the scope of utilitarian analysis to include nonshareholder interests. Evan and Freeman's approach, in other words, still operates under a utilitarian rationality, but is one based on stakeholder rather than shareholder or managerial interests.

What kinds of needs would be raised by stakeholders? The specific needs, of course, would vary from company to company. But there are certain basic human needs likely to be raised by stakeholders if given the opportunity. Modern psychologists have documented the noneconomic needs of individuals in the workplace as well.[80] These social needs, primarily and best met in small, mediating institutions are consistent with the Kantian approach taken in stakeholder theory. The point is that corporations ought to be managed so that individuals are treated as "ends" not as "means." In a corporate mediating institution, the ends-means issue is approached by a structure that requires individuals to take into account others as human beings. A mediating institutions approach would also question the range of duties one has. Rather than a set of open-ended duties to all stakeholders affected by corporate action, it would place primary duties on meeting the social needs of internal constituents such as employees and shareholders.

BMI AND STAKEHOLDER THEORY

The business as mediating institution approach can be integrated, to some degree, with a liberal stakeholder approach. It draws upon a limited notion of stakeholder theory. Like social contract theory and virtue theory,[81] it recognizes the importance of community determination of proper behavior and the community's role at inculcating moral identity. It draws upon a human nature that requires small groups in order to develop that identity and to stress the importance of participation.

Other popular, contemporary theories such as "open-book management"[82] offer similar notions, but the theme of empowered workers championed by BMI is not the same as a full-fledged workplace democracy. Probably the most influential management strategists today, Gary Hamel and C. K. Prahalad argue that while "bureaucracy can strangle initiative and progress, so too can a large number of empowered but unaligned individuals who are working at cross-purposes."[83] Instead, they argue that employees also want a sense of direction set by management, a notion of what they call "strategic intent."[84] So too, BMI does not call for worker plebiscites in order to operate a company. It does, however, call for corporations to recognize that they are communities and as communities interpersonal relationships are important. Because they are important, so are ethical duties, because relationships are sustained by ethical rules and principles. Creating such organizations has already been done. BMI is a way to build on those successes on a wider scale.

It is important to note that the mediating institutions position does not claim to offer a complete solution to ethical dilemmas in business. The mediating approach is essentially a theory of the firm proposing a new model of corporate governance. Even in this regard, such a theory has many additional questions to answer, but for the purpose of normative thought, the approach argues not that businesses should not be Good Samaritans, but that we will never learn to be Good Samaritans until we learn that we are responsible for others. Learning that lesson is hard to do if one has not been socialized to see it. This is exactly what mediating institutions do.

Relatedly, noting that we may be naturally adapted (or designed) to look first to members of our communities is not to confuse "what is" and "what ought to be," but to note that we will never understand "what ought to be" if we demand duties beyond our ability to absorb. Simply making corporations into mediating institutions would dramatically change the way they operate. It might be working out the kinds of mediating approach before trying the more complex work of full-blown stakeholder theory.

CONCLUSION

Corporations that are structured as mediating institutions owe primary duties to internal constituents. Those include shareholders and employees. It is important for employees to have some kind of representation on the board itself. Moreover, if a corporation is a community; that is, a mediating institution in which individuals learn both rights and responsibilities, particular work must be structured so as to provide some type of affective meaning.[85]

The rationale for this approach is that it takes advantage of the valuable aspects of stakeholder theory, manifested legally by corporate constituency statutes, as well as other business ethics theories. It does not, however, ask corporations to do more than they are capable of doing. By proposing a "mediating" position between full-blown stakeholder theory and traditional shareholder responsibility, corporations may be able to be more like communities in which moral identity as well as economic efficiency is fostered.

7

Social Contracting

This chapter assesses an approach that is significantly advanced over that of agency contractarianism. Social contractarianism, however, is not without weaknesses. I begin by providing a background of the social contractarian approach and go on to focus specifically on the most advanced social contract application to business: Donaldson and Dunfee's integrative social contracts theory (ISCT). In the last section, I offer three critiques of ISCT: that it gives a too-thin assessment of community, a too-thin understanding of nature, and a too-thin understanding of transcendence.

BACKGROUND OF THE SOCIAL CONTRACT THEORY OF BUSINESS ETHICS

Thomas Donaldson is acknowledged as the pioneer of social contract theory in business ethics.[1] Donaldson argues that in our modern social contract, corporations are given protections such as limited liability and continuity of life in return for being efficient producers of goods and services and for not abusing those who provide them with these rights, such as customers and employees.[2] Thus, "[w]hen Donaldson places the basic contract above derivative duties, he sets the stage for a frontal assault on the conventional wisdom of much of corporate America, that shareholder wealth maximization is the great Good for business."[3]

Michael Keeley applies social contract thinking to the structure of organizations, arguing that corporations should operate according to

136

principles of equality, impartiality, and respect for individuals.[4] Corporations ought to be organized to allow individuals to achieve personal goals within the organization rather than have collective goals imposed upon them.[5]

A second approach is that of extant social contracts. The two leading theorists of this approach are Thomas Dunfee and Steven Salbu. Dunfee argues that the actual legal contracts enacted by a particular community serve as a basis for moral rules.[6] Thus, a business should operate by consulting the basic organizing principles of society to gain clarity on what social consensus has been reached.

Salbu has applied this approach in a number of areas.[7] One example is insider trading regulation.[8] Salbu argues that principles of procedural equality and legitimate mechanisms of property acquisition require an expansive, rather than fiduciary, approach to insider trading.[9] In the "extant" social contracts view of Dunfee and Salbu, societies have agreed upon the rules of the game, and companies should consult these principles rather than attempt to invent new principles of normative behavior.

THE BASICS OF ISCT

Donaldson and Dunfee have now joined these approaches to create a theory called integrative social contracts theory (ISCT). Donaldson and Dunfee combine the power of empirical studies of business behavior with a normative evaluation of that behavior. Thus, this approach purports to take into account both the actual rules enacted by a community or society and a normative understanding of those rules.

Donaldson and Dunfee's argument is based on a normative, hypothetical, macrosocial contract of political economy and on the social contracts found in various commercial and noncommercial communities.[10] Unlike the family, economic organizations are not natural; they are "artifactual."[11] Because of human, bounded rationality and the artifactual nature of economic life, ISCT requires "moral free space" with room for differentiated cultural and religious norms that specify the particular rules for each economic enterprise.[12]

"Moral free space" suggests that there are no universal norms. Donaldson and Dunfee address this moral relativism by proposing limits to the moral norms a "community" can devise. They present a two-step analysis to provide real moral support to a community's norms. First, an "authentic" norm is one to which members of a community have consented in an informed way.[13] Consent must be real.[14] To guarantee that, Donaldson and Dunfee argue that consent must be reinforced by a right to exit the community.[15] If a community has enacted norms and those norms have been freely accepted, they are then "authentic."[16]

What has generated a good deal of attention since ISCT first debuted is the notion of "hypernorms." In order for the local norms to be obligatory (or legitimate), the norms must also be in accord with formal philosophy. Donaldson and Dunfee provide an elaboration of the notion of hypernorms in their recent book, *Ties That Bind*. Paralleling Charles Taylor's notion of hypergoods, they define hypernorms as "second-order moral concepts because they represent norms sufficiently fundamental to serve as a source of evaluation and criticism of community-generated norms."[17]

One of the more interesting aspects of the book is Donaldson and Dunfee's refusal to identify the source of a hypernorm. Several scholars in the field have pushed Donaldson and Dunfee to specify the source of hypernorms. Bill Frederick, for instance, has encouraged Donaldson and Dunfee to locate hypernorms in the processes of nature,[18] while Don Mayer has argued for locating them in reason.[19]

In response, Donaldson and Dunfee first rely on the human capacity to recognize a hypernorm. Regardless of the source (reason or nature or something else), a convergence of intellectual thought and the evidence of them as global norms is sufficient to identify them. Second, they argue that scholars have used ISCT's second-order hypernorms successfully. Thus, unless someone is able to show how such quests to find and apply hypernorms fail, in light of the success other scholars have had in finding and applying them, Donaldson and Dunfee remain unconvinced that further specification of the source of hypernorms is necessary.[20] Of course, even the strategy of recognition gets one only so far. If recognition of a hypernorm is central to its status as a hypernorm, how do we come to recognize them? Donaldson and Dunfee respond to this question quite specifically. They list the following eleven kinds of evidence that suggest the existence of a hypernorm and argue that if two or more of these confirm a widespread recognition of any ethical principle, a decision maker should take that as a rebuttable presumption that a hypernorm exists. The eleven kinds of evidence are

1. Widespread consensus that the principle is universal.
2. Component of well-known global industry standards.
3. Supported by prominent nongovernmental organizations such as the International Labour Organization or Transparency International.
4. Supported by regional government organizations such as the European Community, the OECD, or the Organization of American States.
5. Consistently referred to as a global ethical standard by international media.
6. Known to be consistent with the precepts of major religions.

7. Supported by global business organizations such as the International Chamber of Commerce or the Caux Round Table.
8. Known to be consistent with precepts of major philosophies.
9. Generally supported by a relevant international community of professionals, e.g., accountants or environmental engineers.
10. Known to be consistent with findings concerning universal human values.
11. Supported by the laws of many different countries.[21]

In providing this list, Donaldson and Dunfee thus provide a significant amount of specificity to what a hypernorm is and how we can find it. In a sense, they use these extant manifestations of norms in order to reinforce and perhaps identify philosophical criteria for moral behavior. "What is" thus has a great deal to do with "what ought to be" or "what is" at least points toward what "what ought to be" might look like. This is an interesting phenomenological straddle, which may or may not be intellectually convincing to critics, but which allows Donaldson and Dunfee to plausibly argue that the burden of proof ought to be shifted to their critics. In legal terms, they have constructed a prima facie case for the establish of any particular hypernorms.

In a sense, the argument Donaldson and Dunfee make seems to be most akin to a kind of natural law. If there is an innate moral sense in every human being, then one would expect to find manifestations of it in every human culture. Moreover, if human beings have the ability to reason about the good, then we may be able to specify the moral goods that are important for human life. Donaldson and Dunfee do exactly this when they seek to ground the existence of hypernorms in extant norms and do so while maintaining the necessity of formal moral philosophy in examining such norms. This parallel is not to argue that Donaldson and Dunfee should locate their argument in natural law. I would expect that they would respond to such a proposal as they have to the arguments of critics already mentioned. That is, they would probably remain agnostic about the source of hypernorms. It seems, however, that a natural law approach that takes seriously the laws of nature is an approach very compatible with Donaldson and Dunfee's project.

Donaldson and Dunfee elaborate three kinds of hypernorms: procedural, structural, and substantive. Procedural norms are those conditions essential to support consent in microsocial contracts. These would include notions of exit and voice, which permit Donaldson and Dunfee to characterize a community norm as authentic. Structural hypernorms are those principles that establish and support the essential background institutions in society. This would include a legal system designed to assure fair trials. Substantive hypernorms are fundamental concepts of the right and the good, such as promise keeping and respect for human dignity.

As an example of the application of hypernorms, Donaldson and Dunfee consider the perennial global ethics question concerning bribery. Donaldson and Dunfee identify "necessary social efficiency" as a hypernorm. By this they mean that an action or policy is efficient "when it contributes toward the provision of necessary social goods sufficient to sustain the least well-off members of society at a level of reasonable possibility concerning liberty, health, food, housing, education, and just treatment."[22] They establish this hypernorm by arguing that two necessary goods are fairness and aggregate welfare.[23] In order to actualize these goods, one must have institutions such as private property. Following Aristotle's argument against Plato, they argue that property is more likely to be utilized efficiently and productively for the benefit of all members of society if it were in private ownership than in a system in which there was no private ownership.

Therefore, the economic structure of a society must be organized so that resources in which society has a stake will be efficiently utilized and individuals will discharge their role duties stemming from the economizing parameters of efficiency strategies in which they participate. In other words, the least well-off have the best chance of reaching basic goods if resources are used efficiently, and society should be structured to allocate resources efficiently and individuals should fulfill their roles in such a structure.

This sounds abstractly enough like a hypernorm, and it also has a practical implication. Focusing on bribery, Donaldson and Dunfee make three arguments from the perspective of ISCT. First, bribery may violate a role duty in a principal-agent relationship. An agent may extort a bribe for the benefit of the agent herself rather than for the benefit of the principal.

Second, in those communities in which a norm of bribery is accepted, Donaldson and Dunfee argue that, in fact, the norm is not authentic. They note that bribery is outlawed in *all* countries. In addition to this evidence that bribery then is not a community norm, they cite interviews conducted with executives in countries where bribery is frequent and record the disgust of executives at the practice. One may wonder if this reaction was for the benefit of the audience (an ethicist), but Donaldson and Dunfee make their point sufficiently well to conclude that bribery may occur, but that does not mean that it is viewed as moral even by members of communities where it does occur.

Third, bribery violates the hypernorm of necessary social efficiency. It does this in two ways. One way is that political participation is harmed when governmental officials accept bribes. When a government official makes a decision on the basis of a bribe, he is allocating public resources in a manner not subject to the political control of the public. Accordingly, there is a violation of the norm of a society structured to provide the least well off the possibility of pursuing basic goods.

A second way that bribery violates the hypernorm of necessary social efficiency is that it skews the efficient distribution of resources. A common rationalization for bribery is that no one gets hurt. Under Donaldson and Dunfee's analysis, however, the skewing of resources resulting from bribery may very well hurt the least well-off. It would surprise me if this assessment of bribery is not found by most ethicists to be a very helpful schema.

THREE CRITIQUES OF SOCIAL CONTRACTING

It is important to note the advances Donaldson and Dunfee have made over agency contractarianism. By insisting upon a social contract in which those citizens who bargain for corporate existence—employees and customers—stakeholders are entitled to have corporations treat them in a nonabusive way. It is not sufficient, as the agency contractarians allow, for a manager to focus on shareholder profitability with no more than an ideological assumption that doing so will reward other stakeholders. Donaldson and Dunfee's theory does consider benefit to nonshareholder constituents, making corporations accountable for the consequences of all their actions, not just those affecting a particular group.

Their two-step approach also has significant merit. Human beings' moral identity is shaped in communal relationships. This communitarian nature must be recognized; individual communities and cultures must have the freedom to develop moral norms according to the history of the organization and its historical interaction with the community in which it is situated. Relying only upon communities to identify moral norms, however, is tantamount to endorsing moral relativism and tribalism. Particularly in a global business environment, some global ethics are necessary for the ongoing engagement of international business. Thus, ISCT includes several worthy ideas.

There are critiques, however, that question Donaldson and Dunfee's reliance on contractual methodology to achieve the results they desire. Instead of contracts, a richer notion of nature provides a more meaningful identification of the community norms necessary for moral development—and even the hypernorms necessary for restricting tribalism. Such a notion of nature, in fact, ultimately becomes a transcendent check on corporate activities.

A Too Thin Communitarianism: Consent and Embeddedness

Donaldson and Dunfee endorse the importance of community, but the view they provide of community is very thin. Because individuals develop their identity in mediating institutions, members learn that they are not autonomous beings but relational, social persons. As relational beings, our "self" is inextricably tied up with our ethical duties. In ways very similar to those noted by Wilson regarding our attraction to family members and persons "like" us,[24] persons become nurturing and affectionate toward others within the mediating institution group.[25] Such organizations, even business organizations, are efficient at inculcating virtue when they view their institution as a family.[26]

Banded Contracts: An Anthropological Evolution

Anthropologist Kent Flannery, whom we have seen already, provides a helpful distinction between social evolution and cultural evolution in anthropology. Cultural evolution is about the "shared beliefs, values, cosmologies, ideologies, customs, and traditions that distinguish one group of people from other groups, giving it its ethnic identity."[27] Social evolution occurs at a different level of organizational complexity, such as "when a small society based on egalitarian relationships becomes a larger society based on hierarchical relationships."[28] Culture gives rise to identity; society leads to various forms of organization. Society, like an organ, undergoes a different kind of evolution from the species. Culture, however, is akin to "what biologists call divergent evolution—the rise of two or more new forms from a common ancestor."[29]

When societies are structured to require individuals to exist in associations other than their "natural" small bands, an inherent instability results from the coercive necessity of living together.[30] The most basic unit of extrafamilial human organization throughout prehistory was the hunter-gatherer band.[31] Such bands generally comprised twenty-five to thirty-five persons and subsisted nomadically on wild plants and animals.[32] Their structure, still common into the nineteenth century, had "[n]o hereditary differences in rank or authority and their leadership was ephemeral, based on differences in age, experience, skill, and charisma. Divisions of labor were largely along the lines of age and gender, and most hunter-gathering bands had an egalitarian ethic that downplayed any differences in prestige that arose."[33]

The adoption of agriculture, however, led to "autonomous village societies."[34] Such communities, according to Flannery, were larger than the bands, but generally still displayed no hereditary differences in rank, and had no authority over smaller villages nearby.[35] In some places, a third level of society, rank society, arose.[36] In rank society, egalitarianism was replaced by an ideology in which individuals were unequal at birth and leaders came from a hereditary class.[37] In such societies, small villages lost their autonomy to larger nearby villages.[38] In some cases, this led to an even greater amalgamation of villages under the authority of chiefdoms.[39] The difficulty with these larger sizes is that they also increased coercion. "Once large villages begin to break down the autonomy of the small villages around them, ambitious chiefs can bring very large territories and thousands of people under their control," a result that seems to follow megastructures.[40]

On the other hand, if transcending bands claim to serve for the benefit of the entire community, then the new larger group may be more productive. Yet enlarging the group may not be for the community's collective benefit. An archaic state sometimes arose from competing chiefdoms,[41] kingdoms with social strata including nobles, merchants, and slaves.[42] These states could be conquered and grouped into multiethnic empires.[43] The result was that "empires were the largest and least stable. Most broke down within two hundred years or less, perhaps telling us something about the upper size limits of human social organization."[44]

It is difficult not to see similarities in the world of business. An interesting feature of the bands described above, moreover, is that they were founded on an egalitarianism that seems to be the historical purpose of social contracting. Decisions in bands place a premium on consensus, consent, and community. The contracts of these groups are not "bounded" but "banded." In short, it is not just any community that fosters the desire to be ethical, but a small one—a mediating institution. In such a mediating institution, contracts are not based on consent alone, but have a socialized content—a "banded contract."

Social Contracting and Mediating Institutions

According to sociologist Robert Nisbet, the Enlightenment social contract offered to guarantee freedom and equality in exchange for loyalty to the state, rather than to mediating institutions.[45] Legal systems developed to replace private dispute resolution; taxation, regulation, and education placed the state in the role of problem solver.[46] In each legal system, the state guaranteed individuals the freedom to choose and to be treated impartially by powerful mediating institutions. Wilson goes so far as to characterize many of the dominant ideologies of the nineteenth and twentieth centuries as founded on the replacement of the idea of commitment to a community with the idea of choice.[47]

To Tocqueville, such a social contract, even in democratic form, was a dangerous thought. Protecting freedom and equality can throw a per-

son "back forever upon himself alone and threatens in the end to confine him entirely within the solitude of his own heart."[48] When that happens, "the social tie is destroyed, and each workman, standing alone, endeavors simply to gain the most money at the least cost. The will of the
customer is then his only limit."[49] Tocqueville's concern was that the
moral and political quest for equality and liberty could engender excessive selfishness and the rejection of any willingness to seek individual
sacrifice for a common good. It could muzzle the communitarian nature of humanity, thereby undermining the very social structures necessary to develop individuals' ability to make appropriate, rational decisions based on consent.

In short, the political social contract has undermined the communities that give rise to personal identity. The same will be true in business
unless a strong mediating institution preserves communal identity. By
magnifying the needs of stakeholders who are now free to voice needs
and to participate in decisions, the pursuit of individual needs assumes
greater legitimacy because each person has an equal right to speak up
and join in. This can be a beneficial corrective to the oppressive hierarchies that communities can foster, but the pursuit of individual needs
can also lead to the self-interested pursuit of economic greed that often
characterizes capitalism and to politics where voting for the common
good is subordinated to self-interest. Thus, sewn in the quest for freedom and equality were the philosophical and sociological seeds of self-
interest disconnected from social responsibility. While freedom and
consent may be good values, they cannot be abstracted from the community that gave them meaning. The meaning of consent must be given
form by a certain kind of community: a mediating institution.

I want to be clear that Donaldson and Dunfee do not necessarily fall
prey to this social contract problem. Yet, to the extent their view of community stays away from anthropological underpinnings, the threat of a
direct attempt to relate individuals to hypernorms unmediated by community is present and can thereby undercut the role of the communitarian aspects they wish to endorse. The business as mediating institution approach, however, provides this anthropological underpinning in
a way that can complement Donaldson and Dunfee's approach and do
so in a way that preserves both a communitarian and hypernorm-like
kind of accountability.

A Too Thin View of Nature:
The Naturalistic Fallacy's Fallacy

Another issue that Donaldson and Dunfee raise from time to time, but
do not dwell upon, is the notion that human beings may be hardwired
to be ethical. This is a view advocated recently by biologists and evolu-

tionary psychologists. James Q. Wilson and Robert Wright exemplify the position. Their argument is that there is a "moral sense" among human beings, a conviction substantiated by economist Robert Frank, who reports that cheaters do not dominate in the long term. Donaldson and Dunfee also consider Bill Frederick's case for grounding ethics in nature and note that ethicists can use the argument that nature requires cooperation as well as competitiveness as a weapon against executives who paint a narrow portrait of Darwinian struggles for survival. For Donaldson and Dunfee, the issue is important because authentic norms are the product of human interactions.[50] Perhaps a better way to tap into the biological human nature would be to characterize human beings as Aristotle and Darwin did. Larry Arnhart has recently argued that Aristotle and Darwin can be linked because, at least in part, they both carefully considered biological evidence to conclude that human beings are social creatures. By virtue of being social creatures, they must elaborate rules by which they live together. Those rules are the cultural specifications of moral behavior.[51] Thus, as social creatures, human beings can use their reasoning capacities to figure out what rules are necessary to live together. Human beings must in some sense contract with each other. The basis for this is not so much that there is an instinct toward altruism, but rather simply that human beings are social creatures.

The danger in relying on a "moral sense" is that it suggests that such a sense does not thereafter need cultural cultivation. One could simply advise individuals to tap into their biological instincts. Such an approach would be more therapeutic than moral. A "moral sense" obtains its ethical character, however, by the reality of human sociability. As Frederick argues, a central evolutionary adaptation of human beings is our ability to create culture through natural technosymbolic capacities. I hardly think that Donaldson and Dunfee are prepared to advocate for a view of business ethics absent from this cultural, philosophical explication of moral duties. In raising the notion of human "hardwiredness," I simply wish to note that (1) this natural characteristic in fact could be an advantageous recognition by the field (against a narrower notion of Darwinism) while (2) placing the recognition in a human nature of sociability to preserve the necessity of cultural and philosophical specification. Taking account of human sociability, it seems, fits more easily into Donaldson and Dunfee's framework and does so while doing justice to anthropological studies of human nature.

The historically demonstrated danger of the naturalist approach is that the theory becomes deterministic. Sociobiology leaves little room for individual initiative and creativity. Business ethicist Bill Frederick, who relies upon naturalist justifications to ground his approach, finds a way out of this, however: one naturally recurring characteristic of human beings is our technologizing ability.[52] Technologizing does not

mean only the creation of gadgets, but more broadly that human beings have an evolutionary adaptation to think symbolically and abstractly.[53] Such thinking was first evidenced in toolmaking, when human
beings took raw materials and reconfigured them for a new use.[54]
Human technologizing ability is also our ability to use language, to
think philosophically, to interpret the world theologically, and to create
cultures.[55] Human beings can reconstruct and reformulate the world—
and this capacity for fostering constant change prevents Frederick's
theory from becoming deterministic.

Thus, one way to reformulate business ethics is to blend economizing
(our need for converting resources into productive energy) and ecologizing (our physical need to live in an integrated, interconnected community) value clusters. Human beings do this by technologizing. Biological and anthropological research may inform the study of business
and its ethics. Rather than attempting to explain moral values by biology, however, Frederick uses empirical evidence only to bolster the legitimacy of extant social contracts and of philosophical reflection on those
contracts. With such a well-constructed platform, Frederick is probably
reluctant to more completely rely upon nature to ground business
ethics, for fear of committing the naturalistic fallacy.

Yet the difficulties with the naturalistic fallacy can, at least to some extent, be overcome in other additional ways. First, the naturalistic fallacy
is overstated. Every normative theory commits the naturalistic fallacy, at
least in part. For instance, in defining hypernorms, Donaldson and
Dunfee rely upon a cross-cultural convergence of norms. Thus, the
identification of hypernorms depends upon norms that already exist.
Donaldson and Dunfee attempt to abstract these norms so that they do
not immediately run afoul of the naturalistic fallacy. In fact, hypernorms
are nevertheless derived from empirical evidence—and therefore suffer
the same naturalistic fallacy as any theory deriving the "ought" from
what "is." This is actually a compelling feature of Donaldson and Dunfee's argument: if many cultures repeatedly articulate the same norm,
that norm is evidence of a "natural law" that all persons must take into
account in making moral judgments. For example, the fact that all
world religions, as well as higher primates, have a social rule of reciprocity[56] indicates that this norm may be stitched into our moral nature.

Similarly, social contractarians, including Donaldson and Dunfee, rely
upon a fictional rational negotiating group or thinker, producing social
agreements that are rational and are rationally articulated. But, argues
legal philosopher Michael Perry, "[t]here is no noncircular way to justify
[the claim that one ought to be rational] because any putative justification would be rational and thereby presuppose the authority of that
which is at issue: rationality."[57] There simply is no way to make our

moral positions objective. Whatever criteria we use to justify our moral norms cannot be noncircularly justified. This is exactly the circular reasoning problem faced by the naturalistic fallacy. Thus, all moral thinking relies on the same theoretical underpinnings as the naturalistic fallacy.[58]

The second solution to the naturalistic fallacy is a sense of transcendence that extends beyond human cognitive abilities: if business ethics do not take into account the effects of corporate actions on nonshareholder constituents, who will object? Cannot society adopt any norm that is rationally chosen? Why choose one set of norms over another? In short, why worry about being ethical in business? The answer is in notions of transcendence.

A Too Thin View of Transcendence

Donaldson and Dunfee are remarkably open to the influence of religion in ethical practices. They relate their approach to the "compact" with God in the Torah and to the imaginary agreement among members of Plato's state.[59] This openness to notions of transcendence, however, should be extended further. What if ethical rules are not constituted simply by real or hypothetical negotiations, but instead are the result of dealing with something larger?

Part III of this book will more fully address this possibility. One can recognize, however, four "universal" aspects of nature with which any culture's moral norms must deal. Becoming aware of these aspects is itself an important step in ethical reflection. Ethical responsibilities are sometimes learned through an experience with a transcendent reality, typically a religious experience. A Hindu finds his *brahman-atman*[60]; Saul encountered Christ on the road to Damascus.[61] In each, and undoubtedly in many others as well, ethical awareness comes from an experience with transcendence.

Nature itself is a transcendent force. The naturalistic fallacy is troublesome in its "that's the way things are, so there's nothing we can do to change it" form. It is equally troublesome to confuse what ought to be with what is. One naturalist complains that this is exactly the problem of the political correctness movement; in its obsession with what ought to be done, it does not take into account the realities of the way people act.[62] As much as some ethicists wish that human beings did not have economizing needs, the world is competitive as well as cooperative. In competition, there are losers. Society may be structured to limit loss and pain, and this will dovetail well with ethical behavior. But it is impossible to remove reality—what nature is—from plausible accounts of human nature; some competitive battles are part of our nature.

"If There Is No God, Then Nothing Is Immoral"

Another aspect of transcendence is Dostoyevsky's classic notion that without God, crime becomes not only possible, but also inevitable.[63] However one defines the identity of "God," it is fundamentally a notion of an ultimate good to which human beings are ultimately accountable. For Dostoyevsky, as he relates most famously in "The Legend of the Grand Inquisitor," religion is dangerous because it causes people to stop thinking for themselves, preferring instead to defer their thinking to a leader.[64] Individuals thus forfeit, to use Frederick's term, their technologizing ability. An equally problematic difficulty, however, is that an individually, or even socially, constructed "God" can become the product of rationalization and negotiation, ultimately producing rationalization of or agreement upon the "legitimacy" of crime.

It is possible, of course, to dismiss the need for some ultimate good ungrounded in reality. Naturalistic evidence, however, demonstrates that human beings have a natural reflective impulse grounded in our symbolic nature. Anthropologists trace evidence of human symbolic ability to roughly 40,000 years ago.[65] At that time, not only art and language appeared, but also religious ritual.[66] Indeed, as Frederick argues, at least one of the characteristics that differentiates human beings from nonhuman life is our religious (as well as other symbolic) dimension.[67] Thus, it may well be true not only that Dostoyevsky was correct that the consequences of law (and ethics) without religion are unacceptable, but also that the connection of spiritual realities and ethics is rooted in human nature and culture. In addition to the description of various forces and clusters that recur throughout all human societies, a notion of transcendence of some kind is also necessary to ground any social ethic. If this is true, then there should be evidence of at least some common social ethic, of various cultures repeating the same moral norms—evidence of a more deeply rooted source, human nature, for the norm itself.

Other Transcendences: Bands and Reciprocity

A third form of transcendence is the evidence that human beings are most naturally at home in band groups. Bands require and depend upon characteristics of moral behavior praised by many ethicists: equality, identity, altruism, and solidarity.

The fact that virtually all of human history was lived in bands, and that band moral values are still considered to be important, is evidence of the enduring, cross-cultural legitimacy of those values. They are, in short, communitarian virtues. Yet it is not in the large megastructure of society where characteristics such as equality, solidarity, altruism, and identity are formed, but in mediating institutions. More important, bands foster empathy. Small bands are required for moral development even in business organizations.

Moral empathy answers the question of why one should be moral. Agency and social contractarianism have trouble answering that question. Finance professor John Dobson's term "technical universe" generally corresponds to what we have called agency theory. And for Dobson, the theory's failure to answer the "why be moral" question reveals its intellectual incoherence:

> [Technical universe] fails in terms of its own standards of logic and rationality; it conjures a business milieu of opportunistic individuals pursuing wealth maximization within a contractual nexus, yet it provides no mechanism within its construct for the adequate (that is, economically efficient) enforcement of these contracts. Without such enforcement, the rationally determined economic goal of material advancement is thwarted. In short, a dominant epistemology of individualistic wealth maximization ensures that individuals within that universe never maximize wealth; it is a classic "catch-22" scenario. As Aristotle and others have pointed out, to really achieve what is one's self-interest, one cannot directly pursue what one perceives to be in one's self-interest; the Technical Universe lacks the philosophical sophistication to realize this.[68]

Similarly, contemporary moral philosophy, of which ISCT is an example, has difficulty answering the question: "ISCT, like business ethics theory in general, suffers from all the internal inconsistencies and incoherence characteristic of modernity. Simply put, there is no such thing as a hypernorm. Ethics is always contextual."[69]

The final universal characteristic of transcendence is the basic moral norm of reciprocity. In human society, some variation of the Golden Rule exists in nearly every culture.[70] Yet differences among the formulations of the notion of reciprocity are not without significance. Doing to others what they have done to you is quite different from doing to others as they would like you to do to them, or from treating others as you would like to be treated. Human societies with a moral system, however, will typically include some form of the rule of reciprocity. Thus, reciprocity may be a moral principle with global appeal.[71]

These four examples of transcendent principles demonstrate that human beings are, in fact, subject to "forces" beyond our control. There are forces within us that are part of our nature that must be considered when formulating ethical rules for business. Too often, "hard-headed" realists argue that business is "survival of the fittest."[72] But nature is more complex than that. Nature is the survival of the fit, not necessarily the fittest. Nature is also about individuals in small bands cooperating with one another, establishing bonds that lead them to treat others altruistically, to practice solidarity and reciprocity, and to inculcate moral identity.

The forces that transcend human control, whether Dostoyevksy's

God, Nature, or even Yoda's "force" are not simply the product of a contract. In a community of the right size, a banded contract reveals that our nature is about more than consent. These small mediating institutions are the best means for restructuring the modern corporation.

AMBIGUITIES

I specifically want to acknowledge that nature is ambiguous. While it is naïve to think we can escape certain hardwired dimensions of our nature, it is also ingenuous to think that our nature does not provide us with the capacity to culturally favor some kinds of behavior over others. To fail to note both is to fail to appreciate the dialectical dimension of human nature. What then might be problematic with a corporate model that is consciously holistic?

Social contractarian Michael Keeley provides many of the most persuasive arguments against what he calls an "organismic" model.[73] Such a model relies upon biological analogues, as well as a strand of anthropology, suggesting that organizations take on their own life separate and apart from the combination of the members of the organization. As Keeley rightly notes, such a conception of an organization as an "emergent property" can easily be used to deemphasize the rights of individuals within the organization to the extent that basic human rights are abridged.[74] This is why he argues, for instance, that James Madison insisted that a bill of rights be appended to the U.S. Constitution.[75] Keeley also notes that although premodern societies did not have a modern notion of "rights," there were appropriate claims to what many call rights. In Hebrew society, these included claims to physical security, to basic necessities, and to participation in community governance. Such checks on power are important, according to Keeley, because they provide for a dispersal of power that safeguards participants from exploitation.[76] Thus, Keeley argues that institutions that challenge managerial authority may be appropriate; these institutions may include unions and government.[77]

Keeley also argues that organizational models that provide members of organizations with enhanced decision-making control over manufacturing processes are not necessarily something to be admired. He notes that German munitions minister Albert Speer eschewed mechanistic organizational models in favor of "collegial decision making, fluidity of organizational structures, temporary organizational structures, and industrial self-responsibility [for local managers]."[78] Speer's approach proved productive and engendered enthusiasm among his managers.[79] Of course, the workers carrying out the directives of the managers were conscripted slaves, and the munitions that were produced went to the direct service of the goals of the Third Reich. Thus, Keeley argues that contemporary managerial mantras endorsing decentralized, participatory workplaces ought not to be too quickly embraced. They are not an ethical panacea.

Even more problematic are shallow, contemporary attempts to foster a notion of teamwork. Teams, of course, seem to be something of a contemporary business mantra. Business schools organize students into teams for projects, and corporations rely on teamwork in order to achieve their objectives. Teams and communities, however, are not necessarily the same things.

In their analysis of paper mills, Steven Vallas and John Beck note that although firms reconstruct jobs in order to follow total quality management notions of team building and decentralization, which depend upon worker involvement, the centralization of statistical analysis and the centralized determination of job requirements outside of a team-driven process simply discourage workers.[80] Portraying such efforts as community building can only be justified in a contractual manner, in which it is assumed that both parties have freely consented to the new way of doing work. It is clear that efforts like those studied by Vallas and Beck have not even minimally considered what makes a community. As a result, to reject a business-as-community approach because of the manipulation of "communities" through sham quality efforts is similar to criticizing a small chamber orchestra because the large symphony that replaced it doesn't sound like a chamber group.

Similarly, Richard Sennett has argued that managerial models of teamwork destroy personal character, because, at least in part, membership in any particular business team is temporary. Learning to be a team player means learning how to display certain traits of rhetoric and superficial cooperativeness. Such traits are masks appearing to demonstrate consensus. In reality, this apparent consensus is ordered acquiescence to centralized management, with little relationship between identifying one's well-being and the common good of the group, rather than virtues formed in mediating associations.[81] Moreover, Sennett found that peer pressure within the groups to conform to a goal can be harsh, and the goal is typically not what the group members view as important, but simply that of enhancing the bottom line.[82] This effectively coerces individuals to work harder under the guise of team action, while simultaneously exempting upper management from responsibility for "cracking the whip."[83] Again, such efforts have utterly no relationship to what constitutes a mediating institution; that is, a small community where members of the mediating institution have a relationship in the activities they undertake, not to the exclusion of outside goals, but not in complete deference to the interests of such outside megastructures either.

In this chapter, I am prepared to endorse the efforts of those attacking bureaucratic structures. I am not prepared to do so in the name of a subsequent sole reliance on entrepreneurial initiative, nor on a hegemonic gimmick of teamwork. Simply put, a choice between a centralized bureaucracy dominating individuals and gimmicky teams doing senior management's dirty work is no choice. I propose another kind of community—a mediating institution—in critiquing contractual theories of the firm.

Nowhere in any of these critiques is there a discussion about the sizes of the organizations in question. They simply present a dichotomy between individual protection and organizations. In this chapter, I am speaking of a community that is sufficiently attuned to human nature, and in which the goals of an organization are largely synonymous with the goals for an organization.[84] Describing a notion of businesses as mediating institutions is a dialectical task attending to *both* individual and organizational dynamics of corporate life. It is not one or the other, nor is it a false choice between domination and hegemony; it is a fresh initiative.

In arguing for these small institutions, I am not advocating turning AT&T or Ford Motors into contemporary hunter-gatherer bands selling telecommunications equipment and automobiles. Large, multinational corporations are here to stay, and our proposal to emphasize decentralization is one made in order to balance bureaucratic trends with human needs, not to reject large organizations in their entirety.

The naturalist implications of business ethics begin from the premise that, "[b]iologically, we are just another ape. Mentally, we are a new phylum of organisms."[85] It is the human symbolic ability to recreate, recombine, and analyze that distinguishes us from our closest relatives in the animal kingdom. But again, however, we are not romanticizing hunter-gatherer bands. The aim is not to glorify our banded past, but to note its reality and to integrate its benefits into a contemporary business structure. Corporations ought to be structured to allow individuals to develop their moral identity within relatively small groups, resolve their own disputes, and have representation in the megastructures that inevitably will exist in our global, capitalistic world. The result, while similar to Donaldson and Dunfee's social contract structure, will seek to describe a more precise communitarian view of human nature.

CONCLUSION

Business ethics can be strengthened by the kinds of anthropological resources I have relied upon. Megastructures carry with them coercion and conflict. Kent Flannery notes, for example, that in the late 1770s, four of the Hawaiian Islands (Hawaii, Maui, Oahu, and Kauai) had native chiefs ruling over a chiefdom.[86] The competition among them, particularly that of Oahu and Maui for the smaller islands of Lanai and Molokai, produced a period of intrigue, warfare, and usurpation that ultimately allowed Kamehameha to conquer all the islands under the power of a single state.[87] Hawaii, of course, is hardly a unique example. The amalgamation of bands into larger organizations requires coercion in direct confrontation with social harmony and virtue. With multinational corporations sometimes equal in size—and often in wealth—to some nation-states, advice to political organizations is equally applicable to business.

There is, therefore, a need to restructure workplaces into communities of relatively small groups that can foster a sense of moral virtue and identity. In these places, individuals can acquire a self-interest that is more than opportunistic behavior and that is connected to the common good. In the face of individualistic entropy, the maintenance of egalitarian norms is crucial to band selection.[88] Norms of equality, solidarity, and altruism will not be found in big bureaucratic institutions, but in small groups in which individuals in bands negotiate the relational rules that create win-win rather than win-lose contracts.

As in Donaldson and Dunfee's integrative social contracts theory, the notion of business as mediating institution recognizes the importance of community contracts and overarching norms to control the tribal excesses that small communities could indulge. The notion of a community in business as mediating institution theory, however, has additional specified requirements in order to accord with human nature: small numbers, internal group dispute resolution, and individual participation.

Beyond these community norms, cross-cultural norms must also be identified. One such norm might be a notion of reciprocity, the content of which will vary according to the level of selection. Within a mediating institution, reciprocity may mean treating others as the actor would like to be treated. Among institutions or among the individual representatives of institutions in a sequential hierarchy, reciprocity might be "generous tit-for-tat"[89] (reflecting the actions of the other party with occasional forgiveness for negative outcomes to prevent a degenerative cycle of retribution and revenge). Undoubtedly, there are other cross-cultural norms, such as participation in group decision making,[90] which suggests a greater role for employees on boards of directors. In every norm, there will persist the ongoing tension between the recurring limitations of human nature and the human symbolic technologizing ability to recombine and recreate to find new structures of organization.

Social contracting theory also must be supplemented by a much more explicit understanding of the communal nature of human beings. That understanding is best gained by learning from those who specifically study human nature. The small mediating institutions necessary to nurture our natural communal identity require specific forms of corporate structure before the social contract theory can begin to analyze the authenticity of norms provided by other "communities" and to draw upon norms from around the world. Moreover, without a sense that not everything can be negotiated, and without a sense of transcendence, social contracting provides little justification for being ethical. Thus, an important first step is to consciously recognize the interconnected identity of human beings with one another and with nature as a whole. The second step is to recognize the importance of size, a factor that will become even more important in the next chapter.

8

Business as Community

First, Goldilocks tasted Papa Bear's great big bowl of porridge. "Oh my, this is too hot!" she said, dropping the spoon from the table. Then, Goldilocks tasted Mama Bear's middle-sized bowl of porridge. "Oh, no, this is too cold!" she said, pushing the bowl away. Finally, Goldilocks tasted Baby Bear's wee little bowl of porridge. "Oh yes," she said, "this is just right!"[1]

This chapter argues that one of the more promising fields of ethical inquiry in business, virtue theory, requires an understanding of human nature derived from the natural world, so that community-based virtues are neither too weak nor too strong, but just right. By focusing their attention on the common good of large megastructures, communitarians can undermine individual autonomy. Such a "strong" version of communitarianism is, as Goldilocks would say, "too hot." Those advocating an autonomy-based moral theory of business, however, threaten to leave the individual disconnected from the relationships that fulfill life and that form moral identity. Although there is some commitment to community, this "weak" form of communitarianism is, as Goldilocks would say, "too cold."

Business ethics requires authentic communities that form respect for individual dignity. These "mediating institutions" must be small to form moral identity while empowering individuals. In these "wee little bowls," business ethicists and corporate theorists will find a mix that is, as Goldilocks found, "just right."

155

The first section of this chapter describes representative communitarian conceptions outside of business ethics. The second shows how community-based notions are manifested in business ethics, usually in the form of virtue theory. In the third section, I address problems with a community-based approach even when one "downsizes" communitarianism into those "wee little bowls" known as mediating institutions. The last section takes this analysis back to a larger argument about public morality in the form of civic republicanism, which will set the stage for part III of this book.

THE COMMUNITARIAN IMPULSE

Communitarianism has been an increasingly influential approach to the moral problems of contemporary society. The perception that we live in an American culture that overemphasizes individualism—a result, one could argue, of a political emphasis on autonomy-based ethics—has led to calls for a communitarian politics from both liberal and conservative sources.

In the late 1980s, a "republican revival"[2] and communitarian sociology fostered liberal (in the contemporary political sense) claims that national politics ought to be about more than self-interested, autonomous freedom, but instead ought to be about the common good. Conservative scholars made similar arguments, but couched them in terms of the kind of republic and community to which Americans had originally "contracted" through the Constitution.[3]

Perhaps the most prolific spokesperson for communitarianism has been Amitai Etzioni, who argues that the United States must be constituted as a "community of communities" with "megalogues" about the nature of the common good, particularly as that good relates to the restraint of corporate power and business practices.[4] These positions can be referred to as "strong" notions of communitarianism, because they look to the community on the large scale of the nation-state as the defining ground for the common good and the virtues relevant for achieving that good.

Introduction to Etzioni: Communitarian Choirs

A popular characterization of a message geared to those who already agree with the speaker is "preaching to the choir." As the phrase suggests, it is often applied to those who are religious, but it need not be so limited. In his book *The New Golden Rule*, Amitai Etzioni gives us a glimpse of the choral analogy when he writes that, based on his experience, bowling associations, chess clubs, and choirs may provide some degree of social bonding, but not much of a moral culture.[5] He parenthetically admits that his experience with choirs is much more limited than his experience with bowling and chess. As one who has sung in close to fifteen hundred concerts or performances, I would like to suggest that choirs are actually a good metaphor for Etzioni's task.

Members of choirs are, to be sure, often devoted and devout and therefore may already agree with what the preacher says. Even those who are compensated to sing in choirs are usually deeply devoted to the art and to the transcendent purpose for which they sing. Beyond that, however, choirs are comprised of very different individuals.

Particular choirs, however, are very different, depending upon their membership. Many choirs are comprised of pious, serious singers. Others are filled with irreverent and playful jokesters who rarely leave a cleric or ritual unskewered. Many singers are the epitome of harmony. Others are not. Dramatic sopranos rarely like to flatten their vibrato to blend with others singing a plainsong chant. Many think no bass has ever sung a low note softly by choice. In short, behind the veneer of devoted participants to a common cause is a wide variety of individualists, hopeful soloists, and team players, the combination of which makes each group different. Once accomodating these idiosyncracies, however, the beauty comes in a unified sound of different voices and timbres that is far more than the arithemetical addition of voices.

Because individual choirs are different, they are also responsive to a variety of successful leadership styles. They can be "inspired" by a conductor's intimidation, joy, weirdness, legend, or sweetness. The elements uniting conductors whom I have seen practicing each one of these styles are commitment to a transcendent purpose for which the music is placed in service, to the art itself, and to the members' "voice"—not only in the sense of the musical voice, but also in the governance sense of having some participation in the substantive development of the musical "product." ("I don't think our section has measure forty right; can we sing it again?" is a question heard in every successful choir.) Even conductors, at least the successful ones, who lead by intimidation are wise enough to encourage individuality and participant-directedness.

If one wants a choir to fail, the strategy is not difficult to devise. Still the "voice" of the members, ignore their interests. deemphasize the contribution they make to the greater community, and question their motives. Take away their ability to participate in the direction of the group. Do these things, and voluntariness is replaced by weary duty, participation loses its relationship to a transcendent purpose, and the resulting loss of joy will solidify hierarchies as the attention of those remaining in the choir turns to status. Finally, people will stop singing.

If this is not enough to discourage new recruits, then a sure way to do so is to make sure prospective members think there is nothing distinctive about the choir (particularly if these prospects have other places to sing). Size is also a factor. Big choirs tend to sound like big choirs (which can actually be quite exciting). Small choirs tend to sound like the individual timbres of particular voices; they are nearly always distinctive.

In short, choirs are pretty much like most other organizations. We want the organization to meet our interests and satisfy our need to belong to something bigger than our individual selves. Our enthusiasm for giving up our individualistic pursuits is fueled by the commitment to this larger result that is grander than the sum of the individual voices (i.e., transcendent) and because individual singers see the connection between their self-interest and the good of this larger community. And the common good of the choir is particularly close to individual preferences when the size of the group is small enough to foster empowerment. So how does this relate to politics?

Etzioni articulates a vision of communitarianism in which one should "respect and uphold society's moral order as you would have society respect and uphold your autonomy."[6] Interestingly, he chooses not to preach to those who are already committed to sing in a communitarian choir. How does he approach the difficult task of forming an ensemble? He finds a common enemy.

In making religious conservatives the common enemy against which he wants to rally others around his communitarianism, he essentially asks religious communitarians of any stripe to keep quiet. His tactics lead to some strange consequences. For instance, he frequently refers to Richard John Neuhaus, a Catholic priest usually grouped with neoconservative thinkers. Etzioni characterizes neoconservatives, however, as interested in autonomy rather than communitarianism. Nonetheless, he identifies Neuhaus as an endorser of an Etzioni-endorsed communitarianism,[7] but also as representative of a backward-looking Catholic hierarchy where autonomy is granted as long as one thinks like the Church.[8]

In diminishing the religious voice, he thus gets trapped in such paradoxical caricatures of those who, like him, try also to bridge the autonomy-communitarian gap. Rather than getting other communitarians to join in his choir, he seems more interested in arguing for a communitarianism that stills the voice of those who might have a part to sing in his choir. There seems to be no part for them to sing in his choir; they are limited to singing a different song. He may well be right that social conservatives pose difficulties for his choir, but their departure or injury may drain helpful communitarians away from the song he wants to sing.

Substance of Etzioni's Communitarianism

Mike Keeley argues that differences among individuals is the lurking problem for communitarians.[9] Because individuals have different notions of the good, it seems that one cannot articulate a singular common good. One must instead emphasize individual goods. Etzioni, however, hopes to enlist support for communitarianism as a national public ethic by demonstrating that we would freely consent to a social contract based on a balance of community and autonomy.[10]

Etzioni recognizes that communities can be oppressive and hierarchical.[11] Because "the quest for community often involves domination for some and subordination for others,"[12] Etzioni concedes that there is reason to fear that communitarians "want us to live in Salem."[13] He attributes such fears, however, to an image of premodern communities in which there were rigid boundaries separating old villages, which were "total communities."[14] Today, however, the availability of attachments to multiple communities prevents any one community from overwhelming an individual.[15] Moreover, one avoids many of the authoritarian features of community if one rejects religious conservatism.[16]

To avoid these rigid kinds of community while simultaneously contending for some kind of communitarianism, Etzioni argues for a community that balances autonomy and community through the practice of a "New Golden Rule." A community such as this, for Etzioni, is one that is entitled to respect from individuals because such a moral order respects individual autonomy. Thus, by practicing the New Golden Rule, in which you should "respect and uphold society's moral order as you would have society respect and uphold your autonomy,"[17] you create a reciprocity whereby community and autonomy are both enhanced.

For the United States, which meets his definition of a community,[18] this requires a commitment to constitutional democracy (as a substantive rather than procedural value), "layered loyalties" to the many communities that comprise our polity, a sense of voluntariness to membership in the community, tolerance for the beliefs of others, a reduction of the use of "identity politics," megalogues and smaller communal dialogues, and reconciliation with those estranged from us.[19]

One cannot dismiss Etzioni's argument quickly. Unlike the civic republicans, Etzioni is concerned with constructing a community whose common good is developed by all individuals in the society, not just the elites. He also takes seriously the hierarchical problems that plague community-based normative structures. Thus, he insists upon a community that values individual autonomy. Perhaps his best insight, though, is that, in a diverse society where individuals have many attachments, the risk of oppressive community structures is much less than was the case in the past. The multiplicity of communities has become a protection against communitarian excesses.

Missing Elements

Etzioni's communitarianism lacks a number of elements. Two of these missing elements are worth emphasizing. The first is the importance of small groups in forming moral virtues, a theme replete throughout this book and which needs no further elaboration. Etzioni does not reject these mediating structures. Indeed, he notes that the moral infrastructure of society depends upon the four formulations of families, schools, communities, and the "community-of-communities."[20] However, by focusing his theory on the "community-of-communities," Etzioni fails to give a rationale for how individuals can cognitively inculcate the "moral voice" necessary for virtuous democracy.[21] It is not likely that we will learn to sing well in a large symphony chorus if we have not first been trained to sing well in smaller choirs.

Second, Etzioni minimizes the importance of transcendence. Etzioni uses the Golden Rule as a criterion for his balanced, virtuous democracy. His Golden Rule, he argues, is an improvement over the "old" Golden Rule, because the latter is concerned with "merely interpersonal" relationships.[22] His reading of the old Golden Rule obscures its historically social nature and by doing so, also obscures its transcendent element.

For instance, the Confucian formulation of the Golden Rule is set within a context of defined social relationships, such as those between father and son and husband and wife. These social relationships are not simply interpersonal, however, but are sanctioned by an entire cosmology of earthly existence. Similarly, when Plato places Socrates, in the *Crito*, in the dilemma of whether to obey an unjust law, he uses Golden Rule thinking to uphold society's rules, not to simply resolve an interpersonal conflict. Finally, when Rabbi Hillel offered his summary of the Hebraic law as practicing the Golden Rule, he went beyond interpersonal relationships to identify an entire legal and social order that was dependent upon and which also stood behind this ethical norm.[23]

Behind these formulations of the Golden Rule are connections with transcendent ideals. Hebraic law was not simply created out of a negotiated, interpersonal agreement, but within a social context embedded with limitations on what society could enact. Indeed, Golden Rule thinking was connected to the rationale of concern for the less fortunate as exemplified by the condemnation of King David for having taken Bathsheeba by sending her husband to die in battle.[24] The "Old Golden Rule," thus, was much more than interpersonal.

In Etzioni's understandable desire to avoid divisiveness and to promote an approach with national consequences, however, he brushes over exactly the supports necessary for the citizenship he desires. Mediating institutions, which form individuals to see a transcendent reality in their communal identity, must be a part of a contemporary republicanism/communitarianism. Such structures must reach to all citizens, not just the elite, so these citizens can develop their own communal voice and identity. Because our society is so much more diverse than it was in the past when a community was a "total community," and because modern technology prevents any one total community, we can advocate for a community-based approach with less fear of its past problems. This is so provided our communities are more geared toward those that empower all voices in large megastructures where otherwise only shouting is heard, not music.

BUSINESS AS COMMUNITY

Community and Virtue

Not surprisingly, community thinking was quickly transported into business ethics. It is important, however, to keep in mind that "business as community" (BAC) operates, or should operate, on a scale different from communitarianism. The difficulty with BAC is that its proponents have not specified the size of the corporate community where virtues flourish. BAC proponents thereby leave themselves open to the critiques made of strong notions of communitarianism.

Though careful to disassociate himself from "nostalgic" versions of communitarianism, Robert Solomon explicitly states that the corporation is a kind of a community, and like any community, the virtues and character relevant in other aspects of life are applicable within business.[25] Solomon argues that businesses are human institutions, so that virtues practiced in any other social endeavor ought also to be valued in business.[26] To be sure, certain virtues are more applicable in business than in other endeavors (virtues applicable to chess are not necessarily applicable to marketing), but the point is that business requires cooperation, and cooperation requires virtues defined by a community.[27] When individuals internalize such virtues through regular practice, they develop character.[28] Like similar practices in total quality management systems, virtues continually integrate morality and business decisions and thereby head of an intractable dilemma.[29]

The virtue-ethics school focuses on the development of character through which persons achieve moral excellence. It rejects the existence of an autonomous negotiator of any contract, hypothetical or otherwise. Thus, although contracts analogies can be helpful, Janet Mc-Cracken and Bill Shaw write that their "usefulness . . . comes from, and must be understood in terms of what it is about us that *makes us want to live together* in states or communities."[30]

Without an affective commitment to being ethical, no specification of rights, justice, or utilitarianism is likely to produce any kind of truly ethical person. Like Solomon, Ed Hartman relies upon Aristotelian theory, although he speaks of corporations as "commons" rather than "community."[31] Solomon sympathizes with Hartman's avoidance of the term "community" and writes: "[C]ommunity has become a buzz-word, an excuse for the persecution and/or exclusion of minorities, a plea for protection, a demand for immunity and isolation, a warm and cozy metaphor for some mythical extended family left over from the commune days of the late sixties."[32] Solomon goes on to note that Michael Sandel critiques John Rawls in the name of community without ever suggesting what "community" might mean and that Alasdair MacIntyre endorses community, but rejects communitarianism.[33]

These philosophical articulations of BAC stress how communities form the moral character of individuals. More will be said about this later, but it is important to show that BAC has strong proponents in the legal community as well. In particular, legal scholars have reemphasized the social nature of human identity, the importance of individual roles within the corporate enterprise, and the need to avoid relativism.

Writing with Janet McCracken, Bill Shaw argues that Aristotelian theory grounds a conception of a *good business person* in both "the technical and the moral sense."[34] With Fran Zollers, Shaw argues that Etzioni has relevance for the description of corporations as communities and as citizens of the larger public community, particularly in attacking economic descriptions of individuals as rational actors.[35] Jeffrey Nesteruk has emphasized how law creates roles that individuals play within corporate communities, and in how law defines excellence.[36] In noting that communitarians emphasize the external interface between corporations and society, Nesteruk writes:

> My account of the law's influence over the moral lives of those in the business environment suggests the need for a broadened perspective in the development of communitarian corporate theory. Communitarians should consider anew the internal relationships of the corporation. By attending to effects of corporate law upon the nature of roles, the kinds of choices, and the character of community within the corporation, communitarians can significantly bolster their case for a multifiduciary model of managerial responsibility. This is because the superiority of the multifiduciary model lies in how it affects the moral development of individuals occupying managerial positions within the corporate hierarchy.[37]

While Caryn Beck-Dudley warmly reviews Solomon's work, the relativism of goods defined by particular communities troubles her, so "[c]learly, much more work is needed to identify the universality of the human community and of human nature. This is where research in moral development and cognitive science can be useful."[38]

In this book I have also defined forms of BAC "business as mediating institution" (BMI) in which the corporate purpose is to benefit internal constituents of shareholders and employees, so as to mediate between the larger superstructures of society and the individual. In varying degrees, all these theories posit the authority of communities to define relevant business ethics. Nesteruk is on to an important point in relating the scope of corporate community to the internal workings of the organization. Beck-Dudley, as well as Donaldson and Dunfee, appropriately recognizes the importance of empirical research in identifying universal norms. Only BMI addresses the importance of a community's size.

Why this enthusiasm for corporations as communities? Why have philosophical and legal scholars found this approach superior to economic positivism and Kantianism? One can answer these questions by listing three key reasons.

Three Reasons for Business as Community

Corporations Were Historically Public Institutions

First, there is a strong sense that corporations ought to benefit the public generally as opposed to being solely profit-driven. This argument has its roots deep in American legal history.[39] As indicated previously, early legislative bodies chartered corporations only if the proposed activity benefited the public, such as in building bridges or incorporating municipalities.[40] With the democratization of many parts of American law in the Jacksonian revolution, along with the increasing demand for charters that outstripped legislative capacities to deliberate about each individual incorporation request, and within an increasingly (Adam) Smithian understanding of capitalism, granting incorporation charters became a ministerial rather than a legislative act.[41]

In this century, corporate purposes have become defined more by managerial than by shareholder design.[42] The split between management and shareholder control has led some to argue that shareholders require more protection from managers than they currently have.[43] It is even more difficult for nonshareholder constituents, so-called stakeholders, to have much impact on managerial decision making.[44] The important point, however, is that the call for corporations to be like communities is one that is rooted in a recognition that many individuals do not have a voice in corporate actions that affect them, that corporations once did have a more explicit public role, and that it is possible to recreate them to fulfill this role in the sense that they recognize communitarian responsibilities.

Weak and Strong Forms of Communitarianism

The second reason for the communitarian approach to business ethics reaches much deeper. It challenges the idea of the economic rational actor—*homo economicus*—who is able to rationally choose according to his or her self-interest.[45] The ethical challenge to the economic model is that it does not adequately take into account one's responsibilities toward those who lay outside of one's self-interest. The rational-actor mode, Shaw argues, reduces moral norms to individual preferences, which leads to utilitarian moral decision making.[46] To the extent moral norms are implemented, they can be accounted for as efficient economic (or legal) positivism, but such positivism does not account for noneconomic factors necessary for "the good life."[47]

Kantian and contractarian business ethics react to this economic theory as well. Under these ethical positions, the autonomous decision maker is moral when exercising authority that treats individuals as ends rather than means. Stakeholder theory, rights theory, and social contract theory all accord a strong right for individuals to define what is important to them. But there is a significant communitarian component in both positivism and autonomy theory. Exercising authority implies that there is some reason that we ought to care about those who live around us. And that concern implies that we live in some sort of community; otherwise we should not care about those who live around us. Although few Kantians are likely to accept the designation, their principle can be characterized as a weak form of communitarianism insofar as they are concerned with how communities operate and the respect for individuals that must be a defining element of a good community. Positivists also have communitarian elements as they acknowledge a greater good for a community that is beyond individual preferences of will. It strains definitional credulity to actually rename these positions as communitarian, and like Mama Bear's porridge, they supply a very cold notion of moral character.

Autonomy ethics challenges economic rationality's moral adequacy. Virtue ethics likewise challenges economic rationality, but on the basis of human nature. Although not writing out of a virtue ethics framework, Ed Conry claims that no business ethics contractarians "are explicit in focusing on our empirical understanding of the moral dimension of human nature. Indeed, they all move further and further away from any specific assessment."[48]

Human Nature

The epistemological void that communitarianism fills is that which demonstrates how the moral self is formed. Philosophers such as MacIntyre[49] and Taylor,[50] along with theologians such as Stanley Hauerwas,[51] uncompromisingly argue that it is the community that forms the self, so that the self can learn to "see" what is morally at stake in a given dilemma. The autonomous individual, according to these theorists, is simply nonexistent. This communitarian attack thus takes on not only the rational economic person, but the morally autonomous person. Indeed, one can argue that the morally autonomous person's moral choices, and the economic person's economic choices, are so based on individual preference as to provide no grounds for demonstrating any reason as to why one person's choices are morally superior to another's. This anthropology tends to play directly into the arguments of the law-and-economics literature that gives up trying to determine which "choices" are morally superior and instead tries to maximize individual preferences by efficient distribution of goods.[52]

In short, communitarians argue that corporations ought to be considered communities and that both economic rationality and individual autonomy misleadingly posit a decision maker abstracted from the community that formed her moral self.

Business as Mediating Institution

While the same principles drive both communitarianism and BAC, the relative scope each gives to the relevant community makes a qualitative difference. On the other hand, in mediating institutions theory, the community is relatively small.[53] Individuals are empowered by understanding their relational identity and by living in a structure small enough to have an impact on the community through one's own actions.[54]

First, mediating institutions typically are defined to be structures such as family, voluntary organizations, neighborhoods, and religious institutions[55] (as well as small choirs). A central criterion is that they are structures where each member has face-to-face interaction with others in the structure so that one is able to see the consequences of one's action.[56]

Second, these institutions are communal. They form the moral identity of individuals.[57] One's family, for instance, forms one's moral identity and, precisely because one never has the ability to leave the community behind, one must learn to adapt one's behavior to the expectations, praise, and coercion of the community. It is true that one may disassociate oneself with the ongoing interactions of, say, family members, but it is very difficult, if not impossible, to rid oneself of the formative experiences of families or other mediating institutions.

Third, individuals are empowered in such organizations. This may seem illogical based on the previous paragraph, but it remains true in two ways. One way is that one has developed a moral character, so that one habitually knows what one's actions ought to be.[58] One does not need to agonize over the number of choices a person could make, but one has a moral character that indicates a narrower range of choices. Of course, such an "internal script" can confine too much if there is not also freedom. A person of character, however, knows how to exercise that freedom.

A second way the mediating institution is individually empowering is that because the institution is small, an individual can have an impact on it.[59] One is not lost in a huge organizational bureaucracy, when there are relatively few other individuals in the group. Accordingly, one can be empowered by having a greater responsibility in the organization itself.[60]

The notion of BMI, like BAC, is that work is a human activity. Given the fact that we spend a significant percentage of our waking hours working, it is only logical that our moral identities are formed not only in families and churches, but at work as well. Thus, businesses are communities that form identity; the question is whether they are mediating institutions that empower individuals. By being a mediating institution, a business has a culture that respects both community and autonomy, by orienting the business community to the empowerment of the individual.

There are four central benefits to BMI in relation to this discussion. The first is moral: it bridges the weak and strong forms of communitarianism, or, if one prefers, it bridges communitarian-based and autonomy-based institutions. It thus synthesizes these two moral approaches in a way that respects both and draws upon the benefits of each. It does not simply do so by compromise, but by integrating a deeper understanding of nature than has been philosophically or legally articulated to date in business ethics.

The second benefit is economic: self-organizing work groups—which are essentially a kind of mediating institution—have been increasingly relied upon in business through managerial techniques such as total quality management. Thus, BMI is not only morally beneficial, but economically realistic. The third benefit is legal: the mediating institution approach can draw upon political history to understand how small subunits of an organization and the larger organization can be integrated and balanced.

There is a fourth benefit as well. Given the acidic nature of the debate between community-based theorists and autonomy-based theorists, it may well be that a fresh name is required to describe the community-based model. The difficulty is that communitarianism and autonomy theory each draw such reaction from those on the opposing side that it may be difficult for either side to accept anything with the other's name on it.

The other major difference, however, between Etzioni's insistence on the "community of communities" and BMI is that individuals need to have small structures by which to obtain identity. Again, BAC theorists do not necessarily ignore this, but, to the extent that they underspecify the necessity for small communities to provide moral identity, they are vulnerable to associations with Etzioni-like, strong communitarianism. The driving forces of communitarianism and mediating institutions may be the same, but the sizing of each of them is quite different because mediating institutions theory is more alert to the need to empower individuals to have control over the actions that affect them. Like the porridge in Baby Bear's wee little bowl, mediating institutions are "just right."

PERSISTENT PROBLEMS

One can question whether the approach that describes the downsized form of community is naive, nostalgic, and blind toward the abuses perpetrated by communities. Two important critiques are worth exploring in more depth. Stated differently, if autonomy-like communitarianism is too weak, and if Etzioni-like communitarianism is too strong, can one still claim that BMI is "just right"? One can offer two strong critiques of both business as community and business as mediating institution

A Lousy History

The first argument against the community approach is that communities, regardless of what they are called, have a troublesome history of hierarchy and oppression. The communitarian movement is one that dangerously and nostalgically looks back to a supposed purer time. Michael Keeley articulates this position as well as anyone.[61] The difficulty, according to Keeley, is that attempts to read what the community's virtues were according to the perspective of those who were in power say little about how those in power treated those without power. Just as reading a corporate annual report skews what really goes on in the corporation, so reading the reports of those in power in any community tends to obscure the hierarchies and unfairness within the organization.[62]

An associated problem is that communities do not tend to treat their neighbors well, particularly when those neighbors are deemed to be "different." This, according to Keeley, is the story of slavery.[63] In short, the problem with communities is that their leaders do not respect rights of those inside and outside of their borders, or at least treat those who are not in power as means rather than as ends. This is why Keeley says that the problem with communitarianism is that it doesn't satisfactorily account for people's differences.[64]

Keeley is writing about communitarianism generally, but his critique also applies to mediating institutions. He is correct, of course, that powerful persons in communities often treat those without power quite shabbily. He is also correct that communities are prone to "de-humanize" those outside of the community's borders. This criticism, however, does not challenge the notion that as human beings we always do exist in communities and that we learn our moral obligations through the habits we form in communities. Bad or good, we must deal with our communitarian nature

It is true that communities can be oppressive, but people do not typically leave communities to live in a hermit's cell. When they do leave, they join communities more to their liking. This is what happens when people move from job to job; in exiting communities, people end up in communities. Defenders of autonomy thus fairly ask what kind of community is good, but the point is that, for better or worse, community is inevitable. Moreover, as will be developed in the next section, if we look backward—really backward—we are likely to find that our biological structure requires that we live in relatively small communities and it is in those communities where we can develop our identity and learn our moral obligations.

Keeley, a strong defender of individual autonomy, is critiquing a strong version of communitarianism from what might be called a position of a weak communitarianism. Keeley indicates that "individualists" do join communities, but he insists that the good community is one that respects individual dignity; in short, he espouses a liberal community.[65] Regardless of whether one joins Keeley in his critique or continues to espouse the benefits of a strong communitarianism, one must admit that Keeley is right that communities can be lousy places for those not in power and that it can be difficult for an outsider to see how lousy it can be, since those in power are the ones with the ability to convey information about the community to the outside world. In short, while it would be unfair to actually transform autonomy-based ethics into some kind of communitarianism, there is more commonalty than what might be expected. One can hold on to both, as I have done in this chapter and book, if one preserves the accuracy of Keeley's critique concerning the dangers of communities, whether they are large megastructures or small mediating institutions.

Short-Sightedness

The second charge against BAC is that it misses the forest for the trees. That is, while there may be benefits for human beings in the theory of business as a community, the more important issues for business today relate to larger extracommunity affairs. Don Mayer summarizes this position well:

> Both ISCT [Donaldson and Dunfee's integrative social contracts theory, which blends notions of autonomy and community] and mediating institutions have provided useful ideas for business ethics and the law, but both have left the most pressing agenda items wide open. This is more an observation than a criticism. . . . In the case of ISCT, there is an as-yet undefined role for global "hypernorms" that would overrule a particular community's errant moral consensus, but as Donaldson and Dunfee candidly acknowledge, the search for hypernorms is a difficult one and is left largely for the future. In Fort's mediating institutions, the work of finding internal and external structures to encourage corporate transformation is left for the future. Given the unique historical relations among business, governments, people, and the natural environment, the major agenda items of "hypernorms" cannot begin soon enough, nor can finding the means to reshape corporations into mediating institutions that serve individual human needs and real human communities wait much longer.[66]

Mayer focuses much more specifically on mediating institutions than does Keeley, although his critique subsumes communitarianism as well. His argument also has a great deal of truth to it. Focusing on how to treat those within the corporate walls says little about important issues such as environmental degradation. Mayer's argument can be seen as a critique from a strong communitarianism, one that considers the ecology of the planet as the relevant community. But two points must balance this critique.

First, saying that there are environmental issues does not eliminate the importance of issues within the corporate walls. Those issues remain important. Issues of discrimination, harassment, conflicts of interest, wages, work rules, honesty, and firing are important issues that ought not be diminished.

Second, legal restrictions are entirely appropriate to prevent corporate misconduct. But "seeing" our lives as communal teaches a person that there are duties other than narrow self-interest, and it is exactly that recognition that can be enhanced so as to "see" environmental duties. BAC is not the entire answer for business ethics, but it is a necessary part of any answer of business ethics because otherwise one simply either conforms to the power of positivist coercion or can individually choose to be ethical or unethical. The problem with the former is that complying with coercion is not particularly inspiring. The problem with the latter is that autonomy theory offers no compelling reason for describing why a person ought to be ethical.

CIVIC REPUBLICANISM

The Claims of Civic Republicanism

The 1980s revival of republicanism as a political theory had both conservative and liberal components that appealed similarly to communitarian sentiments. The movement revitalized the philosophies of judicial restraint and originalism.[67] The originalist perspective was linked to civic republicanism by Gordon Wood, who argued that the United States was founded as a republic, not as a liberal democracy.[68] On the other hand, the movement was also committed to the notion of quests for the common good rather than reliance upon individual autonomy. The task of this civic republicanism was to find a way to teach moral empathy and political citizenship.

The Substance of the Theory

The republican revival in America has centered on developing a notion of citizenship based in the public good. The most prominent theme of the revival revolves around subordinating self-interest to a notion of civic virtue. Interest group liberalism, the republicans argue, does not allow for a conversation about the public good.[69] Instead, individuals (particularly members of the judiciary and intellectual elites)[70] must replace the pursuit of self-interest with concern for the common good.

Thus, there must be a rethinking of our politics in order to create the room and incentives for consideration of the common good. This is the second theme of the republican revival. The common good, the republicans argue, can be defined by a deliberative political structure in which discussion of the good itself becomes the defining feature of politics. The heart of the revival, then, is that there must be open dialogue between citizens (particularly intellectual elites) in defining the common good. It is a procedural commitment to rational discussion via "dialogical structures."

Frank Michelman relies upon the notion of "jurisgenesis" (by which he means the disclosure of actual consensus through dialogue) to create this quest for the meaning of the common good.[71] Michelman views politics as the point where private-regarding individuals "dialogue" by means of their own shared narratives, so they know how to live.[72] That process, he believes, will transform vice to virtue via a common set of beliefs that can be uncovered through dialogue. The result is the creation of self-government and a government of laws rather than individual leaders.[73]

Michelman essentially argues that by requiring the individuals to dialogue with other individuals they will find that their interests are not as different as they originally thought. They will discover shared visions of the common good. Michelman does not identify the content of that good, but rather emphasizes the necessity of the dialogue by which individuals discover and define their mutual good. "Jurisgenesis," as its translation suggests, "creates law" through dialogue so that the law is formed for the common good.

Whereas Michelman advocates a notion of jurisgenesis, Cass Sunstein offers the notion of liberal republicanism.[74] Sunstein uses the term because he wishes to disassociate republicanism from classical and militaristic manifestations.[75] These forms of republicanism, he argues, led to oppression. Sunstein wants to preserve the protection of individual rights that liberal democratic politics defends, while creating some way to define a common good with direct exercise of that freedom.[76]

For Sunstein, there are four republican commitments. First, there is a commitment to deliberative government.[77] By this, Sunstein means that politics should not be about the imposition of beliefs by groups.[78] Instead, political actors are "to achieve a measure of critical distance from prevailing desires and practices, subjecting their desires and practices to scrutiny and review."[79] The goal, then, is for citizens to deliberate in order to build a consensus as to what constitutes the common good.[80]

Second, there must be a commitment to political equality. This requires that all people should have an equal opportunity to participate in the political process.[81] When power and wealth become unbalanced, equality is gravely endangered.[82]

Third, there must be a regulative notion of universality or agreement. By this, Sunstein means that the deliberative process will seek to identify a common good. Under interest group pluralism, he argues, no substantive notion of the common good can be articulated; it is either mystical or tyrannical.[83] Both are oppressive. He does believe, however, that a common good can be achieved through republicanism, although he comments that religious belief should play no part in that deliberation.[84]

Fourth, there must be a fully developed understanding of citizenship. Through political participation, Sunstein argues, citizens learn empathy, virtue, and feelings of community.[85] These characteristics, of course, lead to concern for more than narrow self-interest and reinforce the quest for defining the common good.[86]

Sunstein argues that only by making liberalism into a caricature of its tradition can it be opposed to republicanism. He correctly argues that possessive individualism and modern neo-Lockeanism were not central at the founding of the country. The founding liberals placed great emphasis on deliberation and on the capacity of political dialogue to improve the outcomes and to undermine unjustified disparities of power.[87] While collectivist republicanism and atomistic individualism are at odds, more moderate forms of liberalism deny self-interest as a sufficient basis for political outcomes because rights are not prepolitical. They are the product of a "well-functioning deliberative process."[88] Thus, liberalism and republicanism can be mutually supportive.

Is there a more concrete notion of the common good than that of process? Is political dialogue among elites sufficient to transform narrow self-interest? Is there a role for moral education so that persons view dialogue as constructive rather than competitive? If so, what does that moral education look like? What is its source? And what kinds of institutions are necessary for its dissemination? These questions raise the point of what elements are missing in the republican revival.

Missing Elements in Civic Republicanism

While Sunstein and Michelman advance a process by which persons may be able to grow beyond narrow self-interest, one can categorize the shortcomings of their theory in four parts. First, they neglect to adequately describe human nature, which leads to an impoverished substantive content of the common good. Second, they dramatically shortchange religion and its potential to foster the kind of concern for the common good they wish to see. Third, they fail to account for the possibility of oppression, a problem directly related to their resistance to the notion of transcendence. Fourth, they underestimate the potential for mediating institutions to play a role in this process.

Human Nature and Substantive Content. Jonathan Macey has noted that the republican theorists are fundamentally optimistic about human nature.[89] Rather than assuming that human beings are essentially self-interested, the republican theorists assume that human beings can conduct deliberative debate beyond their narrow self-interest.[90] That assumption, according to Macey, which is neither justified nor developed by Michelman and Sunstein, makes a very big difference in one's view of the potential efficacy of republicanism.[91]

Macey's skepticism about republican optimism, however, begs the question of whether self-interested persons can ever form a common good. Can the "first man" really find a common good with other "first men"? Both Sunstein and Macey place self-interest as a fact positioned in opposition to the common good. Such an opposition makes any transformation away from self-interest deeply problematic. Richard Epstein recognizes this problem. He has argued that a republican collectivist vision requires substantive criteria of the good.[92] For Epstein, procedural dialoguing structures are not sufficient for such a transformation.

Epstein's position, however, is itself overstated. A commitment to dialogue presupposes an end of humanity—peacefulness, rationality, goodwill, and solidarity—that can be a teleological goal itself.[93] Thus procedure can be substantive because it recognizes the inherent status of other persons and provides criteria for the dialogue itself.[94] If, as Durkheim would argue, "individuals" are not autonomous, discrete beings, but manifestations of a single, unitary, and transcendent force, then dialogue is not procedural, but a constitutive aspect of self-identity. The problem with civic republicanism is that neither Sunstein nor Michelman really contends for a substantive good that justifies their procedural recommendations. This failure does leave their common good vulnerable to Epstein's critique.

There is, however, a substantive, albeit undeveloped, good underlying their commitment that ought to be identified and ought to challenge the assumptions of Macey and Epstein. The commitments to communication, dialogue, and mutual respect reflect a human nature very different from that of pure self-interest. It is not procedure alone that transforms self-interest, but procedure together with nourished moral empathy and sympathy resting upon the notion that there is a transcendent, interconnected reality that makes moral duties concomitant with self-identity.

To be sure, a procedural notion of justice could be simply a good designed for individualistic pursuit of self-interest. In fact, this is exactly what procedural justice becomes without transcendence and mediating institutions. If Epstein is insisting that a republican common good requires a Quebec-like substance,[95] republicanism is surely lifeless in the United States. That is, a common good may be defined in terms of particular uses of language, culture, and religion as it is in Quebec, but those characteristics are not likely to be found in the United States.

While Epstein may be wrong to insist upon the necessity of a structured, substantive common good, he is right that a stronger articulation of the republicans' procedural *qua* substantive common good is necessary. Unless one directly grapples with the substantive issues of human nature and self-interest, there is no rationale to explain how procedural dialogue will guide self-interest toward the common good. Unless one knows the nature of what is being transformed, how can one know if it has been transformed or whether, in the attempt at transformation, violence (rather than deliberation) will occur? If human beings are deeply self-interested and isolated, and if dialogue does not resolve disputes, the necessary social structures required for civilized life may be implemented through bloodshed and/or coercion. It is only by empathy, sympathy, solidarity, and respect for dignity that one can rely upon dialogue as a means to the common good. Unfortunately, Sunstein and Michelman do not ground their procedure at this level, perhaps to avoid the religious and/or metaphysical arguments it necessarily triggers.

The Role of Religion in Republicanism. Religion is the "loser" in Michelman and Sunstein's republicanism.[96] That loss undermines their theory. Without a perspective that explains and teaches the evident, basic, anthropological elements of human life, the procedural approach is insufficient. The kind of prophetic critique—a "depth-hermeneutic"[97]—provided by religion prevents any common good (substantive or procedural) from becoming blind to the abusive practices that a common perspective fosters.[98] That is, consensus and dialogue are not guarantors of communal politics. Engaging substantive issues of human nature, however, will lead to the kind of theological and metaphysical philosophy that Michelman and Sunstein marginalize.[99] In short, Sunstein and Michelman marginalize exactly the questions that their common good requires.

Why is such dialogue problematic for Michelman and Sunstein? In general, they wish to avoid the polemic dialogue that religious debate can foster.[100] Religion, as a powerful social force, can foster intolerance, hatred, and oppression as much as it can foster goodwill and generosity.[101] Such attributes are very good reasons to fear any introduction of religious belief into political dialogue. While Sunstein and Michelman essentially propose a common good that floats away from any particular comprehensive moral view,[102] they ultimately cannot avoid the need for comprehensive moral views, including religious ones. Although the republican theorists avoid making the substantive argument for it, goods such as tolerance and solidarity are normative ends because the republicans believe human beings are "good" enough to discuss differences peaceably and because they value the respect inherent in such a dialogical structure.

I fully agree that these are good ends, but Epstein rightly raises the question about the need for clarity in articulating the substance of the common good. That substance acts as the core of a prophetic critique of actions that drift from the common good. It acts act as a depth-hermeneutic to which procedural dialogue can be subject. More specifically, goods such as tolerance and solidarity are a transcendent reality to which citizens are accountable. In short, Sunstein and Michelman are exactly right in what they propose, but by failing to acknowledge the substantive good they pursue, they also eliminate the structures that can sustain that good.

There are also two practical reasons why the absence of religion is a problem for republican theory. The first relates to citizen education. Democratic moral self-governance requires significant confidence in

the ability of citizens throughout the society to deliberate in an informed, disciplined way.[103] Thus, if republicanism is to be a full-blown
citizen-based theory, it must identify the ways in which citizens themselves understand that their "self" includes concern for others. This educational process must link itself with institutions that teach those lessons. Because the task involves moral predispositions, however, those
institutions involved in moral formation—such as religious institutions—are vital to the republican task.

Second, if the republican process is to allow individuals to share their
narratives, and if the participation in the dialogue is to have any kind of
popular involvement, then one must be prepared for the fact that narratives often will have some element of religious belief.[104] In other words,
religious belief is meaningful to many citizens, and to engage their participation, one might want them to be free to rely on what is meaningful
to them.

The Risks of Oppression When There Is No Transcendence. Derrick Bell and
Preeta Bansal add another, related problem: to avoid oppression, one
must have some transcendent rules.[105] They worry that unless principles
are guaranteed, there is no reason to be confident that dialogue will
transform prejudice.[106] The purely democratic deliberation Michelman
and Sunstein propose, according to Bell and Bansal, may not be sufficient to protect minorities from oppression.[107] Their procedural account of equality, disconnected from its underlying teleology, does not
avoid practices such as slavery, because no moral sense—no prophetic
critique or depth-hermeneutic or transcendence—stands as a limit to
popular sovereignty. This, of course, is precisely what Abraham Lincoln
saw in slavery: oppression is not necessarily prevented by popular sovereignty.[108] The transcendent rules Bell and Bansal appeal to require exactly the kind of moral (including religious) dialogue about the good
that Sunstein and Michelman marginalize.

While religion is often blamed for being intolerant and itself oppressive (and blamed for good reasons), dialogue requires religion if republicanism is to sustain the kinds of virtues Sunstein and Michelman
rightly admire. This is so because religion deals with transcendence.
Without such engagement, deference to contractual agreements and
consensus gives rise to the Douglas position permitting slavery, a position that Lincoln resisted.

This is not to say that religion has had no part in perpetuating oppression. It can both support and undermine oppression.[109] The difficulty is that any social construction, even that of language, privileges
those who articulate the customs of a community at the expense of
those who are marginalized.[110] Thus, even the construction of moral
principles through dialogue entails oppression insofar as the partici-

pants to the dialogue are limited. A community dialogue among any population less than all members of the community, even one motivated and practiced in good will, will lurch toward the marginalization of those outside the norm.[111] This problem becomes even more pronounced when one recognizes that any community relies not only on current members of the community, but on those whose participation comes through remembering them.[112] The practical counterweight to this marginalization and to the impossibility of involving everyone in dialogue is that of virtues tied to transcendence.[113] In a sense, transcendence becomes a guarantor against marginalization.

Apart from the complex relationship between oppression and virtue generally, sociologist Robert Jackall's analysis of corporate life supports this concern. In Jackall's study, he argued that the "moral mazes" managers must experience result from ethical principles that are entirely constructed within the confines of the organization with no relationship to an external standard that clarifies what virtuous behavior is.[114] When virtue is merely socially constructed, as Jackall found in his study, moral behavior in corporate life becomes merely bureaucratic efficiency and fealty to hierarchy.[115]

The Role of Mediating Institutions. The civic republican theory of Sunstein and Michelman fails to consider mediating institutions adequately. The absence of a significant role for mediating institutions is related to, but is also distinct from, the exclusion of religion. To be sure, Sunstein does argue that mediating institutions serve "as areas for the cultivation and expression of republican virtues,"[116] although he also argues that mediating institutions can be oppressive.[117] As places where individuals learn responsibilities to others, however, mediating institutions become critically important institutions, places where one's view of one's self is connected or fails to be connected to a common good. Whether they are oppressive, as Sunstein fears, whether they enhance a distance from public life,[118] or whether they foster individual responsibility depends upon the existence of the altars and temples (and not only religious ones) that the "first man" can no longer find. It also depends upon the size of the community.

As Kathryn Abrams notes, mediating institutions (including religious institutions, as well as voluntary organizations and local governments) were relied upon by the founders, who knew that a citizen's relation to the polity was shaped by popular political institutions.[119] To foster republicanism, she argues, one needs to foster mediating institutions because they are highly visible, provide easy opportunity for involvement, initiate participants into the self-governing process, provide a way for individuals to grasp common norms, and reduce coercion.[120] In short, the benefits of mediating institutions are the same benefits Sustein and

Michelman champion in terms of dialogue. Both civic republicanism and mediating institutions foster notions of citizenship, goodwill, tolerance, and solidarity for particular communities.

There is no one form of mediating institution required to assure the success of republicanism. As Paul Brest notes, to encourage republicanism, one must reduce the fascination with judicial exclusivity and focus on private spheres.[121] Mediating institutions need not be, indeed are best not, governmental associations, but include families, churches, and corporations. Brest cites Hannah Pitkin, who explains the role of mediating institutions, which by fostering actual participation in a community, make us realize our connections with others so that we claim entitlement to a good rather than a desire for a good and, in doing so, make a claim that "becomes negotiable by public standards themselves, about our stake into the existence of standards, of justice, of our community, even of our opponents and enemies in the community; so that afterwards we are changed. Economic man becomes a citizen."[122]

The purpose of mediating institutions, according to Brest, is to create space for citizens and nonjudicial institutions to participate in common discourses and decision making.[123] That is particularly true, Brest argues, in the business sector. In fact, Brest argues that the key to republican participation is to develop a notion of participation in the workplace.[124] Regardless of the particular form of the mediating institution, however, the important task is the creation of nongovernmental places in which one learns that one's self is inevitably connected to and dependent upon associations with others. Such a definition of the self, however, goes directly to the heart of what is missing from the republican theory.

Michelman and Sunstein assume the self is properly constituted as an entity that should concern itself with others. Even if one agrees with their assessment, how does one change an attitude of narrow self-interest? This transformation of self-interest cannot simply be done through deliberative politics. Civic virtue only becomes desirable if one understands the personal benefit of promoting such virtue. That is a moral task, not a political one. It explains why Bell is right to worry about oppression. Without a transcendent sense of moral belief in the wrongness of discrimination, deliberative politics is not sufficient to extend the identification of the self to solidarity with the poor, oppressed, or simply different.[125] It requires a moral transformation of the self that can only be done in conjunction with interdependence with others learned through mediating institutions that allow that self to be concretely broadened.

Thus, a recovery of republicanism requires more than the good start in dialogue. It also requires a moral depth-hermeneutic that demonstrates why, and depends on an understanding that self-interest is best conceived in interdependence with others and a set of structures through which authentic, popular dialogue can effectively occur.

CONCLUSION

Notions of "business as community" or "business as mediating institution" remind ethicists that human nature is communal, for better or for worse. Since our moral identity is formed through community, the goodness of communities themselves becomes an important issue for business ethics. Because communities can be oppressive and are often skewed to advantage those in power, methods must be devised to protect individuals. Because communities can be short-sighted, methods must be devised to protect the environment as well.

The naturalist approach offers criteria to restrain such communitarian shortcomings without destroying the notions of "business as community" or "business as mediating institution." The naturalist approach reminds us that economic affairs must strike a balance between values of economizing, ordering, and ecologizing, including a balance between profitability and sustainability. The reason for this is because we are inextricably linked with one another and with our natural world through logic and through scientific reality. Nature teaches that while our nature is communal, our moral identity is formed in small mediating structures. If business is to be moral, it must also provide mediating structures, so that individuals are empowered to have meaningful participation in the actions that affect them. As Goldilocks would say, business ethics should not be "too hot" nor "too cold," but will find its best formation in the "wee little bowls" that are "just right."

III

Theology
and Business

One may fairly think that in relying upon nature as a normative resource, I have already caused enough trouble. Yet I need to make things more contentious in this part of the book by talking about religion. Not only that, I want to link theology with nature and do so in order to deepen the integration of my mediating institutions approach with the philosophical approaches of stakeholder, social contract, and virtue theory. I fully understand that proponents of these philosophical approaches and proponents of various religious traditions may want nothing to do with this kind of integration. It is for this reason that this part of the book comes last. I believe that mediating institutions and philosophical business ethics can be linked with the arguments of parts I and II. Yet, because the impetus for this linkage is based on the theological naturalism described in this part III, it would be disingenuous of me not to make the argument linking theology, nature, and business ethics. I am somewhat content, however, if scholars are comfortable with the linkage of parts I and II and find part III unnecessary.

As problematic as theology and naturalism are for some ethicists to swallow, they are both valuable. This part of the book seeks to integrate them by drawing upon a relatively new school of thought developing in theological circles and in some scientific communities that, for purposes of this chapter, I will call "theological naturalism." Some refer to the school as naturalistic theology, but others object to this characterization because the school does not attempt to describe theology in terms of nature, but nature in terms of theology. For this reason, others prefer the designation "theology of the natural." For brevity, I will simply refer to the school as "theological naturalism."

9

Theological Naturalism

Let me begin by proposing an integration of William Frederick's naturalism with theology. I would like to take Frederick up on an invitation he first implied in his book *Values, Nature and Culture in the American Corporation* and then explicitly extended in his address to the Social Issues of Management Section of the Academy of Management (SIM), revised and published in the journal *Business and Society*.[1] In his book, Frederick notes convergence among world religions around central moral principles.[2] The implication is that dialogue with and among world religions may produce insights for moral principles in business.

Frederick went further in his 1996 SIM address. In it, he proposed three directions for corporate social responsibility ("CSR" in Frederick's terms): an increasing awareness of the cosmological (another way to read the "C" in CSR) processes of all life, including business[3] and the increasing importance of science (the other "S" in CSR) in understanding these natural processes. A third direction was an increased emphasis on the phenomenon of religious belief (the other "R" in CSR) in business.

He provides several reasons for emphasizing religion. Most important, he argues that, like it or not, human beings have a "metaphysical impulse" rooted in neurological processes that generate a "constant stream of symbolic-creative-imaginative-curiosity-play impulses."[4] These impulses lead to an inquiry of what a person's place in the natural order might be. In short, it leads to religion. Frederick is careful to point out that he is not arguing that this should be the case, only that it is the case and has to be taken into account.

More normatively, he notes that on grounds of legitimacy, fairness, and honest disclosure, it may be worth considering that a person with strong religious beliefs should be entitled to rely upon those beliefs in making a business decision and to also rely upon those beliefs in explaining the decision. Noting, while not endorsing the whole of Laura Nash's work on evangelical CEOs, he points to the fact that many business leaders do in fact have strong religious beliefs and those beliefs may have a positive impact on the ethicality of the business. Underlying each of these rationales is the conviction that religion is an undeveloped resource for the motivation to practice ethical business behavior and for finding cross-cultural moral principles.[5]

There are dangers in opening this door. As Hume noted, "[E]rrors in religion are dangerous; those in philosophy only ridiculous."[6] Theologians often agree. Stanley Hauerwas argues that once one thinks one knows what is "natural," then one can much more easily punish, perhaps even torture, something or someone who is "unnatural."[7] Moreover, Frederick himself warns that natural processes dictate no one religious dogma.

> [D]on't count on finding your own religious philosophy written on the face of the cosmos. Rather, what you *can* count on is a personal need to make the search [for cosmic meaning]. Some people *create* their own meaning; for them, personal significance is not "out there" awaiting discovery. Most people fall short of this kind of religious creativity and simply *accept* the metaphysical meanings given to them by their culture.[8]

This chapter argues that when we take account of contemporary notions of naturalist theology, we will find ourselves in a position in which (1) there is a transcendent good to which all business persons are accountable, (2) the fate of business persons is that of freedom of choice, wrestling with difficult moral issues, and (3) business persons become responsible for integrating the various elements of life, including ethics in business. Before making this argument, two important delimitations are necessary.

First, this approach runs a great risk of making no one happy. To philosophers, adding religion to Frederick's already controversial naturalism could be like throwing gasoline on a fire. To those with strong religious convictions, naturalist theology can come across as flabby and pantheistic. This chapter, however, neither seeks to challenge philosophy nor to evangelize. Instead, it seeks to use natural theology's increasingly sophisticated integration of religion and science to make applied philosophy more relevant and to identify this basic transcendence that religions interpret diversely. Second, this chapter does not provide a comprehensive analysis of naturalist theology nor of naturalism, nor of the relation between these approaches and corporate bureaucracy. It only suggests why some beginning integration might be fruitful.

Moreover, there are strong reasons to attempt the integration. Simply in terms of strategic reasons to motivate ethical behavior, one must ask, where do business students and business leaders get their ethics? Frankly it is unlikely that many get them from philosophy or empirical survey studies, methodologies that have dominated the field of business ethics. This is not to diminish the importance of both of these approaches; indeed, I think business ethics without these approaches would be monumentally impoverished. But Laura Nash and Bob Solomon each point to the ways in which many business leaders or students draw upon, respectively, religious belief and nature.

In her book *Believers in Business,* Nash has identified the seriousness with which evangelical CEOs rely upon their religious beliefs in making business judgments. And the results, on the whole, are not too bad. Nash notes the prevalence of equality and participation in the workplace, an attempt to make work meaningful, an insistence upon honest and fair dealings, and a lower ratio between top and bottom compensation levels than exist generally in corporate America.

This is not to argue that religion always correlates with ethical business behavior, nor is it to argue that one must be religious to be ethical. It is to suggest that recognition of a spiritual transcendent reality is a meaningful motivation for many to be ethical in business. One must recognize that moral formation still occurs in churches, synagogues, mosques, and temples, and that business persons may well reach for those languages when analyzing a moral dilemma. This is true whether or not one is particularly religious. One can think instead of "transcendence" in a way that Emile Durkheim used the notion of "force."[9]

In describing Australian aborigines, Durkheim argues that although there is not among them a notion of "God" in the Western sense, there is a notion of "force," which is an energy existing within all creatures, especially within members of a community, and which continues on for generations.[10] This unifying spiritual force is the result of a power greater than the arithemetically aggregated forces of individuals within the community.[11] Two aspects of this term are important for my purposes.

First, Durkeim characterizes this "force" as a spiritual reality and a religious one. By that, he does not mean that there is only one such authentic religious manifestation, but that some description of a transcendent reality binds the community by its awareness of this religious force. Hence, the reality is transcendent: it is beyond any particular person or collection of persons to change the mores of a society by some kind of individual choice.

Durkeim states that he is not using the term "force" in a metaphorical sense; instead, these principles "behave like real forces. In a sense, they are even physical forces that bring about physical effects mechanically."[12] The important aspect is not the name "Force" or "Power" or

"God" or "Nature" but a reality transcending individual creatures. This transcendent reality connects individuals to their community and to nature, to history, and to cosmos.

The second important point about this notion of transcendence is that human beings are accountable to it. The transcendent reality to which one is accountable could be Yawheh, but it could also be Shiva, Allah, or nature. It could also be a nonsupernatural conception of a transcendent reality. Whatever the name, there is a moral component implied in the use of the name.[13] The "individual" fears, loves, and respects the "sacred" being or transcendent reality and also is bound by communal identity.[14] As a result, duties toward others create kinship.[15] Thus, to the extent one is in a community, a sense of commitment to a force larger than oneself is part of a strong motivation for and linguistic description of ethics.

In his book *Ethics and Excellence* (1993), Robert Solomon deconstructs a model of business that is based on a Darwinian survival of the fittest. In the model Solomon attacks, business is a jungle populated by individuals for whom life is a Hobbesian struggle. Solomon's enemy is indeed stitched into the language of business. Thus, drawing upon a methodology that demonstrates to such individuals that there is more to science—particularly biology and physics—than competitive battles for survival, is to take away a central argument such individuals use to claim that a scientific approach is "harder" than the "soft" approach of normative theory. In short, a methodology that combines theology and nature addresses many—I will not attempt to claim whether the number qualifies as "most" or a "majority"—of the ways business persons live.

A second reason for integrating theology and business is partly strategic, but also is important in terms of notions of basic respect. When one engages in the ethical issues in international business, one simply cannot do so in terms of Western philosophical (or religious) traditions. One needs to respect the moral culture of the lands in which one is working. Thus, it would be disrespectful to consider a problem of business ethics in India without at least an understanding of Hinduism, and being able to relate one's ethical theory to the meaning of how one becomes *braham-atman* may well be important. Given the globalization of business, such respect can be desirable anywhere. While U.S. academic circles have largely secularized normative debate, international circles do not always do so. Basic respect for other cultures requires that discourse at least be familiar with terms phrased outside of language we may be used to.

As some have argued, at the basis of every culture is religion. Even a secularized society has remnants—the Protestant work ethic or Puritan litigiousness would be two examples in the United States—of a religious tradition. Every culture must also deal with nature. The gifts and impediments nature gives to a culture make a difference in one's view of reality. And a view of reality influences, if not determines, a culture's normative rules. Thus, theology and nature speak in a language that helps to meet cultures where they are.

The third reason is substantive. Whether one wishes to characterize "God" in personal terms as traditionally done in Western faiths, or to make "God" into a basic (dare I say a Star-Warsian) force as would be more typical in, say, Hinduism, or even in terms of a Tillich-like nature (about which more will be said), transcendence keeps human choice accountable. It may be possible to describe such a spirit in modern philosophical terms and maybe even in terms of rational, economic self-interest. Both of these approaches stress the importance of autonomous, human choice. But both struggle with how to rule some choices inappropriate when they cause harm to others.

This is particularly a problem of business leaders. Ethicists ask business leaders to be ethical because in the long term it is good business and because we should want to be as we should be. But unethical business actions do not always add up to profitability, and unless the long run has connotations of reincarnation or some other afterlife, punishment for wrongdoing may well be viewed as simply wishful (a characterization often made of the prospect of the afterlife). Further, while it is a tautology to provide an argument for why we should be as we should be, this approach founders on what I shall later describe as the philosophical version of the naturalistic fallacy.

My approach does not seek to replace either philosophy or empirical study. Heaven knows, so to speak, that without the rigor of philosophical logic and empirical study, theology can launch into wild speculation and naturalism can suffer from Spencerism. Instead, this chapter attempts to sketch an approach that augments traditional ethics by consulting a new school of thought that may well resonate with business experience.

THE COMMITMENTS OF THEOLOGICAL NATURALISM

As this is an emerging school, one hesitates to attempt to definitively describe the commitments of theological naturalism. Nevertheless, there are certain characteristics that are worth noting. I will first characterize them generally, and then make a more explicit integration of the characteristics, which can then be transferred to the field of business ethics.

Removing the Faith-Science Divide

An important commitment is to remove the gulf between science and theology. One is more likely to characterize the gulf as an ocean. Evolutionary biology and physics (both in terms of astronomy and in molecular substructure) have performed an incredible deconstruction of religious descriptions of the world in the last half of the last millennium. Gone are turtle-carried flat worlds, earth-centered universes, the Garden of Eden, and a host of other notions whose demise was fought, often violently, by the church. Even today, science and faith are uneasy partners at best. But in the midst of this deconstruction, scientists have noted several things.

First, with any small variation of the laws of thermodynamics, gravity, and other "natural laws," life (as we know it) would not exist. Richard Dawkins's precious monkeys aside,[16] it is simply extraordinarily improbable that this kind of fine-tuning could occur without some direction. Thus has been born the "anthropic principle," which has weak and strong forms.

The strong form states that life must have been specifically designed for human life. Such a traditional design argument thereby suggests a designer. This argument, of course, has generated debates among theologians, philosophers, and cosmologists for years, with little end in sight.[17]

The weak anthropic principle is more subtle and less dramatic, but perhaps more profound. Although it has various forms,[18] it essentially has two parts. First, scientists have noted the improbable coincidences that allow life to exist. A universe would have to be rather old to have cooled sufficiently for carbon-producing stars to have formed and, consequently, for carbon-based life forms to appear.[19] The creation of such stars depends on the expansion of the universe. If it were expanding more rapidly, solar systems like our own would be too unstable to support life.[20] If expansion were occurring more slowly, hydrogen would be burned up before carbon compounds could form.[21] If the strong nuclear force integral to the pace of expansion were 5 percent weaker, there would be only hydrogen and no helium; if it were 2 percent stronger, hydrogen would convert into helium.[22] Similar kinds of "fine-tuning" apply to electronic magnetic forces and gravity.[23] What the fine-tuning produces is a life form and, further, an intelligence that engages with these physical forms. In a counterintuitive way, there may be no material structures such as electrons, protons, and neutrons per se. They do exist in some energy-matter form, but they become an object that one can observe when one in fact does observe them. From this argument, the weak anthropic principle states that the universe has a relationship with some kind of intelligent being.

Either anthropic approach thus requires a special intelligence. The strong anthropic principle, of course, appeals directly to God, who has designed natural laws. This principle may or may not have deistic elements; a creative God viewed in terms of on ongoing life force could still be actively creating. But whether deistic or not, the point is that explaining the existence of the finely tuned universe, the strong anthropic principle suggests a plan, which then suggests a planner. The weak anthropic principle appeals to a connecting force or reality that links physical laws with human perception and existence. It suggests that the perception of the existence of the universe is dependent upon our intelligence and engagement with the relationality of the natural order. It is in intelligent engagement with all dimensions of existence that the world, in a very basic sense, exists. In this form, "God" may not be a designer, but instead a relational glue that binds existence together. As Zycinski points out "to explain the nature of cosmic design, one can refer to a force or a form of energy, imposing rational structures on the physical processes. The neo-Platonic Logos of the philosophers' Absolute would be enough to explain the cosmic design disclosed by anthropic principles."[24]

Morality and Technology

Technology is a major concern for business ethics and for theological naturalism. To place it into an understandable context, I would like to return again to Frederick and compare his approach to that of theologian Paul Tillich. As we have seen, the methodological heart of Frederick's naturalist approach is to argue that in all life, there are three distinct value clusters[25] of economizing,[26] power aggrandizing,[27] and ecologizing.[28] Any biologically based moral approach risks the attack of determinism. Frederick avoids this dilemma by arguing that our biologically rooted ability to think symbolically and abstractly allows us to invent and create. These are "technologizing values." Some inventions can be gadgets. But Frederick conceives of this creative aspect of humanity more broadly, as the ability to integrate, innovate, design, and reflect.

Similarly, for any naturalist theory, it is necessary to confront Hume's so-called naturalistic fallacy.[29] The fallacy, of course, is that one cannot derive an "ought" from an "is." Several things can be said about the fallacy. I will limit myself to two: Hume is right and Hume is wrong.

Every business ethicist has been confronted at some point with the argument "That's just the way things are" from a student, colleague, or business person. This argument could justify a whole laundry list of distressing actions. Beyond such a weak form of the fallacy, Hume was after theologians whose religious dogma ultimately relied on a descriptive rather than a normative argument.

Hume is wrong, however, if his position means that "what is" does not have a great deal to do with "what ought to be." Nature does constrain what we ought to do. More importantly, Hume is also wrong if our ability to construct an "ought" is the quality that allows us to reach toward a cosmological essence that lies beyond our particularity. At that point, "ought" is an expression of "is." The naturalist fallacy has its greatest weight when "ought" is confused with an attempted universalization of a particular normative form, but is weightless when "ought" stands beyond the particular form.

Frederick invites us to see if we can preserve the "is" from which we drive the "ought" without confusing the language of the "ought" with what "is." In other words—and not in Frederick's words—Frederick asks us to see if religion can motivate ethical business behavior and thereby make business life meaningful while keeping a cosmological essence free from being captured by any one theological tongue.

If nature is the transcendent reality of our existence from which we develop into who we are, then what we ought to be is simply part of our extended nature. Paul Tillich puts this theologically when he writes: "[T]he superior law is, at the same time, the innermost law of man himself, rooted in the divine ground which is man's own ground: the law of life transcends man, although it is, at the same time, his own."[30]

In this formulation, what ought to be is a subset of what is. The particular form of this subset, however, varies according to culture and community. This means that there is an existentialist, autonomous point where the question of what ought to be is made within the community to which one belongs and with regard to a transcendent reality.

Tillich makes a distinction between naturalist theology and theology of the natural. The term "naturalist theology" is misleading, he argues, because, at least in terms of ethics, we live in terms of culture.[31] It is through culture that we learn our moral duties, not through an unmitigated revelation through nature, although nature can provide insight.[32] Thus, as seen in Frederick's work, we experience nature through the communities in which we live.

What then is this nature and what is God's relation to it? For Tillich, God is Being. God is not "a" being, but God is power that transcends all beings and the totality of beings. God is the ground of being and God is the structure of being.[33] God is not a grand old man sitting up in heaven, but is more like a Buddhist energizing force that supports, structures, and moves through all beings. Religion, then, is directedness toward this unconditional, transcendent element.[34] God, in a very real sense, is the phenomenon of life, and religion is a particular group's experience with that phenomenon.

Tillich's God sounds a great deal like Frederick's nature. For both, God/nature is that which is life, and because that God/nature has a certain structure, there are lessons we can learn by reflecting on that structure. The structure or force is not embodied fully in any particular culture, but particular communities structure themselves according to their experience with and reflection on it.

There are more specific corollaries. Frederick emphasizes, as we have seen, the human ability to use symbols. This ability is the heart of technologizing values. Theologically, this ability to grasp and to use symbols emphasizes the meaningfulness of business activity. Symbols, according to Tillich, "are directed toward the infinite which they symbolize *and* toward the finite through which they symbolize it."[35] Our work in business attempts to make sense of such work in light of a transcendent reality and empowers our work as a symbol. In this light, business is not only a (technologizing) symbol of Frederick's value clusters, but business becomes important and meaningful because of what it reflects. In short, business is not "just business" but links existential work to transcendence itself.

There is a second, important symbol: the notion of participation. Its "meaning" lies in the fact that the transcendent participates in life.[36] This leads to the notion of God as Person, because people participate. That is the symbol. The meaning behind the symbol is that there is human interaction with the transcendent because the ground of being, God/nature, is a participating force in lives.

A third important symbol is destiny. For Tillich, secular culture is troubled by the fact that it has no teleology directing it and none toward which it is directed. Religion, however, deepens the meaning and purpose of culture by tying it to a transcendent reality.[37] Such a teleology shapes our destiny in a way that emphasizes our particularity and individuality. To lose teleology causes us to lose the meaningfulness of life.[38]

There is one final point to make about this all-too-brief reprise of Tillich's thought. Because of his understanding of the particularity of culture, Tillich is quite open to other religions. Indeed, he describes the revelation of this God-as-Being as "universal."[39] Thus, the type of convergence work Frederick describes is not only an interesting phenomenon of what people share, but a revelation of transcendence itself. Thus, three main themes for Tillich—God as the being of life, symbol (with elements of meaningfulness, participation, and destiny), and culture—describe a transcendent force of life whose presence dramatically raises the stakes in business ethics.

Of course, noting overlaps is only a moderately persuasive reason to admit theology to business ethics discussion. One could respond, and many do: why admit such controversial notions when one can talk about ethics or even nature without then? Those who would rather keep the religious voice quiet may see little reason to admit it, but others might equally see the voice as valuable. In fact, if there is a "metaphysical impulse" practiced diversely, then there is a critical need for multiple moral languages. No side needs to convert others to using any one language. Overlaps suggest a point for agreement about what ought to happen, while different languages provide ownership for the speaker of why that action is personally meaningful.

If I read Frederick's invitation correctly, this is very much his point. Speaking in a religious language, as well as a secular one, allows a person to connect with a meaningful source. Some business persons may not see why Rawls is compelling in requiring consideration of the health conditions of factory workers, but they can understand the same obligation through the parable of the Good Samaritan. Similarly, many business persons are fond of applying Darwinian analogies to business. Showing a moral side to nature, as Frederick and naturalist theology do, speaks in a language more difficult for a competitive business person to dismiss than Kant's.

A theology of nature also poses a challenge to religions that absolutize their dogma. The more one can find corollaries and common ground among religions and with nature, the harder intolerance is to practice. While I am not naive about the risks of linking theology and nature, doing so may enhance the motivation for being ethical in business while limiting the likelihood of intolerance.

Naturalism and naturalist theology provide a rationale for why business ethics matters. They do so by linking the importance of moral behavior in terms of transcendence and personal meaningfulness. Tillich's theology of the natural provides a helpful jumping-off point for developing a model of business for theological naturalism.[40] Three aspects are worth noting.

God and Life

As noted, Tillich does not insist that God is like life, or in life, or learned through life—although all these may be true—but that God *is* life. God is a force, a spirit, and being who is life itself. Wherever there is life, there is God. This insight has several implications.

First, one can learn about God by studying not just human life, but all life. Nature, not just humanity, becomes revelatory. Like Frederick, we can look at the processes of reality not in order to replicate nature, but to learn from nature, and from the interaction of life with life. One of the things Frederick notices in this interaction is that life is about economizing, which in its most basic form is metabolism or photosynthesis. That is, each life form must transform raw materials into energy in order to survive. Corporations do this on an organizational level when they transform raw materials into goods and services.

Second, Frederick also points out that power aggrandizing is common in nature. Whether one looks at a pride of lions or the executive floor of a modern corporation, there is an attempt to dominate and control. Frederick's third "value cluster" is ecologizing, which is the deep-rooted (often literally) orientations for the survival of the species. Thus, an individual will sacrifice its own life for the welfare of the herd.

Nature thus helps us understand the entirety of life. In addition to Frederick's value clusters, and implicit in them, is the notion of competition. Competition is a fact of life, and it in fact helps life flourish. But competition is not the whole story. Altruism, mutual support, and (at least among higher primates and human beings) affection impact behavior as well. The important point is that, if a transcendent spirit is at the bottom of life, then there is a commensurate indication to respect that life and the things that allow that life to flourish.

Culture and Nature

Tillich is careful to argue that individuals do not simply appropriate nature's values, but cultures describe nature's values and teach them to individuals. This is a communitarian notion of values, but that does not undermine human autonomy. Frederick is clear here. Like Tillich, he focuses on culture's intermediary role between individuals and nature, but individuals, as individuals and through cultures, have the ability to put things together in different ways in order to solve problems. This is our technologizing ability, and it is rooted in our ability to think symbolically.

Thinking symbolically is something on Tillich's mind as well. Tillich notes that humans think symbolically, and, by doing so, transform an ordinary thing into something extraordinary. The symbol brings meaning to the mundane by infusing it with a connection with transcendence, as the mechanism of this transference gains in stature. To take a traditional example, sprinkling water on someone's head (or dunking them in water) is a mundane activity. But when this becomes a symbol of one's bond to God, then baptism transforms the act into something of great significance.

Human beings appear to be the only creatures who worship religious beings, and our ability to communicate seems advanced precisely because we are able to manipulate symbols. This ability is creative in the sense that it in fact creates. And thus, the connection with the divine life that Tillich argues is God comes full circle. In our creativity, not just in the instincts we share with our primate cousins, we participate in the creation of the world.

Thus, theological naturalism has no place for deterministic sociobiology or a modern form of predestination. Individual choice and participation is part of our human nature. But the description of reality that we have is provided to us through our cultures; it is not brought to us in unmediated fashion.

This suggests that a topic for business ethics is the design of the cultures that describe business reality in terms other than the Darwinian jungle to which Solomon so strenuously objects. Corporate governance is thus a critical issue. The structure of our organizations goes a long way toward communicating the ethical duties individuals believe they have in business. It reinforces the anthropology grounding the mediating institutions model.

If there is a transcendent reality/force/God/nature, then why would basing an ethic on that model be such a bad thing? Let me suggest two reasons why it would not be a bad thing. First, as already noted, *every* moral theory commits its own version of the naturalistic fallacy. We find a characteristic of human (or nonhuman) nature that we find compelling and adjudicate moral norms accordingly. The characteristic could, for instance, be love. It could be survival. More typically it is rational and logical. This is the position of philosophy and, in its own version, economics. Modern versions of both proceed on the basis that individuals are rational persons and that persons should have the choice to determine what they should be able to do.

Notice, however, that what they should do is determined according to the rationality of their choice. But why rationality and logic (particularly in Western form)? Why not build back in love and survival?

Rationality is, to be sure, one defining human characteristic. But it is not uniquely human. Animals, particularly higher primates use rationality, just as they demonstrate affection. Animals, particularly higher primates, use tools and language. Human rationality may be more sophisticated, just as human affection may be more profound and altruistic, and just, as human language may be more complex. But anthropologists have not found the "great divide" between human and nonhumans. Our lives are more complex than any of these traits, and we commit the naturalistic fallacy when we value rational logic just as we do when we value nature.

The antidote for the naturalistic fallacy in any form is to confront an instance of it with other characteristics of life. Thus, neither nature nor theology ought to claim that it can describe the reality of the world, including the business world. Each requires help from economics, empirical business ethics, philosophical business ethics, and other disciplines. The present point is that appealing to theological naturalism is not doomed because of the so-called naturalistic fallacy.

There is another argument against the naturalistic fallacy, this time from eastern religions. The basis of Asian faiths such as Hinduism and Buddhism is the experience with one's connection with divine spirit. Thus, the yogi experiences a complete melting of subject and object relationship when in *asana*. In earlier Hindu times, a brahman's freedom from the suffering experienced by all the world resulted from an "awakening" that "I am" the *braham-atman*. That is, that the person is in fact the divine spirit.

From this encounter, one develops moral duties. Or, more specifically, one is freed from the greed and desires of life that cause pleasure and pain. It is this disengagement that allows reengagement with temporal affairs. As Krishna would say, one can participate and create in the world without becoming attached in the world. Or as Buddha would draw from a similar experience, one follows a middle way rather than the extremes of asceticism or gluttony. Following a middle way calls for following the Eightfold Path, which, to come full circle, comes from the four Noble Truths arrived at by an Awakening in which one recognizes the transitoriness of life and the fulfillment (salvation in Hinduism, nirvana in Buddhism) of life in the annihilation of suffering through connection with the divine.

The important point to note is that ethical virtues are derived from the experience of the divine. One models behavior on the creative but unattached model of Vishnu when one imitates Vishnu's ninth incarnation in Krishna. It is difficult to find an application of the naturalistic fallacy in this system in any way other than to completely undermine it. To undermine it in this way, however, raises questions about the cultural limitations of the naturalistic fallacy. In short, the naturalistic fallacy has its primary weight when one is attempting to derive moral duties from moral norms when ruling out transcendence models. If transcendent models are admissible in modeling ethical behavior, then one cannot simply rule out transcendence on the basis of a preference for philosophical derivation or discipline of rational thought.

Forces and Nature

Perhaps the most artful elaboration of the attack on the faith-science debate comes from German theologian Wofhart Pannenberg. Pannenberg pioneered the notion of field forces in theology. Stretching at least to Newton, physics traditionally has held that forces such as gravity derive from a mass or body. If this is true, what kind of force could God, who has no body, have?[41] One might logically conclude that spiritual ideas (of God) and scientific ideas (of forces) are simply two separate realms of knowledge. Indeed, this two-knowledge approach is part of what underlies Richard DeGeorge's critique of theology. Secular knowledge can be researched (i.e., it is akin to a science) whereas theology cannot (i.e., it is the subject of belief).[42]

Yet contemporary physics messes up a good deal of this neat distinction. To Michael Farraday, for instance, a body was simply a manifestation of a force resulting from a concentration of a force in a field at a particular place and time.[43] This, of course, would be consistent with the idea of God as a spirit linking all of life as a field of existence, a conception that would explain all sorts of so-called miracles.[44] It also connnects with biblical notions of spirit, breath, wind, and storm.[45] God then, like Tillich's life, and Frederick's nature, is the whole of which existential reality is a component part. If this is true, then there is no part of human life that stands outside of this spirit of God. Not only might this dramatically increase the stakes of any action, including business action, but it also places a new twist on a perfectly understandable statement of DeGeorge, who claims that philosophers approach issues from a secular point of view.[46] Under Pannenberg's conception, there is no secular point of view.

Now I can imagine three immediate, strong objections to this line of argument. First, is it true? Is Pannenberg correct? No one I know can prove or disprove his position. But it is every bit as plausible to understand life in this fashion as it is in a Newtonian one. Moreover, the immediate and inescapable engagement with the divine in business action and an understanding of our self as interrelated with others place ethics on a more meaningful level. Why be ethical? Because I am directly engaged with the creative spirit of the world and because that other person (at work) is really another part of me. It is not surprising that the previous sentence could just as easily be phrased along the lines of "Love your God with all your heart, soul, mind, and strength, and your neighbor as yourself."[47] Finally, this conception is hardly limited to the Judeo-Christian tradition; in fact, it may even be better characterized by Eastern faiths:

> In Buddhism there are corresponding features. *Dharmakaya* corresponds to *Braham,* pervading all material bodies, and the *Avatamsaka* sutra stresses the ubiquitous interrelatedness of things, which, under the propulsion of the "body of being," or ultimate reality, are in constant flux and change. . . . Taoism has similar characteristics. . . . the *Tao* is the way, and also the unity of opposites, the recognition of which it brings. All things dispose themselves as opposites, according to this teaching, but they are also complementary and ultimately mutually identical. . . . [T]he *Tao* is not represented as a god, but it is the infinite whole, and it does manifest itself in series of opposites that unite and are identical; and the aim of human endeavor is to become one with it and to think and act in accordance with its flow. In Chinese thought, the ideal for humankind is final and total union with the universe in its unbroken wholeness.[48]

The second strong objection is whether I have just magically converted atheists and agnostics into some sort of believers who simply aren't smart enough to figure out that God is in everything. The answer is no, I have not done this, for two reasons. First, to the extent an atheist or agnostic is an atheist or agnostic because of objection to the conception of God often portrayed in organized (or unorganized) religion, nothing I have said really challenges the ground of their objection. (Actually, I anticipate that my description of theological naturalism is likely to provoke more animosity from traditional religious approaches than it is from atheists and agnostics.) Second and perhaps more deeply, one can still choose to reject this theological naturalism in favor of a more Newtonian or Darwinian description. There is nothing coercive in this description.

A third objection is the old (and important) one of theodicy: how can a loving God allow evil? Obviously, answering this question could produce (and has produced) multiple tomes. Let me briefly relate an answer from Errol Harris:

> Evil is always the concomitant of finitude and is only its privative aspect. It is the consequence of the self-contradiction and conflict that results from the self-assertion of the finite as independent, in disregard and neglect of its necessary dependence on its complement, on its environment, on its social context, and ultimately on the absolute whole which determines the natures and the operation of all of these. . . . To be omnipotent, to be God, the deity must, as it were, empty himself of his glory, pour himself out as a physical world and that issues from it. He must create. A created world, however, essentially involves finitude. So to create a world without evil is really a meaningless and nonsensical demand. And is it is no derogation from omnipotence, or from benevolence, to be both unable and unwilling to produce the nonsensical and logically impossible, the existence of evil is incompatible neither with God's omnipotence nor with his infinite goodness.[49]

The heart of such responsibility is to experience one's part of a greater wholeness. In doing so, one gains a sense of solidarity with others, because one sees the other as part of oneself. Because of the structure of our brains, we are most likely to experience this knowledge in mediating institutions. Practicing solidarity within the mediating institution only is not sufficient; it still must be open to others and seeing some of these others outside of one's mediating institution is a vital experience of spiritual and moral growth. But solidarity is first nourished in each of these mediating institutions on which live throughout our lives.

If there is no clean differentiation between science and spirit, theological naturalism's holistic understanding provides an account for what is meaningful as well. Ethical behavior is meaningful not because it accords with a principle (legal or philosophical), but because individuals transcend themselves by linking themselves to others and to God. According to Nancey Murphy and George Ellis, "[S]elf-renunciation for the sake of the other is humankind's highest good."[50] There is danger in this insofar as one ignores one's life and needs. Thus, I propose to mitigate this commitment to total self-sacrifice with a Tillich/Frederick commitment to life (for Tillich) and survival and flourishing (for Frederick) so that cooperative solidarity rather than sacrificial emolation may be the normative goal, at least in business.

THEOLOGICAL NATURALISM AND BUSINESS ETHICS

Having described this transcendent reality in terms that link theology and Frederick, the next question is what, if anything, this has to say about business ethics.[51] One can identify three major themes in which the reality of transcendence makes ethics a necessary component of business.

First, Dostoyevksy's point about the need for God was that human determination of the good was insufficient if it was unhinged from a transcendent reality. In business terms, business persons often think that any activity is allowed, provided it does not violate the law (and sometimes not even then). This view considers economizing values and, to the extent the law can be characterized as an instrument of power, power-aggrandizing values. It says nothing about what is necessary to build a community of people living together. Frederick's naturalist transcendent reality argues that business is not exempt from community-building realities. This need is one reason ethics is critical to business. To the naturalist theologian, business is subject to the being, the life force, that is God. Some research indicates that reciprocity is a universal norm[52] and that its practice is biologically required by and enhanced in small mediating institutions. Business then becomes a symbol for opening up human lives to the transcendent reality of the natural need for community and raises the stakes for business. Cultures and individuals do vary, and therefore many values are relative, but not everything is allowed.

The work of theorists such as Frans de Waal demonstrate that traits such as affection are not isolated in human beings.[53] Perhaps, one would not want to cavalierly state that since bees, for instance, are social, they hold their societies together through bonds of affection. But when one studies the activities of the higher primates, those creatures most closely related to human beings, one sees exhibitions of affection tied to norms of behavior. De Waal, following Robert Trivers, explains that for bonobos, reciprocal altruism is an effective mechanism of keeping the group together.

More complexly, game theorists have demonstrated that the most effective strategizers in prisoners' dilemma games do not practice just reciprocal altruism. Such a strategy is vulnerable to someone who takes advantage of such trusting behavior. Nor do they practice "tit for tat," because, while this assures that one will not be taken advantage of, it provides no escape for the downward spiral of revenge.

The most effective strategy is something called "generous tit for tat." In this approach, one generally reciprocates the behavior shown, but occasionally one must break out of this reciprocity to treat another as one would like to be treated. This strategy may sound like a way to move from an eye-for-an-eye approach to that of a Gospel Golden Rule, but it is, in fact, a strategy practiced by de Waal's bonobos.

Thus, if one is asked what moral principles ought to govern business behavior (and provided that one does not mind committing the naturalistic fallacy), one could respond that one should treat other stakeholders in a way that they generally treat management (a basic contract approach), but that management could raise the ethical bar by treating stakeholders in a way one would like to be treated. Why? Because it is a basic principle of human nature demonstrated by world religions and also confirmed by the natural world. Thus, the first methodological principle is that world religions can be understood as anthropological evidence of aspects of human nature. Nature itself can then be used as confirmatory evidence of this nature.

A second theme is that of freedom. Our technologizing efforts of innovation, creativity, and reflection are not simple tasks. In business terms, this human freedom is double-edged. Business persons and business students ask for a great deal of freedom. They want to be free of many things, including governmental and moral constraints. But they also often want business ethicists to tell them what the right "rule" is and become quite unhappy when the professor responds with a way to analyze the problem rather than providing a fast rule.

If, however, our very being is that of a transcendent participation in life and in creatively responding to the openness of the opportunity to participate in life, then we must also be free creatures, at least to some degree. Our ethics are not determined, nor are we to be rote followers of oppressive hierarchical regimes, but nature provides us with technologizing capabilities that require us to accept an existential challenge of choice.

The third theme is responsibility. Executives foster a culture, create incentives for certain kinds of behavior, and even give orders, but often when the consequences of those orders are negative, they maintain "plausible deniability" so they will not be blamed. But if one does not integrate the transcendent elements of life, then one is subject to the participation of that element, regardless of whether one likes it or not. In biblical times, this would be known as God's punishment. A less dramatic but no less painful example is acid rain as the natural result of pollution. In short, nature ultimately demands responsibility.

Business is thus subject to universal moral laws of a transcendent good, of having to wrestle with tough ethical choices, and of being responsible. Transcendence requires choice and responsibility; it does not determine behavior. Transcendent being and nature thus mandate an integration of values, because transcendent reality participates in life itself. Transcendence raises the stakes of business activity; freedom and participation make individual effort meaningful.

CONCLUSION

Theological naturalism does not require any particular belief. Yet it supports calls for ethical business behavior. Why treat a stakeholder respectfully? Because that stakeholder is a part of our very self and connects us with the ultimate force of the universe. Why focus on forming business communities? Because our cognitive capabilities lend themselves to these kinds of mediating institutions in order to see our connection with others. Why a two-tiered social contract? To balance this need for community with an ultimate standard of mutual solidarity, the essence of a hypernorm.

10

The Dark Side of Religion in the Workplace and Some Suggestions for Brightening It

Several years ago when I was writing an article about Supreme Court church-state jurisprudence, a judge on a U.S. circuit court asked incredulously if I thought I could make sense of it. Indeed, the second half of the twentieth century regularly witnessed bewildering litigation over religion's proper role in a constitutional democracy.[1] The product of this litigation is immense, confusing, and contentious.

There are many reasons for this jurisprudence, among them being the difficulty of balancing a moral system strongly influenced by a religious history with a tremendously diverse population that has rights to individual expression of religious belief, and a right to no belief at all. As difficult as this subject may be in a diverse United States, however, even more problems appear when one considers how global corporations can possibly deal with religious diversity in their worldwide operations.

This complex issue becomes more difficult when one considers the calls being made for businesses of all sizes to be more ethical and for penalties on businesses that fail to adopt ethical compliance. A manager who responds to calls for ethical business behavior must consider how to do so when the content of any such ethical behavior may touch upon and perhaps gravely offend some of those who work for the company.

Take the following as an example. Several years ago, my MBA ethics class developed a hypothetical drug-testing policy. The class decided to allow drug testing of employees upon entry to the company, and thereafter on a random basis. To protect against "false positives," any person testing positive would be retested prior to any further action. If the person tested positive again, the company would offer a substance abuse rehabilitation program at the company's expense and the employee would be placed on probation. While the employee was placed on probation, she would be fired only if she dropped out of the program or tested positive again (subject to the "false positive" double-testing that would accompany any drug test).

One week later, a recently retired, deeply religious executive spoke to the class about business ethics. A student asked him what his drug-testing policy would look like. The CEO repeated nearly verbatim the class's policy from the previous week (and he had no knowledge of that policy), except that he added three things.

First, he would not fire an employee even if the person failed the program or a subsequent test. Second, he, the CEO, would personally accompany the troubled employee to rehabilitation sessions if the employee so desired. Third, the reason for having this policy, the CEO said, was because, as a Christian, he should take all steps necessary to help a neighbor in need. He substantiated this duty by quoting a series of biblical passages.

My students were angered by his comments, because he had justified his position on the basis of his religious beliefs, thereby "proving" that he was a "religious bigot." Although my students later thought that they may have been the ones practicing a form of prejudice, their reaction was a telling sign of the incendiary additive religious belief brings to a debate, even in determining ethical business behavior.

There is another danger. Throughout this book, I have occasionally referred to Dostoyevsky's *The Brothers Karamazov* and the notion of the necessity for the belief in God. From another perspective, legal scholar William Marshall reminds us of the dark side of religion. Marshall relies on the tale of the Grand Inquisitor from *Karamazov*. In the story, Jesus, who for Dostoyevsky provides the gift of freedom, returns to inquisitorial Seville. The people are initially drawn to him, but the Grand Inquisitor imprisons Jesus and tells him that people do not want freedom, but happiness, and that happiness is not fostered by freedom but by the Grand Inquisitor telling people what to do. It is out of the Grand Inquisitor's love of humanity that he removes freedom and allows people to be happy.[2] It is this dark side of religion, the side that removes freedom, Marshall argues, that itself causes problems.[3] The final consequence is that "[t]he more rigid and expansive the doctrine, the more the believer is shielded from the tremendum. Eventually, because of the strength of its appeal, doctrine replaces God as the center of religious experience."[4] A similar process occurs when ritual replaces God.[5]

Marshall has a valid point. There is a disturbing history of religious ugliness in the workplace as well as in the public square that could undermine the appeal I make for a more inclusive presence of religion. Trends suggest that the presence of religion may be increasing, which raises these concerns to a more acute level. *Time* magazine ran a cover story in November 1999 featuring the growing presence of spirituality in corporate America.[6] From accommodating religious practices by holding prayer meetings to noting that spiritual people "are less fearful, less likely to compromise their values, and more able to throw themselves into their jobs,"[7] the story emphasized the fact that religion, like it or not, simply won't go away.

RELIGION IN THE WORKPLACE

Nearly every Establishment Clause scholar notes the overwhelmingly religious nature of the American people. However, they draw very different conclusions from this fact. A strict separationist like Kathleen Sullivan, for instance, argues that spiritual expression and commitment are fostered when government stays out of religion.[8] Thus, a high "wall of separation" between church and state helps religion.[9] Scholars such as Michael McConnell draw the opposite conclusion. For him, the religious orientation of the American people is both a current reality and a historically significant context that requires a lower wall between church and state interaction.[10] Putting to the side which interpretation is more accurate, the point is that there is a strong consensus that the country has a strong religious orientation. Polls regularly substantiate this as well.[11]

A second question is whether this orientation is deep or superficial.[12] Relatedly, some have asked whether being religious makes any difference to one's behavior, particularly in business.[13] While the *Time* article noted religion's empowerment of ethical behavior, sociologist Robert Wuthnow argues that the evidence shows that religious belief makes little difference to the actions individuals take in business.[14] The prevailing ethic, Wuthnow argues, is a sense of honesty interpreted subjectively by the individual person making a decision, so that exceptions to when one must be honest are easily made.[15] Thus, one can conclude that America's religious orientation makes little difference in business.

One can also conclude that there is an implicit "wall of separation" between church and corporation that raises a bar to religious discourse about business issues. Two examples support this interpretation.

First, popular corporate theorist Tom Peters, in discussing spiritually oriented managerial practices, complains: "[W]hen talk turns to the spiritual side of leadership, I mostly want to run. It should be enough if I work like hell, respect my peers, customers and suppliers, and perform with verve, imagination, efficiency and good humor. Please don't ask me to join the Gregorian Chant Club too."[16] This desire to keep corporation and church separated is also supported by a 1988 study indicating that business persons do not see the involvement of clergy as a helpful way to improve the ethical business climate,[17] evidence that demonstrates a certain queasiness among business persons at the blending of religion and work.

Second and more indirectly, Frederick Bird studied the reasons managers give for "doing the right thing" at work.[18] The primary conclusion he drew was that managers are often very reluctant to justify a decision on moral grounds for fear that it will appear "soft" or "weak."[19] In the rough-and-tumble corporate world, one needs to relate one's decisions to self-interest, not moral virtue.[20] If this is true, then it would seem likely that there is also a constraint against making an argument on the basis of "love of neighbor" or "mercy" or "peace" or "religious duty."

Nash recognizes the good that religiously motivated managers can do, but she also says that religiously conservative CEOs have a "blind spot" with regard to the equal treatment of women.[21] The relationship between this blind spot and the power CEOs have wielded over women, power that has resulted in harassment cases, is something that I expand upon in the next subsection. Beyond the issue of the role of women, however, there is also a horror list of bad and ugly things that can happen in the workplace when religion is turned loose. As Terry Dworkin and Ellen Piece write:

> For example, in *Compston v. Borden,* the first case to recognize religious harassment, Compston was continuously referred to both within and outside his presence as a "Jew-boy," "the kike," "the Christ-killer," the "damn Jew," and "the goddam Jew," after casually mentioning to his supervisor that he believed in the basic tenets of Judaism. In a later case, *Weiss v. United States,* Weiss was similarly taunted by a coworker and his supervisor for two years with slurs such as "Jew faggot," "resident Jew," "rich Jew," and "Christ-killer," when they discovered he was Jewish.[22]

In *Meltebeke v. Bureau of Labor and Industries,*[23] the owner of a painting business first told a worker that he was going to hell for living with his girlfriend, then told him that he must be a good Christian to be a good painter, then told him that he only wanted to work with Christians since they would not steal, and finally fired him.[24] In another case, employers held required devotional services during work.[25] The interesting thing about these cases is not that the employers held strong religious beliefs, but that, offering a secular reason for their ethic, they felt that those religious beliefs were good business.

Power and Employee Rights

Because executives in the corporate world have significant authority over those who work for them, their exercise of that power is important for any business ethic. Because religion can be incendiary, and because someone with power could use that power in order to proselytize or embarrass another person, any freedom for religious expression in the workplace must take into account uses of power traceable to someone expressing her religious views. In essence, just as the Establishment Clause prevents government from, among other things, dictating religious belief but does not prevent government from looking at the behavior associated with the belief, so religious freedom in the business world requires similar attention. In particular, the protection of those not in power from being coerced by those with power is analogous to governmental frameworks. This makes comparisons with workplace harassment law worthwhile.

Harassment Analogies

In their review of harassment law, Dworkin and Pierce consider several different rationales for balancing an employer's freedom of religious expression with that of an employee. They reject as inadequate an "animus" standard that would prohibit an employee from making statements and taking actions along the lines of *Compston*.[26] The difficulty, they argue, is that this standard would not protect *Meltebecke* situations where the conduct and/or speech is harassing, but is done by the employer because the employer sincerely believes he or she has an obligation to witness to his or her belief and to correct sinful behavior.[27] Similarly, they reject a "directed speech test"[28] because it likewise gives insufficient protection for an employee who must work in an environment quite hostile to her beliefs, even if statements are not directly targeted toward her.[29] Dworkin and Pierce offer an example of a poster that could create a very hostile environment, more offensive than a private bigoted remark.[30]

Dworkin and Pierce, recognizing a unique status of religion, also reject the transference of a "reasonable victim" standard applied in sexual harassment cases. This is an approach taken in 1993 by the Equal Employment Opportunity Commission in publishing its very controversial, and subsequently withdrawn *Guidelines on Harassment Based on Race, Color, Religion, Gender, National Origin, Age or Disability*.[31] The determination, under the guidelines, of harassing conduct creating a hostile or abusive work environment was to be made according to "whether a reasonable person in the same or similar circumstances would find the conduct intimidating, hostile, or abusive."[32]

Dworkin and Pierce argue that the difficulties with this "reasonable victim" standard are that its vagueness allows for too much discretion by "idiosyncrasies of protected classes" and is "too narrowly drawn to protect the First Amendment rights of the religious.[33] They note that given the results of a sexual harassment case where the mere possession of sexually explicit photographs could create a hostile environment, one could similarly interpret the guidelines as preventing the possession of religious symbols or photographs (such as on one's desk or neck) that would offend another person.[34]

Rather than any of these standards, Dworkin and Pierce propose a "reasonable person" standard, which would determine the harassing nature, if any, of speech or action.[35] This "more objective" (than that of the reasonable victim) in (sexual) harassment cases means, according to the courts, "that 'no ordinary person' would welcome such comments and conduct."[36] Moreover, relying upon its development in tort law, Dworkin and Pierce note that "[t]he reasonableness test is intended to reflect changing social mores as well as to represent an objective standard which imposes the same behavior on everyone, thereby limiting political decision-making by a judge."[37]

Dworkin and Pierce recognize that this standard errs on the side of religious expression.[38] They also argue that religious expressions such as wearing a cross or having a picture of Jesus on one's desk are fundamentally different, under the reasonable person test, than the "girlie pictures" of *Robinson*.[39] While "girlie pictures" are demeaning, they argue, because they portray women as sexual objects rather than workers, the display of religious objects "is not generally seen by the reasonable person as demeaning."[40] Instead, they may be expressions of a person's faith.[41] Moreover, a reasonable person, they argue, is more likely to find expression by a coemployee less intimidating than that by an employer.[42] A reasonable person standard can make this distinction.[43]

The Danger of "The First Man"

These dangers of harassment are real. But there is also danger in the loss of the sense of connectedness and transcendence that religion provides. Consider, for instance, this quote:

> An enormous oblivion spread over them, and actually that was what this land gave out, what fell from the sky with the night over the three men returning to the village, their hearts made anxious by the approach of night, filled with that dread that seizes all men in Africa when the sudden evening descends on the sea, on the rough mountains and the high plateaus, the same holy dread that has the same effect on the slopes of Delphi's mountain, where it makes temples and altars emerge. But on the land of Africa the temples have been destroyed, and all that is left is this soft unbearable burden of the heart.[44]

In this passage from Albert Camus's unfinished novel, *The First Man*, the solitary loneliness, because of the absence of temples and altars, is not only a description of the Africa of which he wrote, but of humanity. As in other works of Camus, the self is alone. The dark absurdity of the

evil-wielding, death-dealing universe gives one no hope for identity beyond that which the individual provides for herself. A commitment to
reduce the suffering of the world is Camus's rational choice by the "first
man" who could, however, have also chosen evil and solitude.

This isolation is neither fictional nor dated. It remains a factor now as
well. Corporate downsizing has left the loyalty of employees unrequited.
Once, an employee's loyalty and commitment to a company provided a
sense of identity and meaning. Today, "[t]hey've got to appreciate their
value apart from the corporation."[45] It is increasingly difficult for individuals to find a sense of long-term identity in corporate America. The
"company man" has become the "first man."

The "first man" and today's "company man" have little reason to seek
the common good. Their notions of the good have been constructed
from the perspective of self-interest: a good that is individually described
and defined. If we are all "first men," what hope do we have for a politics
concerned with communal welfare? What religion does is provide a sense
of connectedness with others and with a transcendent source. As I have
argued, this is an important connection, but one that has to be cautiously
approached because of the harassing behavior it can promote.

THREE APPROACHES TO RELIGION IN
THE WORKPLACE

To claim that religion has only recently begun to engage actively in
questions of business ethics is, of course, to make an absurd statement.
The religions of the world have made business affairs the subject of ethical analysis for thousands of years. In a recent issue of a prominent business ethics journal, Jewish ethicists Ronald M. Green, Elliot N. Dorff,
and Meir Tamari all demonstrate the modern applicability of millennia-
old religious principles to economics.[46] It is a fair guess that many clergy
comment upon economic affairs in their weekly services today. Thus,
one can hardly say that religious institutions and their leaders have been
mute, although it is possible that religious managers have been quiet.

Nevertheless, Stewart Herman is on the mark when he writes that in
the past ten years, the emerging field of business ethics has not heard
much from theologians.[47] Indeed, since Richard DeGeorge's seminal
challenge that religion has little to teach philosophical business ethics,[48]
authors of theological contributions to the field of business ethics have
struggled to emerge.

Given this recent history, there is a concern as to whether religion
ought to be a participant in prescribing normative behavior for business
practices. It is a concern whose dimensions have been developed by
those arguing about the proper role of religion in political matters.

Thus, to explicate why religion should be a participant in developing moral business practices, it is worth recapping the salient features of the religion-politics debate. In that debate, which is concerned with the morality, rather than the constitutionality, of relying upon religious belief in making political choices and in justifying those choices, one can identify, with only moderate oversimplification, three main positions. The next subsection describes the strict exclusionist view. The following subsection describes two attempts at describing a moderate view. The third subsection follows the writings of, to my mind, the most insightful and precise thinker in the field—Michael Perry—whose work places the issue of religion in public life in its most accurate formulation.

The Strict Exclusionist Position

The strict exclusionist position (SEP) states that one should not rely upon religion, at least not to justify one's position on religious grounds. Instead, one should rely on "shared values." This position has taken a variety of forms, but each essentially relies upon the development of a neutral set of moral principles generally excluding direct religious influence on public ethics.

Bruce Ackerman, for instance, attempts to derive what he termed "neutral" legitimate political argument through a three-step process. First, at any time a person exercises power, he must present reasons explaining the exercise. Second, those reasons must be consistent with the reasons uses to justify other uses of power.[49] Third, and most relevant, some reasons should be excluded from public justifications of the use of power; those justifications include religious ones.[50] The reason for excluding religious justifications is that religious reasons suggest that the power holder is "intrinsically superior" to others.[51] Instead of asserting moral superiority "whenever one citizen is confronted by another's question, he cannot suppress the questioner nor can he respond by appealing to (his understanding of) the moral truth; he must instead by prepared, in principle, to engage in a restrained dialogic effort to locate normative premises both sides find reasonable."[52]

The reason my students found the CEO in our class to be so threatening, I suspect, is not that they were horrified that religion had something to say about drug testing. Instead, it was a fear that a person with the power a CEO has could use such religious beliefs in ways that were troubling. Although there was no substantive distinction between his position on drug tests and that of the class, he offered no neutral principles to explain the exercise of his power. While my students seemed very quick—too quick—to stereotype him as a bigot because of his rationale, they were onto an important problem: the exercise of power explained only by religious reasons can be very offensive in a pluralistic society.

Like Ackerman, Thomas Nagel attempts to create an "impartial" language.[53] Nagel argues that the power holder should not attempt to coerce another person on grounds that person can reasonably reject.[54] The difficulty with relying upon religious belief to justify an exercise of power is that the listener is not able to share the religious believer's experience. The believer still has something that the listener does not have. By relying on impartial reasons, however, Nagel argues that one can eliminate this problem.[55]

The difficulty with this shared values approach is that it is both over- and underinclusive. Michael Perry, for instance, has suggested that in many cases, individuals can appreciate experiences even when one party has not had direct, identical experience. He offers the example of a conversation between a drug user and the spouse of a drug user.[56] Neither would have direct experience of what the other "has," but it is likely that they would be able to share a good deal of their experience. Likewise, it may well be true that a nonbeliever may strongly disagree with the believer's account of her experience, but it is another to assume that constructive conversation cannot take place.

It may also well be true that a person who claims that "God has told me to fire any nonbeliever working for me" will be unable to share fully that experience with the fired employee. But not all religious belief is so singularly revelational. A good number of religious believers hold that their belief is rational in whole or in part. Even the CEO in my class, who offered no neutral or impartial principles, could be drawn into a dialogue of what the best way is to love one's neighbor. His religious belief did not dictate method, but a direction and duty. Thus, the SEP school underincludes the ability of individuals to understand differing experience and overincludes all religious belief as belief that is inherently not shareable.

Moreover, it is a fact that many Americans do rely upon religious belief in making decisions that affect others. Michael Perry cites statistics showing that 95 percent of American adults profess belief in God[57] and 70 percent belong to a church or synagogue.[58] As Perry writes, the issue of religion in politics cannot possibly be marginal: "If few Americans were religious believers, the issue of the proper role of religion in politics would probably be marginal to American politics. But most Americans are religious believers. Indeed the citizenry of the United States is one of the most religious—perhaps even the most religious—of the world's advanced democracies."[59]

With religion having such a presence, it seems odd to ask a religious person to compartmentalize her beliefs. When a person does have religious beliefs, one cannot simply compartmentalize them as "private." They are likely to become constitutive elements of a person's entire moral framework. This is why Richard Jones writes that religion "does

not govern only limited areas in the life of the religious—it is not reducible to something exclusively personal or private. Instead, religion is
comprehensive in the sense that all aspects of one's life are related in one
degree or another to this fundamental framework."[60]

Many have made similar claims but have also noted the difficulty in
relying upon religious reasons in public.[61] Because Jones is right to
identify the unrealistic requirement to compartmentalize religious belief, some scholars have developed more moderate positions than that
of the SEP position exemplified by Ackerman and Nagel.

A Moderate Position

John Rawls and Overlapping Consensus

The moderate position takes two forms. In the first form, championed
by John Rawls, religious belief is recognized as an important rationale
for private individuals when they make political choices.[62] In "background" structures such as churches and families, public reason is not
necessary. Rawls, in fact, goes further to recognize that any kind of comprehensive moral position can be important for individual judgment,
but in the liberal democracy of the United States, one must create a
"public reason" for moral discourse. The United States, he argues, is too
diverse to anchor its political judgments on religious or any other comprehensive moral ground. Instead, one ought to derive a public reason
from the overlaps found in the various comprehensive moral positions.
In making arguments in public, one should rely upon the reasons found
in this "overlapping consensus."

Rawls's position certainly gives more room for reliance upon religious belief in "mediating institutions" than can be found in the SEP
school. Nevertheless, there remain several problems with this kind of
approach.

First, public beliefs are still important to believers, so the arguments
against the unrealistic requirement of compartmentalizing one's religious beliefs apply as much to Rawls's position as to Ackerman's and
Nagel's.[63]

Second, one must ask what sustains Rawls's notion of an overlapping
consensus. Religious statements can and have acted as a prophetic de-
nunciation of overlapping consensus. Martin Luther King Jr.'s insistence
on civil rights, for instance, was rooted in religious belief, justified in religious language, and violative of the racist overlapping consensus he
was born into. If one only admits established consensus to public debate, one diminishes the ability of any society to correct itself. Jurgen
Habermas has argued that.[64]

The same holds true in business. Total quality management, for instance, was completely rejected in the United States after World War II.[65] It was not part of any sort of established consensus. Instead TQM theorists such as W. Edwards Deming and Joseph Juran found receptive ears in Japan.[66] It was only after U.S. manufacturing interests, particularly the automotive industry, were being consistently routed by Japanese companies practicing TQM that Americans invited TQM theorists back home. Adopting TQM strategies, including Deming's and Juran's insistence that TQM was a "new religion,"[67] then turned around many companies. The point is that the overlapping consensus eliminates self-correction when it insists upon arguments made within the language and thinking of that consensus.

Of course, Rawls's advice that one should use language that others can find acceptable does have strategic value. One may very well build political coalitions on this basis. But such a reason for excluding religion from public debate is different from determining whether it is fair to rely upon comprehensive beliefs. Because Rawls's position is unrealistic in rejecting that reliance and because it removes an important method of correction, his more moderate position fails for the same reasons as those of Ackerman and Nagel failed.

Kent Greenawalt and Accessible Rationales

A second scholar, Kent Greenawalt, has taken a position more open to religion than Rawls. In his moderate position, one may rely upon religion in making public justifications of one's moral positions, but should refrain from doing so in certain circumstances, for example, when one is influential and when the position amounts to an imposition. The heart of Greenawalt's argument is to recognize (1) that individuals can and should honestly rely upon what motivates their positions but (2) that because religious justifications of public positions can cause social conflict, influential individuals ought to refrain from using such language, except as a last resort, even if hiding one's belief is somewhat deceptive.[68] Although Greenawalt attempts to provide a basis for this distinction on the basis of his "accessible rationales," which he claims are different from "shared values," there is no meaningful difference between the two.[69]

Greenawalt's philosophical distinction is less compelling than his consequentialist argument. Relying upon the work of William Marshall,[70] Greenawalt worries about the unrest that could result if influential individuals justified public positions on the basis of religious belief.[71] One reason Greenawalt says those justifications could cause unrest is because of the notion that religion is essentially private and a decision of individual choice. In terms of business ethics, however, a person's ethical stance, religious or otherwise, is about the treatment of others and therefore can never be private. While belief is undoubtedly a matter of private conscience, the ethical duties derived from such beliefs are, at least to some degree, public. Thus decisions made about politics or business ethics can neither be compartmentalized nor kept private.

It is worth noting that in Greenawalt's definition of who is influential, business executives are included.[72] Since they are in positions of power, the arguments I have provided regarding religion and politics are applicable to their reasons for how they conduct their businesses. Since executives and general counsels often are the ones promulgating ethical codes, they possess the kind of influence that would worry Greenawalt. There are costs, then, to the application of Greenawalt's position to business.

First, it would seem that one cost of becoming influential is to forfeit one's ability to rely upon religious belief. But if one's influence is tied to religious belief, such as that of Martin Luther King Jr., for instance, why should that influence suddenly become illegitimate? Relatedly, of course, the determination of exactly when one becomes influential and therefore required to abandon evidence of faith, is problematic.

Second, Greenawalt assumes, as does the SEP school, that many religious beliefs are essentially nonaccessible and cannot be shared. But keeping important beliefs private can sow as much dissension, mistrust, and hatred as can open dialogue. Greenawalt is wise to note the unrest religious belief can cause, but silence can cause unrest as well. As long as religious belief and, more important, ethics derived from religious belief are viewed as idiosyncratically personal, then dialogue itself becomes problematic. If religious belief is not simply private, then one can conduct debate about it. The only way to conduct such dialogue is to challenge the notion that religion is essentially private.

In spite of these criticisms of any variation of the shared values approach, however, there is an inherent wisdom in requiring that normative positions be justified according to some kind of objective standard. The SEP school and Greenawalt do this by making the standard that of secular justification. But one can acknowledge the need for a standard that is not idiosyncratically personal without eliminating religious belief. This leads to a third school of thought.

Michael Perry's Inclusionist Position

Ecumenical Politics and Full Inclusionism

The position legitimating debate among religions, and among religious and nonreligious belief about normative goods, is the one Michael Perry has adopted. Perry had once advocated a position not dissimilar to Greenawalt, in which Perry argued that one could rely religious belief in making political decisions, provided one presented arguments that were accessible to others, and as long as one acknowledged the possible fallibility of one's position.[73] Perry advocated an "ecumenical politics" in which religious beliefs were admissible rather than being relegated to the side because they were not "neutral." Indeed, Perry's critiques of Ackerman, Nagel, and Rawls are extensive and (more completely than provided herein) make the criticisms laid out to date in this chapter. While it is admissible in public debate, however, Perry recognizes that the dialogue featured by his ecumenical politics required arguments that were accessible and a humility about the fallibility of one's position. As we have seen by the fact that he now recognizes more clearly that individuals with similar but not identical experiences (a drug user and a spouse of a drug user) can "access" each other's experience, Perry's view of accessibility is much now wider than it once was, and wider than we have seen in Greenawalt's position, let alone those of Ackerman, Nagel, and Rawls.

Perry relies more upon the sincerity and authentic good will of the speaker in presenting reasons than on the characterization of those reasons by the listener. Under the SEP schema, if a listener cannot comprehend the descriptions provided, then the position is not accessible and ought not be offered. Under Perry's schema, if the speaker thinks the reasons are reasonable and shareable, then he meets the accessibility standard.

In an interesting later article,[74] Perry scaled back his position to a degree. He argued that his position amounted to one that sought to advocate his kind of religion—one based on dialogue, accessibility, and fallibilism—to the exclusion of religious beliefs that did not value such traits.[75] This seems to have led to a full inclusivist position (FIP), in which he argues that a believer ought to justify her decisions on whatever sincerely motivated the position.[76] Not only does this position have the benefit of honesty, but Perry challenges several deeply held assumptions about the view of religion in politics that are important to understand. Two are particularly important.

First, Perry challenges the notion that by relying upon religious beliefs in justifying political choice, we risk social unrest. Religious differences, he argues, may have resulted in bloodshed hundreds of years ago, but Americans are hardly in that predicament now.[77] As he put it in a still later article (to be discussed in a few paragraphs): "[I]t is implausible to believe that in the context of a liberal democratic society like the United States, governmental reliance on religiously based moral arguments in making political choices (even coercive ones) is *invariably* destabilizing—or that is invariably *more* destabilizing than governmental reliance on controversial secular moral arguments."[78]

A second implicit, but equally important argument, is Perry's confidence in debate. While Greenawalt[79] and Marshall[80] worry about the intolerance religion can perpetrate, Perry worries about religious illiteracy that precludes debate:

> Religious discourse about the difficult moral issues that engage and divide us citizens of liberal democractic societies is not necessarily more problematic—more monological, say—than resolutely secular discourse about those issues. Because of the religious illiteracy—and, alas, even prejudice—rampant among many nonreligious intellectuals, we probably need reminding that, at its best, religious discourse in public culture is not less dialogic—it is not less open-minded and deliberative—than is, at its best, secular discourse in public culture. (Nor, at its worst, is religious discourse more monologic—more closed-minded and dogmatic—than is, at its worst secular discourse.[81]

In Perry' s position, one should permit honest reliance (with some exceptions, such as that of a Nazi sincerely telling a Jew that the Jew is inferior)[82] upon the grounds that motivate an individual taking a moral position. Once made, we then ought to debate the validity of the position. Perry's willingness to engage in such debate is a statement of his confidence in the validity of his positions, on, for instance, abortion and homosexuality.[83] Indeed he not only is willing to allow reliance on religious beliefs in conducting debate, he argues that we ought to encourage it.[84]

Secular Corollaries

In this advocacy for open debate, Perry has continued to describe the ways in which argument can be made. He does not back down from his willingness to allow individuals, even influential ones, to rely on religious reasons for making political choices, but he adds an interesting corollary. That is, one should offer a "secular" argument in addition to the religious argument.[85] Perry gives three reasons supporting this approach.

First, he claims that most religious believers take a secular agreement with a religious position as proof of the validity of the position.[86] In particular, Perry cites Catholics, Episcopalians, Lutherans, Methodists, and Presbyterians as doubting the truth of a religious argument if there is no corresponding secular support.[87] There does not necessarily need to be agreement or consensus among a large group as to the validity of the secular argument, but the believer ought to think that the secular argument is persuasive.[88] The central reason for this position returns Perry to his position on accessibility and, even more importantly, fallibilism:

> [R]eligious believers—even religious believers within the same religious tradition—do not always agree with one another about what God has revealed. Moreover, many religious believers understand that human beings

are quite capable not only of making honest mistakes, but even of deceiving themselves, about what God has revealed—including what God might have revealed about the requirements of human well-being.[89]

It is important to note the ground Perry relies upon to make his argument. It is that of natural law. Because God's revelation is open to all human beings, one can conduct rational argument about what has been revealed by nature.[90] Thus, his second reason for requiring a secular argument is that we all, not just the mainline Christian churches he cites, have the ability to reason to the knowledge of the good.

Even further, Perry describes the "human propensity to be mistaken and even to deceive oneself about what God has revealed" as "ubiquitous."[91] An argument only relying on revelation, that is, one that is unsupported by a secular argument, is one that is particularly vulnerable to manipulation, self-deception, and mistakenness. In short, human fallibility requires a secular argument as a check against these human frailties. Thus, his third argument for considering a secular reason in addition to a religious reason is that our human weakness requires it as a check against self-deception and manipulation.

Perry anticipates a negative reaction against this position from fundamentalists for whom reason itself is corrupted.[92] He makes three key arguments to counter such objections that arise directly out of the above-described rationale. First, because Christians believe that basic requirements for human welfare are inherent in every human being—the natural law position grounded in Romans 2:14–16—one cannot dismiss secular arguments as not having a part of the divine.[93] He confirms this through the work of evangelical scholar Mark Noll, who says that, "Nature is as truly a revelation of God as the Bible, and we only interpret the Word of God by the Word of God when we interpret the Bible by science."[94]

Second—and probably the most controversial position Perry takes—he argues that conservatives must also take into account the fallenness of themselves and, therefore, of religiously based arguments, because both religiously based arguments and secular arguments "are, finally, human arguments."[95]

A third reason is that religious believers have little hope of influencing a liberal democracy unless they do rely on a secular confirmation of their moral position.[96] Noting the work of Richard John Neuhaus, Perry notes that any religion wanting to give witness in this democracy must subject itself to self-critical rationality and must develop a *mediating* language to describe its insights to the larger community.[97]

In both positions, Perry stresses the importance of making accessible arguments and recognizing fallibility, not as restrictive hurdles one must overcome in order to be allowed to speak, but as requisite characteristics for religious belief to be taken seriously. Perry thus creatively uses the criteria of secular arguments as a strategic device to gain influence, and as a check against self-deception, while preserving the full freedom of an individual to rely upon religious belief in justifying a public position.

NATURAL LAW AND BUSINESS ETHICS

The real importance of Perry's position is not that he threads the minute needle of acceptable religious justification for a public position, although that threading is impressive and helpful. The real importance is his claim that religious belief need not be, and in fact becomes suspicious when it is, purely personal and idiosyncratic. If religion can be tied to more objective reality, an argument that I read Perry to be willing to undertake and not merely assume, then its legitimacy as a normative criterion for political, business, and any other kind of public decision grows dramatically. Its accessibility increases and its "debatibility" opens. Because of this, one should not exclude religious belief from business ethics debate from policies or from theories. If a person has a sincerely held religious belief that addresses the propriety of business practices, that belief is as worthwhile and worthy of respect as any other normative belief. The exclusionism advocated by all the described theorists except Perry are not only inapplicable to the political setting, but they are inapplicable to the business setting as well. As opposed to Tom Peters's comment, reliance on religion in managerial decision making does not necessarily lead to requests for singing in the Gregorian Chant Club. But because there is legitimate concern for imposition of religious belief on others, Perry's proposal for a secular, corollary justification to a religious belief is appropriate for any proposed religiously based business ethic.

The ground for Perry's position is natural law. There are, of course, several different kinds of natural law, some religious and some not.[98] These variations of "traditional natural law" attempt to find basic normative principles of conduct through philosophical and/or theological reflection.[99] As I will argue in the following sections, there are understandings of natural law that rely on other sources as well, such as custom and science. However, the important point to note here, which will be developed more fully in the next section, is that the justification of a religious argument that is acceptable in public discourse cannot be predicated on an epistemological understanding of religion as idiosyncratically personal. If it is predicated on such a basis, then it runs great risk of falling prey to accurate assessments by the SEP school and by Greenawalt. It also becomes more likely to be incendiary if a justification for religious belief is simply individual understanding and not something that has at least a secular corollary, if not a corresponding secular justification.

Perry's position allows and even encourages religious believers to offer their insights in public debate. His concern is the political world, but Greenawalt is correct to note that corporate leaders, as influential individuals, are subject to the same concerns that arise when political leaders rely upon religious justifications for making moral and political decisions. In fact, this recognition of the power of corporate leaders is important to consider further.

Corporations, Power, and Religion

The only difficulty in applying Perry's position to the business world consists in the importance of power differentials. In his articles, he contends for an approach that legitimates the use of religious language against those who are in good positions to defend themselves. To argue, for instance, that intellectuals should be free to rely upon religion in making political arguments, or that legislators should, or that judges should—even if such reliance does also have a secular corollary—is to describe a dialogue in which the person not relying on religion, or relying on a religion different from one who has power, and who is relying on religious belief in making her argument, is probably capable of defending herself. Further, when the religious person is making a decision that has coercive consequences, if she is not relying on religious belief, she will have recourse to mechanisms of correction. That is, given Perry's emphasis upon religious pluralism as a check against any one religion or any one religious belief from becoming too powerful or spawning bloodshed, someone not happy with a religiously justified political choice has ready access to political resources to overturn a decision.

Perry is not unmindful of the importance of power differentials. But because the debate in which he is engaged in the academic or jurisprudential world largely rejects the use of religious language, his argument is not really addressed to the situation where a religious believer is in a position of power, and the person, whether a believer or nonbeliever who does not rely upon religious justifications, and perhaps finds such justifications offensive, is in a position of little power. This, however, is exactly the situation an employee could find himself in if a corporate ethics policy was adopted by corporate executives who seek to integrate religious belief in policies.

In the arguments of the SEP school and Greenawalt, there is a concern that the religious person will be a power holder whose actions could be detrimental to someone without power. Thus, they are concerned with the coercive impact of the exercise of this power. Without a standard of accessibility,[100] neutrality,[101] public reason,[102] or impartiality,[103] the stage could be set for abuse of power by those religious persons who have no checks placed upon them.

The concern can be more acute in the corporate world than the political world. In business, the chief executive officer often holds the role of king of a fiefdom.[104] Not only can this structure undermine a requirement for the rational explanation of a position that seems to acquire or retain power, as would be the case in a democracy, but the corporate world has far fewer checks to reign in an executive who views the workplace as fertile grounds for evangelizing. Indeed, the temptations of power explain executive action that leads to unethical behavior in the form of, for instance, harassment and excessive compensation, as well as actions that provide personal prestige without regard to economic performance.[105] In short, while the corporate world is freer from constitutional restrictions concerning religion than is the political process, its structure also poses more acute questions regarding the use of power.

Perry's proposal for accessibility depends upon a structure that makes accountable actions that must be explained in accessible terms. His requirement for fallibility may be less pronounced in a corporate structure that is not democratic. Thus, in addition to Perry's proposal of offering a secular reason for an action in addition to a religious one, the corporate world requires a proviso that cautions the power holder to accord an employee the same ability to rely on religious justifications. In addition to accessibility, one must also equalize power, at least to some extent, so that the exercise of corporate power is not harassing.

Many, perhaps most, issues in business will not be ones in which one must make judgments about the moral propriety of an action. But many will be moral judgments. In particular, given the fact that 95 percent of Americans hold a belief in God, one should not then be surprised that at the place where a very large part of their waking hours is spent—at work—religious beliefs should have an important role to play in defining what ethical business is.

THE DANGER OF PHILOSOPHICAL
AND LEGAL RULES

Nearly forty years ago, Jacques Ellul wrote a small book, *The Theological Foundation of Law*,[106] in which he makes an argument about law, religion, and politics that is directly relevant to the present impulse for corporate codes.[107]

Ellul describes his approach as one based on natural law, but his notion of natural law is entirely different from that relied upon by Perry and that typically used by natural law scholars.[108] Traditional natural law, Ellul argues, fails because it attempts to provide a meeting ground between Christians and non-Christians,[109] an effort analogous to the secular arguments proviso advocated by Perry. Instead, Ellul conceives of natural law as a specific event within a culture's history during which moral conduct spontaneously or naturally is understood without appeal to refined principles of analysis. Indeed, the need for refined principles indicates a deeply troubled culture.

I do not wish to follow Ellul's argument in whole. But there is an important kernel of truth within it that business ethicists ought to consider, particularly when the demand for preciseness is most acute, as it is when religious belief enters the picture. Thus, it is worth sketching the four-part development of law in Ellul's schema.[110]

The Four-Part Typology and the Need for Spontaneity

In its origin, Ellul argues, all law is religious.[111] A priest or shaman acts as the spokesperson for God or the gods and acts as the spokesperson for articulating the divine requirements for the particular village, tribe, or community.[112] At this point, there is no differentiation between religious and political power; they are one and the same.[113]

Gradually, the political and religious realms become separate. There is a political power independent from those individuals who are responsible for the spiritual welfare of the community.[114] According to Ellul, this is the point where natural law emerges. There is still a uniformity of custom that unites the attitudes of the people toward right and wrong, but there is no imposition by political authority of what that right and wrong might be.[115] Law is not directed by the state nor by the religious institution in toto, but comes from the common consciences of the people.[116]

Ellul has particular historical moments in mind when he describes this stage, but his point is accessible in contemporary terms as well. Custom is a powerful driver of morality. It is unlegislated and may very well not have any precise articulation by a religious institution, but people naturally understand that one should not, for instance, roll a bowling ball down the aisle of a funeral home when a funeral is in process, or throw rotten tomatoes at a professor during a lecture (at least one hopes so). Even if such behavior could be deemed a disturbing of the peace, the reason one refrains from such activities is not to stay out of legal trouble, but not to violate unspoken community norms. Indeed, in business, one of the first things one must learn when joining a company is what the local customs are.

Thus, Ellul's point is not simply historical but stands for the entirely reasonable idea that many, perhaps most, of the more important normative regulators of behavior are exactly those that are not precisely specified. But Ellul does not stop here. Instead he goes much further and becomes much more controversial.

In stage 3, law becomes more rationalized and theorized. Here, scholars begin to reflect on the customs that have guided the relevant community and attempt to rationally articulate the defensible, consistent principles that can be applied in the future to similar cases.[117] Ellul cites fourth-century B.C.E. Greece, first-century B.C.E. Rome, and eighteenth-century England and Germany as examples of this stage.[118] The danger of this stage, according to Ellul, is that law ceases to become something that is part of one's life and instead becomes something outside of one's life.[119] It is external to one's way of life; one has a weaker connection to it.

One reason this analysis and formalization may occur is because of religious diversity, where the underlying ideas of what is right and wrong have been undermined by differing conceptions of the good. For instance, I have elsewhere argued that eighteenth-century Connecticut exemplifies Ellul's argument. There, the effects of the Great Awakening and Second Great Awakening undermined what had previously been a population with a very uniform religious approach.[120] With a more diverse understanding of what was required by God, one could not rely on custom, but needed more precise principles of law.[121] Business, of course, prefers such specificity to chaos because it allows for planning. And that economic pressure, in combination with diversity and the quest for power, leads to Ellul's final stage.

In stage 4, the law is corrupted because it loses its connection between its logic and the lives of people. This occurs, according to Ellul, when the law is solely the creation of the state, because the law can then be manipulated by those with the power to interpret it or legislate it for their advantage. Those with money can pay for the best and brightest jural talent to bend the law to designs most appropriate for commercial interests.

One need not go so far as to make this development into a planned conspiracy.[122] Ellul's fourth stage need not, in fact probably is not one of intentional design. More likely, it is the logical result of a time in a culture's history when the normative rules are the object of study rather than that of custom. They have become precise.

One need only look to the lobbyists in the halls of Congress to see evidence of laws that are implemented with very little popular involvement. The U.S. Tax Code, one piece of legislation that applies to nearly everyone and which is nearly impenetrably obtuse, even for the experts,[123] has little to do with the experience of justice in everyday life which is one reason why it is so despised. It is difficult to explain why in estate taxation, the right of a spouse to spend the interest of trust principal for himself qualifies the trust for a marital deduction creating no tax, while the right of the same spouse to withdraw income for his daughter disqualifies the trust and subjects to it estate taxation.[124]

It is when the law is so abstracted from everyday life that respect for law is undermined. Law is then simply a game played by those with the resources to influence its drafting, implementation, and interpretation. Similarly, a corporate code of ethics that is long, detailed, and precise still may not provide specificity, because no one reads it. Philosophical principles that require extensive analysis of complex social factors may likewise be dismissed as having little to do with the experience of work life, no matter how brilliant they may be.

Ellul's Natural Law and Business Ethics

Natural law, as Ellul conceives it, is thus not a set of basic principles that specify what is appropriate, but a spontaneous understanding of what one ought to do. Its very elusiveness, at least in rational terms, is that which is part of its vibrancy. The danger, of course, is a sort of know-nothingness that rejects sophisticated analysis of any kind. But this is true only if one takes Ellul's typology to an extreme. There are more moderate interpretations of the kernel of truth his schema exposes.

In terms of business ethics and corporate codes, this spontaneous natural law is that aspect of working life that is not specified by philosophical or legal principles. The need for spontaneity suggests two things. First, issues of ethical business conduct are not so much about fine-grained analysis but about a corporate culture that inculcates certain behavior on a regular basis. Second, corporate codes and standards of ethical behavior ought not be alien to the experience of those who work in the company. If it is true that Americans have a strong religious dimension, then ethical principles that do not resonate with that experience violate the "lived" experience of which Ellul writes. For this reason, principles of business ethics can follow Perry's proposal of offering secular arguments, but such arguments should not stray too far from the experience, even if religious, of business persons.

There are many points where I do not wish to follow Ellul. For instance, I am unwilling to accept the notion that the clear articulation of ethical principles is an inevitably slippery slope to legal corruption. It may be a slippery slope to the ethics for a particular community, but communities inevitably grow into different shapes and forms. That which prevents the forms from settling disputes through warfare is likely to be an approach featuring negotiation, dialogue, and the working out of common principles. Such dispute resolution often requires clear articulation of principles that have been forgotten, half-remembered, or selfishly manipulated.

Nevertheless, there is an important point here: ethics is not only about precise legal rules or philosophic principles, but needs to connect with an affective side of human nature.[125] An affective side is not always, and may rarely be, describable in precise, rational, and logical terms, but is anchored in elusive elements of love, friendliness, spontaneity, reciprocity, forbearance, and solidarity. Indeed, one of the most important contributions religion can make to business ethics is the engagement of this affective side. It is that side that often makes people want to be ethical, a topic poorly addressed by business ethics scholars.

Whether Ellul's typology is a fully accurate history of law and religion I put to the side. It does demonstrate an important point whose truthfulness can be seen in the way citizens react to the laws of their government. The more bureaucratic abstract rules become, and the less people participate in the rules governing them, the less compelling the principles behind the rules will be. This is true not only of tax law, but of the ethical principles corporations use to inspire ethical behavior.

If business ethics turns into extensive corporate codes and policies that are difficult to read and interpret, and which employees do not have a share in developing, they set the stage for an ineffectual program. If business ethics is about refined philosophical principles, they will also be ineffectual. Both legal codes and business ethics theory may be helpful for the development of the field in general, but to be effective, both law and ethics must engage individuals on how the rules enable them to have a more fulfilling life. In short, they must interact with why people would want to be ethical. And one very important reason for wanting to be ethical is because of religious conviction.

Why Be Ethical? The Religious Component

There are really four reasons why a person in business would want to be ethical. The first is simply that, to some degree, the law requires it. In addition to the provisions of the Federal Sentencing Guidelines, legislatures have enacted a variety of consumer, environmental, and labor laws that insist that the law will punish business when it harms consumers, the environment, and employees. So obedience to the law is one rationale for restraining corporate profitability.

A second reason is that it can be good business. As LaRue Hosmer has effectively argued, trust depends upon a perception that one has been treated fairly, and such treatment is dependent upon being ethical.[126] Once one gains trust, one can build better relationships with creditors, the community, and employees.[127] Ethics, in other words, can be an effective business strategy.

In their thoughtful critique of Hosmer's work, Bill Shaw and John Corvino state, but themselves do not adopt, the classic philosophical conundrum that prevents solid analysis of another reason a person might want to be ethical. As Shaw and Corvino put it, to ask the question Why be ethical? is to pose the tautological question Why should I be as I should be?[128] Because I should be ethical, then I need no further motivation; indeed asking for it would in a sense be illogical.[129] Business ethicists generally do not go to this extreme in explaining this third reason for being ethical. Their unwillingness to probe further behind why a person should want to be honest, loyal, fair, and so on breaks the link between the actual lives of individuals working in business and the principles, often quite good ones, offered by ethicists. Nearly every business ethicist can relate many instances of students and executives asking why they ought to bother with being ethical. And after one has exhausted the legal and good business reasons, there is not much left.

At least there is not much left unless one brings in the fact that many will want to be ethical because of their religious convictions. Religion helps to address the "Why be moral?" question.[130] This fourth reason for wanting to be ethical then draws us directly to what benefits and costs accrue to a business that attempts to be ethical, but does so out of, at least in part, religious conviction. This was the case with the CEO in my class.

In short, because it is necessary to engage an affective spirit in order to be ethical, one must offer more than legal or economic reasons. One may also find that one will want to be ethical for religious reasons. Helping such a person be ethical requires that any corporate code or business ethics policy interface with the experience of the person, which may very well be religious.

I do not wish to argue that every business person is religious and thereby make an argument that the refusal to engage religious experience is fatal to business ethics. Such an argument would be absurd. But it is not absurd to note that religious conviction may foster ethical behavior, and that many workers and managers will evaluate corporate codes and their commitment to such codes according to (an often held) experience connected with religion.

11

Bright Dots, Dot Coms, and Camelot?

A law was made a distant moon ago here
July and August cannot be too hot
And there's a legal limit to the snow here
In Camelot.[1]

David Messick has proposed an account of evolutionary altruism bolstered by contemporary findings in social psychology. In this book, I have essentially embraced a significant portion of Messick's methodology. Rather than being tepid about his methodology, I hope I have shown that a naturalist approach is a strong ally for philosophical business ethics and has potential for substantive reconfiguration of corporate governance structures that take advantage of aspects of human nature in order to construct organizations that foster ethical business behavior.

At the heart of my argument is an acceptance of Messick's readily supportable observation that human beings categorize others (including themselves) into "in-groups" and "out-groups"[2] and that such a grouping tendency need not be genetic or biological.[3] Indeed, the determining reason for grouping could be bright "dots on noses."[4] In other words, the criteria we use to count some as "us" and others as "them" could be anything. As long as these "dots" do not also sit so heavily on our eyelashes[5] so as to blind us to the human ability to modify, to some extent, our biology, naturalist business ethics can point to a corporate governance structure where ethical business behavior is enhanced.

ETHICS AND EVOLUTION

Messick asks how natural selection might have shaped human beings' willingness to offer self-sacrificial help to others.[6] In evolutionary terms, this altruistic aspect[7] of our human nature must be related to the fitness of a population if the population is to survive. Thus, Messick argues that two constraints, efficiency and discrimination, must be present.[8] If a behavior is not efficient, then it will be eliminated through natural selection.[9] The other aspect, discrimination, is at the heart of Messick's argument, however, because the question for ethics is whether a human tendency to categorize can be manipulated so as to be "fit" while not being nasty and brutish.

Messick argues that one might take altruistic acts pursuant to the discriminatory criterion of "kin." This rather deterministic kind of categorization, however, is not the only one. Messick notes that Robert Trivers demonstrated that provided there was a community where promises can be enforced and where reputation is valuable, nonrelated individuals are better off (i.e., more fit) to perform some level of altruism even when they are not related to the beneficiaries of the act.[10] The important point is that categorizations need not be, and often are not, based on race, gender, or geography. The reason for determining who belongs to an in-group, and therefore a person for whom one might perform altruistic acts, could be nothing more than "a dot on the nose."[11] This means that there is some malleability regarding what we discriminate in favor of or against. In Bill Frederick's terminology, human beings have a natural "technosymbolic" ability to reconstruct, redesign, and (within limits) modify natural tendencies; we are not slaves to biology.[12]

In this book I have tried to recognize certain naturalist limitations to what we as human beings can do and to also note that the study of human history and human nature gives clues for organizational arrangements conducive to fostering ethical business behavior. At the same time, one of the characteristics of our humanity is that, as Donna Wood argues, we are "creatures of living spirit [and] as symbol users, as people of will, we can choose the attributes we think are necessary for survival. We can choose *not* to use race or sex as discriminators."[13] Because of this capacity, as I have argued, we are able to shape our corporate governance structures in order to make work environments more participatory and where we can foster virtue by connecting experience with principles. We can enhance communication, and we can design structures that model natural law notions of checks and balances in order to inhibit abusive behavior. Doing so takes advantage of both a natural capacity to create and our natural limitations. Moreover, as creatures of spirit, we leave out a considerably important rationale for ethical business behavior if we exclude religious belief from the workplace. Even if ethicists are concerned about the dangers religion may bring to the workplace, one can integrate stakeholder, contract, and virtue thinking in the workplace by creating mediating institutions in the workplace.

Although stakeholder theory may be broad, a mediating limitation to primarily consider and give voice to the interests of shareholders and employees would provide an effective broadening of stakeholder concerns while also being practicable. Social contract theory may provide a viable model for allowing for communal diversity subject to overarching norms, but can be strengthened by a more precise understanding of what a community most importantly is (a mediating institution); it can also be subject to a robust notion of overarching norms tied to nature itself. Virtue theory provides the explanation for our moral development both individually and structurally when linked to a mediating specification of what constitutes the relevant community in which virtue flourishes. Thus, what the business as mediating institution approach provides is a way to articulate a practical convergence of the leading theories of business ethics in a way that can give rise to a practicable legal regime fostering ethical business behavior.

The anthropological findings noted in this book substantiate Messick's point that the ingrouping tendency is not necessarily one of sexism and racism. It may be more benign in terms of our cognitive ability to process large numbers of relationships. In fact, there may be more likelihood for moral business practices if corporations are structured in relatively small, autonomous subgroups that can be called mediating institutions. If so, this suggests an important way for business ethics to proceed in suggesting corporate governance structures that foster ethical business behavior.

Edwin Hartman suggests that a difference between his critique and Messick's approach is one of principles versus virtue.[14] Certainly, to the extent that one is comparing abstract, evolutionary principles of altruism and discrimination to concrete, communal human virtues, Hartman rightly notes their incommensurability. I have suggested in this book, however, that the insight regarding small numbers allows contemporary business ethics to blend principles and virtue. Aristotle, after all, was both philosopher and biologist. He argued that human beings are by nature social and political and have certain natural impulses.[15] A thinking, speaking, and altruistic nature would be a human nature receptive to the importance of treating others in one's community well.[16] For our purposes, the interesting point is that the *natural* human ability to think, to create, to categorize, and to symbolize is an adaptive evolutionary

characteristic made efficacious and moral through a community's education of individuals. The difficulty, however, arises if one's community
becomes so large that the individual is unable to understand the meaning of one's actions.

In small organizations, however, individuals have more direct relationships with others in the community and have more relative power
vis-à-vis the community's normative structure. In a group of 150, one
generally has more relative power than if the community is 250 million.
Further, in a small organization, one cannot escape the consequences of
one's actions. One has to live with them because those actions affect
others with whom one is in direct contact. Thus in these small institutions, individuals have habits formed by their communities and have a
relatively more empowered position from which they can exercise their
choices.

Such institutions are, in fact, mediating structures.[17] They are the
relatively small places where moral identity is formed through face-to-
face interactions with others. Such structures have a communal identity.
They also provide the place for the development of moral identity because one must deal with the consequences of one's actions rather than
having those actions disappear into an amorphous megastructure (the
recipe, by the way, for embezzlement).

These groups exhibit Messick's in-grouping tendency, but they do so
because of our limited ability to process relationships. Institutions such
as the Montana Freemen or a city gang also have a very troubling side.
Might technology help mitigate this aspect? Might it be possible to have
just one in-group in which no discrimination would be tolerated? Given
technological advances, one should not rule anything out. If, however,
the in-grouping tendency is a result of neural ability, then one should
have grave worries about the technology that might literally play around
with our heads. It is not clear that technologies such as the Internet extend our ability to identify with others as much as they rearrange the individuals with whom we do identify. More important, technology or no
technology, there are three ways in which we might create a new, inclusive in-group.

First, we might acknowledge that we already live in an inclusive in-
group by examining the extent to which our very lives and those of our
children depend upon ecological responsibility. Given the diversity of
humankind, it is not clear exactly what normative principles might arise
from this recognition, but even a Spinozoan, universal connecting force
would be a good start.[18] For most religions, after all, the first step in normative knowledge is the recognition of a transcendent reality.[19]
Whether identified as religious or not, ecological interconnectedness is
a step in this direction.

Second, we can study cultures to determine what rules are consistently adopted in communities. If one finds repeated normative rules, they may suggest an evolutionary adaptiveness that is universal. This seems, in part, the role of hypernorms in Tom Donaldson and Tom Dunfee's work.[20]

Third, we can build on the insights of Messick, Wood, and Hartman. If we are creatures of spirit and will and if we can redesign rules and if our nature for in-groups is not based on sexism or racism but instead on neural abilities, then the law can play a role in counteracting these frailties. Simply put, corporate law may not be able to help create one in-group, but it may be able to encourage people to reconsider who is in their in-group and thereby blur distinctions otherwise made on the basis of race, gender, and geography.

Antidiscrimination laws, for instance, can require us to deal with those different from us in terms of race and gender as an incident of our small number. To balance the meaningfulness of ethical rules with regulation of the hostility small groups can exhibit to outsiders, the Federal Sentencing Guidelines (to take just one example), could be modified so that these small groups are given a level of autonomy to create the rules appropriate for them in exchange for a clear articulation of the "aims" of the group that are subject to regulation. This kind of clarity is akin to Messick's recommendation regarding hiring criteria and also may allow for a joining of Kantian principles and communal virtues along the lines proposed by Joshua Margolis.[21] Kantian principles, such as dignity "discipline the mind in observance of duty."[22] Thus, while Kant may never be squared with Darwin, Kant and Aristotle might be linked to argue for mediating institutions that nurture communal virtue while remaining accountable to the outside world.

Corporate constituency statutes could be limited so as to place a tighter focus on what constitutes a community (i.e., internal constituents of a corporation), rather than creating a stakeholder understanding of corporate life so broad that it short-circuits our ability to deal with its requirements. Rather than making managers accountable to all stakeholders, it may be efficacious to make them accountable to internal constituents such as shareholders and employees, whose voice could be heard on a regular basis, and who in fact might also serve as proxies for other stakeholders.

As a way to encourage corporate mediating institutions to "flirt" with the outside world, tax laws could provide corporate deductions for adoption of core not-for-profit groups (such as schools, homeless centers, and hospices) that are extraneous to the purposes of the corporate subgroup itself. A corporate subgroup would not be required to consider this kind of social responsibility, but (in a virtue ethics strategy) such corporate policies would reward this kind of behavior.

Thus, the identification of naturalist categorization tendencies can be used to ethical advantage. The ideas sketched in this book suggest the practical legislation that might be available for creating the organizational structures that will foster ethical business behavior using evolutionary and anthropological insights. It is indeed hubris to think that we can discard 99 percent of our human history in the development of our contemporary economic and political megastructures. Recognizing that our in-grouping tendencies are the result of our anthropology does not doom us to tribalism, sexism, or racism. Instead, the recognition is important knowledge that might allow for a business ethics with insight and efficacy.

ETHICS IN AN E-COMMERCE AGE

In the millennium issue of *Business Ethics Quarterly,* senior scholars looked to the issues confronting business and business ethics. There was a good deal of discussion of globalization and integration. Of course, the e-commerce age must deal with issues of privacy (both within the workplace and in the collection of marketing data), fraud, pornography, and even charges of a new form of colonialism.[23] More than one commentator has glibly equated the "www" of the World Wide Web to the Wild Wild West.[24] Some of the more interesting attempts to get a handle on the changes the Internet makes to the economic, political, and moral landscape are in comparisons of the Internet to the building of the transcontinental railroad, where a new method of moving things linked previously unlinkable places with breathtaking speed while upsetting previously existing order.[25]

Although the notion of mediating institutions may sound nostalgic, the e-commerce age will need them if we are to foster ethical behavior. If I am anywhere close to being right about the need for communities to foster ethical behavior, then building the communal structures in the e-commerce age is a necessary step for business ethics. Noting and combating violations of privacy and incidents of fraud are also necessary, of course, but if individuals are to take ethical responsibilities seriously then business ethicists, particularly those with either organizational or legal skills, need to attend to how the character of those individuals are formed. Corporate governance proposals, such as the one I have made in this book, are one step in that direction, but my proposal is only one. While fostering internal interdependencies is necessary, there is much to do in creating a sense of interdependence outside of the corporation as well.

In making proposals for these additional structures, I offer the notion of mediating institutions as a template. I do so because I think it takes the best of the best business ethics thinking and links it to empirical realities. I also offer it because I think it provides a way to reach another goal that ought to become a serious consideration among ethics in a globalized, technologically driven age of business. That goal is how business relates to peace.

One of the justifications used for globalized business is that trade fosters peace. Phil Nichols has written that countries that trade are less likely to go to war.[26] Anthropologist Lawrence Keeley is less optimistic, noting that historically those with whom any group trades is also the group with whom one is mostly like to go to war.[27] To prevent trade from erupting into war, Keeley suggests that it is important to "treat trading partners with special care since they are our most likely enemies" and to "create largest social, economic and political units possible ideally encompassing the whole world, rather than allowing those we do have to fragment into mutually hostile ethnic or tribal enclaves."[28]

It would seem that global business will provide the means for communication and economic integration of the world, a step that may help to mitigate some tribal rivalry. Nevertheless, it is not the tribal that causes warfare, but a certain kind of tribalism. In his study of nonviolent socieites, anthropologist David Fabbro notes the following attributes that are present in peaceful societies: small and open communities with face-to-face interpersonal interactions; an egalitarian social structure; generalized reciprocity; social control and decision making through group consensus; and nonviolent values and enculturation.[29]

I discovered Fabbro's list long after writing the vast majority of the text of this book. The interesting thing about his list is that the characteristics are virtually identical to my description of mediating institutions, at least those with a normative character. A central task for business ethicists is to figure out how to create these structures in an age dominated by a technology and an economic model that shrinks the world. It is in this combination of mediating institutions in a global village where business ethics will find the significance of its work in linking justice and business to sustainable peace.

FINALLY

Ten years ago, I wrote an op-ed piece for the *Chicago Tribune*. At the time, the notion of business as mediating institution was not even one I had considered. In retrospect, however, the notion provides the answer to the questions I posed and the structure for the solution I desired when I wrote the piece. I conclude, then, with a slightly modified reprise of that piece.

Shortly after World War II, the French writer Albert Camus wrote one of his great novels, *The Plague*. It told the frightening story of the town of

Oran, which had been held hostage by the bubonic plague. Because of the plague, the town was cut off from the rest of the world; no one entered or left Oran.

The heroes of Camus's story were not glamorous. They were the doctor, the town clerk, and others who simply struggled to do their jobs as best they could with no headlines, thanks, or praise. Camus's story was a metaphor for his view of the world, in which evil could not be conquered but where a person could struggle against it.

A less dramatic but perhaps more insidious threat confronts us in business ethics. Ethical lapses are not hard to document, whether they be insider trading, embezzlement, or environmental degradation. They have reawakened the periodic demand that the mess get cleaned up.

Who does the cleaning up? Who deals with the plague of ethical misconduct?

Politicians try by enacting new laws. Prosecutors try by sharpening legal weapons like the Federal Sentencing Guidelines. Schools try by putting ethics courses into the curriculum. Religion tries by recalling the truth of sacred wisdom. The press tries by exposing the "bad guys." Many others make worthy attempts as well.

Such efforts are good and should be commended, although any attempt to punish others has inherent dangers of excessiveness that should always be monitored. A crusade for ethics could lead to a new McCarthyism for the new millennium. The greater danger, though, is that well-intentioned crusaders, and the public, will become disillusioned when the plague does not surrender unconditionally.

The struggle for ethics in society is a battle of human nature, not simply the product of the "greedy eighties" or "rich nineties." The materialism of the last part of the twentieth century may have loosened the restrictions on the seamy side of human nature, but it certainly did not cause it. To think that we can simply construct an ethical society in response to these problems is, as Friedrich Hayek said in a slightly different context, a fatal conceit. If we measure the efforts of these well-intentioned crusaders in terms of whether unethical behavior is eradicated, we will ultimately become frustrated and disillusioned when another round starts.

By what standard should we determine whether we have dealt successfully with our plague? How do we fight the battle against unethical behavior? How do we motivate people to ethical behavior without overreaching our ability to produce?

We do it by the same method Camus described in Oran. We struggle against unethical behavior, we do our job (however mundane) the best we can, and we maintain our own integrity against the evil. We do this by offering a competing vision to the one Camus showed us in Oran. Our vision is one of Camelot. Not the misty-eyed dreaminess of a place where there is a limit to the snow, but one where we see the vision of peace and justice through an organization where power is shifted from the hands of a king to those around a table.[30]

That method may not grab headlines, but it will prove effective in the long run. Our goal must not be to change everyone, but to be an example to the person working next to us. Who will clean up the mess? Every one of us.[31] And for each of us to have a chance to contribute, to influence the person around us, and to be accountable for our actions, we must work in a corporate mediating institution.

Notes

1. Touchstones

1. This story is used with permission of my former client on the condition that names be withheld.

2. See generally, Peter Berger & Richard John Neuhaus, *To Empower People: The Role of Mediating Structures in Public Policy* (1977). Berger and Neuhaus's work will be central to the discussion of chapter 2.

3. Oliver Wendell Holmes, *The Common Law* (Mard Dewolfe Howe ed., 1963). For an interesting theological commentary on this aspect of Holmes's thought, see, James T. Butchaell, *Philemon's Problem: The Daily Dilemma of the Christian* 66 (1973).

4. See John Hasnas, "The Normative Theories of Business Ethics: A Guide for the Perplexed," 8 *Bus. Ethics Q.* 19, 31 (1998).

5. Ian R. MacNeil, "Contracts: Adjustment of Long-Term Economic Relations Under Classical, Neoclassical, and Relational Contract Law," 72 *Nw. U. L. Rev.* 854 (1978).

6. Timothy L. Fort, "Trust and Law's Facilitation Role," 34 *Am. Bus. L.J.* 205 (1997), noting Ian R. MacNeil, *Contracts: Exchange Transactions and Relations* 181–209 (2d ed. 1978).

7. Steven R. Salbu, "Law and Conformity, Ethics and Conflict: The Trouble with Law-Based Conceptions of Ethics," 68 *Ind. L.J.* 101, 112–14 (1992).

8. Id. at 110 n.42.

9. See Jacques Ellul, *The Theological Foundation of Law* (1960). For an application of Ellul's critique of precise rules in business, see Timothy L. Fort, "Mediating Law and Religion in the Workforce Naturally," 12 *Notre Dame J.L. Ethics. & Pub. Pol'y.* 121 (1998).

10. Id. at 19.

11. Id.

231

12. Id.

13. Steven R. Salbu, "The Decline of Contract as a Relationship Management Form," 46 *Rutgers L. Rev.* 1271, 1295–96 (1995).

14. Id. at 1296.

15. Id. at 1297.

16. Id.

17. Id. at 1298.

18. Id.

19. Id. at 1303.

20. Id. at 1303–04.

21. Tom Chappell, *Soul of a Business: Managing for Profit and the Common Good* 61–62 (1993).

22. Robbin Derry, "The Mother-Child Paradigm and Its Relevance to the Workplace," 38 *Bus. & Soc.* 217 (1999).

23. Id. at 218.

24. Id. at 222, commenting of William Frederick's allusion to Virginia Held. Derry elaborates on the Held position in integrating with Frederick's work. Much more will be said about Frederick throughout the course of this book.

25. Id. at 223.

26. William Damon, "The Moral Development of Children," *Sci. Am.* 73 (Aug. 1999).

27. Salvador Minuchin & H. Charles Fishman, *Family Therapy Techniques* 11 (1981).

28. Id. at 11–27.

29. Jeffrey Nesteruk, "Reimagining the Law," 9 *Bus. Ethics Q.* 603, 606–07 (1999).

30. Id. at 604.

31. Id. at 611–15.

32. This story is used with permission of my former client on the condition that names are withheld.

2. Some Catholic Notions

1. Infra chapter 4.

2. See Louis Fischer, *The Life of Mahatma Gandhi* 129 (1950). I make some interpretation to support this claim. In the cited material, Fischer indicates the closeness of Gandhi's ashram and reports that Gandhi said that all India was his family. In the context of Gandhi's decision to live in the ashram as a place of egalitarian simplicity, it seems a fair interpretation to claim that the ashram experience was the daily experience of solidarity that Gandhi also applied to his politics.

3. Pope John Paul II, *Sollicitudo Rei Socialis* United States Catholic Conferences, (Washington, D.C.) (1988), para. 38.

4. LaRue Tone Hosmer, *Moral Leadership in Business* 78 (1994).

5. Id.

6. Id. at 78–79.

7. Peter Berger & Richard John Neuhaus, *To Empower People: The Role of Mediating Structures in Public Policy* 2 (1977).

8. Charles Hampden-Turner, *Creating Corporate Culture: From Discord to Harmony* 58–59 (1990).

9. William Byron, "Core Principles of Catholic Social Thought," *America*, October 31, 1998, at www.americapress.org/articles/Byron.htm.

10. John Paul, supra note 3.

11. Byron, supra note 9.

12. Meir Dan Cohen, "Between Selves and Collectivities: Toward a Jurisprudence of Identity," 61 *U. Chi. L. Rev.* 1213 (1994).

13. Robert G. Kennedy, "God's Project: A Catholic Vision of Business," Presentation at 3d Annual John F. Henning Conference (March 5, 1999) (manuscript, at 7–8, on file with author).

14. Id. at 3.

15. Alexis De Tocqueville, *Democracy in America* 131 (Phillips Bradley ed., 1945).

16. Robert A. Nisbet, *The Quest for Community: A Study in the Ethics of Order and Freedom* 50 (1990).

17. John Haughey, S.J., *The Holy Use of Money: Personal Finance in Light of the Christian Faith* 3–6 (1986).

18. James T. Burtchaell, c.s.c., *Philemon's Problem: The Daily Dilemma of the Christian* 101 (1973).

19. Nisbet, supra note 16, at 255–56.

20. Iwao Taka, "Business Ethics: A Japanese View," 4 *Bus. Ethics Q.* 53 (1994).

21. Robert N. Bellah, Richard Madsen, William M. Sullivan, Ann Swidler, & Steven M. Tipton, *The Good Society* 92 (1991).

22. Patricia H. Werhane, *Adam Smith and His Legacy for Modern Capitalism* 113 (1991).

23. F. A. Hayek, *The Fatal Conceit* 136–37 (1988).

24. Juliet B. Schor, The Overworked American: The Unexpected Decline of Leisure 27–48 (1992).

25. Berger & Neuhaus, supra note 7, at 2.

26. Id. at 3.

27. Id. at 34.

28. Richard B. Madden, "The Larger Business Organization as Mediating Structure," in *Democracy and Mediating Structures: A Theological Inquiry* (Michael Novak ed., 1980).

29. Id. at 110–11.

30. Richard John Neuhaus, *Doing Well and Doing Good: The Challenge to the Christian Capitalist* 269 (1992).

31. Michael Novak, *Business as a Calling: Work and the Examined Life* 139–45 (1996).

32. John Paul, supra note 3, at para. 6.

33. Id., at para. 43.

34. Gary Dorrien, *The Neoconservative Mind: Politics, Culture and Ideology* 252 (1993).

35. Novak, supra note 31.

36. Robert Jackall, *Moral Mazes, The World of Corporate Managers* (1988).

37. Id. at 193.

38. Michael Novak, *The Spirit of Democratic Capitalism* 132 (1991).

39. Berger & Neuhaus, supra note 7, at 41.

40. Id., at 3.

41. Richard John Neuhaus, *Doing Well and Doing Good: The Challenge to the Christian Capitalist* 150–51 (1992).

42. Robert K. Greenleaf, *Servant Leadership: A Journey Into the Nature of Legitimate Power and Greatness* 143 (1977).

43. Ronald Takaki, *A Different Mirror: A History of Multicultural America* 426 (1993).

44. Berger & Neuhaus, supra note 7, at 43.

45. Berger & Neuhaus, supra note 7, at 43.

46. William C. Frederick, "Complexity, Corporation, Community: How Nature Shapes Business's Civic Role," Address to the Midwest Division of the Academy of Management 12 (April 18, 1998) (manuscript on file with author).

47. Cf. Errol E. Harris, *Formal, Transcendental & Dialectical Logic: Logic and Reality* (1987).

48. Frederick, supra note 46, at 21.

49. Id., at 21.

50. Id., at 21–22.

51. Neuhaus, supra note 41, at 62.

3. Natural Law and Laws of Nature

1. Bruce Wasserstein, *Big Deal: The Battle for Control of America's Leading Corporations* 5 (1998).

2. Robert Jackall, *Moral Mazes* (1988).

3. William C. Frederick, *Values, Nature, and Culture in the American Corporation* (1995).

4. LaRue Tone Hosmer, *Moral Leadership in Business* 51, 52 (1994).

5. Id. at 52 (citing Bryan Burrogh and John Helyar, *Barbarians at the Gate: The Fall of RJR Nabisco* 96 (1990)

6. Robert C. Solomon, *Ethics and Excellence: Cooperation and Integrity in Business* 9 (1993).

7. This is sometimes known as the "superman," but I follow the translation provided by Walter Kaufman. See Nietzsche, *Thus Spoke Zarathustra: A Book for None and All* (Walter Kaufman trans., 1978).

8. Id., 23–24.

9. Frank H. Easterbrook & Daniel Fischel, *The Economic Structure of Corporate Law* (1991).

10. See Anthony Sampson, *The Company Man: The Rise and Fall of Corporate Life* (1995).

11. Nietzsche, supra note 7, at 112.

12. Id. at 101.

13. Id. at 199.

14. Alasdair MacIntyre, *After Virtue* 103 (1981).

15. Id. at 103.

16. Id. at 104–05.

17. Id. at 105.

18. Id. at 105.

19. Marshall Sahlins, *Islands of History* 142 (1985).

20. MacIntyre, supra note 14, at 107.

21. Id. at 105.

22. Id. at 106.

23. Valerio Valeri, *Kingship and Sacrifice: Ritual and Society in Ancient Hawaii* (Paula Wissing trans. 1985); see also J. D. Bisignani, *Kauai Handbook* 19–39 (3d ed. 1997) for a concise and surprisingly accurate introduction to Hawaiian history for a beginning orientation.

24. Sahlins, supra note 19.

25. Alasdair MacIntyre, *Three Rival Versions of Moral Enquiry: Encyclopaedia, Genealogy, and Tradition* 184 (1990).

26. Id. at 185

27. MacIntyre, supra note 14, at 106.

28. Id. at 107–11.

29. Nietzsche, supra note 7, at 288.

30. Steven R. Salbu, "Law and Conformity, Ethics and Conflict: The Trouble with Law-Based Conceptions of Ethics," 68 *Ind. L.J.* 101, 110 (1992).

31. Id. at 108.

32. Id. at 110.

33. See, e.g., Richard De George, "Theological Ethics and Business Ethics," 5 *J. Bus. Ethics* 421 (1986).

34. See John Finnis, *Natural Law and Natural Rights* 30 (1980).

35. John Finnis, "Natural Law and Legal Reasoning," in *Natural Law Theory: Contemporary Essays*, 136–37 (Robert P. George ed., 1994).

36. Finnis, supra note 34, at 176.

37. Id. at 176.

38. Jeffrey Wattles, *The Golden Rule* (1996).

39. See Hosmer, supra note 4, at 78, 117–21, for a good, concise summary of these religious and Kantian positions.

40. Finnis, supra note 34, at 83–84.

41. Salbu, supra note 30, at 108 (citations omitted).

42. See Michael J. Perry, *Morality Politics and Law* 29 (1988).

43. See generally, Jack Cohen & Ian Stewart, *Discovering Simplicity in a Complex World* (1994).

44. See James Gleick, *Chaos: Making a New Science* (1987) for a good overview of the topic.

45. Id. at 30.

46. Id. at 308.

47. Id.

48. See Wasserstein, *supra* note 1.

49. Finnis, supra note 34, at 147.

50. Joseph Birdsell, "On Population Structure in Generalized Hunting and Gathering Populations," in 12 *Evolution* no. 2, at 196–99 (1958).

51. Gregory Johnson, "Organizational Structure and Scalar Stress," in *Theory and Explanation in Archaeology* (C. Renfrew, M. J. Rowlands, & B. A. Segraves eds., 1982).

52. Robin Dunbar, *Grooming, Gossip, and the Evolution of Language* 56 (1996).

53. Id. at 56–57.

54. Id. at 57–63.

55. Id.

56. Id. at 63.

57. Id.

58. Id at 71–73.

59. Id at 72.

60. Id. at 71–73.

61. Id. at 74–76.

62. Peter Berger & Richard John Neuhaus, *To Empower People: The Role of Mediating Structure in Public Policy* (1977).

63. See, e.g., Cass Sunstein, "Beyond the Republican Revival," 97 *Yale L.J.* 1539 (1988).

64. Id.

65. Roy A. Rappaport, *Ecology, Meaning, & Religion* (1979).

66. Joseph Boyle, "Natural Law and the Ethics of Traditions," 10–11, in *Natural Law Theory: Contemporary Essays* (Robert P. George ed., 1992).

67. Manuel Velasquez & F. Neil Brady, "Natural Law and Business Ethics," 7 *Bus. Ethics Q.* 83 (1997).

68. Id. at 92.

69. Id.

70. Id.

71. Id. at 93–94.

72. Id. at 95.

73. Id. at 96.

74. Id. at 97.

75. Id.

76. Id.

77. Id.

78. Id. at 98.

79. Id. at 99.

80. Id. at 100.

81. Douglas W. Kmiec & Stephen B. Presser, *The American Constitutional Order: History, Cases, and Philosophy* 1 (1998).

82. Larry Arnhart, *Darwinian Natural Right: The Biological Ethics of Human Nature* 51 (1998).

83. Id. at 3.

84. Id. at 29.

85. Alasdair MacIntyre, *Dependent Rational Animals: Why Human Beings Need the Virtues* (1999).

86. Arnhart, supra note 82, at 30.

87. James Q. Wilson, *The Moral Sense* (1993).

88. MacIntyre, supra note 85, at 1–4, 63–68.

89. Id. at 68–71, 82–86.

90. Id. at 71–72, 87–95.

91. Id. at 99–118.

92. Lon Fuller, *Anatomy of the Law* 181 (1968)

93. Arnhart, supra note 82, at 4.

94. Id. at 4.

95. Id. at 24.

96. Frederick, supra note 3

97. Rappaport, supra note 65, at 131.

98. Finnis, supra note 34, at 272 (citations omitted).

99. Perry, supra note 42, at 37.

100. G. K. Chesterton, *Orthodoxy* 14 (1990). My thanks to Mike Naughton for calling my attention to this statement.

101. *A Judicial and Civil History of Connecticut* 9 (Dwight Loomis & J. Gilbert Calhoun eds.) (1895).

102. Timothy L. Fort, *Law and Religion* 71 (1987); see 69–76 for a fuller explanation of this aspect of Connecticut legal history.

103. Mary Jeanne Anderson Jones, *Congregational Commonwealth: Connecticut, 1636–1662,* at 70–71 (1968).

104. Fort, supra note 102, at 71. The general court, however, did delegate functional responsibilities to specialized bodies that included courts.

105. Id.

106. See e.g., Martina Duechler, *The Confucian Transformation of Korea* 107–11 (1992).

107. Thomas Aquinas, *Treatise on Law* 7 (from *Summa Theologica* Questions 90–97).

108. Finnis, supra note 34, at 360.

109. Fuller, supra note 92, at 186.

110. Richard Pipes, Property and Freedom 116 (1999).

111. Id. at 64–120.

112. Id. at 79.

113. Id. at 80.

114. Id. at 86.

115. Id. at 87.

116. Id. at 92–97.

117. Id. at 7–8.

118. Id. at 8.

119. Id. at 17.

120. Id. at 34.

121. Id. at 5.

122. Id. at 121–58.

123. Matt Ridley, *The Origins of Virtue: Human Instincts and the Evolution of Cooperation* 231–46 (1997).

124. Stephen B. Presser, *Recapturing the Constitution: Race, Religion, and Abortion Reconsidered* 62 (1994).

125. Finnis, supra note 35, at 135.

126. See Frederick, supra note 3.

127. Id. at 9.

128. Id. at 9.

129. Id.
130. Id. at 168–244.
131. Michael Novak, *The Spirit of Democratic Capitalism* (1991)
132. See Frederick, supra note 3, at 166.
133. Id.
134. Novak, supra note 131.
135. Lyall Watson, *Dark Nature: A Natural History of Evil* 20 (1995).
136. Id. at 22.
137. Frederick, supra note 3.
138. Watson, supra note 135, at 152.

4. Nature and Self-Interest

Portion of this chapter are drawn from previous work published with my coauthor James J. Noone. My thanks to him for allowing me to include them in this book.

1. Al Gini, "Soul as an Ethic," 7 *Bus. Ethics Q.* 157 (1997) (reviewing Allan Cox, *Redefining Corporate Soul: Linking Purpose and People* [1996]).

2. *The Empire Strikes Back* (Lucasfilms-Twentieth Century Fox 1980).

3. See 2 Mircea Eliade, *A History of Religious Ideas* 91–106 (Willard R. Trask trans., 1982).

4. See id. at 44–46.

5. See generally Mircea Eliade, *Yoga: Immortality and Freedom* (Willard R. Trask trans., 2d ed. 1969).

6. See Peter J. Paris, *The Spirituality of African Peoples: The Search for a Common Moral Discourse* 28–33 (1995); Vine DeLoria, Jr., *God Is Red: A Native View of Religion* 88–95 (1994); Scott Cunningham, *Hawaiian Religion and Magic* (1994).

7. See, e.g., *Meister Eckhart: Selected Writings* (Oliver Davies trans., 1994).

8. This list of world religions is not meant to be exhaustive. For a sustained treatment of the notion of a connecting force that lies at the basis of all religious life, see Emile Durkheim, *The Elementary Forms of Religious Life* (Karen E. Fields trans., 1995).

9. See Paul Tillich, *Theologian of the Boundaries* 165 (Mark Kline Taylor ed., 1991) (noting Spinoza's claim of the inability to escape the infinite).

10. See generally Alfred North Whitehead, *Process and Reality: An Essay in Cosmology* (David Ray Griffin & Donald W. Sherburne eds., 1978).

11. See, e.g., Rosemary Radford Ruether, *Gaia and God: An Ecofeminist Theology of Earth Healing* (1992).

12. See, e.g., Errol E. Harris, *Formal, Transcendental, and Dialectical Thinking: Logic and Reality* (1987). Another approach, which also stresses thoroughgoing connectedness, but in a very materialist, nonspiritual sense, are the writings of many neo-Darwinians such as Richard Dawkins, *The Blind Watchmaker* (1986).

13. A philosophical version of nature law does not necessarily lend itself to notions of transcendence. Indeed this is a point by Robert Rodes, a legal ethics scholar, who views a weakness of natural law in its ability to contemplate human beings' ability to transcend. Robert E. Rodes, Jr., *Pilgrim Law* (1998). As will be-

come clearer later in this book, nature can be transcendent in a spiritual way when one views nature as an expression of the divine. This is a position taken by the naturalist theology movement. For now, I simply intend to view nature as transcendent insofar as it limits the human ability to choose whatever a person attempts to choose. In that sense, even this restricted notion of nature transcends humanity.

This chapter makes no claim to speak for the entirety of anthropology. Like any discipline, anthropology possesses a variety of perspectives and paradigms. Rather, the goal of this chapter is, in part, to present anthropology as a viable and rich resource for information on the study of humans and as a source of information on the human condition, some of which is contrary to key premises held by current contract theoreticians.

In the most general sense, as the study of humanity and culture, anthropology is perhaps best positioned among the social sciences to examine the variety of the human experience. More specifically, anthropology has grappled, since its inception, with the relationship between individuals, the environment, and culture.

What I present in this chapter is not by any means a cross-section of current anthropological thought. It is rather a selection of significant research, readily applicable to the issues at hand, drawn from different areas within anthropology. Each has something important to contribute to the current debate. In addition, to facilitate informed debate and the exchange of ideas, I have chosen well-known and readily available research. (I am grateful to James Noone for his assistance in developing this footnote and others in this chapter directly related to anthropology.)

14. See Frank H. Easterbrook & Daniel R. Fischel, *The Economic Structure of Corporate Law* (1991).

15. See F. A. Hayek, *The Fatal Conceit* (1988).

16. See Oliver E. Williamson, *Markets and Hierarchies: Analysis and Antitrust Implications* (1975).

17. See, e.g., Steven R. Salbu, "Insider Trading and the Social Contract," 5 *Bus. Ethics Q.* 313 (1995).

18. See, e.g., Michael C. Keeley, *A Social-Contract Theory of Organizations* (1988).

19. See Thomas Donaldson & Thomas W. Dunfee, "Toward a Unified Conception of Business Ethics: Integrative Social Contracts Theory," 19 *Acad. Mgmt. Rev.* 252 (1994).

20. See James M. Gustafson, *Intersections: Science, Theology, and Ethics* 144–45 (1996).

21. See, e.g., John Boatright, "What's So Special About Shareholders?" 4 *Bus. Ethics Q.* 393 (1994); William M. Evan & R. Edward Freeman, "A Stakeholder Theory of the Modern Corporation: Kantian Capitalism," in *Ethical Theory and Business* 97 (Tom L. Beauchamp & Norman E. Bowie eds., 3d ed. 1988); and Kenneth E. Goodpaster, "Business Ethics and Stakeholder Analysis," 1 *Bus. Ethics Q.* 553 (1991).

22. See, e.g., Robert C. Solomon, *Ethics and Excellence: Cooperation and Integrity in Business* 115–17 (1992); Janet McCracken & Bill Shaw, "Virtue Ethics and Contractarianism: Towards a Reconciliation," 5 *Bus. Ethics Q.* 297 (1995); Jeffrey

Nesteruk, "Law and the Virtues: Developing a Legal Theory for Business Ethics," 5 *Bus. Ethics Q.* 361 (1995).

23. See, e.g., Patricia H. Werhane, *Persons, Rights and Corporations* (1985).

24. See Keeley, supra note 18; Donaldson & Dunfee, supra note 19; Salbu, supra note 17.

25. See, e.g., William C. Frederick, *Values, Nature and Culture in the American Corporation* (1995).

26. Errol E. Harris, *Formal, Transcendental, and Dialectical Thinking: Logic and Reality* (1987).

27. See id.

28. See id.

29. See id. at 57–58.

30. See id.

31. Timothy L. Fort, "Corporate Constituency Statutes: A Dialectical Interpretation," 15 *J.L. & Com.* 257, 267 (1995).

32. For a critique of Kant outside of dialectical theory, see Alasdair MacIntyre, *After Virtue* (1984).

33. See Steven R. Salbu, "The Decline of Contract as a Relationship Management Form," 47 *Rutgers L. Rev.* 1271, 1298 (1995).

34. See Ian R. MacNeil, "Contracts: Adjustment of Long-Term Economic Relations Under Classical, Neoclassical, and Relational Contract Law," 72 *Nw. U.L. Rev.* 854 (1978).

35. This ideal, for instance, could be one of autonomy, freedom, and basic human rights—the commitments made in the U.S. Declaration of Independence and the Constitution.

36. See Williamson, supra note 16.

37. See Daniel A. Farber & Suzanna Sherry, *A History of the American Constitution* 16–17 (1990); and Gordon Wood, *The Creation of the American Republic, 1776–1787*, at 114–15 (1969).

38. Jeffrey Nesteruk, "Law, Virtue, and the Corporation," 33 *Am. Bus. L.J.* 473 (1996).

39. See Hayek, supra note 15, at 70.

40. See id. at 12.

41. See id.

42. See id. at 17.

43. See id. at 19.

44. See id. at 14.

45. See id. at 20.

46. Id. at 70.

47. Id. at 19.

48. Id. at 70.

49. Id. at 15.

50. Id. at 23.

51. See id. at 74.

52. Geoffrey M. Hodgson, *Economics and Evolution: Bringing Life Back into Economics* 152 (1996).

53. Id. at 160.

54. Id. at 40.

55. Jon Elster, "Marxism, Functionalism, and Game Theory," 11 *Theory & Soc'y* 453, 453 (1982).

56 Hayek defines the individual not only as the locus of evolutionary change but also as the level most relevant to any incisive study of society. The work of Malinowski and Durkheim demonstrates that, at the very least, the individual is not always the most fruitful object of study, particularly if the goal is to understand a society or culture rather than simply the actions of an individual. In fact, a broad perspective, which considers a person to be, at least in part, a social creature, suggests that the study of an individual as an isolated subject can never be truly explanatory or predictive.

While more recent work has investigated the relationships between individuals and societies, Durkheim and Malinowski were chosen for this chapter for two reasons. First, the two authors shaped subsequent work; both historically and chronologically, their work offers an excellent starting point for the students of such relationships. Second, and more important, both Durkheim and Malinowski were concerned with very broad questions, questions that have seldom been framed as broadly since. As a result, these authors offer basic information and insight, based on observations and grounded in the real world, which are readily comprehensible and applicable.

Hayek also argues that the individual is the locus of evolutionary change. Within the discipline of anthropology, and particularly within the subfield of archaeology, however, a debate on the role of the individual in cultural evolution has been in progress (in its most recent incarnation) for over ten years. Very recently, however, research has inserted some new insights into the debate, particularly in the realm of methodology for study. See Christopher Boehm, "Emergency Decisions, Cultural-Selection Mechanics, and Group Selection," 37 *Current Anthropology* 763 (1996). Boehm's paper, and a subsequent critical analysis by Polly Wiessner, effectively summarize the positions taken and the evidence used by those on both sides of the current debate. See Polly Wiessner, "On Emergency Decisions, Egalitarianism, and Group Selection," 39 *Current Anthropology* 356 (1998). For my purposes in this chapter, the basic conclusion from their research is that viewing biological evolution and cultural evolution as the same is dangerous.

57. See generally Emile Durkheim, "Rules for the Explanation of Social Facts," in *High Points in Anthropology* 233 (Paul Bohannan & Mark Glazer eds., 1973).

58. Id. at 244 (emphasis removed).

59. See Bronislaw Malinowski, "The Group and the Individual in Functional Analysis," in *High Points in Anthropology*, supra note 57, at 275.

60. Id. at 291.

61. Of course, methodological individualism is compelling, insofar as it points to a specific set of criteria and direction for decision making. If one knows that one should make decisions according to profitability, then a great deal of work is eliminated in assessing other options. Such a single-minded focus is effective for many kinds of decision-making issues, ranging from one issue politics to "Winning isn't everything—it's the only thing" in sports to ethnic cleansing. Single-minded clarity may be powerful, but it is not morally compelling.

62. See Hodgson, supra note 52, at 148.

63. Id. at 155.

64. See Errol E. Harris, *Cosmos and Theos: Ethical and Theological Implications of the Anthropic Cosmological Principle* (1992).

65. See Hayek, supra note 15.

66. Hodgson, supra note 52, at 162.

67. See id. at 181.

68. Id. at 182–83.

69. See id. at 183–84.

70. See id.

71. Kent V. Flannery, "Prehistoric Social Evolution," in *Research Frontiers in Anthropology* 3 (Carol R. Ember & Melvin Ember eds., 1995).

72. Id. at 20.

73. Id. at 19.

74. See id.

75. See id. at 21.

76. See id.

77. Hodgson, supra note 52, at 175–76.

78. See David Sloan Wilson, "Altruism and Organism: Disentangling the Themes of Multilevel Selection Theory," 150 *American Naturalist* S122, S123 (Supp. 1997).

79. See id. at S122.

80. See id.

81. See id. at S124.

82. Id.

83. Id. at S126.

84. Alasdair MacIntyre, *Dependent Rational Animals: Why Human Beings Need the Virtues* 48 (1999).

85. Id.

86. Id. at 21.

87. Id. at 24–27

88. Wilson, supra note 78, at S128. For a good overview of organizational theory literature on these matters, including that of a group mind, see James P. Walsh, "Managerial and Organizational Cognition: Notes from a Trip Down Memory Lane," 6 *O.S.* 280 (1995).

89. Wilson, supra note 78, at S126.

90. See id. at S132.

91. See id.

92. This too is borne out in anthropological literature. In many discussions of trade among aboriginal populations, it has been observed that strict rules of fairness and behavior are enforced with great strength close to home, but that the enforcement of such rules diminishes with social and geographic distance. See Douglas L. Oliver, *A Solomon Island Society: Kinship and Leadership Among the Siuai of Bougainville* (1955); and Marshall Sahlins, *Stone Age Economics* (1972) (particularly ch. 5). Both of these authors note and discuss the importance of "good relations" with those who are most important. Sahlins offers a succinct summation of the situation:

[There is] a tendency for morality, like reciprocity, to be sectorally organized in primitive societies. The norms are characteristically relative and
situational rather than absolute and universal. A given act, that is to say, is
not so much in itself good or bad, it depends on who the "Alter" is. The
appropriation of another man's goods or his woman, which is a sin
("theft," "adultery") in the bosom of one's community, may be not merely
condoned but positively rewarded with the admiration of one's fellows—if
it is perpetuated on an outsider.

Id. at 199.

93. Easterbrook & Fischel, supra note 14, at 16.

94. See Ian Maitland, "The Morality of the Corporation: An Empirical or
Normative Disagreement?," 4 *Bus. Ethics Q.* 445 (1994).

95. Easterbrook & Fischel, supra note 14, at 36.

96. See John R. Boatright, "Business Ethics and the Theory of the Firm," 34
Am. Bus. L.J. 217, 222–23 (1996).

97. See id.

98. See John Hasnas, "The Normative Theories of Business Ethics: A Guide
for the Perplexed," 8 *Bus. Ethics Q.* 19 (1998). Hasnas points out that the stock-
holder approach of Fischel and Easterbrook, the stakeholder approach of Boatright, and the social contract approach all rely upon a notion of consent to justify moral obligations.

99. Boatright, supra note 96, at 223.

100. Easterbrook & Fischel, supra note 14, at 38.

101. Id. at 38–39.

102. Id. at 38.

103. See Jonathan R. Macey, "An Economic Analysis of the Various Rationales for Making Shareholders the Exclusive Beneficiaries of Corporate Fiduciary Duties," 21 *Stetson L. Rev.* 23 (1991).

104. See Katherine Van Wezel Stone, "Employees as Stakeholders Under
State Nonshareholder Constituency Statutes," 21 *Stetson L. Rev.* 45, 70–71
(1991).

105. See Stephen B. Presser, "Thwarting the Killing of the Corporation: Limited Liability, Democracy, and Economics," 87 *Nw. L. Rev.* 148 (1992) (critiquing
Fischel and Easterbrook and warning of the dangers of playing with founda-
tional corporate building blocks such as limited liability).

106. See Easterbrook & Fischel, supra note 14, at 1.

107. Boatright, supra note 96, at 233.

108. See id.

109. Eric W. Orts, "Shirking and Sharking: A Legal Theory of the Firm," 16
Yale L. & Pol'y Rev. 265 (1998).

110. See id.

111. See id.

112. Williamson, supra note 16, at 9.

113. See id. at 21–22.

114. Id. at 9.

115. Id. at 4.

157. Id.
158. Id.
159. Easterbrook & Fischel, supra note 14, at 15–16.

5. The Velvet Corporation

An earlier version of this chapter was published as an article with my coauthor Cindy A. Schipani. My thanks to her for allowing me to use substantial portions of that article in this book.

1. Vaclev Havel, *Disturbing the Peace* 14 (1987).
2. Peter J. Richerson & Robert Boyd, "Complex Societies: The Evolutionary Origins of a Crude Superorganism," 10 *Human Nature* 253 (1999).
3. Id.
4. Roy A. Rappaport, *Ecology, Meaning, and Religion* 76 (1979).
5. Larry Kramer, "The Confidence of the People: Size, Representation, and the Constitutional Role of Political Parties," Presentation at the Legal Theory Workshop, University of Michigan Law School (Nov. 5, 1999) (manuscript on file with author).
6. Id. at 10.
7. See id. at 24.
8. Larry Kramer, "Madison's Audience," 112 *Harv. L. Rev.* 611 (1999).
9. Kramer, supra note 5, at 4.
10. Id. at 5.
11. Id. at 26.
12. Id., at 27 (citing New York governor George Clinton).
13. Id. at 30–31 (citations omitted).
14. Id. at 35.
15. Id. at 38.
16. Id. at 42 (citing New York governor George Clinton).
17. Id. at 81.
18. Id. at 81.
19. Id. at 88.
20. Id. at 45 (quoting Brutus in John DeWitt, 1 *American Herald* [Oct–Dec. 1747] in 4 *Complete Anti-Federalist* 300–301).
21. Kramer, supra note 5, at 62.
22. Id. at 76.
23. Id. at 85.
24. Steven G. Calabresi, "Political Parties as Mediating Institutions," 61 *U. Chi. L. Rev.* 1479 (1994).
25. Michael Keeley, "A 'Matter of Opinion, What Tends to the General Welfare': Governing the Workplace," 10 *Bus. Ethics Q.* 243, 247 (2000).
26. Id. at 246.
27. Id. at 248.
28. Id.
29. Id.
30. Id. at 250.

31. Id.

32. Id.

33. Id. at 251.

34. Id.

35. Id. at 252.

36. See, e.g., David Postman, "Resistance Takes Fast Track—Protesters Training Now for Sit-ins, Blockades," *Seattle Times*, Sept. 10, 1999, at A1; Lynda Gorov, "The Varied Foes of WTO Unite in Seattle Protests," *Boston Globe*, Nov. 30, 1999, at A1.

37. See, e.g., Jane Perlez, "At Trade Forum, Clinton Pleads for the Poor," *N.Y. Times*, Jan. 30, 2000, at 8; David Greising, "Shades of Seattle Riot as Clinton Addresses Elite Economic Forum," *Chi. Trib.*, Jan. 30, 2000 at C13.

38. Amitai Etzioni, *The New Golden Rule* (1996); See also Antonin Wagner, "Communitarianism: A New Paradigm of Socioeconomic Analysis," 24 *J. Socio-Econ.* 593, 598 (1995); Amitai Etzioni, "Freedom and Community: The Politics of Restoration," *Economist*, Dec. 24, 1994, at 33.

39. For general background on the debate, see Michael Bradley, Cindy A. Schipani, James P. Walsh, & Anant K. Sundaram, "The Purposes and Accountability of the Corporation in Contemporary Society: Corporate Governance at a Crossroads," 62 *Law & Contemp. Probs.* 9, 33–45 (Summer 1999). For views on the corporation as a natural entity, see David Millon, "Theories of the Corporation," 1990 *Duke L.J.* 201 (1990); Thomas Lee Hazen, "The Corporate Persona, Contract (and Market) Failure, and Moral Values," 69 *N.C. L. Rev.* 273 (1991); David Millon, "New Directions in Corporate Law: Communitarians, Contractarians, and the Crisis in Corporate Law," 50 *Wash & Lee L. Rev.* 1373 (1993). For arguments from the law and economics literature depicting the corporation as a nexus of contracts, see Ronald Coase, "The Nature of the Firm," 4 *Economica* 386 (1937) (emphasizing the nature of the firm as a center of contracts to reduce the transaction costs of business); Armen A. Alchian & Harold Demsetz, "Production, Information Costs, and Economic Organization," 62 *Am. Econ. Rev.* 777 (1972); Michael C. Jensen & William H. Meckling, "Theory of the Firm: Managerial Behavior, Agency Costs and Ownership Structure," 3 *J. Fin. Econ.* 305 (1976).

40. See, e.g., Bradley et al., supra note 39, at 61.

41. For example, see infra note 82 for a listing of over forty states adopting statutes permitting corporate directors to consider the interests of nonshareholder constituencies in making various corporate decisions.

42. See Bradley et al., supra note 39, at 66–68.

43. *The LGT Guide to World Equity Markets 1997*, at 500 (1997).

44. Id.

45. See Organization For Economic Cooperation and Development, *OECD Economic Surveys: 1995–5* [hereinafter OECD], at 88, table 23.

46. See id.

47. For stock market data, see International Finance Corp., *Emerging Stock Markets Factbook* 17 (1998). For GDP data, see International Monetary Fund, *International Financial Statistics* 315, 397, 745 (July 1998).

48. *The Merger Yearbook* 1999, at 15, 22–23 (Securities Data Exchange).

49. See Stephen Prowse, *Corporate Governance in an International Perspective: A*

Survey of Corporate Control Mechanisms Among Large Firms in the United States, the United Kingdom, Japan, and Germany, BIS Economic Papers No. 41 (Bank for International Settlements, July 1994), at 47.

50. Bradley et al., supra note 39, at 58; see also "A Texas Raider Rocks Club Japan," *U.S. News & World Report,* Apr. 17, 1989, at 15.

51. Rafael La Porta, Florencia Lopez-De-Silanes, & Andrei Shleifer, "Corporate Ownership Around the World," *J. of Fin.,* Apr. 1, 1999, at 470. See also Roy C. Smith, "Restructuring Japanese Financial Institutions," *Washington Q.* (Summer 1999), at 181, for a discussion of cross-shareholding and its effect on merger and acquisition activity.

52. See Prowse, supra note 49, at 47.

53. Between World War II and 1993, there were only four hostile takeovers in Germany. Julian Franks & Colin Mayer, *German Capital Markets, Corporate Control, and Obstacles to Hostile Takeovers: Lessons from Three Case Studies,* London Business School Working Paper (1993).

54. Bradley et al., supra note 39, at 55; see also Prowse, supra note 33, at 46–54.

55. See Prowse, supra note 49, at table 5, 28–29

56. Id.

57. See Securities Exchange Act of 1934, ch. 404, 48 Stat. 881; 7 Louis Loss & Joel Seligman, *Securities Regulation* 3448–66 (1991).

58. See Mitsuhiro Fukao, *Financial Integration, Corporate Governance, and the Performance of Multinational Corporations* 119 (1995).

59. See id.

60. German tax laws generally explain this choice of accounting rules. See id. at 120–21.

61. Nancy Rivera Brooks, "Advisory May Imperil Worker Stock Options," *Los Angeles Times,* Jan. 22, 2000, at A1, A7.

62. NCEO Library, "ESOPs, Stock Options, and 401(k) Plans Now Control 8.3% of Corporate Equity," <wysiwyg://63http://www.nceo.org/library/control_eq/html> (Mar. 3, 2000).

63. Id.

64. Adam Bryant, "After 7 Years, Employees Win United Airlines," *N.Y. Times,* July 13, 1994, at A1.

65. See UAL, "Company Profile, Hoover's Online," <wysiwyg://129http://www.hoovers.com/premium/profile.0/0,2147,11520,00.html> (Mar. 3, 2000). See also United Airlines, DEF14A Proxy Statement, Mar. 23, 2000.

66. See Steven Greenhouse, "The U.P.S. Walkout: News Analysis; High Stakes for 2 Titans," *N.Y. Times.,* Aug. 5, 1997, at A1.

67. Nichole M. Christian, "3,400 Strike G.M. Plant; Assembly Put at Risk," *N.Y. Times.,* June 6, 1998, at A7.

68. "Business Headlines, *Dayton Daily News,* Feb. 25, 2000, at 2E.

69. "No Country for Old Men," *Economist,* May 1, 1999, at 60, 61.

70. See Stephen M. Banker, "Climate for M&A in Japan Shifts, Country Appears to be Overcoming Its Traditional Cultural and Legal Barriers," *N.Y. L.J.,* Nov. 15, 1999, at S4.

71. See "Structural and Regulatory Developments in OECD Countries," *Fin. Market Trends,* Nov. 1, 1998, at 17; see also Bruce Kelly, "Corporate Governance Is

Key: Investors' Demands Lead to Increased Changes Worldwide," *Pensions & Investments*, Dec. 14, 1998, at 16; Greg Steinmetz, "German Shift on Cutbacks May Lift Stock," *Wall Street J.* (Europe), Jan. 13, 1997, at 13.

72. See OECD, supra note 45, at 120.

73. See Fukao, supra note 58.

74. Michael J. Phillips, "Corporate Moral Personhood and Three Conceptions of the Corporation," 2 *Bus. Ethics Q.* 435, 437 (1992) (citing John Marshall at 434 in Trustees of Dartmouth College v. Woodward, 17 U.S. (4 Wheat) 518 (1819)); see also Justice Brandeis's dissent in Liggett v. Lee, 288 U.S. 517, 549 (1933) (observing that "there was a sense of some insidious menace in large aggregations of capital, particularly when held by corporations. So at first, the corporate privilege was granted sparingly; and only when the grant seemed necessary in order to procure for the community some specific benefit otherwise unattainable."); Millon, supra note 39, at 207.

75. Stephen B. Presser, "Thwarting the Killing of the Corporation: Limited Liability, Democracy, and Economics," 87 *Nw. U. I. Rev.* 148, 156 (1992).

76. Id.

77. In 1919, the Michigan Supreme Court decided in favor of private accountability to the shareholders. Dodge v. Ford Motor Co., 170 N.W. 668, 684 (Mich. 1919). In the early 1930s, two highly respected legal theorists, Adolf A. Berle of Columbia Law School and E. Merrick Dodd of Harvard, took up the debate in their classic series of articles. See A. A. Berle Jr., "Corporate Powers as Powers in Trust," 44 *Harv. L. Rev.* 1049 (1931); E. Merrick Dodd Jr., "For Whom Are Corporate Managers Trustees?," 45 *Harv. L. Rev.* 1145 (1932); A. A. Berle Jr., "For Whom Corporate Managers Are Trustees: A Note," 45 *Harv. L. Rev.* 1365 (1932); E. Merrick Dodd Jr., "Is Effective Enforcement of the Fiduciary Duties of Corporate Managers Practicable?," 2 *U. Chi. L. Rev.* 194 (1935). For a more modern view of the debate, see A. A. Sommer Jr., "Whom Should the Corporation Serve?: The Berle-Dodd Debate Revisited Sixty Years Later," 16 *Del. J. Corp. L.* 33 (1991).

78. Delaware General Corporation Law § 102(a)(3). The Revised Model Business Corporation Act similarly provides that "every corporation incorporated under this Act has the purpose of engaging in any lawful business unless a more limited purpose is set forth in the articles of incorporation." Revised Model Business Corporation Act § 3.01.

79. Dodge v. Ford Motor Co., 170 N.W. 668, 684 (Mich. 1919).

80. American Law Institute, Principles of Corporate Governance §2.01 (1994).

81. Connecticut requires a director of a publicly held corporation to consider a standard list of factors "in determining what he reasonably believes to be in the best interests of the corporation." However, this requirement is not imposed on the director for any other decisions. Conn. Stock. Corp. Act § 33-313(e). The following statutes permit directors to consider the interests of non-shareholder constituencies in any appropriate context: Conn. Gen. Stat. § 33-756(d) (1997) (mandating consideration of nonshareholder constituencies); Fla. Stat. ch. 607.0830(3) (Supp. 1999); Ga. Code Ann. § 14-2-202(b)(5) (Supp. 1998); Haw. Rev. Stat. § 415-35(b) (1997); Idaho Code § 30-1702 (1996); 805 Ill. Comp. Stat. 5/8.85 (West 1993); Ind. Code § 23-1-35-1(d) (1995); Iowa Code §

491.101B (1991); Me. Rev. Stat. Ann. tit. 13-A, § 716 (West Supp. 1998); Mass. Gen. Laws Ann. ch. 156B, § 65 (West Supp. 1998); Minn. Stat. § 302A.251(5) (Supp. 1999); Miss. Code Ann. § 79-4-8.30(d) (1998); Nev. Rev. Stat. § 78.138(3) (1994); N.J. Stat. Ann. § 14A:6-1(2) (West Supp. 1998); N.M. Stat. Ann. § 53-11-35(D) (Michie 1997); N.Y. Bus. Corp. Law § 717(b) (McKinney Supp. 1999); N.D. Cent. Code § 10-19.1-50(6) (Supp. 1997); Ohio Rev. Code Ann. § 1701.59(E) (Anderson 1993); Or. Rev. Stat. § 60.357(5) (Supp. 1996); 15 Pa. Cons. Stat. § 515 (1995); Wis. Stat. § 180.0827 (1992); Wyo. Stat. Ann. § 17-16-830(e) (Michie 1997). The following statutes permit directors to consider the interests of nonshareholder constituencies in the context of transactions for corporate control: Ala. Code § 10-2B-11.03(c) (1994); Ariz. Rev. Stat. §§ 10-2702, 10-1202(c) (1996) (sale of assets); Ark. Code Ann. § 4-27-1202(C) (Michie 1996) (sale of assets); Colo. Rev. Stat. §§ 7-106-105(7) (reverse splitting of shares), 7-111-103(3), 7-114-102(3) (1998) (authorization of dissolution after issuance of shares); Ky. Rev. Stat. Ann. §§ 271B.11-030(2)(b), 271B.12-020(3) (Banks-Baldwin 1989) (sale of assets); L. Rev. Stat. Ann. § 12:92(G) (West 1994); Mo. Ann. Stat. § 351.347 (West 1991); Mont. Code Ann. §§ 35-1-815(3), 35-1-823(3) (1997) (sale of assets); N.H. Rev. Stat. Ann. §§ 293-A:11.03(c), 293-A:12.02(c) (Supp. 1996) (sale of assets); N.C. Gen. Stat. §§ 55-11-03(c), 55-12-02(c) (1990) (sale of assets); R.I. Gen. Laws § 7-5.2-8 (1992); S.C. Code Ann. §§ 33-11-103(c), 33-12-102(c) (Law. Co-op. 1990) (sale of assets); S.D. Codified Laws § 47-33-4 (Michie 1991); Tenn. Code ANN. § 48-103-204 (1995); Tex. Bus. Corp. Act Ann. art. 5.03 (West Supp. 1999); Utah Code Ann. § 16-10a-1103(3) (1995); Vt. Stat. Ann. tit. 11A, §§ 11.03(c), 12.02(c) (1997) (sale of assets); Va. Code Ann. § 13.1-718(C) (Michie 1993); Va. Code Ann. § 13.1-724(C) (Michie Supp. 1998) (sale of assets); Wash. Rev. Code §§ 23B.11.030(3), 23B.12.020(3) (1994) (sale of assets). The following states and territories do not have specific legislation regarding consideration of the interests of nonshareholder constituencies: Alaska, California, Delaware, District of Columbia, Kansas, Maryland, Michigan, Nebraska, Oklahoma, Puerto Rico, Virgin Islands, and West Virginia.

82. See Delaware Div. of Corps., "DELAWARE: The Corporate Choice" (last modified Feb. 1, 2000), <http://www.state.de.us/corp/index.htm> (Mar. 3, 2000); E. Norman Veasey, "An Economic Rationale for Judicial Decisionmaking in Corporate Law," 53 *Bus. Law.* 681 (May 1998).

83. See generally, Rima F. Hartman, "Note, Situation-Specific Fiduciary Duties for Corporate Directors: Enforceable Obligations or Toothless Ideals?," 50 *Wash. & Lee L. Rev.* 1761 (1993); James J. Hanks Jr., "Playing with Fire: Nonshareholder Constituency Statutes in the 1990s," 21 *Stetson L. Rev.* 97 (1991); William J. Carney, "Does Defining Constituencies Matter?," 59 *U. Cin. L. Rev.* 385 (1990).

84. See Eric W. Orts, "Beyond Shareholders: Interpreting Corporate Constituency Statutes," 61 *Geo. Wash. L. Rev.* 1, 14, 91-92 (1992).

85. Alejandro Reyes, "Playing a New Tune," *Asia Week*, Nov. 19, 1999, at 64.

86. Bradley et al., supra note 39.

87. Yutaka Imai, Reinvigorating Business Dynamism in Japan, OECD *Observer*, Jan. 1999, at 6. But see Martin Lipton and Steven A. Rosenblum, "A New System of Corporate Governance: The Quinquennial Election of Directors,"

58 *U. Chi. L. Rev.* 187, 222 (asserting that the structure of stock ownership within Japanese corporations has aligned the interests of management and stockholders).

88. Bradley et al., supra note 39, at 51.

89. See Detlev F. Vagts, "Reforming the "Modern" Corporation: Perspectives from the German," 80 *Harv. L. Rev.* 23, 40 (1966).

90. See id. at 41.

91. See Bradley et al., supra note 39, at 51.

92. See OECD, supra note 45, at 84. See also Stefan Wagstyl, "Crumbs from the Table," *Fin. Times*, Sept. 25, 1996, at 15 (noting that the German language does not include a phrase for the words "shareholder value").

93. Robert Nisbet, *The Quest for Community* (1991).

94. See Bureau of Census, U.S. Dep't of Commerce, *Statistical Abstract of the United States* 524 tbl.808 (1997).

95. See Stephen L. Nesbitt, "Long-Term Rewards from Shareholder Activism: A Study of the CalPERS Effect," *J. Applied Corp. Fin.*, 75 (Winter 1994).

96. See OECD, supra note 45 at 88, table. 23.

97. See id.

98. Bradley et al., supra note 39, at 56; see generally E. Berglof & E. Perotti, "The Governance Structure of the Japanese Financial Keiretsu," 36 *J. Fin. Econ.* 259 (1994); David Flath, "Shareholdings in the Keiretsu, Japan's Financial Groups," *Rev. Econ. & Stat.* 249 (1993); Hesna Genay, "Japan's Corporate Groups," 15 *Econ. Persp.* 20 (1991); Ronald Gilson & Mark J. Roe, "Understanding the Japanese Keiretsu: Overlaps Between Governance and Industrial Organization," 102 *Yale L.J.* 871, 894–95 (1993); W. Carl Kester, *Japanese Takeovers: The Global Contest for Corporate Control* (1991).

99. See Paul Sheard, "The Main Bank System and Corporate Monitoring and Control in Japan," 11 *J. Econ. Behav. & Org.* 399, 402 (1989).

100. See Robert Lightfoot & W. Carl Kester, "Note on Corporate Governance Systems: The United States, Japan, and Germany" 69–74 (1991).

101. Mary Ann Maskery, "Safety Net; Web of Ownership Between Banks, Auto Industry Keeps Companies Alive," *Automotive News*, Aug. 6, 1990.

102. See Richard Pascale & Thomas P. Rohlen, "The Mazda Turnaround," 9 *J. Japanese Stud.* 219 (1983)

103. See id.

104. See Brenton R. Schlender, "Japan's New Realism: Don't Count This Superpower Out," *Fortune*, Oct. 31, 1994, at 117, 118.

105. "Auto Parts Sales to Japan Rise," *Chi. Trib.*, Jan. 22, 1995, at 11.

106. Id.

107. James B. Treece, "Nissan Untethers Suppliers and Itself," *Automotive News*, April 12, 1999, at 26.

108. "Japan Inc. Faces Radical Change," *Banker*, Oct, 1, 1999, at 4; see also "Merge-or-Submerge Fever Spreads as Keiretsu Die Out," *Daily Yomiuri* (Tokyo), Dec. 21, 1999, at 9.

109. "Japan Inc. Faces Radical Change," supra note 108.

110. Bradley et al., supra note 39, at 57.

111. Ronald J. Gilson & Mark J. Roe, "Essay: Lifetime Employment: Labor

Peace and the Evolution of Japanese Corporate Governance," 99 *Colum. L. Rev.* 508, 529 (Mar. 1999).

112. Masahiko Aoki, "The Japanese Firm as a System of Attributes: A Survey and Research Agenda," in *The Japanese Firm: The Sources of Competitive Strength* (Masahiko Aoki & Ronald Doe eds., 1994), at 11, 18.

113. See Prowse, supra note 49, at 1123, 1126.

114. Id. at 1124–26.

115. Smith, supra note 51, at 181.

116. Kathy Matsui, *Mergermania—Premature Euphoria,* Goldman Sachs Japan Economic Research Group, Jan. 25, 1999 (cited in Smith, supra note 51, at 181).

117. See OECD, supra note 45, at 88.

118. See Fukao, supra note 58, at 27.

119. See id.

120. See OECD, supra note 45, at 120.

121. See "Stakeholder Capitalism: Unhappy Families," *Economist,* Feb. 10, 1996, at 23, 25.

122. See Edward Carr, "Survey, Business in Europe: Fortress Against Change," *Economist,* Nov. 23, 1996, at 12.

123. See Revised Model Business Corporation Act § 8.08; Delaware General Corporation Law §141(k).

124. See James Abbeglen & George Stalk Jr., *Kaisha: The Japanese Corporation* 183 (1985); Fukao, supra note 58, at 98.

125. See Prowse, supra note 49, at 42.

126. "No Country for Old Men," supra note 69.

127. Id.

128. Id.

129. Id.

130. Almost 78 percent of japanese directors are promoted from among employees. See Fukao supra note 58. A recent article in the *Economist* opened by quoting a young Japanese politician exclaiming, "(D)amn these old bastards," in reference to the aging Japanese company men who are thwarting the radical change sought by Japan's younger businessmen and politicians. "No Country for Old Men," supra note 69.

131. "No Country for Old Men," supra note 69.

132. Id.

133. Id.

134. Id.

135. Brian Bremmer, "The Stock Option Comes to Japan," *Bus. Week,* Apr. 19 1999, at 39.

136. "No Country for Old Men," supra note 69.

137. Id.

138. Id.

139. Gilson & Roe, supra note 111, at 535.

140. Mark J. Roe, "German Codetermination and German Securities Markets," 1998 *Colum. Bus. L. Rev.* 167, 171–173 (1998).

141. See OECD, supra note 45, at 86.

142. Bradley et al., supra note 39, at 52.

143. See OECD, supra note 45, at 86. In companies with fewer than two thou-

sand employees, the ratio of employee to nonemployee representation is one-to-two.

144. See OECD, supra note 45, at 86. For more details about German boards, see Prowse, supra note 49; see also Alfred F. Conrad, 'Corporate Constituencies in Western Europe,' 21 *Stetson L. Rev.* 73 (1991); Fukao, supra note 58, at 100–101; Jonathan R. Macey & Geoffrey Miller, 'Corporate Governance and Commercial Banking: A Comparative Examination of Germany, Japan, and the United States," 48 *Stan. L. Rev.* 73 (1995); Mark J. Roe, "German 'Populism' and the Large Public Corporation," 14 *Int'l Rev. L. & Econ.* 187 (1994); Mark J. Roe, "Some Differences in Corporate Structure in Germany, Japan, and the United States," 102 *Yale L.J.* 1927 (1993); Vagts, supra note 89.

145. See Klaus J. Hopt, "Labor Representation on Corporate Boards: Impacts and Problems for Corporate Governance and Economic Integration in Europe," 14 *Int'l Rev. L. & Econ.* 203, 205 (1994).

146. See Philip Glouchevitch, *Juggernaut—The German Way of Doing Business* 136 (1992); see also Lightfoot & Kester, supra note 100, at 10.

147. Bradley et al., supra note 39, at 52.

148. See generally M. Aoki, "Toward an Economic Model of the Japanese Firm," 28 *J. Econ. Lit.* 1 (1990); Gilson & Roe, supra note 111, at 510.

149. Wai Shun Wilson Leung, "The Inadequacy of Shareholder Primacy: A Proposed Corporate Regime That Recognizes Non-Shareholder Interests," 30 *Colum. J.L. & Soc. Probs.* 587, 630.

150. Gilson & Roe, supra note 111, at 530.

151. See Fukao, supra note 58, at 59

152. Jennifer Reingold & Ronald Grover, "Executive Pay," *Bus. Week*, Apr. 19, 1999, at 72.

153. Id.

154. Id.

155. Shirley Fung, "How Should We Pay Them?" *Across the Board*, June 1, 1999, at 36.

156. The Financial Executive Institute is an Arthur Anderson entity composed of 88 percent U.S. and 12 percent Canadian companies. Id.

157. For example, out of a sample of 119 large Japanese firms, none used stock options for top executive compensation. In contrast, all of the 111 large U.S. corporations included in the sample used stock options to compensate their top executives. See Steven N. Kaplan, "Top Executive Rewards and Firm Performance: A Comparison of Japan and the United States," 102 *J. Pol. Econ.* 510, 534–536, table 4 (1994).

158. "Who Wants to Be a Billionaire?," *Economist*, May 8, 1999.

159. Id.

160. Id.

161. See Bremner, supra note 135.

162. See Jon Choy, "Hashimoto Lights Fuse for "Big Bang" in Japan's Financial Sector," *JEI Rept.*, Nov. 22, 1996, at 1; "Laying the Charge for the Big Bang," 147 *Banker* 108, July 1, 1997, at 108. See generally "A Survey of Japanese Finance, "*Economist*, June 28, 1997, at 56.

163. See "Structural and Regular Developments in OECD Countries," *Financial Market Trends*, Nov. 1, 1988.

164. See Carr, supra note 122, at 12.

165. This notion of ownership is akin to a property-like interest in one's work. The property notion, of course, has long been linked to work. John Locke, of course, "introduced the notion that the origin of material property lies in labor. . . . Property comes into existence when an individual applies labor to objects belonging to no one." Richard Pipes, *Property and Freedom: The Story of How Through the Centuries Private Ownership Has Promoted Liberty and the Rule of the Law* 35–36 (1999). Locke held that the mixing of labor with property created a property interest in the resulting product and that the protection of property rights was the raison d'etre for government (id. at 37). Abraham Lincoln concurred that labor is prior to, and independent of, capital. Capital is only the fruit of labor and thus could not be without it. "Labor is the superior of capital, and deserves the higher consideration. Capital has its rights, which are as worthy of protection as any other rights. Nor is it denied that there is, and probably always will be, a relation between capital and labor, producing mutual benefits. The error is in assuming that the whole labor of a community exists within that relation." "Reply to a Committee from the Workingmen's Association of New York" (Mar. 21, 1864) in *The Collected Works of Abraham Lincoln* (Roy P. Balser ed., 1953).

166. James T. Burtchaell, *Philemon's Problem* 101 (1973).

167. Thomas J. Andre Jr., "Some Reflections on German Corporate Governance: A Glimpse at German Supervisory Boards," 70 *Tulane L. Rev.* 1819 (1996). One of the more frequent criticisms of the German model is that the shareholder representative component of the supervisory boards of German companies tends to be dominated by representatives of a few large German banks, with a small number of other individuals, many of whom also have close business or professional relationships to the company on whose board they sit. The implicit suggestion in the criticism is that the interrelationships among these individuals may sometimes be too close to allow effective monitoring of corporate management.

168. Bradley et al., supra note 39, at 10.

169. See generally, Mitsuhior Umezu, "Relational Ethics and the Context of Trust: Understanding the Ethical Basis of Paternalistic Japanese Business," 4, Presentation at Meeting of the Society of Business Ethics (1999) (manuscript on file with author).

170. Id. at 5.

171. Id.

172. Id. at 6 (following Japanese philosopher Watsuji).

173. Id.

174. Id. at 9.

175. Id. at 10–11 arguing that the West tends not to make distinctions among these three.

176. Richerson & Boyd, supra note 2.

177. Id.

178. Id.

179. Id. at 13.

180. Id. at 14–15.

181. Gail G. Whitchurch & Larry L. Constantine, "Systems Theory" 325, in

Sourcebook of Family Theories and Methods: A Contextual Approach (Pauline G. Boss, William J. Doherty, Ralph LaRossa, Walter R. Schumm, and Suzanne K. Steinmetz eds., 1993).

182. Id. at 331–34.

183. Benjamin Benson, "Do You Keep Too Many Secrets?," 402–3, in Ward & Astroff, *Family Business Sourcebook*, reprinted from *Nation's Bus.* (Aug. 1989).

184. Bernard Black & Reiner Kraakman, "A Self-Enforcing Model of Corporate Law," 109 *Harv. L. Rev.* 1911, 1916 (1996).

185. Rob Goffee & Gareth Jones, "What Holds the Modern Company Together," *Harv. Bus. Rev.* 113–34 (Nov–Dec. 1996).

186. On "too many masters," see, e.g., Robert Clark, *Corporate Law* § 1:2.4, at 21–22 (1986). On "managerial authority," see, e.g., Katherine Van Wezel Stone, "Employees as Stakeholders Under State Non-Shareholder Constituency Statutes, 21 *Stetson L. Rev.* 45, 54–55, 70–71 (1991). On "gridlock," see, e.g., James J. Hanks Jr., "Playing with Fire: Non-Shareholder Constituency Statutes in the 1990s", 21 *Stetson L. Rev.* 97, 111 (1991).

187. William C. Frederick, *Values, Nature, and Culture in the American Corporation* 30 (1995).

188. Roberta Romano, "A Guide to Takeovers: Theory, Evidence, and Regulation," 9 *Yale J. Reg.* 119 (1992).

189. Pipes, supra note 165, at 80.

190. Id.

191. John Locke, *Two Treatises of Government* (Peter Laslette ed., 1960).

192. Lincoln, supra note 165.

193. See Rushworth M. Kidder, *How Good People Make Tough Choices: Resolving the Dilemmas of Ethical Living* 90–92 (1995).

194. Kramer, supra note 5, at 30–31.

195. See Michael C. Keeley, *A Social Contract Theory of Organizations* 129 (1988).

196. See e.g., Edward Deming, *Out of the Crisis* 583–85 (1982).

197. See John S. Oakland, *Total Quality Management* 29–41 (1990).

198. Pipes, supra note 165, at 121–58.

199. Nisbet, supra note 93.

200. Id.

201. Richard Sennett, *The Corrosion of Character* (1998).

202. David Bollier, *Aiming Higher* 303 (1997).

203. Joshua Margolis, "Psychological Pragmatism and the Imperative of Aims: A New Approach for Business Ethics," 8 *Bus. Ethics Q.* 409 (1998).

204. See, e.g., Oliver Williamson, *Markets and Hierarchies: Analysis and Antitrust Implications* (1975).

205. Id. at 41–56.

206. Gregory Johnson, "Organizational Structure and Scalar Stress," in *Theory and Explanation in Archaeology* (C. Renfrew, M. J. Rowlands, & B. A. Segraves eds., 1982).

207. *Ethics and Agency Theory: An Introduction* 6 (Norman E. Bowie & R. Edward Freeman eds. 1992).

208. Id. at 392–98.

209. Id.

210. Lon Fuller, *The Morality of Law* 186 (1969).

211. Cass Sunstein, "Beyond the Republican Revival," 97 *Yale L.J.* 1539 (1988); Frank Michelman, "Law's Republic," 97 *Yale L.J.* 1493 (1988).

212. Karen E. Mishra, Gretchen M. Spreitzer, & Aniel K. Mishara, "Preserving Employee Morale During Downsizing," *Sloan Mgmt. Rev.* 86 (Winter 1998).

213. Id.

214. Id. at 86.

215. Id. at 87–88.

216. Id. at 89–91.

217. Id. at 92.

218. Id. at 92–94.

219. For a more skeptical view of the importance of corporate culture, see Charles M. Yablon, "Mergers and Acquisitions: Corporate Culture in Takeovers," 19 *Cardozo L. Rev.* 553 (1997). Yablon compares corporate culture to arguments about God. To some, he says, God/culture is worthy of intense study; to "atheists," culture plays no role in takeovers. And to the agnostics, culture might well exist, but because of the difficulties associated with it, it is better to act under the assumption that it is not really there. Id. at 554–55.

220. See Alexis DeTocqueville, *Democracy in America* 23 (1945).

221. See Robert E. Cole, "Quality Circles," in *Quality Management Handbook* (Loren Walsh, Ralph Wurster, & Raymond Kimber eds., 1986).

222. Charles Hampden-Turner, *Creating Corporate Culture: From Harmony to Discord* 58–59 (1990).

223. Richerson & Boyd, supra note 5.

224. Rappaport, supra note 4, at 139.

225. Frederick, supra note 189, at 30–42.

226. Id. at 144. Frederick refers to the goal of homeostatic succession and notes that radical shifts diminish the supportive system of life's web. Of course, this is not to say that all changes must be smooth. There may be some starts and stops in the evolutionary process. The point, however, remains that radical change involves significant risk to the beings living in the midst of such change and that the technosymbolic ability of human beings can be used, particularly in corporate life, to make those changes less rather than more painful.

6. Stakeholder Theory

1. William M. Evan & R. Edward Freeman, "A Stakeholder Theory of the Modern Corporation: Kantian Capitalism" in *Ethical Theory and Business* 97, 101–05 (Tom Beauchamp & Norman Bowie eds., 3d ed. 1988). The authors specifically leave open the notion that the potential list of stakeholders could be quite broad.

2. See Ariz. Rev. Stat. Ann. § 10-1202 (Supp. 1992); Fla. Stat. Ann. § 607.0830 West Supp. 1993); Ga. Code Ann. § 22-202 (b)(5) (Michie Supp. 1992); Haw. Rev. Stat. § 415-35(b) (Supp. 1992); Idaho Code § 30-1702 (Supp. 1992); Ill. Ann. Stat. ch. 32, para 8.85 (Smith-Hurd 1991); Ind. Code Ann. § 23-1-35-1 (Burns Supp. 1992); Iowa Code Ann. § 491.101B (West Supp. 1992); Ky. Rev. Stat. Ann § 271B12-210(4) (Baldwin 1989); La. Rev. Stat. Ann. § 12:92(G) (West

Supp. 1993); Me. Rev. Stat. Ann. tit. 13-A, § 716 (West Supp. 1992); Mass. Gen. Laws Ann. ch. 156B, § 65 (West Supp. 1992); Minn. Stat. Ann. § 302A.251(5) (West Supp. 1993); Miss. Code Ann. § 79-4-8.30(d) (Supp. 1992); Mo. Ann. Stat. § 351.347.1 (Vernon Supp. 1992); Neb. Rev. Stat. § 21-2035(1) (c) (Supp. 1992); N.J. Stat. Ann. § 14A:6.1 (West Supp. 1992); N.M. Stat. Ann. § 53-11-35(D) (Michie Supp. 1992) N.Y. Bus. Corp. Law § 717(b) (McKinney Supp. 1993); Ohio Rev. Code Ann. § 1701.59(E) (Anderson Supp. 1992); Or. Rev. Stat. § 60.357(5) (Supp.1992); 15 Pa. Cons. Stat §§ 1715–1716 (1992); R.I. Gen. Laws § 7-5.2-8 (1992); S.D. Codified Laws Ann. § 47-33-4 (Supp. 1992); Tenn. Code Ann. § 48-35-204 (Supp. 1992); Wis. Stat. Ann. § 180.0827 (West Supp. 1992); Wyo.Stat. § 17-16-830(e) (Supp. 1992).

3. See Timothy L. Fort, "Corporate Constituency Statutes: A Dialectical Interpretation," 15 *J. Law & Comm.* 257 (2995).

4. Eric W. Orts, "Beyond Shareholders: Interpreting Corporate Constituency Statutes," *61 Geo. Wash. L. Rev.* 14, 71 (1992).

5. For the remainder of this chapter I use "stakeholder theory" and "corporate constituency statutes" interchangeably.

6. Id. at 152.

7. In this regard, business as mediating institutions theory is much like that of some contemporary feminist theory. The feminist version of stakeholder theory, in fact, develops this notion and will be described in the second section. I have definite affinities with some parts of feminist thought, and it may well be that a mediating institutions theory can be assisted by an integration of the two. That focus on relationality is not the source for mediating institutions in this chapter nor in the sources cited in this chapter, so that integration will not be done here.

8. For an even more sweeping statement of our relational sense, see Errol E. Harris, *Formal, Transcendental and Dialectical Thinking: Logic and Reality* (1984). Harris argues that the entire physical, biological, and even logical structure of the world is "dialectical" (Harris's philosophical term for what is essentially relationality). Thus, it is not simply that human beings are relational, but the entire physical and philosophical world is a series of complex interrelationships.

9. Thomas Donaldson & Lee E. Preston, "The Stakeholder Theory of the Corporation: Concepts, Evidence, and Implications," 20 *Acad. Mgmt. Rev.* 65–91 (1995).

10. See note 2.

11. In addition to other material cited in this chapter, see e.g., Gary von Stange, "Corporate Social Responsibility Through Constituency Statutes: Legend or Lie?," 11 *Hofstra Lab. L.J.* 461 (1994); Edward D. Rodgers, "Striking the Wrong Balance: Constituency Statutes and Corporate Governance," 21 *Pepp. L. Rev.* 777 (1994); Steven M. H. Wallman, "The Proper Interpretation of Corporate Constituency Statutes and Formulation of Director Duties," 25 *Conn. L. Rev.* 681 (1993); Lawrence A. Mitchell, "A Theoretical and Practical Framework for Enforcing Corporate Constituency Statutes," 79 *Texas L. Rev.* 579 (1992); Walter M. Cabot, "The Free Market Promotes Long-Term Efficiency That Benefits All Shareholders," 21 *Stet. L. Rev.* 245 (1991); David Ruder, "Public Obligations of Private Corporations," 114 U. *Pa. L. Rev.* 209 (1965).

12. Orts, supra note 4, at 20.

13. Id. at 23–26.

14. See A. A. Berle Jr., "Corporate Powers as Powers in Trust," 44 *Harv. L. Rev.* 1049 (1931); E. Merrick Dodd Jr., "For Whom Are Corporate Managers Trustees?," 45 *Harv. L. Rev.* 1145 (1932).

15. Thomas J. Baumonte, "The Meaning of the "Corporate Constituency" Provision of the Illinois Business Corporation Act," 27 *Loy. Chi. L. J.* 1, 14 (1995).

16. The seminal portion of Marshall's opinion reads: "[A] corporation is an artificial being, invisible, intangible, and existing only in contemplation of law. Being the mere creature of law, it possesses only those properties which the charter of its creation confers upon it, either expressly, or as incident to its very existence. These are such as supposed best calculated to effect the object for which it was created." Dartmouth College 17 U.S. (4 Wheat.), at 636.

17. John Boatright, "What's So Special About Shareholders?," 4 *Bus. Ethics Q.* 393, 405 (1994).

18. This is not to suggest, however, that there may not be recurring problems in business or recurring values in business that do take on the character of immutability. It simply acknowledges that we are culturally able to specify the particular things that corporations ought to do in our specific society.

19. Id. Boatright concludes that there is no moral superiority of extending duties solely to shareholders. Instead, it is a matter of public policy.

20. See note 4.

21. Orts, supra note 4, at 24. Orts argues that Rust Belt states such as Pennsylvania, Ohio, Wisconsin, Indiana, Minnesota, and Illinois were among the leaders in passing constituency statutes, citing John C. Coffee Jr., "The Uncertain Case for Takeover Reform: An Essay on Stockholders, Stakeholders, and Bustups," 1988 *Wis. L. Rev.* 435, 437.

22. See, e.g., Robert Clark, *Corporate Law* 20 (1986).

23. See Katherine Van Wezel Stone, "Employees as Stakeholders Under State Nonshareholder Constituency Statutes," 21 *Stet. L. Rev.* 45, 54–55, 70–71 (1991).

24. See, e.g., James J. Hanks Jr., "Playing with Fire: Nonshareholder Constituency Statutes in the 1990s, 21 *Stet. L. Rev.* 97, 111 (1991).

25. Jonathan Macey, "An Economic Analysis of the Various Rationales for Making Shareholders the Exclusive Beneficiaries of Corporate Fiduciary Duties," 21 *Stet. L. Rev.* 23 (1991).

26. Id. at 33.

27. Nell Minow, "Shareholders, Stakeholders and Boards of Directors," 21 *Stet. L. Rev.* 197, 219 (1991).

28. F. A. Hayek, *Law, Legislation, Liberty: The Political Order of a Free People* 3 (1982).

29. It is for this reason that, although unlikely to be upheld by the courts, a "takings" problem might exist.

30. See Macey, supra note 25, at 41–44.

31. "Market forces provide the strongest restraints on the discretion of corporate directors." Baumonte, supra note 15, at 17.

32. Joseph Biancalana, "Defining the Proper Corporate Constituency: Asking the Wrong Question," 59 *U. Cin L. Rev.* 425, 429–30 (1990).

33. Id. at 434–36.

34. Id.

35. William J. Carney, "Does Defining Constituencies Matter?," 59 *U. Cin. L Rev.* 385–424 (1990).

36. Bamonte, supra note 15, at 9–10 (quoting *Shlensky v. Wrigley,* 237 N.E.2d 776, 780 [Ill. App. Ct. 1968]) (other citations omitted).

37. Evan & Freeman, supra note 1, at 101–5.

38. Id.

39. Id.

40. Id.

41. Boatright, supra note 17, at 402.

42. See Kenneth E. Goodpaster, "Business Ethics and Stakeholder Analysis," 1 *Bus. Ethics Q.* 53 (1991).

43. See generally, Boatright, supra note 17.

44. Andrew C. Wicks, Daniel R. Gilbert Jr., and R. Edward Freeman, "A Feminist Reinterpretation of the Stakeholder Concept," 4 *Bus. Ethics Q.* 459, 483 (1994).

45. Id, at 490.

46. See Fort, supra note 3, at 265–70.

47. Donaldson & Preston, supra note 9, at 83.

48. Id.

49. Id. at 84.

50. Id. at 84–85.

51. *The Clarkson Principles* 4 (1999).

52. Ian Maitland, "The Morality of the Corporation: An Empirical or Normative Disagreement?," 4 *Bus. Ethics Q.* 445, 455 (1994).

53. Id.

54. Id. at 453.

55. Id.

56. Stephen Cohen, "Stakeholders and Consent," 14 *Bus. & Prof. Ethic. J.* 3, 13 (1996).

57. Sun-Tzu, *The Art of War* (Samuel B. Griffith trans., 1963). In the fourth paragraph of Sun Tzu's work, he writes that leaders must have moral influence so that people are in harmony with their leaders. Id. at 64.

58. Van Wezel Stone, supra note 23, at 54.

59. Id. at 49–51.

60. See, e.g., W. Edwards Deming, *Out of the Crisis* 83–85 (1982); Charles Hampden-Turner, *Creating Corporate Culture: From Discord to Harmony* 58–59 (1990).

61. See generally, Thomas Donaldson & Thomas W. Dunfee, "Toward a Unified Conception of Business Ethics: Integrative Social Contracts Theory," 19 *Acad. Mgmt. Rev.* 252 (1994).

62. Id.

63. Richard John Neuhaus, *Doing Well and Doing Good: The Challenge to the Christian Capitalist* 240 (1992).

64. It may also be true that conscience is an inherent aspect of human nature. I would support that view, in fact. But it is also at least in part the result of the internalization of the results of having been "caught" by others in a commu-

nity. A child who is disciplined for hitting a sibling, for instance, may eventually internalize the notion that she should not hit her brother, regardless of whether or not she could get away with it.

65. See Robert Solmon, *Ethics and Excellence* (1992); Edwin M. Hartmann, *Organizational Ethics and the Good Life* (1996).

66. See Rob Goffee & Gareth Jones, "What Holds the Modern Company Together?," *Harv. Bus. Rev.* 133 (Nov.–Dec. 1996).

67. Id.

68. Id. at 133–34.

69. Id. at 134.

70. William C. Frederick, *Values, Nature & Culture in the American Corporation* 251 (1995).

71. Id.

72. Id. at 261.

73. Id. at 262.

74. Robin Dunbar, *Grooming, Gossip, and the Development of Language* 70 (1996).

75. Lawrence Keeley, *War Before Civilization* 93 (1996).

76. James Q. Wilson, *The Moral Sense* 23, 41–42 (1993).

77. See Jacques Ellul, *The Theological Foundation of Law* 11–43 (1960).

78. See Robert Wright, *The Moral Animal: The New Science of Evolutionary Psychology* (1994).

79. J. Bronowski, *The Ascent of Man* 45 (1973).

80. See, e.g., C. R. Walker & R. H. Guest, *The Man on the Assembly Line* (1952); F. Herzberg, *Work and the Nature of Man* (1966); D. C. McClelland & D. G. Winter, *Motivating Economic Achievement* (1971).

81. See, e.g., Solomon, supra note 65.

82. John Case, *Open-Book Management: The Coming Business Revolution* (1995).

83. Gary Hamel & C. K. Prahalad, *Competing for the Future* 319 (1994).

84. Id.

85. See Timothy L. Fort, "The Spirituality of Solidarity and Total Quality Management," 14 *Bus. & Prof. Ethics J.* 12 (1995), in which I argue that TQM's efficacy is based on an affective connection between the person and her work that is similar to the solidarity prominent in Catholic social thought.

7. Social Contracting

Portions of an earlier version of this chapter were published with my coauthor James J. Noone. My thanks to him for allowing me to use this material in this book.

1. See, e.g., Thomas Donaldson, *Corporations and Morality* (1982).

2. See id. at 42–54.

3. Edward J. Conry, "A Critique of Social Contracts for Business," 5 *Bus. Ethics Q.* 187, 194 (1995).

4. See Michael Keeley, *A Social Contract Theory of Organizations* 52–53 (1988).

5. See id.

6. See Thomas W. Dunfee, "Business Ethics and Extant Social Contracts," 1 *Bus. Ethics Q.* 23 (1991).

7. See, e.g., Steven R. Salbu, "Insider Trading and the Social Contract," 5 *Bus. Ethics Q.* 313 (1995).

8. See id.

9. See id.

10. See Thomas Donaldson & Thomas W. Dunfee, "Toward a Unified Conceptions of Business Ethics: Integrative Social Contracts Theory," 19 *Acad. Mgmt. Rev.* 259–60 (1994).

11. Id. at 257.

12. See id. at 260–62.

13. Id. at 262.

14. See id. at 263.

15. See id. at 262–63.

16. Id. at 263.

17. Thomas Donaldson & Thomas W. Dunfee, *Ties That Bind* 50 (1999).

18. William C. Frederick, *Values, Nature and Culture in the American Corporation* (1995).

19. Mayer, 1996.

20. Donaldson & Dunfee, supra note 17, at 74–78.

21. Id. at 60.

22. Id. at 119.

23. Id. at 121.

24. See James Q. Wilson, *The Moral Sense* 48–49 (1993).

25. Wilson acknowledges that there are also rivalries within the group, but those are different from the resistance shown to those outside the community. See id. at 48.

26. See Tom Chappell, *The Soul of a Business: Managing for Profit and the Common Good* 61–62 (1993).

27. Kent V. Flannery, "Prehistoric Social Evolution," in *Research Frontiers in Anthropology* 3 (Carol R. Ember & Melvin Ember eds., 1995).

28. Id. at 4.

29. Id. at 3.

30. Id.

31. See id. at 5.

32. See id.

33. Id.

34. Id.

35. See id.

36. See id. at 6.

37. See id.

38. See id. at 7.

39. See id.

40. Id.

41. See id.

42. See id. at 8.

43. See id. at 9.

44. Id.

45. See Robert Nisbet, *The Quest For Community* 134–35 (1992).

46. See id. at 89–108.

47. See David Sloan Wilson, "Altruism and Organism: Disentangling the Themes of Multi-Level Selection Theory," 150 *American Naturalist* S122, S232 (Supp. 1997).

48. Alexis De Tocqueville, *Democracy in America* 105–6 (Henry Reeve trans., Phillips Bradley ed., 1945).

49. Id. at 50–51.

50. Donaldson & Dunfee, supra note 17, at 155.

51. Larry Arnhart, *Darwinian Natural Right* (1998).

52. See Frederick, supra note 18, at 168–69.

53. See id. at 172.

54. See id. at 181.

55. See id. at 185–97.

56. By a social rule of reciprocity, I simply mean that in these populations, there is a norm that one should treat others as one has been treated. Some cultures may stretch that to require that a person should treat another as that person would like to be treated, but there is a basic notion of at least tit-for-tat reciprocity in all primate groupings.

57. Michael J. Perry, *Morality, Politics and Law* 15 (1988).

58. For a similar argument, see Alasdair MacIntyre, *Whose Justice, Which Rationality?* (1988).

59. Donaldson & Dunfee, supra note 17, at 183.

60. See 2 Mircea Eliade, *A History of Religious Ideas* 46–56 (Willard R. Trask trans., 1982).

61. See Acts 9:1–31.

62. See Matt Ridley, *The Origins of Virtue: Human Instincts and the Evolution of Cooperation* 257–58 (1996).

63. See generally Fyodor Dostoyevsky, *The Brothers Karamazov* (Richard Peveart & Larissa Volokhonsky trans., 1990).

64. Id. at 246–64.

65. See Robert Whallon, *Elements of Social Change in the Lower Paleolithic* (1989).

66. See id.

67. See William C. Frederick, "Moving to CSR4: What to Pack for the Trip, or The Dinosaur's Next Footprint," Address to the Social Issues in Management Division of the Academy of Management 21–23 (August 10, 1996) (transcript on file with author).

68. John Dobson, *The Art of Management and the Aesthetic Manager: The Coming Way of Business* 59 (1999).

69. Id. at 69.

70. See LaRue Tone Hosmer, *Moral Leadership in Business* 78 (1994). One can develop many nuances of the Golden Rule. In its most basic form, it simply means, "I know how I like to be treated; and that's how I am to treat others." Jeffrey Wattles, *The Golden Rule* 3 (1996). Wattles elaborates the nuances of the Golden Rule in his book.

71. Reciprocity is a norm even shared by some of our closest primate rela-

tives. Frans de Waal has demonstrated that chimpanzees have sophisticated social norms of reciprocity. The fact that our closest animal relatives have social norms similar to our own should strengthen our commitment to our human sense of morality.

72. See Robert Solomon, *Ethics and Excellence* 26 (1993).

73. Keeley, supra note 4, at 22.

74. Id. at 129.

75. See id.

76. See id. at 154.

77. See id.

78. Id. at 6.

79. See id.

80. See Steven P. Vallas & John P. Beck, "The Transformation of Work Revisited: The Limits of Flexibility in American Manufacturing," 43 *Soc. Probs.* 339, 347–48 (1996).

81. See Richard Sennett, *The Corrosion of Character: The Personal Consequences of Work in the New Capitalism* 106–17 (1998).

82. See id. at 113.

83. Id. at 113–14.

84. See Keeley, supra note 4, at 98 (Keeley uses this language to distinguish between the preferences of individuals within an organization and the goals an organization has for itself).

85. Terrence W. Deacon, *The Symbolic Species: The Co-Evolution of Language and the Brain* 23 (1997).

86. See Flannery, supra note 27, at 15.

87. See id.; see also Kalakaua, *The Legends and Myths of Hawaii: The Fables and Folklore of a Strange People* (R. M. Daggett ed., 1888).

88. See id.

89. Robert M. Axelrod, *The Evolution of Cooperation* 211, 1390 (1984).

90. See John Finnis, *Natural Law and Natural Rights* 146–47 (1980).

8. Business as Community

1. *Goldilocks and the Three Bears: Adapted from an English Folk Tale* (Bernice E. Cullinan ed., 1992). The application of the story of Goldilocks to moral theory, particularly from a scientific approach, I owe to biologist Lyall Watson, *Dark Nature: A Natural History of Evil* 15 (1995), who in turn borrowed it from astrophysicist John Gribbin.

2. See e.g., Cass R. Sunstein, "Beyond the Republican Revival," 97 Yale L.J. 1539 (1988); Frank Michelman, "Law's Republic," 97 *Yale L.J.* 1493 (1988).

3. See generally, Stephen B. Presser, *Recapturing the Constitution: Race, Religion and Abortion Reconsidered* (1994).

4. See Amitai Etzioni, *The New Golden Rule* (1996).

5. Id. at 96.

6. Id. at xviii.

7. Id. at 75.

8. Id. at 16.

9. Michael Keeley, "Community, the Joyful Sound," 6 *Bus. Ethics Q.* 549 (1996).

10. For a more complete review of Etzioni and his book, see Timothy L. Fort, "On Golden Rules, Balancing Acts, and Finding the Right Size," 8 *Bus. Ethics Q.* 346 (1998). The following discussion draws significantly from that review.

11. Etzioni, supra note 4, at 127.

12. Derek L. Phillips, *Looking Backward: A Critical Appraisal of Communitarian Thought* 195 (1993).

13. Amy Gutmann, *Communitarian Critics of Liberalism,* 14 Phil. & Pub. Aff. 319 (1985).

14. Etzioni, supra note 4, at 128.

15. Etzioni, supra note 4, at 128.

16. Etzioni, supra note 4, at xix–xx.

17. Etzioni, supra note 4, at xviii.

18. Etzioni defines community as "a web of affect-laden relationships among a group of individuals, relations that often crisscross and reinforce one another (rather than merely one-on-one or chainlike individual relationships), and second, a measure of commitment to a set of shared values, norms, and meanings, and a shared history and identity—in short, to a particular culture." Etzioni, supra note 4, at 127.

19. Etzioni, supra note 4, at 200–8.

20. Etzioni, supra note 4, at 176.

21. Etzioni is fond of the term "moral voice" and devotes a chapter to it by name. Etzioni, supra note 4, at 123–64.

22. Etzioni, supra note 4, at xviii.

23. Jeffrey Wattles, *The Golden Rule* 33 (1996).

24. 2 Samuel 12:1–7.

25. Robert Solomon, *Ethics and Excellence* 105 (1992).

26. Id. at 105, 187.

27. Id. at 145–52.

28. Id. at 109.

29. See Timothy L. Fort, "The Spirituality of Solidarity and Total Quality Management," 14 *Bus. & Prof. Ethics J.* 12 (1995).

30. Janet McCracken & Bill Shaw, "Virtue Ethics and Contractarianism: Towards a Reconciliation," 5 *Bus. Ethics Q.* 297, 310 (1995).

31. Ed Hartman, *Organizational Ethics and the Good Life* (1996).

32. Robert C. Solomon, "The Corporation as Community: A Reply to Ed Hartman," 4 *Bus. Ethics Q.* 271, 276 (1994).

33. Id. at 276–77.

34. McCracken & Shaw, supra note 30, at 310.

35. Bill Shaw & Frances E. Zollers, "Managers the Moral Dimension: What Etzioni Might Mean for Managers," 3 *Bus. Ethics Q.* 153 (1993).

36. Jeffrey Nesteruk, "Law and the Virtues: Developing a Legal Theory for Business Ethics," 5 *Bus. Ethics Q.* 361 (1995); Jeffrey Nesteruk, "Law, Virtue, and the Corporation," 33 *Am. Bus. L. J.* 473 (1996).

37. Jeffrey Nesteruk, "Law, Virtue, and the Corporation," 33 *Am. Bus. L.J.* 473, 482 (1996).

38. Caryn L. Beck-Dudley, "No More Quandaries: A Look at Virtue through the Eyes of Robert Solomon," 34 *Am. Bus. L.J.* 117, 131 (1996).

39. Michael J. Phillips, "Corporate Moral Personhood and Three Conceptions of the Corporation," 2 *Bus. Ethics Q.* 435.

40. Id. at 436.

41. Stephen B. Presser, "Thwarting the Killing of the Corporation: Limited Liability, Democracy, and Economics," 87 *Nw. U. L. Rev.* 148, 155 (1992).

42. Jonathan Macey, "An Economic Analysis of the Various Rationales for Making Shareholders the Exclusive Beneficiaries of Corporate Fiduciary Duties," 21 *Stet. L. Rev.* 23 (1991).

43. Id.

44. Morey McDaniel, "Stockholders and Stakeholders," 21 *Stet. L. Rev.* 121 (1991).

45. See, e.g., F. A. Hayek, *The Fatal Conceit* (1988).

46. McCracken & Shaw, supra note 30, at 302–3.

47. Id. at 310.

48. Ed Conry, "A Critique of Social Contracts for Business," 5 *Bus. Ethics Q.* 187, 197 (1995).

49. Alasdair MacIntyre, *After Virtue* (1981).

50. Charles Taylor, *Multiculturalism and "The Politics of Recognition"* (1992).

51. Stanley Hauerwas, *The Peaceable Kingdom: A Primer in Christian Ethics* (1983).

52. See, e.g., Richard A. Posner, *An Economic Analysis of Law* (2d ed. 1977); see also Richard A. Posner, *The Economics of Justice* 48–87 (1981), in which Posner contracts a concept of justice on wealth maximization with that of utility maximization. Posner argues against general utilitarian notions in favor of a more explicit test of wealth maximization.

53. See Peter Berger & Richard John Neuhaus, *To Empower People: The Role of Mediating Structures in Public Policy* 28 (1977).

54. Id. at 3.

55. Id.

56. Id. at 3–4.

57. Id. at 3.

58. See generally, Hauerwas, supra note 51.

59. See generally, Berger & Neuhaus, supra note 53.

60. See id.

61. Keeley, supra note 9, at 549.

62. Id. at 550–51.

63. Id. at 551.

64. Id. at 556–57.

65. See generally id.

66. Don Mayer, "On Corporations as Communities or Mediating Institutions," Presentation at the Tri-State Academy of Legal Studies in Business (November 9, 1996) (manuscript on file with author), at 16.

67. See, e.g., Robert Bork, *The Tempting Of America* (1990), for a more complete description of judicial restraint and originalism. Bork, of course, was a central intellectual figure in advocating for this philosophy, and his nomination to the Supreme Court demonstrated the stakes of his methodology.

68. See Gordon Wood, *The Creation of the American Republic: 1776–1787* (1969).

69. Michelman, supra note 2, at 1507.

70. Michelman seems to value his dialogical structure as a judicial, not a popular enterprise. He gives a minor role to people who unself-consciously always participate in achieving consensus through debate as part of every-day life, but a big role to the courts. By doing so, he may energize the courts, but the general population's development of citizenship is not likely to occur. See Kathryn Abrams, "Law's Republicanism," 97 *Yale L.J.* 1591, 1596 (1988).

71. Michelman, supra note 2, at 1504–7.

72. Id. at 1513.

73. Id. at 1502, 1526–27.

74. See generally Sunstein, supra note 2.

75. Id. at 1564.

76. Id. at 1564–65.

77. Id. at 1541.

78. Id. at 1544.

79. Id. at 1549.

80. Id. at 1550–51.

81. Id. at 1552.

82. Id. at 1552, 1576–77.

83. Id. at 1554.

84. Id. at 1555.

85. Id. at 1567.

86. Id. at 1550–58.

87. Id. at 1567.

88. Id. at 1567–69.

89. See generally Jonathan R. Macey, "The Missing Element in the Republican Revival," 97 *Yale L.J.* 1673 (1988).

90. Id. at 1679.

91. Id. at 1683.

92. Richard A. Epstein, "Modern Republicanism—Or the Flight from Substance," 97 *Yale L.J.* 1633 (1988).

93. See, e.g., Timothy L. Fort, "The Spirituality of Solidarity and Total Quality Management," 13 *J. Bus. & Prof. Ethics* 3 (1995).

94. Cf. John Howard Yoder, *The Politics of Jesus* 243–44 (1972). Yoder makes the argument about the status of opponents in relation to war. Both Yoder and the republicans, however, recognize the inherent status of others as ends themselves.

95. See Taylor, supra note 50, at 59 (1992). Taylor argues that liberalism's rights protection can be ensured within a Quebec-styled government, whose "common good" has a very specific cultural content.

96. See Sunstein, supra, note 2, at 1555.

97. See Jürgen Habermas, "A Review of Gadamer's 'Truth and Method,'" in *The Hermeneutic Tradition: From Ast to Ricouer* 254 (Ormiston & Schrift eds., 1990). Habermas describes depth-hermeneutics as follows: "Depth-hermeneutic understanding requires therefore systematic pre-understanding that extends onto language in general, whereas hermeneutical understanding always proceeds from a

pre-understanding that is shaped by tradition and which forms and changes itself within linguistic communication."

98. Id. at 239.

99. One may argue whether philosophy is better positioned to make such arguments. I think it is not (at least in any exclusive sense), but regardless of the settlement of that issue, the kinds of questions raised by these fields of inquiry are critical to the efficacy of republicanism.

100. See Kathleen M. Sullivan, "God as a Lobby: The Culture of Disbelief: How American Law and Politics Trivialize Religious Devotion," 61 *U. Chi. L. Rev.* 1655, 1669 (1994) (book review).

101. See generally William Marshall, "The Other Side of Religion," 44 *Hastings L. Rev.* 843 (1993).

102. See John Rawls, *Political Liberalism* 8 (1993).

103. See "Proceedings and Report of the Commissioners for the University of Virginia," in *Manual of the Board of Visitors of the University of Virginia* (1975).

104. Cf. MacIntyre, supra note 49. If one relies on narratives, one must take into account the realities that people bring religious understanding into their notions of what the good is; religion and narrative are usually bound together.

105. See generally, Derrick Bell & Preeta Bansal, "The Republican Revival and Racial Politics," 97 *Yale L.J.* 1609 (1988).

106. Id. at 1612.

107. Id. at 1617.

108. This is, of course, the position Lincoln took against Stephen Douglas. As Lincoln biographer Carl Sandburg wrote:

> A powerful fragment of America breathed in Douglas' saying at Quincy: "Let each State mind its own business and let its neighbors alone! . . . If we stand by that principle, then Mr. Lincoln will find that this republic can exist forever divided into free and slave States. . . . Stand by that great principle and we can go on as we have done, increasing in wealth, in population, in power, and in all the elements of greatness, until we shall be the admiration and terror of the world . . . until we make this continent one ocean-bound people."

Carl Sandburg, *Abraham Lincoln: The Prairie Years and the War Years,* 129 (1970).

109. Marshall, supra note 106. I leave to the side for now the issue of the equivalency of oppression and marginalization. Suffice it to say that marginalization creates a path for oppression.

110. Habermas, supra note 102.

111. Michael J. Perry, *Love and Power: The Role of Religion and Morality in American Politics* 8–16 (1991). Perry argues against a "neutral" version of political dialogue because in so arguing, those who do have religious beliefs are excluded from participating and are thereby marginalized.

112. Alasdair Macintyre, *Three Rival Versions of Moral Enquiry: Encyclopedia, Genealogy, and Tradition* (1990). The theme of a continued discussion with one's ancestors is a dominating feature of this and most others of MacIntyre's works.

113. Id. at 127–48. Cf. Russell Hittinger, "Natural Law and Virtue: Theories at Cross Purposes," in *Natural Law Theory: Contemporary Essays* (Robert P. George

ed., 1994). Hittinger critiques MacIntyre's association of natural law and virtue.

114. See also Richard Sennett, *The Corrosion of Character: The Personal Consequences of Work in the New Capitalism* (1998). Sennett makes a similar critique, but focuses more tightly on the superficial nature of work tools such as "teams."

115. Robert Jackall, *Moral Mazes: The World of Corporate Managers* 75–100, 192 (1988).

116. Sunstein, supra note 2, at 1572.

117. Id. at 1574, 1578.

118. Jonathan R. Macey, "Packaged Preferences and the Institutional Transformation of Interests," 61 *U. Chi. L. Rev.* 1443, 1475 (1994).

119. Abrams, supra note 70, at 1604–5.

120. Id. at 1604, 1615.

121. Paul Brest, "Further Beyond the Republican Revival: Toward Radical Republicanism," 97 *Yale L.J.* 1623, 1624, 1628–29 (1988).

122. Id. at 1624 (citing Pitkin, "Justice: On Relating Private and Public," 9 *Pol. Theory* 327, 347 [1981], quoting J. Tussman, *Obligation and the Body Politic* 78–81 [1960] [footnotes omitted]).

123. Id. at 1629.

124. Id. at 1626, 1631.

125. Bell & Bansal, supra note 111, at 1610–12.

9. Theological Naturalism

1. William C. Frederick, "Moving to CSR4: What to Pack for the Trip," 37 *Bus. & Soc.* 7 (1998).

2. William C. Frederick, *Values, Nature and Culture in the American Corporation* (1995).

3. Frederick, supra note 1.

4. Id. at 50.

5. Id. at 52.

6. David Hume, *Dialogues Concerning Natural Religion* 30 (M. Bell ed., 1779, 1990).

7. Stanley Hauerwas, *The Peaceable Kingdom: A Primer in Christian Ethics* 61 (1983).

8. Frederick, supra note 1, at 23.

9. Emile Durkheim, *The Elementary Structures of Religious Life* 191 (Karen E. Fields trans., 1995).

10. Id.

11. Id.

12. Id. at 192.

13. Durkheim, supra note 9, at 192.

14. Id.

15. Id. Obviously, this is not to argue that moral duties are the only way to create kinship.

16. Richard Dawkins, *Climbing Mount Improbable* (1996) (noting that given enough time monkeys typing could produce a literary masterpiece).

17. See Joseph M. Zycinski, "The Weak Anthropic Principle and the Design Argument," 31 *Zygon* 115, 116 (1996).

18. See, e.g., John D. Barrow & Frank J. Tipler, *The Anthropic Cosmological Principle* (1986); Paul Davies, *The Mind of God: The Scientific Basis for a Rational World* (1992).

19. Zycinski, supra note 21, at 117.

20. Id.

21. Id.

22. Id.

23. Id.

24. Id. at 128.

25. Frederick, supra note 2, at 7–14.

26. Id. at 27–56.

27. Id. at 57–78.

28. Id. at 134–67.

29. David Hume, *Treatise of Human Nature* 469–70 (1888) (distinguishing between facts and values). Larry Arnhart argues that attributing the naturalistic fallacy is a mistake (*Darwinian Natural Right: The Biological Ethics of Human Nature* 70–75 [1998]). Because of its prevalence, however, I do not believe this is the time and place to resolve the historical question regarding attribution.

30. Paul Tillich, *Theologian of the Boundaries* 121 (Mark Kline Taylor ed., 1946).

31. Id. at 39.

32. Id. at 163–64.

33. Id. at 163–166.

34. Id. at 40.

35. Id. at 168.

36. Id. at 172.

37. Id. at 123–25.

38. Id. at 162.

39. Id. at 316.

40. It is important to note, however, that Tillich's theology of the natural are not regarded as his main work. Yet the descriptions he provides as a theologian seem to be a helpful way to link this approach not only to philosophy but also to nature and to religion.

41. Wolfhart Pannenberg, *Toward a Theology of Nature: Essays on Science and Faith* 38 (Ted Peters ed., 1993).

42. Richard T. DeGeorge, "Theological Ethics and Business Ethics," 5 *J. Bus. Ethics* 421, 430 (1986).

43. Pannenberg, supra note 44, at 38.

44. Id. at 39.

45. Id. at 124.

46. DeGeorge, supra note 45, at 424.

47. Matthew 22:37–40; Mark 12:29–31; Luke 10:27–28.

48. Errol E. Harris, *Cosmos and Theos* 61 (1992).

49. Id. at 186.

50. Nancey Murphy & George F. R. Ellis, *On the Moral Nature of the Universe: Theology, Cosmology, and Ethics* 118 (1996).

51. Although this may seem far afield, I would like to make this connection in terms of Dostoyevksy's *The Brothers Karamazov*. I show the movie version of this novel to my business ethics class each term because its themes are directly relevant to business and are directly related to the prior discussion. The Brothers Karamazov, like all Russian novels, is complicated, and explaining exactly how the movie or the novel gets to these three themes will be too distracting from the purpose of this chapter. See Timothy L. Fort, "The Brothers Karamazov: Ethics and Responsibility," in *The Moral Imagination: How Literature and Film Can Stimulate Ethical Reflection in the Business World* (Oliver F. Williams ed., 1998).

52. Jeffrey Wattles, *The Golden Rule* (1996).

53. See generally, Frans de Waal, *Good Natured: The Origins of Right and Wrong in Humans and Other Animals* (1996).

10. The Dark Side of Religion in the Workplace

1. With regard to United States Supreme Court cases in last third of the twentieth century alone, see, e.g., Mueller v. Allen, 463 U.S. 388 (1983); Witters v. Washington Dept. of Servs. for the Blind, 474 U.S. 481 (1986); Meek v. Pittenger, 421 U.S. 349 (1975); School District of Grand Rapids v. Ball, 473 U.S. 373 (1985); Lemon v. Kurtzman, 403 U.S. 602 (1971); Bowen v. Kendrick, 487 U.S. 589 (1988); Widmar v. Vincent, 454 U.S. 263 (1981); Board of Education v. Mergens, 496 U.S. 226 (1990); Committee for Public Education and Religious Liberty v. Nyquist, 413 U.S. 756 (1973); Woman v. Walter, 433 U.S. 229 (1977); Aguila v. Felton, 473 U.S. 402 (1985); Marsh v. Chambers, 463 U.S. 783 (1983); Allegheny County v. Greater Pittsburgh ACLU, 492 U.S. 573 (1989); Edwards v. Aguillard, 482 U.S. 578 (1987); Epperson v. Arkansas, 393 U.S. 97 (1968); Walz v. Tax Commissioner, 397 U.S. 664 (1970); Wallace v. Jaffree, 472 U.S. 38 (1985); Larsen v. Valente, 456 U.S. 228 (1982); Texas Monthly, Inc. v. Bullock, 489 U.S. 1 (1989); Corporation of Presiding Bishop of Church of Jesus Christ of Latter-Day Saints v. Amos, 483 U.S. 327 (1987); Employment Division of Human Resources of Oregon v. Smith, 494, U.S. 872 (1990); Thomas v. Review Board of Indiana Employment Security Division, 450 U.S. 707 (1981); Welsh v. United States, 398 U.S. 333 (1970).

2. William Marshall, "The Other Side of Religion," 44 *Hastings L.J.* 843, 847–51 (1993).

3. Id. at 854.

4. Id. at 857.

5. Id. at 858.

6. Michelle Conlin, "Religion in the Workplace: The Growing Presence of Spirituality in Corporate America," *Business Week*, Nov. 1, 1999, at 150.

7. Id. at 153–54 (citing Ian I. Mitroff).

8. Kathleen M. Sullivan, "Religion and Liberal Democracy," 59 *U. Chi. L. Rev.* 195 (1992).

9. Id.

10. Michael W. McConnell, "The Origins and Historical Understandings of Free Exercise of Religion," 103 *Harv. L. Rev.* 1409 (1990).

11. See, e.g., Richard N. Ostling, "In So Many Gods We Trust," *Time,* Jan. 30, 1995, at 72 (cited in Michael J. Perry, "Religion in Politics," 29 *U.C. Davis L. Rev.* 729 (1996) [hereinafter Perry, "Religion in Politics"]). Ostling reports that 95 percent of Americans believe in God and that 70 percent of American adults are members of a church or synagogue.

12. See Robert Wuthnow, *God and Mammon in America* (1994).

13. Id.

14. Id.

15. Id.

16. Tom Peters, "Business Leaders Should Be Spirited, Not Spiritual," *Chi. Trib.,* Apr. 5, 1993, at 8.

17. Peter Arlow & Thomas A. Ulrich, "A Longitudinal Study of Business School Graduates' Assessments of Business Ethics," 7 *J. Bus. Ethics* 295 (1988).

18. Frederick B. Bird & James A. Waters, "The Moral Muteness of Managers," in *Ethical Issues in Business: A Philosophical Approach* 237 (Thomas Donaldson & Patricia Werhane eds., 5th ed. 1996)

19. Id. at 240–42.

20. Id. at 242.

21. Laura L. Nash, *Believers in Business* 245 (1994).

22. Terry Morehead Dworkin & Ellen R. Pierce, "Is Religious Harassment 'More Equal?,'" 26 *Seton Hall L. Rev.* 44, 78 (citing *Compston,* 424 F. Supp. 157, 158 [S.D. Ohio 1976], and *Weiss,* 595 F. Supp. 1050, 1053 [E.D. Va. 1984]).

23. 63 Fair Empl. Prac. Cas (BNA) 709 (Or. Ct. App. May 19, 1993).

24. Id.

25. EEOC v. Townley Engineering & Mfg. Co., 859 F2d 610 (9th Cir. 1988), cert. denied, 109 S. Ct. 1527 (1989).

26. Dworkin & Pierce, supra note 2, at 79.

27. Id. at 79–80.

28. See Eugene Volokh, "Freedom of Speech and Workplace Harassment," 30 *UCLA L. Rev.* 1791 (1992).

29. Dworkin & Pierce, supra note 22, at 87.

30. Id.

31. 58 Fed. Reg. 51,266 (1993). These guidelines said:

Harassment is the verbal or physical conduct that denigrates or shows hostility or aversion toward an individual because of his/her race, color, religion, gender, national origin, age, or disability, or that of his/her relatives, friends, or associates, and that: (i) Has the purpose of effect of creating an intimidating, hostile, or offensive work environment; (ii) Has the purpose or effect of unreasonably interfering with an individual's work performance; or (iii) Otherwise adversely affects an individual's employment opportunities.

Harassing conduct includes, but it not limited to, the following: (i) Epithets, slurs, negative stereotyping, or threatening, intimidating, or hostile acts, that relate to race, color, religion, gender, national origin, age or disability; and (ii) Written or graphic material which denigrates or shows hostility or aversion toward an individual or group because of race, color, religion, gender, national origin, age, or disability and that is place on walls, bulletin boards, or elsewhere on the employer's premises, or circulated in the workplace.

Harassment Guidelines, at 51269

32. Id.

33. Dworkin & Pierce, supra note 22, at 75.

34. Id. at 76 (citing Robinson v. Jacksonville Shipyards, Inc., 760 F. Supp. 1486, 1534 [M.D. Fla. 1991]).

35. Dworkin & Pierce, supra note 22, at 89–91.

36. Id. at 65–66 (citing Kotcher v. Rosa and Sullivan Appliance Center., Inc., 957 F2d 59, 61 [2d Cir. 1992]).

37. Dworkin & Pierce, supra note 22, at 65 n.100 (citing W. Page Keeton et al., *Prosser & Keeton on the Law of Torts,* sect. 32, at 174 [5th ed. 1984]).

38. Dworkin and Pierce, supra note 22, at 89–90.

39. Id. at 90.

40. Id. at 90–91.

41. Id. at 91.

42. Id.

43. Id.

44. Albert Camus, *The First Man* 193 (David Hapgood trans., 1996). The word "anxiety" was written as an alternative word by the author at the top of the manuscript. Id. at viii (editor's note).

45. Anthony Sampson, *The Company Man* 226 (1995) (quoting Charles M. Albrecht, who led a consulting team of "employee transition" experts in the downsizing at IBM).

46. Ronald M. Green, "Guiding Principles of Jewish Business Ethics," 7 *Bus. Ethics Q.* 21 (1997); Elliot N. Dorff, "Judaism. Business and Privacy," 7 *Bus. Ethics Q.* 31 (1997); Meir Tamari, "The Challenge of Wealth: Jewish Business Ethics," 7 *Bus. Ethics Q.* 45 (1997).

47. Stewart W. Herman, "Enlarging the Conversation," 7 *Bus. Ethics Q.* 5 (1997).

48. Richard. T. DeGeorge, "Theological Ethics and Business Ethics," 5 *J. Bus. Ethics* 421 (1986).

49. Bruce Ackerman, *Social Justice in the Liberal State* 7–8, 14 (1980.

50. Id.

51. Id. at 11.

52. Bruce Ackerman, "Why Dialogue?," 86 *J. Philosophy* 5–22 (1989).

53. Thomas Nagel, "Moral Conflict and Political Legitimacy," 16 *Phil. & Pub. Affairs* (1987).

54. Id. at 215–40.

55. Id.

56. Michael J. Perry, *Love and Power* 12 (1991) [hereinafter Perry, *Love and Power*].

57. Perry, "Religion in Politics," supra note 11 (citing Ostling, supra note 11).

58. Id. (citing Book Note, "Religion and *Roe:* The Politics of Exclusion," 108 *Harvard L. Rev.* 495, 498 n.21 (1994) (reviewing Elizabeth Meschn & Alan Freeman, *The Politics of Virtue: Is Abortion Debatable?* [1993]).

59. Perry, "Religion in Politics," supra note 11, at 729.

60. Richard Jones, "Concerning Secularists' Proposed Restrictions of the Role of Religion in American Politics," 8 *B.Y.U. J. Pub. L.* 343, 346 (1994).

61. See, e.g., Stephen L. Carter, *The Culture of Disbelief: How American Law and Politics Trivialize Religious Devotion* (1993); Richard J. Neuhaus, *The Naked Public Square: Religion and Democracy in America* (1984); A. James Reichley, *Religion in America* (1985); Larry Alexander, "Liberalism, Religion and the Unity of Epistemology," 30 *San Diego L. Rev.* 763 (1993); Peter Berger, *The Sacred Canopy* (1967).

62. John Rawls, *Political Liberalism* (1993).

63. See Perry, *Love and Power,* supra note 56, at 42.

64. Jürgen Habermas, "A Review of Gadamer's 'Truth and Method,'" in *The Hermeneutic Tradition: From Ast to Ricouer* 239 (Gayle L. Ormiston & Alan D. Schrift eds., 1990).

65. Robert E. Cole, "Quality Circles," in *Quality Management Handbook* 86 (Loren Walsh, Ralph Wurster, & Raymond Kimber, eds., 1986).

66. Id.

67. Mary Walton, *The Deming Management Method* 58 (1986). See also Joseph Juran who said, "The starting point is the *attitude* that a breakthrough is both desirable and feasible. In human organizations, there is no change unless there is first an advocate of change. If someone does want a change, there is still a long hard road before change is achieved. But the first step on that road is someone's belief that a change—a breakthrough—is desirable and feasible. That a change is desirable in mainly an act of faith of belief." Joseph M. Juran, *Managerial Breakthrough: A New Concept of the Manager's Job* 15 (1964).

68. Kent Greenawalt, *Private Consciences and Public Reasons* 139, 163 (1995).

69. Timothy L. Fort, "Religious Belief, Corporate Leadership, and Business Ethics," *Am. Bus. L.J.* 451, 459–65 (1996).

70. Marshall, supra note 2.

71. Greenawalt, supra note 68, at 70.

72. Id. at 45–46.

73. Perry, *Love and Power,* supra note 56.

74. Michael J. Perry, "Religious Morality and Political Choice: Further Thoughts—Second Thoughts—on *Love and Power,*" 30 *San Diego L. Rev.* 703 (1993) [hereinafter "Religious Morality"].

75. Id.

76. Id.

77. See Perry, "Religion in Politics," supra note 11, at 754–55.

78. Id. at 755.

79. Greenawalt, supra note 68, at 69–70.

80. Marshall, supra note 2, at 847–63.

81. Perry, *Religion in Politics,* supra note 11, at 745–46.

82. Id. at 754.

83. See generally id.

84. Id. at 748.

85. Id. In an important qualification too complex to detail here, Perry argues that questions about human worth are exempt from this requirement to offer a secular reason. The reason for this, as Perry has described in "Is the Idea of Human Rights Ineliminably Religious?," in *Legal Rights: Historical and Philosophi-*

cal Precepts (Austin Sarat & Thomas Kearns eds., 1996) is that notions of human worth boil down to religious, or at least nonprovable claims. Perry details a sort of Rawslian "overlapping consensus" to demonstrate that the notion of all life being sacred is a central tenet of religious and secular morality, which serves as a basis for human rights. Nevertheless, since the underlying basis for the morality is religious, this requirement is exempt from the secular requirement. Perry, "Religion in Politics," supra note 11, at 756–67.

86. Perry, "Religion in Politics," supra note 11, at 767–68.

87. Id. at 787.

88. Id. at 777.

89. Id. at 769.

90. Id. at 770–71.

91. Id. at 772.

92. See David M. Smolin, "The Enforcement of Natural Law by the State: A Response to Professor Calhoun," 16 *U. Dayton L. Rev.* 381, 391–92 (cited in Perry, "Religion in Politics," supra note 11, at 788).

93. Perry, "Religion in Politics," supra note 11, at 770–71.

94. Mark A. Noll, *The Scandal of the Evangelical Mind* 207–8 (1994) (cited in Perry, "Religion in Politics," supra note 11, at 789).

95. Perry, "Religion in Politics," supra note 11, at 789.

96. Id. at 772–73.

97. Id. at 773–74 (citing Richard John Neuhaus, "Reason Public and Private: The Pannenberg Project," *First Things,* March 1992, at 55, 57; and Richard John Neuhaus, "Nihilism without the Abyss: Laws, Rights, and Transcendent Good," 5 *J. L. & Religion* 53, 62 [1987]).

98. See Manuel Velasquez & Neil Brady, "Catholic Natural Law and Business Ethics," 7 *Bus. Ethics Q.* 83 [1997] for a good overview of various natural law variations.

99. Id.

100. See Perry, "Love and Power," supra note50.

101. See Ackerman, supra note 49.

102. See Rawls, supra note 62.

103. See Nagel, supra note 53.

104. Robert Jackall, *Moral Mazes: The World Of Corporate Managers* 19 (1988).

105. See William C. Frederick, *Values, Nature and Culture in the American Corporation* 92–99 (1995).

106. Jacques Ellul, *The Theological Foundation of Law* (Marguerite Wieser trans., 1960).

107. For a more complete analysis of Ellul's position, see Timothy L. Fort, *Law and Religion* 19–25 (1987).

108. See, e.g., John Finnis, *Natural Law and Natural Rights* (1980).

109. Ellul, supra note 106, at 10.

110. Ellul actually characterizes as a three-part development, but stages 3 and 4 as I describe them seem to be separate, though certainly related stages within Ellul's original stage 3.

111. Ellul, supra note 106, at 18.

112. Id.

113. Id.
114. Id.
115. Id.
116. Id.
117. Id.
118. Id.
119. Id.
120. Fort, supra note 107, at 69–119.
121. Id.
122. See, e.g., Morton Horwitz, *The Transformation of American Law* (1977). Horwitz did this when he alleged that there was a very broad-based conspiracy of American businesses so that once commercial interests were firmly in power in the nineteenth century, jurists reinterpreted the law for the benefit of these interests.
123. I think here of the annual report shortly before April 15 that tells us that 30 to 50 percent of the answers given to taxpayers on the IRS helpline are incorrect.
124. See Internal Revenue Code sect. 2056.
125. See, e.g., John C. Haughey, S.J., *Converting 9 to 5: A Spirituality of Daily Work* (1989).
126. See LaRue Tone Hosmer, "Why Be Moral? A Different Rationale for Managers," 4 *Bus. Ethics Q.* 191 (1994).
127. Id. at 192–93.
128. Bill Shaw and John Corvino, "Hosmer and the 'Why Be Moral?'Question," 6 *Bus. Ethics Q.* 373 (1996).
129. Id.
130. Herman, supra note 47, at 16.

11. Bright Dots, Dot Coms, and Camelot?

1. Alan Jay Lerner & Frederick Lowe, *Camelot* (Columbia Records, 1960).
2. See generally, David M. Messick, "Social Categories and Business Ethics," *Bus. Ethics Q. Special Issue: Ruffin Series 1,* at 149 (1998).
3. Id. at 153.
4. Id. at 153.
5. With apologies to Rogers & Hammerstein's song "My Favorite Things" from the *Sound of Music.* In the song, the lyric is "Snowflakes that stay on my nose and eyelashes."
6. Messick, supra note 2, at 149.
7. Rather than altruism, Bill Frederick offers the notion of "mutualism." Mutualism takes into account the notion that there is some benefit to an individual for offering assistance that might otherwise appear to be sacrificial. That benefit might be characterized in terms of a connection to one's kin, genes, or group generally. It is a term that I prefer to "altruism" because it seems to characterize the individual's connection to the group more directly than does "altruism." More generally, it means that organisms "help each other out." This distinction,

for purposes of this chapter seems a minor point in the context of Messick's argument. For a description of mutualism, see William C. Frederick, *Values, Nature and Culture in the American Corporation* 157–62 (1995).

8. Messick, supra note 2, at 150.

9. It is important to note that this does not mean "survival of the fittest," a term incorrectly attributed to Darwin. Efficiency behavior does not require that the most efficient behavior take place, but that a behavior sufficient enough to survive take place.

10. Robert Trivers, "The Evolution of Reciprocal Altruism," 46 *Q. Rev. Biology* 35 (1971).

11. Messick, supra note 2, at 153.

12. Frederick, supra note 2.

13. Donna J. Wood, "Ingroups and Outgroups: What Psychology Doesn't Say," *Bus. Ethics Q. Special Issue: Ruffin Series 1,* 176 (1998).

14. Edwin M. Hartman, "Altruism, Ingroups and Fairness: Comments on Messick," *Bus. Ethics Q. Special Issue: Ruffin Series 1,* 179 (1998).

15. Aristotle, *Politics,* in *The Complete Works of Aristotle* 1253a 30–31, 1278b 17–31 (Jonathan Barnes ed., 1984). My thanks to Bob Solomon for first suggesting to me that I explore the connection between Aristotle and biology.

16. Aristotle, *Nichomachean Ethics* 80 (Martin Ostwald trans., 1962).

17. Peter Berger & Richard John Neuhaus, *To Empower People: The Role of Mediating Structures in Public Policy* 28 (1977).

18. Benedict de Spinoza, *The Ethics* 62 (R. H. M. Elwes trans., 1955). My thanks to Tom Donaldson for suggesting that I explore the relationship of Spinoza and naturalist ethics.

19. See, e.g., 2 Mircea Eliade, *A History of Religious Ideas* 44–46, 91–106 (Willard R. Trask trans., 1982); Mircea Eliade, *Yoga: Immortality and Freedom* (Willard R. Trask trans., 1969); Peter J. Paris, *The Spirituality of African Peoples: A Search for a Common Discourse* 28–33 (1995); Vine Delore Jr., *God Is Red: A Native View of Religion* 88–95; Scott Cunningham, *Hawaiian Religion and Magic* (1994); Meister Eckhart, *Selected Writings* (Oliver Davies trans., 1994).

20. Thomas Donaldson & Thomas W. Dunfee, "Toward a Unified Conception of Business Ethics: Integrative Social Contracts Theory," 19 *Acad. Mgmt. Rev.* 252, 265 (1994).

21. Joshua D. Margolis, "Psychological Pragmatism and the Imperative of Aims: A New Approach for Business Ethics," 8 *Bus. Ethics Q.* 409, 410–11 (1998).

22. Id. at 410.

23. See, e.g., Steve Lohr, "Welcome to the Internet, The First Global Colony," *N.Y. Times,* January 9, 2000, sec. 4, in which the author notes concerns around the globe that the Internet is a way to impose American cultural values.

24. See, e.g., Sheryl Gay Stolberg, "Internet Prescriptions Boom in the 'Wild West' of the Web," *N.Y. Times,* June 27, 1999, at 1.

25. John Steele Gordon, "The Golden Spike," *Forbes,* February 21, 2000, at 118; Edward Rothstein, "The Transcontinental Railroad as the Internet of 1869," *N.Y. Times,* December 11, 1999, Arts, A21.

26. Phillip M. Nichols, "Regulating Transnational Bribery in Times of Globalization and Fragmentation," 24 *Yale J. Int'l L.* 257, 263 (1999), citing Robert McGee.

27. Lawrence Keeley, *War Before Civilization* 117–21 (1996).

28. Id. at 181.

29. Leslie E. Sponsel, "The Natural History of Peace: The Positive View of Human Nature and Its Potential," in *A Natural History of Peace* (Thomas Gregor ed., 1996), citing David Fabbro, "Peaceful Societies: An Introduction," 15 *J. Peace Research* 67 (1978).

30. See Julia Marvin, "The Prose Brut Chronicle and the Lessons of Vernacular History," 148–52, Ph.D. dissertation, Princeton University (1997), in which she notes that the ideal for governance through a devolved structure is a parliamentary ideal for governance transforming warriors into peaceful participants in the quest for justice.

31. Adapted from Timothy L. Fort, "Who Will Clean Up the Mess?" Originally published in the *Chicago Tribune* on June 15, 1990.

Bibliography

Articles and Books

Abrams, Kathryn, "Law's Republicanism," 97 *Yale L.J.* 1591 (1988).

Abbeglen, James, & George Stalk Jr., *Kaisha: The Japanese Corporation* 183 (1985).

Ackerman, Bruce, *Social Justice in the Liberal State* (1980).

——, "Why Dialogue?" 86 *J. Phil.* 5 (1989).

Alchian, Armen A., & Harold Demsetz, "Production, Information Costs, and Economic Organization," 62 *Am. Econ. Rev.* 777 (1972).

Alexander, Larry, "Liberalism, Religion and the Unity of Epistemology," 30 *San Diego L. Rev.* 763 (1993).

Andre, Thomas J., Jr., "Some Reflections on German Corporate Governance: A Glimpse at German Supervisory Boards," 70 *Tulane L. Rev.* 1819 (1996).

Aoki, Masahiko, "The Japanese Firm as a System of Attributes: A Survey and Research Agenda," in *The Japanese Firm: The Sources of Competitive Strength* (Masahiko Aoki & Ronald Doe eds., 1994.

——, "Toward an Economic Model of the Japanese Firm," 28 *J. Econ. Lit.* 1 (1990).

Aristotle, *Nichomachean Ethics* (Martin Ostwald trans. 1962).

——, Politics, in *The Complete Works of Aristotle* (Jonathan Barnes ed., 1984).

Arlow, Peter, & Thomas A. Ulrich, "A Longitudinal Study of Business School Graduates' Assessments of Business Ethics," 7 *J. Bus. Ethics* 295 (1988).

Arnhart, Larry, *Darwinian Natural Right: The Biological Ethics of Human Nature* (1998).

Arrow, Kenneth J., "Oral History I: An Interview," in *Arrow and the Ascent of Modern Economic Theory* (George R. Feiwel ed., 1987).

Aquinas, Thomas, *Treatise on Law* (from *Summa Theologica* Questions 90–97).

Axelrod, Robert M., *The Evolution of Cooperation* (1984).

Banker, Stephen M., "Climate for M&A in Japan Shifts, Country Appears to Be

Overcoming Its Traditional Cultural and Legal Barriers," *N.Y. L.J.* Nov. 15, 1999, at 54.

Barrow, John D., & Frank J. Tipler, *The Anthropic Cosmological Principle* (1988).

Baumonte, Thomas J., "The Meaning of the 'Corporate Constituency' Provision of the Illinois Business Corporation Act," 27 *Loy. Chi. L.J.* 1 (1995).

Berglof, E., & E. Perotti, "The Governance Structure of the Japanese Financial Keiretsu," 36 *J. Fin. Econ.* 259 (1994).

Beck-Dudley, Caryn L., "No More Quandaries: A Look at Virtue Through the Eyes of Robert Solomon," 34 *Am. Bus. L.J.* 117 (1996).

Bell, Derrick, & Preeta Bansal, "The Republican Revival and Racial Politics," 97 *Yale L.J.* 1609 (1988).

Bellah, Robert N., Richard Madsen, William M. Sullivan, Ann Swidler, & Steven M. Tipton, *The Good Society* (1991).

Benson, Benjamin, "Do You Keep Too Many Secrets," in Ward & Astroff, *Family Business Sourcebook,* reprinted from *Nation's Bus.* (Aug. 1989).

Berger, Peter, *The Sacred Canopy* (1967).

Berger, Peter, & Richard John Neuhaus, *To Empower People: The Role of Mediating Structures in Public Policy* (1977).

Berle, A. A., Jr., "Corporate Powers as Powers in Trust," 44 *Harv. L. Rev.* 1049 (1931).

Biancalana, Joseph, "Defining the Proper Corporate Constituency: Asking the Wrong Question," 59 *U. Cin. L. Rev.* 425 (1990).

Bird, Frederick B., & James A. Waters, "The Moral Muteness of Managers," in *Ethical Issues in Business: A Philosophical Approach* 237 Thomas Donaldson & Patricia Werhane, eds. (5th ed. 1996).

Birdsell, Joseph, "On Population Structure in Generalized Hunting and Gathering Population," in 12 *Evolution* 2 (1958).

Bisignani, J. D., *Kauai Handbook* (3d ed. 1997)

Black, Bernard, & Reinier Kraakman, "A Self-Enforcing Model of Corporate Law," 109 *Harv. L. Rev.* 1911 (1996).

Boatright, John R., "Business Ethics and the Theory of the Firm," 34 *Am. Bus. L.J.* 217 (1996).

———, "What's So Special About Shareholders?," 4 *Bus. Ethics Q.* 393 (1994).

Boehm, Christopher, "Emergency Decisions, Cultural-Selection Mechanics, and Group Selection," 37 *Current Anthropology* 763 (1996).

Bollier, David, *Aiming Higher* (1997).

Bork, Robert, *The Tempting of America* (1990).

Bowie, Norman E., & R. Edward Freeman, "Ethics and Agency Theory: An Introduction," in *Ethics and Agency Theory: An Introduction* (Norman E. Bowie & R. Edward Freeman eds., 1992).

Boyle, Joseph, "Natural Law and the Ethics of Traditions," in *Natural Law Theory: Contemporary Essays* (Robert P. George ed., 1992).

Bradley, Michael, Cindy Schipani, Anant K. Sundaram, & James P. Walsh, "Corporate Governance in a Comparative Setting: The United States, Germany, and Japan," 62 *L. & Cont. Probs.* 9 (1999).

Bremner, Brian, "The Stock Option Comes to Japan," *Bus. Week,* Apr. 19, 1999, at 39.

Brest, Paul, "Further Beyond the Republican Revival: Toward Radical Republicanism," 97 *Yale L.J.* 1623 (1988).

Brooks, Nancy Rivera, "Advisory May Imperil Worker Stock Options," *Los Angeles Times,* Jan. 22, 2000, at A1, A7.

Bronowski, Jacob, *The Ascent of Man* (1973).

Brutus, in John DeWitt, I, "American Herald" (Oct.–Dec. 1747), in 4 *Complete Anti-Federalist* (300–301).

Bryant, Adam, "After 7 Years, Employees Win United Airlines," *N.Y. Times,* July 13, 1994, at A1.

Buchholz, Rogene A., & Sandra R. Rosenthal, "Toward a New Understanding of Moral Pluralism," 6 *Bus. Ethics Q.* 263 (1996).

Burrogh, Bryan, & John Helyar, *Barbarians at the Gate: The Fall of RJR Nabisco* (1990).

Burtchaell, James T., *Philemon's Problem: The Daily Dilemma of the Christian* (1973).

Byron, William, "Core Principles of Catholic Social Thought," *America,* Oct. 31, 1998, at www.americapress.org/articles/Byron.htm.

Cabot, Walter M., "The Free Market Promotes Long-Term Efficiency That Benefits All Shareholders," 21 *Stet. L. Rev.* 245 (1991).

Calabresi, Steven G., "Political Parties as Mediating Institutions," 61 *U. Chi. L. Rev.* 1479 (1994).

Camus, Albert, *The First Man* (David Hapgood trans., 1996).

Carney, William J., "Does Defining Constituencies Matter?," 59 *U. Cin. L. Rev.* 385 (1990).

Carr, Edward, "Survey, Business in Europe: Fortress Against Change," *Economist,* Nov. 23, 1996, at 3.

Carter, Stephen L., *The Culture of Disbelief: How American Law and Politics Trivialize Religious Devotion* (1993).

Case, John, *Open-Book Management: The Coming Business Revolution* (1995).

Chappell, Tom, *Soul of a Business: Managing for Profit and the Common Good* (1993).

Chesterton, G. K., *Orthodoxy* (1990).

Christian, Nichole M., "3,400 Strike G.M. Plant; Assembly Put at Risk," *N.Y. Times,* June 6, 1998, at A7.

Choy, Jon, "Hashimoto Lights Fuse for "Big Bang" in Japan's Financial Sector," *JEI Rep.,* Nov. 22, 1996, at 1.

Clark, Robert, *Corporate Law* (1986).

Clarkson Centre for Business Ethics, *The Clarkson Principles* (1999).

Coase, Ronald, "The Nature of the Firm," 4 *Economica* 386 (1937).

Cohen, Meir Dan, "Between Selves and Collectivities: Toward a Jurisprudence of Identity," 61 *U. Chi. L. Rev.* 1213 (1994).

Cohen, Jack, & Ian Stewart, *Discovering Simplicity in a Complex World* (1994).

Cohen, Stephen, "Stakeholders and Consent," 14 *Bus. & Prof. Ethic. J.* 3 (1996).

Cole, Robert E., "Quality Circles," in *Quality Management Handbook* (Loren Walsh, Ralph Wurster, & Raymond Kimber eds., 1986).

Conlin, Michelle, "Religion in the Workplace: The Growing Presence of Spirituality in Corporate America," 151 *Time,* Nov. 1, 1999, at 150.

Conrad, Alfred F., "Corporate Constituencies in Western Europe," 21 *Stetson L. Rev.* 73 (1991).

Conry, Edward J., "A Critique of Social Contracts for Business," 5 *Bus. Ethics Q.* 187 (1995).

Cunningham, Scott, *Hawaiian Religion And Magic* (1994).

Damon, William, "The Moral Development of Children," *Sci. Am.* 73 (Aug. 1999).

Davies, Paul, *The Mind of God: The Scientific Basis for a Rational World* (1992).

Dawkins, Richard, *The Blind Watchmaker* (1986).

———, *Climbing Mount Improbable* (1996).

Deacon, Terrence W., *The Symbolic Species: The Co-Evolution of Language and the Brain* (1997).

Deery, Robbin, "The Mother-Child Paradigm and Its Relevance to the Workplace," 38 *Bus. & Soc.* 217 (1999).

DeGeorge, Richard, "Theological Ethics and Business Ethics," 5 *J. Bus. Ethics* 421 (1986).

DeLoria, Vine, *God Is Red: A Native View of Religion* (1994).

Deming, W. Edwards, *Out of the Crisis* (1982).

Dobson, John, *The Art of Management and the Aesthetic Manager: The Coming Way of Business* (1999).

Dodd, E. Merrick, Jr., "For Whom Are Corporate Managers Trustees?," 45 *Harv. L. Rev.* 1145 (1932).

Donaldson, Thomas, *Corporations and Morality* (1982).

Donaldson, Thomas, & Thomas W. Dunfee, *Ties That Bind* (1999).

———, "Toward a Unified Conception of Business Ethics: Integrative Social Contracts Theory," 19 *Acad. Mgmt. Rev.* 252 (1994).

Donaldson, Thomas, & Lee E. Preston, "The Stakeholder Theory of the Corporation: Concepts, Evidence, and Implications," 20 *Acad. Mgmt. Rev.* 65 (1995).

Dorrien, Gary, *The Neoconservative Mind: Politics, Culture and Ideology* (1993).

Dorff, Elliot N., "Judaism. Business and Privacy," 7 *Bus. Ethics Q.* 31 (1997).

Dostoyevsky, Fyodor, *The Brothers Karamazov* (Richard Peveart & Larissa Volokhonsky trans., 1990).

Duechler, Martina, *The Confucian Transformation of Korea* (1992).

Dunbar, Robin, *Grooming, Gossip, and the Evolution of Language* (1996).

Dunfee, Thomas W., "Business Ethics and Extant Social Contracts," 1 *Bus. Ethics Q.* 23 (1991).

———, "Corporate Governance in a Market with Morality," 62 *J. L. & Cont. Probs.* 129 (1999).

Durkheim, Emile, *The Elementary Forms of Religious Life* (Karen E. Fields trans., 1995).

———, "Rules for the Explanation of Social Facts," in *High Points in Anthropology* 233 (Paul Bohannan & Mark Glazer eds., 1973).

Dworkin, Terry Morehead, & Ellen R. Pierce, "Is Religious Harassment 'More Equal?,'"26 *Seton Hall L. Rev.* 44 (1997).

Easterbrook, Frank H., & Daniel Fischel, *The Economic Structure of Corporate Law* (1991).

Eckhart, Meister, *Selected Writings* (Oliver Davies trans., 1994).

Eliade, Mircea, *A History of Religious Ideas* (Willard R. Trask trans., 1982).

———, *Yoga: Immortality and Freedom* (Willard R. Trask trans., 2d ed. 1969).

Ellul, Jacques, *The Theological Foundation of Law* (1960).

Elster, Jon, "Marxism, Functionalism, and Game Theory," 11 *Theory & Soc'y* 453 (1982).

The Empire Strikes Back (Lucasfilms-Twentieth Century Fox 1980).

Epstein, Richard A., "Modern Republicanism—Or the Flight from Substance," 97 *Yale L.J.* 1633 (1988).

Evan, William M., & R. Edward Freeman, "A Stakeholder Theory of the Modern Corporation: Kantian Capitalism," in *Ethical Theory and Business* (Tom L. Beauchamp & Norman E. Bowie eds., 3d ed., 1988).

Etzioni, Amitai, *The New Golden Rule* (1996).

Fabbro, David, "Peaceful Societies: An Introduction," 15 *J. Peace Res.* 67 (1978).

Farber, Daniel A., & Suzanna Sherry, *A History of the American Constitution* (1990).

Finnis, John, *Natural Law and Natural Rights* (1980).

———, "Natural Law and Legal Reasoning," in *Natural Law Theory: Contemporary Essays* (Robert P. George ed., 1994).

Fischer, Louis, *The Life of Mahatma Gandhi* (1950).

Flannery, Kent V., "Prehistoric Social Evolution," in *Research Frontiers in Anthropology* (Carol R. Ember & Melvin Ember eds., 1995).

Flath, David, "Shareholdings in the Keiretsu, Japan's Financial Groups," *Rev. Econ. & Stat.* 249 (1993).

Fort, Timothy L., "The Brothers Karamazov: Ethics and Responsibility," in *The Moral Imagination: How Literature and Film Can Stimulate Ethical Reflection in the Business World* (Oliver F. Williams ed., 1998).

———, "Corporate Constituency Statutes: A Dialectical Interpretation," 15 *J.L. & Com.* 257 (1995).

———, *Law and Religion* 71 (1987).

———, "Mediating Law and Religion in the Workforce Naturally," 12 *Notre Dame J.L. Ethics. & Pub. Pol'y.* 121(1998).

———, "On Golden Rules, Balancing Acts, and Finding the Right Size," 8 *Bus. Ethics Q.* 346 (1998).

———, "Religious Belief, Corporate Leadership, and Business Ethics," *Am. Bus. L.J.* 451 (1996).

———, "The Spirituality of Solidarity and Total Quality Management," 14 *Bus. & Prof. Ethics J.* 12 (1995).

———, "Trust and Law's Facilitation Role," 34 *Am. Bus. L.J.* 205 (1997).

———, "Who Will Clean Up the Mess?," *Chi. Trib.*, June 15, 1990, at 25.

Franks, Julian, & Colin Mayer, *German Capital Markets, Corporate Control, and Obstacles to Hostile Takeovers: Lessons from Three Case Studies,* London Business School Working Paper (1993).

Frederick, William C., "Complexity, Corporation, Community: How Nature Shapes Business's Civic Role," Address to the Midwest Division of the Academy of Management (Apr. 18, 1998) (manuscript on file with author).

———, "Moving to CSR4: What to Pack for the Trip, or The Dinosaur's Next Footprint," Address to the Social Issues in Management Division of the Academy of Management (Aug. 10, 1996) (manuscript on file with author).

———, *Values, Nature, and Culture in the American Corporation* (1995).

Fukao, Mitsuhiro, *Financial Integration, Corporate Governance, and the Performance of Multinational Corporations* 119 (1995).

Fuller, Lon, *Anatomy of the Law* (1968).

Fung, Shirley, "How Should We Pay Them?," *Across the Board,* June 1, 1999, at 37.

Genay, Hesna, "Japan's Corporate Groups," 15 *Econ. Persp.* 20 (1991).

Gilson, Ronald, & Mark J. Roe, "Understanding the Japanese Keiretsu: Overlaps Between Governance and Industrial Organization," 102 *Yale L.J.* 871 (1993).

———, "Essay: Lifetime Employment: Labor Peace and the Evolution of Japanese Corporate Governance," 99 *Colum. L. Rev.* 508, 529 (Mar. 1999).

Gini, Al, "Soul as an Ethic," 7 *Bus. Ethics Q.* 157 (1997) (reviewing Allan Cox, *Redefining Corporate Soul: Linking Purpose and People* (1996)).

Gleick, James, *Chaos: Making a New Science* (1987).

Glouchevitch, Philip, Juggernaut—*The German Way of Doing Business* 136 (1992).

Goffee, Rob, & Gareth Jones, "What Holds the Modern Company Together," *Harv. Bus. Rev.* 113 (Nov.–Dec. 1996).

Goldilocks and the Three Bears: Adapted from an English Folk Tale (Bernice E. Cullinan ed., 1992).

Goodpaster, Kenneth E., "Business Ethics and Stakeholder Analysis," 1 *Bus. Ethics Q.* 553 (1991).

Gordon, John Steele, "The Golden Spike," *Forbes,* Feb. 21, 2000, at 118.

Gorov, Lynda, "The Varied Foes of WTO Unite in Seattle Protests," *Boston Globe,* Nov. 30, 1999, at A1.

Granovetter, Mark, "Economic Action and Social Structure: The Problem of Embeddedness," 91 *Am. J. Soc.* 481 (1985).

Green, Ronald M., "Guiding Principles of Jewish Business Ethics," 7 *Bus. Ethics Q.* 21 (1997).

Greenawalt, Kent, *Private Consciences and Public Reasons* (1995).

Greenhouse, Steven, "The U.P.S. Walkout: News Analysis; High Stakes for 2 Titans," *N.Y. Times,* Aug. 5, 1997, at A1.

Greenleaf, Robert K., *Servant Leadership: A Journey Into the Nature of Legitimate Power and Greatness* (1977).

Greising, David, "Shades of Seattle Riot as Clinton Addresses Elite Economic Forum," *Chi. Trib.,* Jan. 30, 2000, at C13.

Gustafson, James M., *Intersections: Science, Theology, and Ethics* (1996).

Gutmann, Amy, "Communitarian Critics of Liberalism," 14 *Phil. & Pub. Aff.* 319 (1985).

Habermas, Jürgen, "A Review of Gadamer's 'Truth and Method,'" in *The Hermeneutic Tradition: From Ast to Ricouer* (Gayle L. Ormiston and Alan D. Schrift eds., 1990).

Hamel, Gary, & C. K. Prahalad, *Competing For the Future* (1994).

Hampden-Turner, Charles, *Creating Corporate Culture: From Discord to Harmony* (1990).

Hanks, James J., Jr., "Playing with Fire: Nonshareholder Constituency Statutes in the 1990s," 21 *Stet. L. Rev.* 97 (1991).

Hartman, Rima F., "Note, Situation-Specific Fiduciary Duties for Corporate Directors: Enforceable Obligations or Toothless Ideals?," 50 *Wash. & Lee L. Rev.* 1761 (1993).

Hauerwas, Stanley, *The Peaceable Kingdom: A Primer in Christian Ethics* (1983).

Harris, Errol E., *Cosmos and Theos: Ethical and Theological Implications of the Anthropic Cosmological Principle* (1992).

————, *Formal, Transcendental and Dialectical Logic: Logic and Reality* (1987).

Hartman, Edwin M., "Altruism, Ingroups and Fairness: Comments on Messick," 1 *Bus. Ethics Q. Special Issue: Ruffin Series* 179 (1998).

————, *Organizational Ethics and the Good Life* (1996).

Hasnas, John, "The Normative Theories of Business Ethics: A Guide for the Perplexed," 8 *Bus. Ethics Q.* 19 (1998).

Haughey, John C., S.J., *Converting 9 to 5: A Spirituality of Daily Work* (1989).

————, *The Holy Use of Money: Personal Finance in Light of the Christian Faith* (1986).

Havel, Vaclev, *Disturbing the Peace* (1987).

Hayek, F. A., *Law, Legislation, Liberty: The Political Order of a Free People* (1982).

————, *The Fatal Conceit* (1988).

Hazen, Thomas Lee, "The Corporate Persona, Contract (and Market) Failure, and Moral Values," 69 *N.C. L. Rev.* 273 (1991).

Herman, Stewart W., "Enlarging the Conversation," 7 *Bus. Ethics Q.* 5 (1997).

Herzberg, F., *Work and the Nature of Man* (1966).

Hittinger, Russell, "Natural Law and Virtue: Theories at Cross Purposes," in *Natural Law Theory: Contemporary Essays* (Robert P. George ed., 1994).

Hodgson, Geoffrey M., *Economics and Evolution: Bringing Life Back into Economics* (1996).

Holmes, Oliver Wendell, *The Common Law* (Mark Dewolfe Howe ed., 1963).

Hopt, Klaus J., "Labor Representation on Corporate Boards: Impacts and Problems for Corporate Governance and Economic Integration in Europe," 14 *Int'l Rev. L. & Econ.* 203 (1994).

Horwitz, Morton, *The Transformation of American Law* (1977).

Hosmer, LaRue Tone, *Moral Leadership in Business* (1994).

————, "Why Be Moral? A Different Rationale for Managers," 4 *Bus. Ethics Q.* 191 (1994).

Hume, David, *Dialogues Concerning Natural Religion* (M. Bell ed., 1779, 1990).

Imai, Yutaka, "Reinvigorating Business Dynamism in Japan," *OECD Observer* (Jan. 1999).

Issac, Glynn L., "Traces of Pleistocene Hunters: An East African Example," in *Man the Hunter* (Richard B. Lee & Irvin DeVore eds., 1968).

Jackall, Robert, *Moral Mazes: The World of Corporate Managers* (1988).

Jaynes, Julian, *The Origin of Consciousness in the Breakdown of the Bicameral Mind* (1976).

Jensen, Michael C., & William H. Meckling, "Theory of the Firm: Managerial Behavior, Agency Costs and Ownership Structure," 3 *J. Fin. Econ.* 305 (1976).

John Paul II, *Sollicitudo Rei Socialis*, United States Catholic Conferences (Washington, D.C.) (1988).

Johnson, Gregory, "Organizational Structure and Scalar Stress," in *Theory and Explanation in Archaeology* (C. Renfrew, M. J. Rowlands, & B. A. Segraves eds., 1982).

Jones, Mary Jeanne Anderson, *Congregational Commonwealth: Connecticut* (1968).

Jones, Richard, "Concerning Secularists' Proposed Restrictions of the Role of Religion in American Politics," 8 *B.Y.U. J. Pub. L.* 343 (1994).

Juran, Joseph M., *Managerial Breakthrough: A New Concept of the Manager's Job* (1964).

Kalakaua, *The Legends and Myths of Hawaii: The Fables and Folklore of a Strange People* (R. M. Daggett ed., 1888).

Kaplan, Steven N., "Top Executive Rewards and Firm Performance: A Comparison of Japan and the United States," 102 *J. Pol. Econ.* 510 (1994).

Keeley, Lawrence, *War Before Civilization* (1996).

Keeley, Michael, "Community, the Joyful Sound," 6 *Bus. Ethics Q.* 549 (1996).

————, "A 'Matter of Opinion, What Tends to The General Welfare': Governing the Workplace," 10 *Bus. Ethics Q.* 243 (2000).

————, *A Social-Contract Theory of Organizations* (1988).

Keeton, W. Page, et. al., *Prosser & Keeton on the Law of Torts* (5th ed. 1984).

Kelly, Bruce, "Corporate Governance Is Key: Investors' Demands Lead to Increased Changes Worldwide," *Pensions & Investments,* Dec. 14, 1998, at 16.

Kennedy, Robert G., "God's Project: A Catholic Vision of Business," Presentation at the 3d Annual John F. Henning Conference (Mar. 5, 1999) (manuscript on file with author).

Kester, W. Carl, *Japanese Takeovers: The Global Contest for Corporate Control* (1991).

Kidder, Rushworth M., *How Good People Make Tough Choices: Resolving the Dilemmas of Ethical Living* (1995).

Kmiec, Douglas W., & Stephen B. Presser, *The American Constitutional Order: History, Cases, and Philosophy* (1998).

Kramer, Larry, "The Confidence of the People: Size, Representation, and the Constitutional Role of Political Parties," Presentation at the Legal Theory Workshop, University of Michigan Law School (Nov. 5, 1999) (manuscript on file with author).

————, "Madison's Audience," 112 *Harv. L. Rev.* 611 (1999).

La Porta, Rafael, Florencia Lopez-De-Silanes, & Andrei Shleifer, "Corporate Ownership Around the World," *J. Fin.* Apr. 1, 1999, at 470.

Lee, Richard B., *The Dobe/Ju'Hoansi* (1984).

————, *The !Kung San: Men, Women and Work in a Foraging Society* (1979).

Lerner, Alan Jay, & Frederick Lowe, *Camelot* (1960).

Leung, Wai Shun Wilson, "The Inadequacy of Shareholder Primacy: A Proposed Corporate Regime That Recognizes Non-Shareholder Interests," 30 *Colum. J.L. & Soc. Probs.* 587, 630.

Lightfoot, Robert, & W. Carl Kester, "Note on Corporate Governance Systems: The United States, Japan, and Germany" (1991).

Lincoln, Abraham, "Reply to a Committee from the Workmen's Association of New York" (Mar. 21, 1864), in *The Collected Works of Abraham Lincoln* (Roy P. Balser ed., 1953).

Lipton, Martin, & Steven A. Rosenblum, "A New System of Corporate Governance: The Quinquennial Election of Directors," 58 *U. Chi. L. Rev.* 187 (1991).

Locke, John, *Two Treatises of Government* (Peter Laslette ed., 1960).

Lohr, Steve, "Welcome to the Internet, The First Global Colony," *N.Y. Times,* January 9, 2000, at 00.

Loomis, Dwight, & J. Gilbert Calhoun eds., *A Judicial and Civil History of Connecticut* 9 (1895).

Loss, Louis, & Joel Seligman, *Securities Regulation* 3448–66 (1991).

McClelland, D. C., & D. G. Winter, *Motivating Economic Achievement* (1971).

McConnell, Michael W., "The Origins and Historical Understandings of Free Exercise of Religion," 103 *Harv. L. Rev.* 1409 (1990).

McCracken, Janet, & Bill Shaw, "Virtue Ethics and Contractarianism: Towards a Reconciliation," 5 *Bus. Ethics Q.* 297 (1995).

McDaniel, Morey, "Stockholders and Stakeholders," 21 *Stet. L. Rev.* 121 (1991).

Macey, Jonathan, "An Economic Analysis of the Various Rationales for Making Shareholders the Exclusive Beneficiaries of Corporate Fiduciary Duties," 21 *Stet. L. Rev.* 23 (1991).

———, "The Missing Element in the Republican Revival," 97 *Yale L.J.* 1673 (1988).

———, "Packaged Preferences & the Institutional Transformation of Interests," 61 *U. Chi. L. Rev.* 1443 (1994).

Macey, Jonathan R., & Geoffrey Miller, "Corporate Governance and Commercial Banking: A Comparative Examination of Germany, Japan, and the United States," 48 *Stan. L. Rev.* 73 (1995).

MacIntyre, Alasdair, *After Virtue* (1981).

———, *Dependent Rational Selves* (1999).

———, *Three Rival Versions of Moral Enquiry: Encyclopaedia, Geneaology, and Tradition* (1990).

———, *Whose Justice, Which Rationality?* (1988).

MacNeil, Ian R., "Contracts: Adjustment of Long-Term Economic Relations Under Classical, Neoclassical, and Relational Contract Law," 72 *Nw. U. L. Rev.* 854 (1978).

———, *Contracts: Exchange Transactions and Relations* (2d ed. 1978).

Madden, Richard B., "The Larger Business Organization as Mediating Structure," in *Democracy and Mediating Structures: A Theological Inquiry* (Michael Novak ed., 1980),

Maitland, Ian, "The Morality of the Corporation: An Empirical or Normative Disagreement?," 4 *Bus. Ethics Q.* 445 (1994).

Malinowski, Bronislaw, "The Group and the Individual in Functional Analysis," in *High Points in Anthropology* (Paul Bohannon & Mark Glazer eds., 1973).

Margolis, Joshua, "Psychological Pragmatism and the Imperative of Aims: A New Approach for Business Ethics," 8 *Bus. Ethics Q.* 409 (1998).

Marshall, William, "The Other Side of Religion," 44 *Hastings L. Rev.* 843 (1993).

Marvin, Julia, "The Prose Brut Chronicle and the Lessons of Vernacular History Ph.D. dissertation, Princeton University (1997).

Maskery, Mary Ann, "Safety Net; Web of Ownership between Banks, Auto Industry Keeps Companies Alive," *Automotive News*, Aug. 6, 1990, at 128.

Matsui, Kathy, *Mergermania—Premature Euphoria*, Goldman Sachs Japan Economic Research Group, Jan. 25, 1999.

Mayer, Don, "On Corporations as Communities or Mediating Institutions," Presentation at the Tri-State Academy of Legal Studies in Business (Nov. 9, 1996) (manuscript on file with author).

Messick, David M., "Social Categories and Business Ethics," 1 *Bus. Ethics Q. Special Issue: Ruffin Series* 149 (1998).

Michelman, Frank, "Law's Republic," 97 *Yale L.J.* 1493 (1988).

Millon, David, "New Directions in Corporate Law: Communitarians, Contractarians, and the Crisis in Corporate Law," 50 *Wash & Lee L. Rev.* 1373 (1993).

———, "Theories of the Corporation," 1990 *Duke L.J.* 201 (1990).

Mitchell, Lawrence A., "A Theoretical and Practical Framework for Enforcing Corporate Constituency Statutes," 79 *Texas L. Rev.* 579 (1992).

Minow, Nell, "Shareholders, Stakeholders and Boards of Directors," 21 *Stet. L. Rev.* 197 (1991).

Minuchin, Salvador, & H. Charles Fishman, *Family Therapy Techniques* (1981).

Mishra, Karen E., Gretchen M. Spreitzer, & Aniel K. Mishara, "Preserving Employee Morale During Downsizing," *Sloan Mgmt. Rev.* 86 (Winter 1998).

Mitnick, Barry M., "The Theory of Agency and Organizational Analysis," 76 in *Ethics and Agency Theory: An Introduction* 6 (Norman E. Bowie & R. Edward Freeman eds., 1992).

Murphy, Nancey, & George F. R. Ellis, *On the Moral Nature of the Universe: Theology, Cosmology, and Ethics* (1996).

Nagel, Thomas, "Moral Conflict and Political Legitimacy," 16 *Phil. & Pub. Affairs* 215 (1987).

Nash, Laura L., *Believers in Business* (1994).

Nesbitt, Stephen L., "Long-Term Rewards from Shareholder Activism: A Study of the CalPERS Effect," *J. Applied Corp. Fin.* (Winter 1994), at 75.

Nesteruk, Jeffrey, "Law and the Virtues: Developing a Legal Theory for Business Ethics," 5 *Bus. Ethics Q.* 361 (1995).

———, "Law, Virtue, and the Corporation," 33 *Am. Bus. L.J.* 473 (1996).

———, "Reimagining the Law," 9 *Bus. Ethics Q.* 603 (1999).

Neuhaus, Richard John, *Doing Well and Doing Good: The Challenge to the Christian Capitalist* (1992).

———, *The Naked Public Square: Religion and Democracy in America* (1984).

———, "Nihilism Without the Abyss: Laws, Rights, and Transcendent Good," 5 *J.L. & Religion* 53 (1987).

———, "Reason Public and Private: The Pannenberg Project," *First Things* (Mar. 1992).

Nichols, Philip M., "Regulating Transnational Bribery in Times of Globalization and Fragmentation," 24 *Yale J. Int'l L.* 257 (1999).

Nietzsche, Friedrich, *Thus Spoke Zarathustra: A Book for None and All* (Walter Kaufman trans., 1978).

Nisbet, Robert A., *The Quest for Community: A Study in the Ethics of Order and Freedom* (1990).

Noll, Mark A., *The Scandal of the Evangelical Mind* (1994).

Novak, Michael, *Business as a Calling: Work and the Examined Life* (1996).

———, *The Spirit of Democratic Capitalism* (1991).

Oakland, John S., *Total Quality Management* (1990).

Oliver, Douglas L., *A Solomon Island Society: Kinship and Leadership Among the Siuai of Bougainville* (1955).

Orts, Eric W., "Shirking and Sharking: A Legal Theory of the Firm," 16 *Yale L. & Pol'y Rev.* 265 (1998).

Ostling, Richard N., "In So Many Gods We Trust," *Time,* Jan. 30, 1995, at 72.

Pascale, Richard, & Thomas P. Rohlen, "The Mazda Turnaround," 9 *J. Japanese Stud.* 219 (1983).

Pannenberg, Wolfhart, *Toward a Theology of Nature: Essays on Science and Faith* (Ted Peters ed., 1993).

Paris, Peter J., *The Spirituality of African Peoples: The Search for a Common Moral Discourse* (1995).

Perlez, Jane, "At Trade Forum, Clinton Pleads for the Poor," *N.Y. Times,* Jan. 30, 2000, at A8.

Perry, Michael J., *Love and Power: The Role of Religion and Morality in American Politics* (1991).

———, *Morality Politics and Law* (1988).

———, "Religion in Politics," 29 *U.C. Davis L. Rev.* 729 (1996).

———, "Religious Morality and Political Choice: Further Thoughts Second Thoughts—on *Love and Power,*" 30 *San Diego L. Rev.* 703 (1993).

Peters, Tom, "Business Leaders Should Be Spirited, Not Spiritual," *Chi. Trib.,* Apr. 5, 1993, at 8.

Phillips, Derek L., *Looking Backward: A Critical Appraisal of Communitarian Thought* (1993).

Phillips, Michael J., "Corporate Moral Personhood and Three Conceptions of the Corporation," 2 *Bus. Ethics Q.* 435 (1992).

Pipes, Richard, *Property and Freedom* (1999).

Pitkin, Hannah, "Justice: On Relating Private and Public," 9 *Pol. Theory* 327 (1981).

Posner, Richard A., *An Economic Analysis of Law* (2d ed. 1977).

———, *The Economics of Justice* (1981).

Postman, David, "Resistance Takes Fast Track—Protesters Training Now For Sit-ins, Blockades," *Seattle Times,* Sept. 10, 1999, at A1.

Powelson, John P., *The Moral Economy* (1998).

Presser, Stephen B., *Recapturing the Constitution: Race, Religion, and Abortion Reconsidered* (1994).

———, "Thwarting the Killing of the Corporation: Limited Liability, Democracy, and Economics," 87 *Nw. L. Rev.* 148 (1992).

Prowse, Stephen, *Corporate Governance in an International Perspective: A Survey of Corporate Control Mechanisms Among Large Firms in the United States, the United Kingdom, Japan, and Germany,* BIS Economic Papers No. 41 (Bank for International Settlements, July 1994).

Rappaport, Roy A., *Ecology, Meaning, and Religion* (1979).

Rawls, John, *Political Liberalism* (1993).

Reichley, James, *Religion in America* (1985).

Reyes, Alejandro, "Playing a New Tune," *Asia Week,* Nov. 19, 1999, at 64.

Reingold, Jennifer, & Ronald Grover, "Executive Pay," *Bus. Week,* Apr. 19, 1999, at 72.

Richerson, Peter J., & Robert Boyd, "Complex Societies: The Evolutionary Origins of a Crude Superorganism," 10 *Human Nature* 253 (1999).

Ridley, Matt, *The Origins of Virtue: Human Instincts and the Evolution of Cooperation* (1997).

Rock, Edward B., "America's Shifting Fascination with Comparative Corporate Governance," 74 *Wash. U. L.Q.* 367, 369 (1996).

Rodes, Robert E., Jr., *Pilgrim Law* (1998).

Rodgers, Edward D., "Striking the Wrong Balance: Constituency Statutes and Corporate Governance," 21 *Pepp. L. Rev.* 777 (1994).

Rodgers, Richard, & Oscar Hammerstein, "My Favorite Things," *The Sound of Music* CBS Fox video (1965).

Roe, Mark J., "German Codetermination and German Securities Markets," 1998 *Colum. Bus. L. Rev.* 167 (1998).

———, "German 'Populism' and the Large Public Corporation," 14 *Int'l Rev. L. & Econ.* 187 (1994).

———, "Some Differences in Corporate Structure in Germany, Japan, and the United States," 102 *Yale L.J.* 1927 (1993).

Romano, Roberta, "A Guide to Takeovers: Theory, Evidence, and Regulation," 9 *Yale J. Reg.* 119 (1992).

Rothstein, Edward, "The Transcontinental Railroad as the Internet of 1869," *N.Y. Times*, Dec. 11, 1999 (Arts), at A21.

Ruder, David, "Public Obligations of Private Corporations," 114 *U. Pa. L. Rev.* 209 (1965).

Ruether, Rosemary Radford, *Gaia and God: An Ecofeminist Theology of Earth Healing* (1992).

Sahlins, Marshall, *Islands of History* 142 (1985).

———, *Stone Age Economics* (1972).

Salbu, Steven R., "The Decline of Contract as a Relationship Management Form," 46 *Rutgers L. Rev.* 1271 (1995).

———, "Insider Trading and the Social Contract," 5 *Bus. Ethics Q.* 313 (1995).

———, "Law and Conformity, Ethics and Conflict: The Trouble with Law-Based Conceptions of Ethics," 68 *Ind. L.J.* 101 (1992).

———, "Parental Coordination and Conflict in International Joint Ventures: The Use of Contract to Address Legal, Linguistic, and Cultural Concerns," 43 *Case W. Res. L. Rev.* 1221 (1993).

Sampson, Anthony, *The Company Man: The Rise and Fall of Corporate Life* (1995).

Sandburg, Carl, *Abraham Lincoln: The Prairie Years and the War Years* (1970).

Schlender, Brenton R., "Japan's New Realism: Don't Count This Superpower Out," *Fortune*, Oct. 31, 1994, at 117.

Schor, Juliet B., *The Overworked American: The Unexpected Decline of Leisure* (1992).

Sennett, Richard, *The Corrosion of Character* (1998).

Shaffer, Thomas L., "The Legal Ethics of Radical Individualism," 65 *Texas L. Rev.* 963 (1987).

Shaw, Bill, & John Corvino, "Hosmer and the 'Why Be Moral?' Question," 6 *Bus. Ethics Q.* 373 (1996).

Shaw, Bill, & Frances E. Zollers, "Managers in the Moral Dimension: What Etzioni Might Mean for Managers," 3 *Bus. Ethics Q.* 153 (1993).

Sheard, Paul, "The Main Bank System and Corporate Monitoring and Control in Japan," 11 *J. Econ. Behav. & Org.* 399 (1989).

Smolin, David M., "The Enforcement of Natural Law by the State: A Response to Professor Calhoun," 16 *U. Dayton L. Rev.* 381 (1991).

Solomon, Robert C., "The Corporation as Community: A Reply to Ed Hartman," 4 *Bus. Ethics Q.* 271 (1994).

———, *Ethics and Excellence: Cooperation and Integrity in Business* (1993).

Sommer, A. A., Jr., "Whom Should the Corporation Serve?: The Berle-Dodd Debate Revisited Sixty Years Later," 16 *Del. J. Corp. L.* 33 (1991).

Spinoza, Benedict de, *The Ethics* (R. H. M. Elwes trans., 1955).

Sponsel, Leslie E., "The Natural History of Peace: The Positive View of Human Nature and Its Potential," in *A Natural History of Peace* (Thomas Gregor ed., 1996).

Stange, Gary von, "Corporate Social Responsibility Through Constituency Statutes: Legend or Lie?" 11 *Hofstra Lab. L.J.* 461 (1994).

Steinmetz, Greg, "German Shift On Butbacks May Lift Stock," *Wall St. J.* (Europe), Jan. 13, 1997.

Stolberg, Sheryl Gay, "Internet Prescriptions Boom in the 'Wild West' of the Web," *N.Y. Times,* June 27, 1999.

Sullivan, Kathleen M., "God as a Lobby: The Culture of Disbelief: How American Law and Politics Trivialize Religious Devotion," 61 *U. Chi. L. Rev.* 1655 (1994) (book review).

———, "Religion and Liberal Democracy," 59 *U. Chi. L. Rev.* 195 (1992).

Sunstein, Cass, "Beyond the Republican Revival," 97 *Yale L.J.* 1539 (1988).

Sun-Tzu, *The Art of War* (Samuel B. Griffith trans., 1963).

Taka, Iwao, "Business Ethics: A Japanese View," 4 *Bus. Ethics Q.* 53 (1994).

Takaki, Ronald, *A Different Mirror: A History of Multicultural America* 426 (1993).

Tamari, Meir, "The Challenge of Wealth: Jewish Business Ethics," 7 *Bus. Ethics Q.* 45 (1997).

Taylor, Charles, *Multiculturalism and "The Politics of Recognition"* (1992).

Tillich, Paul, *Theologian of the Boundaries* (Mark Kline Taylor ed., 1991).

Tocqueville, Alexis De, 2 *Democracy in America* (Phillips Bradley ed., 1945).

Treece, James B., "Nissan Untethers Suppliers and Itself," *Automotive News,* April 12, 1999.

Trivers, Robert, "The Evolution of Reciprocal Altruism," 46 *Q. Rev. Biology* 35 (1971).

Tussman, J., *Obligation and the Body Politic* (1960).

Turnbull, Colin, *The Forest People: A Study of the Pygmies of the Congo* (1962).

Umezu, Mitsuhior, "Relational Ethics and the Context of Trust: Understanding the Ethical Basis of Paternalistic Japanese Business," Presentation at Meeting of the Society of Business Ethics (1999) (manuscript on file with author).

University of Virginia, "Proceedings and Report of the Commissioners for the University of Virginia," in *Manual of the Board of Visitors of the University of Virginia* (1975).

Vagts, Detlev F., "Reforming the 'Modern' Corporation: Perspectives from the German," 80 *Harv. L. Rev.* 23, 40 (1966).

Valeri, Valerio, *Kingship and Sacrifice: Ritual and Society in Ancient Hawaii* (Paula Wissing trans., 1985)

Vallas, Steven P., & John P. Beck, "The Transformation of Work Revisited: The Limits of Flexibility in American Manufacturing," 43 *Soc. Probs.* 339 (1996).

Veasey, e. Norman, "An Economic Rationale for Judicial Decisionmaking in Corporate Law," 53 *Bus. Law.* 681 (May 1998).

Velasquez, Manuel, & F. Neil Brady, "Natural Law and Business Ethics," 7 *Bus. Ethics Q.* 83 (1997).

Volokh, Eugene, "Freedom of Speech and Workplace Harassment," 30 *UCLA L. Rev.* 1791 (1992).

Waal, Frans de, *Good Natured: The Origins of Right and Wrong in Humans and Other Animals* (1996).

Wagner, Antonin, "Communitarianism: A New Paradigm of Socioeconomic Analysis," 24 *J. Socio-Econ.* 593, 598 (1995).

Wagstyl, Stefan, "Crumbs from the Table," *Fin. Times*, Sept. 25, 1996, at 27.

Wallman, Steven M. H., "The Proper Interpretation of Corporate Constituency Statutes and Formulation of Director Duties," 25 *Conn. L. Rev.* 681 (1993).

Walker, C. R., & R. H. Guest, *The Man on the Assembly Line* (1952).

Walsh, James P., "Managerial and Organizational Cognition: Notes from a Trip Down Memory Lane," 6 *Org. Sci.* 280 (1995).

Walton, Mary, *The Deming Management Method* (1986).

Wasserstein, Bruce, *Big Deal: The Battle for Control of America's Leading Corporations* (1998).

Watson, Lyall, *Dark Nature: A Natural History of Evil* (1995).

Wattles, Jeffrey, *The Golden Rule* (1996).

Werhane, Patricia H., *Adam Smith and His Legacy for Modern Capitalism* (1991).

Wezel Stone, Katherine Van, "Employees as Stakeholders Under State Non-shareholder Constituency Statutes," 21 *Stetson L. Rev.* 45 (1991).

Whallon, Robert, *Elements of Cultural Change in the Lower Paleolithic* (1989).

Whitchurch, Gail G., & Larry L. Constantine, "Systems Theory," in *Sourcebook of Family Theories and Methods: A Contextual Approach* (Pauline G. Boss, William J. Doherty, Ralph LaRossa, Walter R. Schumm, and Suzanne K. Steinmetz eds., 1993).

Whitehead, Alfred North, *Process and Reality: An Essay in Cosmology* (David Ray Griffin & Donald W. Sherburne eds., 1978).

Wicks, Andrew C., Daniel R. Gilbert Jr., & R. Edward Freeman, "A Feminist Reinterpretation of the Stakeholder Concept," 4 *Bus. Ethics Q.* 459 (1994).

Wiessner, Polly, "On Emergency Decisions, Egalitarianism, and Group Selection," 39 *Current Anthropology* 356 (1998).

Williamson, Oliver, *Markets and Hierarchies: Analysis and Antitrust Implications* (1975).

Wilson, David Sloan, "Altruism and Organism: Disentangling the Themes of Multilevel Selection Theory," 150 *Am. Naturalist* S122 (Supp. 1997).

Wilson, James Q., *The Moral Sense* (1993).

Wood, Donna J., "Ingroups and Outgroups: What Psychology Doesn't Say," 1 *Bus. Ethics Q. Special Issue: Ruffin Series*, 179 1998).

Wood, Gordon, *The Creation of the American Republic: 1776–1787* (1969).

Wright, Robert, *The Moral Animal: Evolutionary Psychology and Everyday Life* (1994).

Wuthnow, Robert, *God and Mammon in America* (1994).

Yablon, Charles M., "Mergers and Acquisitions: Corporate Culture in Takeovers," 19 *Cardozo L. Rev.* 553 (1997).

Yoder, John Howard, *The Politics of Jesus* (1972).

Court Opinions

Aguila v. Felton, 473 U.S. 402 (1985).

Allegheny County v. Greater Pittsburgh ACLU, 492 U.S. 573 (1989).

Board of Education v. Mergens, 496 U.S. 226 (1990).

Bowen v. Kendrick, 487 U.S. 589 (1988).

Committee for Public Education and Religious Liberty v. Nyquist, 413 U.S. 756 (1973).

Corporation of Presiding Bishop of Church of Jesus Christ of Latter-Day Saints v. Amos, 483 U.S. 327 (1987).

Dodge v. Ford Motor Co., 170 N.W. 668, 684 (Mich. 1919).

Edwards v. Aguillard, 482 U.S. 578 (1987).

Employment Division of Human Resources of Oregon v. Smith, 494 U.S. 872 (1990).

Epperson v. Arkansas, 393 U.S. 97 (1968).

EEOC v. Townley Engineering & Manufacturing Company 859 F2d 610 (9th Cir. 1988), cert. denied, 109 S. Ct. 1527 (1989).

Kotcher v. Rosa and Sullivan Apple Computer, Inc. 957 F2d 59, 61 (2d Cir. 1992).

Larsen v. Valente, 456 U.S. 228 (1982).

Lemon v. Kurtzman, 403 U.S. 602 (1971).

Liggett v. Lee, 288 U.S. 517, 549 (1933).

Marsh v. Chambers, 463 U.S. 783 (1983).

Meek v. Pittenger, 421 U.S. 349 (1975).

Mueller v. Allen, 463 U.S. 388 (1983).

Robinson v. Jacksonville Shipyards, Inc. 760 F. Supp. 1486, 1534 (M.D. Fla. 1991).

School District of Grand Rapids v. Ball, 473 U.S. 373 (1985).

Shlensky v Wrigley, 237 N.E.2d 776, 780 (Ill. App. Ct. 1968).

Texas Monthly, Inc. v. Bullock, 489 U.S. 1 (1989).

Thomas v. Review Board of Indiana Employment Security Division, 450 U.S. 707 (1981).

Trustees of Dartmouth College v. Woodward, 17 U.S. (4 Wheat. 1819), at 636.

Wallace v. Jaffree, 472 U.S. 38 (1985).

Walz v. Tax Commissioner, 397 U.S. 664 (1970).

Welsh v. United States, 398 U.S. 333 (1970).

Widmar v. Vincent, 454 U.S. 263 (1981).

Witters v. Washington Department of Services for the Blind, 474 U.S. 481 (1986).

Woman v. Walter, 433 U.S. 229 (1977).

Federal Legislation

58 Fed. Reg. 51,266 (1993).

Internal Revenue Code Section 2056.

Securities Exchange Act of 1934, ch. 404, 48 Stat. 881.

State Legislation

Ala. Code § 10-2B-11.03(c) (1994).
Ariz. Rev. Stat. §§ 10-2702, 10-1202(c) (1996).
Ark. Code Ann. § 4-27-1202(c) (Michie 1996).
Colo. Rev. Stat. §§ 7-106-105(7), 7-111-103(3), 7-114-102(3) (1998).
Conn. Gen. Stat. § 33-756(d) (1997)
Delaware General Corporation Law § 102(a)(3).
Fla. Stat. ch. 607.0830(3) (Supp. 1999).
Ga. Code Ann. § 14-2-202(b)(5) (Supp. 1998).
Haw. Rev. Stat. § 415-35(b) (1997).
Idaho Code § 30-1702 (1996).
805 Ill. Comp. Stat. 5/8.85 (West 1993).
Ind. Code § 23-1-35-1(d) (1995).
Iowa Code § 491.101B (1991).
Ky. Rev. Stat. Ann. §§ 271B.11-030(2)(b), 271B.12-020(3) (Banks-Baldwin 1989).
La. Rev. Stat. Ann. § 12:92(G) (West 1994).
Me. Rev. Stat. Ann. tit. 13-A, § 716 (West Supp. 1998).
Mass. Gen. Laws Ann. ch. 156B, § 65 (West Supp. 1998).
Minn. Stat. § 302A.251(5) (Supp. 1999).
Miss. Code Ann. § 79-4-8.30(d) (1998).
Mo. Ann. Stat. § 351.347 (West 1991).
Mont. Code Ann. §§ 35-1-815(3), 35-1-823(3) (1997).
N.H. Rev. Stat. Ann. §§ 293-A:11.03(c), 293-A:12.02(c) (Supp. 1996).
N.J. Stat. Ann. § 14A:6-1(2) (West Supp. 1998).
N.M. Stat. Ann. § 53-11-35(D) (Michie 1997).
N.Y. Bus. Corp. Law § 717(b) (McKinney Supp. 1999).
Nev. Rev. Stat. § 78.138(3) (1994).
N.C. Gen. Stat. §§ 55-11-03(c), 55-12-02(c) (1990).
N.D. Cent. Code § 10-19.1-50(6) (Supp. 1997).
Ohio Rev. Code Ann. § 1701.59(E) (Anderson 1993).
Or. Rev. Stat. § 60.357(5) (Supp. 1996).
15 Pa. Cons. Stat. § 515 (1995).
R.I. Gen. Laws § 7-5.2-8 (1992).
S.C. Code Ann. §§ 33-11-103(c), 33-12-102(c) (Law. Co-op. 1990).
S.D. Codified Laws § 47-33-4 (Michie 1991).
Tenn. Code Ann. § 48-103-204 (1995).
Tex. Bus. Corp. Act Ann. art. 5.03 (West Supp. 1999).
Utah Code Ann. § 16-10a-1103(3) (1995).
Vt. Stat. Ann. tit. 11A, §§ 11.03(c), 12.02(c) (1997).
Va. Code Ann. § 13.1-718(C) (Michie 1993).
Va. Code Ann. § 13.1-724(C) (Michie Supp. 1998).
Wash. Rev. Code §§ 23B.11.030(3), 23B.12.020(3) (1994).
Wis. Stat. § 180.0827 (1992).
Wyo. Stat. Ann. § 17-16-830(e) (Michie 1997).

Miscellaneous Institutional Data Guides, Web Sites, and Articles

American Law Institute, Principles of Corporate Governance §2.01 (1994).

"Auto Parts Sales to Japan Rise," *Chi. Trib.*, Jan. 22, 1995.

Bureau of Census, U.S. Dep't of Commerce, Statistical Abstract of the United States 524 tbl.808 (1997).

"Business Headlines," *Dayton Daily News*, Feb. 25, 2000.

"Changing Japan: Whispering Reform—Against All Expectations, It Looks as If Japan Really Is Reforming Its Economy, *Economist*, Jan. 11, 1997.

"Freedom and Community: The Politics of Restoration," *Economist*, Dec. 24, 1994.

International Finance Corp., *Emerging Stock Markets Factbook* (1998).

International Monetary Fund, *International Financial Statistics* (July 1998).

"Japan Inc. Faces Radical Change," *Banker*, Oct, 1, 1999; see also "Merge-or-Submerge Fever Spreads as Keiretsu Die Out," *Daily Yomiuri* (Tokyo), Dec. 21, 1999.

"Laying the Charge for the Big Bang," 147 *Banker* 108 July 1, 1997.

The LGT Guide to World Equity Markets 1997 (1997).

The Merger Yearbook 1999, at 15, 22–23 (Securities Data Exchange).

"NCEO Library: ESOPs, Stock Options, and 401(k) Plans Now Control 8.3% of Corporate Equity," www.nceo.org/library/control_eq/html>.

"NCEO Library: ESOPs, Stock Options, and 401(k) Plans Now Control 8.3% of Corporate Equity" (visited Mar. 3, 2000), www.nceo.org/library/control_eq/html.

"No Country for Old Men," *Economist*, May 1, 1999, at 60.

Organization for Economic Cooperation and Development, *OECD Economic Surveys: 1994–95*.

"Stakeholder Capitalism: Unhappy Families," *Economist*, Feb. 10, 1996.

"Structural and Regulatory Developments in OECD Countries," *Financial Market Trends*, Nov. 1, 1998, at 17.

"A Survey of Japanese Finance," *Economist*, June 28, 1997, at 56.

UAL, "Company Profile," *Hoover's Online* (visited Mar. 3, 2000), www.hoovers.com/premium/profile.0/0,2147,11520,00.html>.

United Airlines, DEF14A Proxy Statement, Mar. 23, 2000.

"Who Wants to Be a Billionaire?," *Economist*, May 8, 1999, at 15.

Index

Abbeglen, James, 252n. 124
Abrams, Kathryn, 176, 266n. 70, 268nn. 119–20
Ackerman, Bruce, 206–9, 211, 272nn. 49–52, 274n. 101
Adams, John, 90
AFL-CIO, 34
Agency contractarianism, 63, 65, 75–78, 82, 86, 128, 136, 141
Aggression, 70
Alchian, Armen A., 247n. 39
Alexander, Larry, 82, 273n. 61
Allah, 184
Altruism, 67, 72, 73, 78, 79, 83, 148, 153, 191, 196
American Law Institute, 97, 249n. 80
American Stock Exchange, 94
Amish, 38
Andre, Thomas J., Jr., 254n. 167
Annheuser-Busch, 24, 113
Anthropic principle, 70, 186
Anthropology, relation to business, 9, 16, 26, 39, 44, 46, 47, 49, 51, 56, 59, 63, 66, 68, 69, 83–85, 107, 110, 113, 132, 142, 144, 146, 148, 165, 174, 187, 192, 224, 227
Anti-Federalists, 89–92
Aoki, Masahiko, 252n. 112, 253n. 148
Aquinas, Thomas, 27, 45, 52, 55, 58, 237n. 107

Aristotle, relation to business, 27, 39, 40, 43, 45, 53, 55, 56, 59, 88, 89, 140, 145, 149, 224, 226, 276n. 15
Arlow, Peter, 271n. 17
Arnhart, Larry, 54, 145, 236nn. 82–86, 237n. 93, 262n. 51, 269n. 29
Arrow, Kenneth J., 79, 244n. 120
Articles of Confederation, 89
Asana, 192
Ashram, 21, 51
AT&T, 152
Attenborough, Richard, 21
Authenticity, 137, 139, 140, 145
Authority, 24
Automation, 87
Axelrod, Robert M., 263n. 89

Baishu, 94
Band groups, 67, 71, 83, 142, 143, 148, 149
Banker, Stephen M., 248n. 70
Bansal, Preeta, 175, 267nn. 105–7, 268n. 125
Barrow, John D., 269n. 18
Bathsheeba, 160
Baumonte, Thomas J., 125, 258n. 15, 259n. 36
Beauchamp, Tom L., 239n. 21
Beck, John P., 151, 263n. 80
Beck-Dudley, Caryn L., 163, 265n. 38
Bell, Derrick, 175, 267nn. 105–7, 268n. 125

Bellah, Robert N., 29, 233n. 21
Benson, Benjamin, 255n. 183
Berger, Peter, 23, 31, 32, 34, 36, 37, 231n.
    2, 233nn. 7, 25–27, 234nn. 39–40,
    44–45, 236n. 62, 265nn. 53, 57–60,
    273n. 61, 276n. 17
Berglof, E., 251n. 98
Berle, A. A., Jr., 121, 126, 249n. 77, 258n.
    14
Biancalana, Joseph, 124, 258n. 32
Biological anthropology, 49, 51
Biological naturalism, 70
Biology, 26, 39, 71, 83
Bird, Frederick B., 202, 271n. 18
Birdsell, Joseph, 235n. 50, 245n. 143
Bisignani, J. D., 235n. 23
Black, Bernard, 255n. 184
Boatright, John R., 76–78, 121, 126, 239n.
    21, 243nn. 96, 99,107, 258nn. 17, 19,
    259n. 41
Boehm, Christopher, 241n. 56
Bollier, David, 255n. 202
Bork, Robert, 265n. 67
Bounded rationality, 78, 79
Bowie, Norman E., 239n. 21, 255n. 207
Boyd, Robert, 85, 88, 245n. 156, 246nn. 2,
    3, 254nn. 176–86, 256n. 223
Boyle, Joseph, 52, 236n. 66
Bradley, Michael, 247n. 39, 248nn. 50, 54,
    250n. 86, 251nn. 88, 91, 98, 110, 252n.
    142, 253n. 147, 254n. 168
Brady, F. Neil, 236n. 67, 274n. 98
Braham-atman, 192
Bremner, Brian, 252n. 135, 253n. 161
Brest, Paul, 177, 268n. 121
Bribery, 140, 141
Bronowski, Jacob, 83, 245n. 146, 260n.
    79
Brooks, Nancy Rivera, 248n. 61
Brutus, 91
Bryant, Adam, 248n. 64
Buchholz, Rogene A., 82, 244n. 137
Buddhism, 22, 62, 188, 192–94
Bureaucracy, 26, 32–34, 43, 65, 84, 85, 103,
    110, 134, 152, 153, 176, 182
Burrogh, Bryan, 234n. 5
Burtchaell, James T., 28, 231n. 3, 233n. 18,
    254n. 166
Business, 8–15, 26, 27, 30, 33–36, 50, 51,
    58, 61, 62, 65, 72, 88, 97, 98, 106, 120,
    141, 142, 144, 146, 147, 149, 177, 181,
    182, 184, 189, 190, 197, 199, 201, 208,
    216, 218

Business as community, 151, 161–63,
    165–67, 169, 178
Business as mediating institution, 8, 9, 14,
    16, 17, 32, 36, 88, 91, 105, 112–14, 117,
    120, 121, 125, 133, 134, 144, 153, 163,
    166, 167, 178, 228
Business communities, 88, 106
Business ethicists, 14, 53, 91, 121, 187,
    217
Business ethics, 6–9, 13, 35, 38, 56, 60, 63,
    88, 117, 121, 130, 131, 135, 136, 145,
    149, 152, 155, 156, 163, 164, 169, 189,
    192, 196, 200, 202, 205, 209, 214, 219,
    220, 224, 227, 229
Business leaders, 183, 185, 210
Business persons, 115, 182, 190, 202
Business students, 183
Byron, William, 25, 26, 27, 233nn. 9, 11

Cabot, Walter M., 257n. 11
Calhoun, J. Gilbert, 237n. 101
Camelot, 222, 229
Camus, Albert, 204, 205, 228, 229, 272n.
    44
Carney, William J., 124, 259n. 35
Carr, Edward, 252n. 122, 254n. 164
Carter, Stephen L., 273n. 61
Case, John, 260n. 82
Catholic (Roman), 22, 24, 25, 27, 28, 51,
    65, 85
Catholic (universal), 22, 24, 25, 26
Caux Roundtable, 128, 139
Centesimus Annus, 32
Chappell, Tom, 12, 13, 49, 232n. 21, 261n.
    26
Checks and balances, 9, 17, 57, 61, 66, 88,
    89, 91, 113, 115
Chesterton, G. K., 57, 237n. 100
Chiefdoms, 71, 143
Choy, Jon, 253n. 162
Christian, Nichole M., 248n. 67
Christianity, 21, 22, 62, 200, 202
Chrysler, 102
Church, 12, 28, 31, 36, 109, 130, 177
Church of England, 51
Civic republicanism, 111, 156, 159, 170,
    172, 176, 177
Clark, Robert, 255n. 186, 258n. 22
Clarkson Principles, 127, 259n. 51
Classical contracts, 11
Clubs, 106
Coase, Ronald, 126, 247n. 39
Cohen, Jack, 235n. 43

Cohen, Meir Dan, 233n. 12
Cohen, Stephen, 129, 259n. 56
Cole, Robert E., 256n. 221, 273n. 65
Collective mind, 69
Commitment, 16, 33, 55, 98
Common good, 16, 22, 25, 32, 49, 55, 58,
    60, 61, 88, 89, 91, 98, 105, 110, 115,
    117, 144, 151, 156, 158, 170–74, 176,
    205
Communal Notions of Business, 32, 42, 72,
    74, 154
Communication, 58–60, 88, 89, 117
Communitarian, 6, 81, 98, 103, 104, 106,
    113, 155, 156, 164
Communitarian choirs, 156
Communitarianism, 93, 105, 142, 160,
    165–68
Community, 6, 7, 10, 14, 24, 33, 36–38,
    42, 49–51, 54, 58–60, 73, 75, 77, 80–83,
    105, 119, 120, 124, 126, 130, 132–36,
    141–44, 150, 151, 153, 156, 159–65, 168,
    171, 176, 177, 220, 226
Compassion, 16, 22–26, 32, 51, 74, 85
Competition, 43, 53, 70, 112, 130, 191
Competitiveness, 72, 107, 147
Compston v. Borden, 202, 203
Confidence of the people, 89, 90
Conflicts of interest, 169
Confucianism, 22, 58, 160
Confucius, 46
Conlin, Michelle, 270n. 6
Connecticut's Fundamental Orders of
    1639, 57
Conrad, Alfred F., 253n. 144
Conry, Edward J., 164, 260n. 3, 265n. 48
Consent, 82, 84, 137, 141, 143, 150
Constantine, Larry L., 254n. 181
Constitution, 89, 109
Contract protection, 67
Contract theory and analysis, 7, 16, 42, 56,
    63, 76, 77, 197
Contractarian business ethics, 164
Contractarian governance model, 94
Contractarianism, 45, 93, 103, 105
Contracts, 65, 71, 74, 76, 79, 130, 142, 150,
    161
Cook, James, 44
Cooperation, 33, 35, 47, 53, 67, 70, 72, 80,
    106
Corporate code of ethics, 219
Corporate community, 12, 15, 57, 88, 89,
    108
Corporate constituency statutes, 42, 57, 97,

    109, 119–25, 226, 249n. 81, 255n. 185,
    256n. 2
Corporate control, 94
Corporate culture, 130
Corporate governance, 10, 14, 17, 25, 63,
    69, 72, 76, 80, 86–88, 96–98, 109,
    113–15, 117, 120, 121, 128, 134, 191,
    222, 223, 227
Corporate life, 22, 27, 45, 56, 63, 152
Corporate retirement programs, 3
Corporations, 9, 14, 15, 16, 24, 28–29,
    31–37, 39, 42, 47, 49, 53, 56, 67, 70, 72,
    73, 76, 80, 84, 87, 88, 89, 92, 96, 97, 100,
    102, 105, 106, 109, 110, 114, 117,
    121–25, 128, 132, 134, 135, 141, 161,
    163, 164, 169, 177, 190, 205, 215, 216
Corvino, John, 220, 221, 275n. 128
Creativity, 33, 197
Cultures, 69, 73, 75, 141
Cummins Engines, 109
Cunning, 72
Cunningham, Scott, 238n. 6
Custom, 67, 68
Cybernetic corporate community, 89
Cybernetics, 51, 88

Dai-Ichi Kangyo Bank, 99
Daimler-Benz, 102
Daimler-Chrysler, 103
Damon, William, 232n. 26
Dartmouth College, 249n. 74, 258n. 16
Darwin, Charles, 53, 72, 77, 145, 184, 190,
    191, 195, 226, 276n. 9
Darwinian theory, 68, 70, 83
Dawkins, Richard, 186, 238n. 12, 268n. 16
Deacon, Terrence W., 263n. 85
Decentralization, 34, 151
Defined-benefit plans, 3–5
Defined-contribution plan, 4, 5
DeGeorge, Richard, 193, 194, 205, 235n.
    33, 269nn. 42, 46, 272n. 48
DeLoria, Vine, 238n. 6
Deming, W. Edwards, 209, 255n. 196,
    259n. 60
Democracy, 15, 29, 34, 57, 90, 110, 113,
    143, 160, 213
Democratic moral self-governance, 174
Democratization, 58
Demsetz, Harold, 247n. 39
Dependability, 35
Depersonalization, 87
Depth-hermeneutic, 174, 175, 177
Derry, Robbin, 12, 13, 232n. 22

Dialectical theory, 64–66, 74, 75, 82, 120, 152
Dignity, 85, 88, 111
Discrimination, 169
Dobson, John, 149, 262n. 68
Dodd, E. Merrick, Jr., 121, 126, 249n. 77, 258n. 14
Dodge v. Ford Motor Co., 249n. 77
Donaldson, Thomas, 63, 120, 126, 127, 130, 131, 136–42, 144–46, 152, 153, 163, 169, 226, 239n. 19, 240n. 24, 257n. 9, 259nn. 47–50, 61, 62, 260nn. 1–2, 261nn. 10–17, 20–23, 262nn. 50, 59, 276n. 18
Dorff, Elliot N., 205, 272n. 46
Dorrien, Gary, 233n. 34
Dostoyevsky, Fyodor, 148, 149, 196, 200, 262n. 63, 270n. 51
Douglas, Stephen, 175
Duechler, Martina, 237n. 106
Dunbar, Robin, 50, 51, 73, 132, 236nn. 52–61, 260n. 74
Dunfee, Thomas W., 63, 130, 131, 136–42, 144–46, 152, 153, 163, 169, 226, 239n. 19, 240n. 24, 259n. 61, 262n. 50, 261nn. 10–17, 20–23, 276n. 20
Durkheim, Emile, 69, 173, 183, 238n. 7, 241n. 57, 268nn. 9–15
Dworkin, Terry Morehead, 202–4, 271nn. 22, 24, 26, 27, 29, 30, 272nn. 33–43

Easterbrook, Frank H., 63, 76–78, 86, 87, 234n. 9, 239n. 14, 243nn. 93, 95, 100, 105, 106, 245nn. 153, 155, 246n. 159
Eaton, Bob, 102, 103
Eckhart, Meister, 238n. 7, 276n. 19
Ecologizing values, 60, 61, 114, 115, 146, 178, 187, 190
E-commerce age, 227
Economizing values, 60, 61, 107, 114, 115, 132, 146, 178, 187
Efficiency, 13, 14, 41, 42, 55, 56, 76, 77, 79, 80, 87, 93, 99, 103, 107, 109, 114, 115, 120, 128, 135, 136, 140, 176, 223
Egypt, 71
Eightfold Path, 193
Eliade, Mircea, 238n. 3, 262n. 60, 276n. 19
Ellis, George F. R., 195, 269n. 50
Ellul, Jacques, 216–20, 231n. 9, 260n. 77, 274nn. 106, 109–19
Elster, Jon, 68, 241n. 55
Ember, Carol and Melvin, 54, 242nn. 71–76

Empathy, 15, 16, 21–27, 29, 32, 51, 54, 65, 74, 84–86, 98, 110, 149, 171
Employee stock ownership plans, 108, 112, 115
Employees, 4–6, 8, 12, 24, 26, 27, 33, 36, 51, 55, 76, 78, 84, 91, 95, 102, 104, 106, 108, 110, 112, 114, 115, 117, 119, 120, 122, 123, 125, 126, 128–30, 134, 148, 200, 202, 205, 220
Empowerment, 8, 31, 50, 51, 88, 115, 166
Enlightenment, 45, 143
Epstein, Richard A., 172, 173, 266n. 92
Equality, 137, 143, 144, 148, 153
Establishment Clause, 201, 203
Etzioni, Amitai, 156, 158–61, 167, 263nn. 4–7, 264nn. 8–11, 14–22
Evan, William M., 125, 133, 239n. 21, 256n. 1, 259nn. 37–40
Evolution, 65–68, 70–73, 83, 86, 142, 146
Evolutionary psychology, 82, 132
Executive compensation, 102, 113
Extant social contracts, 82, 137, 146
Extended order, 67

Fabbro, David, 228, 277n. 29
Fairness, 221
Families, 8, 12, 28–31, 36, 48, 104–6, 109, 112, 130, 142
Family business, 15, 24
Farber, Daniel A., 240n. 37
Farraday, Michael, 193
Fatal conceit, 67
Federal Sentencing Guidelines, 108, 220, 226, 229
Federalism, 29
Federalists, 89, 90
Feminism, 62, 126, 127
Fiduciary duty, 14
Finnis, John, 39, 45–47, 49, 52, 53, 56–58, 60, 235nn. 34–37, 40, 49, 237nn. 98, 108–9, 125, 274nn. 108
First Amendment, 203
First man, 172, 176, 204, 205
Fischel, Daniel, 63, 76–78, 86, 87, 234n. 9, 239n. 14, 243nn. 93, 95, 100–102, 105–6, 245nn. 153, 155, 246n. 159
Fischer, Louis, 232n. 2
Fishman, H. Charles, 13, 232n. 27
Flannery, Kent V., 71, 72, 142, 152, 242nn. 71–76, 261nn. 27–44, 263n. 98
Flath, David, 251n. 98
Force, The, 62, 63, 150, 183, 186, 190, 198
Ford Motors, 152

Fox, George, 35
Frank, Robert, 82, 145
Franks, Julian, 248n. 53
Frederick, William C., 37, 60, 61, 84, 107,
    131, 132, 138, 145, 146, 148, 181, 182,
    187–91, 194–96, 223, 232n. 24, 234nn.
    46, 48–50, 237nn. 96, 126–28, 238nn.
    132–33, 137, 240n. 25, 245n. 154, 255n.
    187, 256nn. 225, 226, 260nn. 70–73,
    261n. 18, 262nn. 52–55, 67, 268nn. 1–5,
    8, 269nn. 25–28, 274n. 105, 275n. 7,
    276nn. 7, 12
Freedom, 48, 84, 143, 197
Freeman, R. Edward, 119, 125, 126, 133,
    239n. 21, 255n. 207, 256n. 1, 259nn.
    37–40
Friendship, 28
Fuji Bank, 99
Fukao, Mitsuhiro, 248nn. 58, 59, 249n. 73,
    252nn. 118–19, 124, 130, 253nn. 144,
    151
Full inclusivist position (FIP), 211
Fuller, Lon, 58, 237nn. 92, 109, 256n. 210
Functional families, 12–14
Fung, Shirley, 253n. 155

Gandhi, Mahatma, 21–23, 51, 232n. 2
Genay, Hesna, 251n. 98
General Motors, 95
George, Robert, 235n. 35, 236n. 66, 267n.
    113
Germany, 85, 88, 93–98, 100–105, 11, 113,
    117
Gilbert, Daniel R., Jr., 126, 259n. 44
Gilson, Ronald, 251nn. 98, 111, 252n. 139,
    253n. 150
Gini, Al, 65, 238n. 1
Gleick, James, 235nn. 44–47
Glouchevitch, Philip, 253n. 146
Goffee, Rob, 255n. 185, 260nn. 66–69
Golden Rule, 23, 39, 40, 46, 47, 58, 88,
    149
Goldilocks, 61, 155, 160, 178
Good Samaritans, 13, 190
Goodpaster, Kenneth E., 239n. 21, 259n.
    42
Goodwill, 49, 123, 173, 177
Gordon, John Steele, 276n. 25
Gorov, Lynda, 247n. 36
Granovetter, Mark, 81, 244n. 128
Great Awakening, 218
Great Britain, 21
Green, Ronald M., 205, 272n. 46

Greenawalt, Kent, 209–12, 214, 215,
    273nn. 68, 71–72, 79
Greenhouse, Steven, 248n. 66
Greenleaf, Robert K., 35, 234n. 42
Greising, David, 247n. 37
Grover, Ronald, 253n. 152
Guest, R. H., 260n. 80
Guilds, 30, 109
Gustafson, James M., 239n. 20
Gutmann, Amy, 264n. 13

Habermas, Jurgen, 208, 266n. 97, 267nn.
    98, 110, 273n. 64
Hamel, Gary, 134, 260nn. 83–84
Hampden-Turner, Charles, 24, 113, 233n.
    8, 256n. 222, 259n. 60
Hanks, James J., Jr., 250n. 83, 255n. 186,
    258n. 24
Harassment, 169
Harmony, 60
Harris, Errol E., 64, 195, 234n. 47, 238n.
    12, 240nn. 26–30, 242n. 64, 257n. 8,
    269nn. 48–49
Hartman, Edwin M., 162, 224, 226, 260n.
    65, 264n. 31, 276n. 14
Hartman, Rima F., 250n. 83
Hasnas, John, 231n. 4, 243n. 98
Hauerwas, Stanley, 165, 182, 265n. 51,
    268n. 7
Haughey, John C., 28, 233n. 17, 275n.
    125
Havel, Václev, 93, 103, 246n. 1
Hawaiian Islands, 43, 44, 47, 153
Hayek, F. A., 30, 63, 66–68, 70, 71, 74–76,
    79, 123, 229, 233n. 23, 239n. 15, 240nn.
    39–51, 241n. 56, 242n. 65, 258n. 28,
    265n. 45
Hazen, Thomas Lee, 247n. 39
Hegel, 65
Heidegger, Martin, 73
Held, Virginia, 13, 232n. 24
Helyar, John, 234n. 5
Herman, Stewart W., 205, 272n. 47, 275n.
    130
Herzberg, F., 260n. 80
Hillel, Rabbi, 160
Hinduism, 21, 22, 25, 62, 147, 184, 185,
    192, 193
Hittinger, Russell, 267n. 113
Hobbes, Thomas, 53, 66, 67, 81, 184
Hodgson, Geoffrey M., 68, 70, 240nn.
    52–54, 242nn. 62, 63, 66–70, 77, 244n.
    127

Holmes, Oliver Wendell, 10, 11, 14, 231n. 3
Holons, 106
Honesty, 7, 16, 33, 35, 67, 68, 169, 211, 221
Hooker, Reverend Thomas, 57
Hopt, Klaus J., 253n. 145
Horwitz, Morton, 275n. 122
Hosmer, LaRue Tone, 22, 23, 25, 40, 220, 232nn. 4–6, 234n. 4, 262n. 70, 275n. 126
Human dignity, 25, 26
Human equality, 25
Human nature, 53, 55, 65, 66, 69, 70, 73, 75, 78–84, 134, 152, 154, 155, 165, 172, 178, 197, 220, 222, 223, 229
Hume, David, 54, 182, 268n. 6, 269n. 29
Hunters and gatherers, 67, 142
Hutterites, 50
Hypernorms, 130, 138–41, 144, 169, 198, 226

Identity, 32, 33, 148
Ideology, 85, 88
Impartiality, 58–61, 85, 88, 89, 115, 117, 137
Implied contracts, 10
Incorporeal rights, 59
India, 21, 23, 184
Individualism, 28, 156
Industrial Bank of Japan, 99
Industrialization, 87
Innovation, 197
Integrative social contracts theory (ISCT), 130, 136–38, 140, 141, 149, 153, 169
Interfaith Center on Corporate Responsibility, 128
Islam, 22
Israel, 28, 85
Issac, Glynn L., 83, 245n. 148

Jackall, Robert, 33, 40, 176, 233n. 36, 234n. 2, 268n. 115, 274n. 104
Jackson, Andrew, 96, 163
Jainism, 22
Japan, 88, 93–105, 112, 113, 117, 209
Japanese ethics, 29
Jaynes, Julian, 83, 132, 245n. 149
Jefferson, Thomas, 26, 90, 91
Jensen, Michael C., 247n. 39
Jesus, 46, 200, 204
Jewish law and Judaism, 21, 23, 46
Johnson, F. Ross, 40–42
Johnson, Gregory, 236n. 51, 255n. 206
Jones, Gareth, 260n. 66

Jones, Mary Jeanne Anderson, 237n. 103
Jones, Richard, 208, 273n. 60
Juran, Joseph M., 209, 273n. 67
Jurisgenesis, 170–71
Justice, 53, 58, 68, 127, 131, 177, 230

Kamehameha, 153
Kamehameha II, 44
Kant, 44–46, 52, 64, 125–27, 131, 133, 163, 164, 190, 226
Kaplan, Steven N., 253n. 157
Kaufman, Walter, 234n. 7
Keeley, Lawrence, 132, 228, 260n. 75
Keeley, Michael, 63, 91, 136, 150, 151, 159, 167–69, 239n. 18, 240n. 24, 246nn. 25–35, 255n. 195, 260n. 4, 263nn. 73–79, 84, 264n. 9, 277n. 27
Keiretsu, 98, 99
Keizai Doyukai, 101
Kelly, Bruce, 248n. 71
Kennedy, Robert G., 26, 27, 56, 233n. 13
Kester, W. Carl, 251n. 98, 253n. 146
Kidder, Rushworth M., 255n. 193
King, Martin Luther, Jr., 208, 210
Kmiec, Douglas W., 236n. 81
Kraakman, Reinier, 255n. 184
Kramer, Larry, 89, 91, 246nn. 5, 8–23, 255n. 194
Krishna, 193
Kumulipo, 44

Lamarckian, 68
Laws of nature, 9, 48, 49, 60, 92, 117, 121
Lee, Richard B., 245n. 143
Legend of the Grand Inquisitor, The, 148, 200
Legitimate institutions, 85, 88, 105
Leung, Wai Shun Wilson, 253n. 149
Liberal republicanism, 171
Liberal theory, 88
Liberals, 91
Lightfoot, Robert, 251n. 100, 253n. 146
Limited liability, 136
Lincoln, Abraham, 175, 254n. 165, 267n. 108
Lipton, Martin, 250n. 87
Locke, John, 49, 59, 255n. 191
Lohr, Steve, 276n. 23
Loomis, Dwight, 237n. 101
Lopez-De-Silanes, Florencia, 248n. 51
Loss, Louis, 248n. 57
Love, 28
Loyalty, 6, 12, 16, 23, 38, 66, 81, 221

Macey, Jonathan, 122, 172, 173, 243n. 103, 253n. 144, 258nn. 25–26, 30, 265nn. 42, 43, 266n. 89

MacIntyre, Alasdair, 43–45, 48, 53, 54, 54, 73, 162, 165, 234n. 14, 235nn. 25–28, 236nn. 85, 88–89, 240n. 32, 242nn. 84–87, 262n. 58, 265n. 49, 267nn. 104, 112, 268n. 113

MacNeil, Ian R., 10, 231n. 5, 240n. 34

Madden, Richard B., 31, 32, 233n. 28

Madison, James, 37, 89–91, 150

Madsen, Richard, 233n. 21

Maimondes, 46

Maitland, Ian, 128, 130, 243n. 94, 259n. 52

Malinowski, Bronislaw, 69, 241nn. 56, 59–60

Mao Tse-Tung, 65

Margolis, Joshua, 226, 255n. 203, 276n. 21

Marshall, John, 121, 249n. 74

Marshall, William, 200, 209, 212, 267n. 101

Marvin, Julia, 277n. 30

Marx, Karl, 33, 65

Maskery, Mary Ann, 251n. 101

Matsui, Kathy, 252n. 116

Matsushita, 101

Mayer, Colin, 248n. 53

Mayer, Don, 138, 169, 261n. 19, 265n. 66

Mazda Motors, 98, 99

McClelland, D. C., 260n. 80

McConnell, Michael W., 201, 270n. 10

McCracken, Janet, 162, 239n. 22, 264n. 30, 265nn. 46–47

McDaniel, Morey, 265n. 44

Meckling, William H., 247n. 39

Mediation institutions, 7–9, 12–14, 16, 17, 21–23, 25, 28, 30–32, 35–39, 51, 54, 59–61, 65, 106, 108, 142–44, 148, 150–52, 155, 156, 160, 161, 165, 166, 168, 169, 172, 176, 179, 195, 208, 225, 226, 230

Megalogues, 156

Megastructures, 9, 23, 29, 31, 32, 34, 35, 50, 86, 98, 104, 105, 109, 143, 151, 152, 168, 227

Meltebeke v. Bureau of Labor, 202, 203

Mergers and acquisitions, 40–43, 56, 94

Messick, David M., 222–26, 275nn. 2–4, 6, 276nn. 8, 11

Methodological individualism, 63, 66, 68, 69, 74, 79, 80, 82, 84

Mexico, 71

Michelman, Frank, 170–72, 174, 175, 177, 256nn. 2, 11, 263n. 2, 266nn. 69–73

Miller, J. Irwin, 109

Millon, David, 247n. 39, 249n. 74

Minow, Nell, 258n. 27

Minuchin, Salvador, 13, 106, 232n. 27

Mishra, Karen E., 256nn. 212–18

Mitchell, Lawrence A., 257n. 11

Mitsubishi, 101

Miurisura, 94

Monopolization, 87

Montesquieu, 89

Moral free space, 137

Moral Mazes, 33

Moral sense, 145

Morale, 33

Mother-child paradigm, 13

Multi-level selection theory, 66, 72, 79

Multinational corporations, 16, 22, 23, 26, 40, 50, 85, 152, 153

Multiple masters, 77

Murphy, Nancey, 195, 269n. 50

Muslims, 21

Nagel, Thomas, 207–9, 211, 272nn. 53–55, 274n. 103

NASDAQ, 94

Nash, Laura L., 182, 183, 202, 271n. 21

National Collegiate Athletic Association, 34

Natural law, 9, 25, 39, 40, 45, 46, 48, 49, 51–53, 56–58, 60, 61, 63, 85, 88, 89, 114, 117, 139, 146, 186, 213, 214, 216, 217, 219, 223

Naturalism, 63, 70, 178, 190, 222

Naturalist theology, 182, 190

Naturalistic Fallacy, 144, 146, 147, 185, 187, 188, 192. 193, 197

Nature, 54, 55, 61–65, 70, 71, 136, 141, 149, 150, 179, 183–85, 187–89, 197

Naughton, Michael, 237n. 100

Necessary social efficiency, 140, 141

Neighborhoods, 8, 16, 31, 32, 165

Neoclassical contracts, 10

Neocortex, 50, 73

Nesbitt, Stephen L., 251n. 95

Nesteruk, Jeffrey, 14, 162, 163, 232nn. 29–31, 239n. 22, 240nn. 22, 38, 264nn. 36, 37

Neuhaus, Richard John, 23, 31, 32, 34, 36–38, 158, 213, 231n. 2, 233n. 7, 234nn. 39–41, 44–45, 51, 236n. 62, 259n. 63, 265nn. 53–57, 273n. 61, 274n. 97, 276n. 17

New Golden Rule, 159

New York Stock Exchange, 94
New York Times, 76
Newton, Isaac, 190, 194, 195
Nexus-of-contracts, 8, 42, 63–66. 74–76, 80, 126
Nichols, Philip M., 228, 276n. 26
Nicklaus, Jack, 41
Nietzsche, Friedrich, 41, 42, 44, 45, 234n. 7, 235n. 29
Nisbet, Robert A., 28, 29, 43, 109, 143, 233nn. 16, 19, 251n. 93, 255nn. 199–200, 262n. 45
Nissan, 100, 101
Noble Truths, 193
Noll, Mark A., 213, 274n. 94
Nonshareholder constituents, 97, 101, 102, 119, 121–23, 141, 249n. 81, 255n. 186
Noone, James J., 238
Notorri, 94
Novak, Michael, 32–34, 60, 61, 233nn. 31, 35, 234n. 38, 238nn. 131, 134
Nuremberg Trials, 129

Oakland, John S., 255n. 197
OECD, 95, 247n. 45, 249n. 72, 251nn. 96–97, 252nn. 117, 120, 141, 253n. 144
Offset Pension plan, 4
Oliver, Douglas L., 242n. 92
Open-book management, 134
Orts, Eric W., 78, 121, 243nn. 109–11, 250n. 4, 257n. 84, 258n. 21
Ostling, Richard N., 271n. 11
Oversight boards, 104

Pakistan, 21
Pannenberg, Wofhart, 193, 194, 269n. 41
Paris, Peter J., 238n. 6
Participation, 25, 26, 38, 49, 58, 84, 85, 103, 106, 130, 140, 151, 177, 189, 197
Pascale, Richard, 251n. 102
Peace, 60, 83, 173, 202, 228, 230
Perlez, Jane, 247n. 37
Perotti, E., 251n. 98
Perry, Michael J., 57, 146, 206, 207, 210–17, 219, 235n. 42, 237n. 99, 262n. 57, 267n. 111, 271n. 11, 272nn. 56–57, 273nn. 59, 63, 73–78, 81–85, 274nn. 86–91, 93, 95–97, 100
Peters, Tom, 201, 214, 271n. 16
Phillips, Derek L., 264n. 12
Phillips, Michael J., 249n. 74, 265n. 39

Philosophers' Formula, 131, 133
Pierce, Ellen R., 202–4, 271nn. 22, 26–27, 29, 30, 272nn. 33–43
Pipes, Richard, 59, 237nn. 110–12, 254n. 165, 255nn. 189–90, 198
Pitkin, Hannah, 177, 268n. 122
Plato, 59, 140, 147, 160
Pleistocene Era, 113
Pope John Paul, 21–23, 32, 232n. 3, 233n. 10
Porta, Rafael La, 248n. 51
Posner, Richard A., 265n. 52
Postal Service, 26
Postman, David, 247n. 36
Power aggrandizing values, 60, 61, 84, 109, 114, 115, 187, 190
Practical reasonableness, 53
Prahalad, C. K., 134, 260n. 83
Prayer, 28
Presser, Stephen B., 60, 236n. 81, 237n. 124, 243n. 105, 249nn. 75–76, 263n. 3, 265n. 41
Prestige, 28
Preston, Lee E., 120, 126, 127, 257n. 9, 259nn. 47–50
Principal of Corporate Legitimacy, 125
Promise keeping, 6, 23, 51, 68
Property, 47, 59, 60, 85, 88, 89, 107, 123, 127, 140
Property rights, 60, 105, 107, 109–11, 114, 115, 126, 127
Protestant reformers, 59
Protestant work ethic, 184
Prowse, Stephen, 247n. 49, 248n. 52, 252nn. 113–14, 125, 253n. 114

Quakers, 35
Quarantining institutions, 14, 17, 23, 37, 38, 48, 51
Quasi contracts, 10
Quebec, 173

Rank society, 143
Rappaport, Roy A., 56, 88, 114, 236n. 65, 237n. 97, 246n. 4, 256n. 224
Rationality, 173
Rawls, John, 81, 131, 162, 190, 208, 209, 211, 267n. 102, 273n. 62, 274n. 102
Recognition, 28
Reflection, 197
Reichley, James, 273n. 61
Reingold, Jennifer, 253nn. 152–54
Relational contracts, 10, 11, 39, 65

Religion, 22, 28, 47, 52, 138, 147, 148, 172, 174–76, 179, 181, 184, 188, 189, 197, 199, 202, 206–11, 216, 225, 229

Religious, 23, 65, 91, 158, 159, 200, 201, 203, 204, 217

Religious belief, 38, 46, 182, 183, 201, 203, 207, 214, 215

Religious believers and groups, 50, 212, 215

Religious illiteracy, 212

Religious institutions, 8, 16, 30, 31, 165, 175, 176

Religious justification, 214

Religious norms, 137

Renault, 100

Republicanism, 86–88, 113, 156, 170–77

Reputation, 123

Respect, 15, 21, 27, 32, 55

Revolutionary War, 66

Reyes, Alejandro, 250n. 85

Richerson, Peter J., 85, 88, 245n. 156, 246n. 2, 254nn. 176–80, 256n. 223

Ridley, Matt, 59, 237n. 123, 262n. 62

Right of association, 25, 26

Rights, 53, 59, 63, 87, 88, 105, 130, 164

RJR Nabisco, 40, 41

Rodes, Robert E., 238n. 13

Rodgers, Edward D., 257n. 11

Roe, Mark J., 251n. 111, 252nn. 139–40, 253n. 150

Rohlen, Thomas P., 251n. 102

Romano, Roberta, 255n. 188

Rosenblum, Steven A., 250n. 87

Rosenthal, Sandra R., 82, 244n. 137

Rothstein, Edward, 276n. 25

Ruder, David, 257n. 11

Ruether, Rosemary Radford, 238n. 11

Sahlins, Marshall, 235nn. 19, 24, 242n. 92

Salbu, Steven R., 10, 11, 12, 14, 45, 46, 48, 63, 81, 137, 231n. 7, 232nn. 13–20, 235nn. 30, 41, 239n. 17, 240nn. 24, 33, 244n. 136, 261nn. 7–9

Sampson, Anthony, 234n. 10, 272n. 45

Sandel, Michael, 162

Scalar stress, 50

Schipani, Cindy, 246, 247n. 39

Schlender, Brenton R., 251n. 104

Schools, 12, 106

Schor, Juliet, 30, 233n. 24

Schrempp, Jurgen, 102, 103

Schumpeter, Joseph, 69

Sears Roebuck, 34

Second Great Awakening, 218

Segmented hierarchies, 85

Self-help groups, 12, 16

Self-interest, 12, 24, 27, 35, 42, 54, 55, 62, 65, 67, 70, 71, 74, 149, 158, 164, 172, 173, 177, 205

Self-interest rightly understood, 28, 29

Seligman, Joel, 248n. 57

Senate, U.S., 25

Sennett, Richard, 151, 255n. 201, 263nn. 81–83, 268n. 114

Separation of powers, 57

Sequential hierarchies, 110, 116

Shareholders, 5, 6, 8, 15, 36, 41, 76–78, 93, 95, 97, 100, 103, 107, 119, 122, 125, 128, 133–35, 163

Sharking, 78

Shaw, Bill, 162, 164, 220, 221, 239n. 22, 264nn. 30, 35, 265nn. 46–47, 275n. 128

Sheard, Paul, 251n. 99

Sherry, Suzanna, 240n. 37

Shirking, 78, 80

Shiva, 184

Shleifer, Andrei, 248n. 51

Sikhism, 23

Simon, Herbert, 78

Simpson, O. J., 41

Simultaneous hierarchies, 110

Small groups, 24, 29, 49–51, 67, 68, 83, 85, 88, 91, 108, 110, 112, 117, 132, 133, 153, 226

Smith, Adam, 29, 30, 96

Smolin, David M., 274n. 92

Sociability, 53

Social contract theory, 9, 65–66, 68, 117, 127, 130, 134, 136, 141, 143, 144, 152, 154, 164, 179, 198, 224

Social embeddedness, 75, 81

Social evolution, 71, 142

Socialism, 67

Sociobiology, 82

Socrates, 160

Sodalities, 110, 116

Solidarity, 6, 16, 21–27, 32, 33, 35, 38, 39, 51, 67, 72, 74, 78, 79, 85, 86, 98, 126, 148, 153, 173, 174, 195, 198

Solomon, Robert C., 161–63, 177, 183, 184, 191, 234n. 6, 239n. 22, 260n. 65, 263n. 72, 264nn. 25–28, 32–33

Sommer, A. A., Jr., 249n. 77

Sony, 100, 101

Speer, Albert, 150

Spencerism, 70, 185

Spinoza, Benedict de, 62, 225, 238n. 9, 276n. 18
Spirituality, 13, 15, 21, 24–28, 148, 183, 201
Sponsel, Leslie E., 277n. 29
Stakeholder Fiduciary Principle, 126
Stakeholder management, 6, 121
Stakeholder theory, 8, 9, 16, 42, 56, 63, 77, 78, 119, 123, 135, 164, 179, 224
Stakeholders, 86, 87, 91, 92, 95, 97, 99, 104, 106, 107, 127–30, 133, 141, 144, 163
Stalk, George, Jr., 252n. 124
Stange, Gary von, 257n. 11
Stewardship, 25
Stewart, Ian, 235n. 43
Stolberg, Sheryl Gay, 276n. 24
Stone, Katherine Van Wezel, 243n. 104, 255n. 186, 258n. 23, 259nn. 58–59
Strict exclusionist position (SEP), 206, 208, 210, 211, 214, 215
Subsidarity, 24–26, 28, 34, 39, 49, 58, 59, 61, 88, 89, 109, 117
Sullivan, Kathleen M., 201, 267n. 100, 270n. 8
Sumitomo, 98, 99
Sundaram, Anant. K., 247n. 39
Sunstein, Cass, 172, 174–77, 236n. 63, 256n. 211, 263n. 2, 266n. 96, 268nn. 116–17
Sun-Tzu, 129, 259n. 57
Supervisory boards, 101
Survival of the fittest, 71
Swidler, Ann, 233n. 21

Taka, Iwao, 29, 233n. 20
Takaki, Ronald, 35, 234n. 43
Tamari, Meir, 205, 272n. 46
Taoism, 194
Taylor, Charles, 83, 138, 165, 245n. 152, 265n. 50, 266n. 95
Teams, 33, 151, 152
Technical universe, 149
Technologizing values, 60, 89, 132, 145, 146, 148, 187, 189, 191, 223
Theological naturalism, 179, 181, 185, 190, 191, 194–96, 198
Tillich, Paul, 187, 189–91, 194, 195, 238n. 9, 269nn. 30–40
Tipler, Frank J., 269n. 18
Tipton, Steven M., 233n. 21
Tokyo Stock Exchange, 96
Tolerance, 174, 177

Too many masters argument, 106, 122, 123, 126
Toqueville, Alexis de, 28, 143, 144, 233n. 15, 256n. 220, 262nn. 48–49
Torah, 147
Total quality management, 151, 208
Tradition, 67, 68
Transactional contracts, 10, 11, 79
Transcendence, 136, 141, 143, 147, 148, 154, 157, 158, 161, 174–77, 182, 183, 189, 191, 193, 197, 204
Transcendent reality, 62, 183, 184, 188, 192, 196, 225
Transparency, 16, 96, 103, 104, 115, 160
Transparency International, 138
Treece, James B., 251n. 107
Trivers, Robert, 196, 223, 276n. 10
Trump, Donald, 42
Trust, 16, 27, 33, 66
Truth telling, 6, 7, 23, 35, 47, 51, 68
Turnbull, Colin, 83, 132, 245n. 147
Two masters argument, 77

Ulrich, Thomas A., 271n. 17
Ultra vires, 124
Umezu, Mitsuhior, 105, 254nn. 169–75
United Airlines, 95
United Kingdom, 93
United Parcel Service, 95
United States, 88, 89, 93–96, 98–104, 107, 111, 112, 117, 159, 170, 173, 184, 208, 209, 211
U.S. Constitution, 66
Utilitarianism, 45, 63

Vagts, Detlev F., 251nn. 89–90, 253n. 144
Valeri, Valerio, 235n. 23
Vallas, Steven P., 151, 263n. 80
Velasquez, Manuel, 236nn. 67–80, 274nn. 98–99
Virtue theory, 9, 16, 63, 117, 134, 155, 164, 179, 224
Virtues, 6, 8, 23, 32, 39, 52, 55, 66, 67, 73, 90, 116, 151, 160, 161, 171
Vishnu, 193
Voice, 88, 106, 130, 139, 144
Volokh, Eugene, 271n. 28
Voluntary associations, 8, 16, 20, 31, 36, 109, 130, 165, 176

Waal, Frans de, 82, 244n. 138, 263n. 71, 270n. 53
Wages, 169

Wagner, Antonin, 247n. 38
Wagstyl, Stefan, 251n. 92
Walker, C. R., 260n. 80
Wallman, Steven M. H., 257n. 11
Walsh, James P., 242n. 88, 247n. 39
Walton, Mary, 273n. 67
Washington, George, 90–92
Wasserstein, Bruce, 40, 49, 234n. 1
Waters, James A., 271n. 18
Watson, Lyall, 61, 238nn. 135–36, 138
Wattles, Jeffrey, 235n. 38, 262n. 70, 264n. 23, 270n. 52
Wee little bowls, 155, 156, 167, 178
Werhane, Patricia H., 30, 233n. 22, 240n. 23
Whallon, Robert, 245n. 143, 262n. 65
Whitchurch, Gail G., 254n. 181
Whitehead, Alfred North, 62, 238n. 10
Wicks, Andrew C., 126, 259n. 44
Wiessner, Polly, 241n. 56
Wild Wild West, 227
Williamson, Oliver, 63, 78–80, 84, 239n. 16, 240n. 36, 243nn. 112–15, 244nn. 121–26, 255n. 204

Wilson, David Sloan, 242n. 78, 262n. 47
Wilson, James Q., 54, 82, 83, 132, 145, 236n. 87, 245nn. 141–42,144, 260n. 76, 261n. 24
Winter, D. G., 260n. 80
Wood, Donna J., 223, 226, 276n. 13
Wood, Gordon, 170, 266n. 68
World Series, 25
World Wide Web, 227
Wright, Robert, 82, 83, 145, 245nn. 139–40, 260n. 78
Wuthnow, Robert, 201, 271nn. 12–15

Yablon, Charles M., 256n. 219
Yawheh, 184
Yoda, 62, 63, 150
Yoder, John Howard, 266n. 94
Young, Brigham, 51

Zarathustra, 41–43
Zollers, Frances E., 162, 264n. 35
Zycinski, Joseph M., 187, 269n. 17